ADVENTURE GUIDES

SOUTHERN AFRICA

ADVENTURE GUIDES

SOUTHERN AFRICA

Produced by AA Publishing
© Automobile Association Developments Ltd 2001
Maps © Automobile Association Developments Ltd 2001
Coloured maps produced by the Cartographic Department,
The Automobile Association
Black and white maps produced by Advanced Illustration,
Congleton, Cheshire
A CIP catalogue record for this book is available from
the British Library
ISBN 0-7495-2359-X

The contents of this publication are believed correct at the time of
printing. Nevertheless, the publishers cannot be held responsible for any
errors or omissions or for changes in the details given in this guide or for
the consequences of any reliance on the information provided by the
same. Assessments of sights, accommodation, restaurants and so forth are
based upon the authors' own experience and, therefore, descriptions
given in this guide necessarily contain an element of subjective opinion
which may not reflect the publisher's opinion or dictate a reader's own
experience on another occasion.
We have tried to ensure accuracy in this guide, but things do change
and we would be grateful if readers would advise us of any inaccuracies
they may encounter.
The areas covered in this guide can be subject to political, economic,
and climatic upheaval, so readers should consult tour operators,
embassies and consulates, airlines, e.t.c. for current requirements and
advice before travelling. The publishers and authors cannot accept
responsibility for any loss, injury, or inconvenience, however caused.

Published by AA Publishing, a trading name of Automobile Association
Developments Limited, whose registered office is Norfolk House, Priestley
Road, Basingstoke, Hampshire RG24 9NY.
Registered number 1878835.

Visit our website at www.theAA.com

Colour separation by Chroma Graphics, Singapore
Printed and bound by G Canale & C. s.p.a., Torino, Italy
Previous page: *The camp at Domwe Island, Malawi (➤ 116)*
Inset: *Victoria Falls from the Zambia side*

CONTENTS

INTRODUCTION

Southern Africa is a region that boasts magnificent mountains, vast plains, wilderness deserts, raging rivers and wondrous coastal reef systems. It includes some of the countries that head the list of dream destinations for many people. Talk of safaris and it is this region that springs to mind. Mention impressive waterfalls and Victoria Falls will drop effortlessly into the conversation. From the Maasai tribe in the Serengeti to the wildlife-rich Okavango Delta, southern Africa oozes adventure travel opportunities. Despite being laden with these famous locations, there are plenty of lesser-known but equally spectacular places to explore too. Madagascar is renowned for its unique wildlife, in particular the fabled lemurs, and in Uganda you can spend time with the awe-inspiring mountain gorillas. If you are looking for some whitewater thrills then rafting on the Nile should satisfy your thirst, while in Kenya you could experience your first mountain climb to the top of Kilimanjaro, Africa's highest mountain. Travel in Africa is more demanding than in many other parts of the world but the rewards are suitably sweeter. So, if you can bear roughing it a little and don't mind getting a bit of dust in your hair, then you could hardly pick a more exciting region to travel in.

Mist filters through the forest on the Marangu Trail, Tanzania
Inset: *A dance troupe at the entrance to Bourkes Luck Potholes on the Panorama Route, Mpumalanga, South Africa*

About the Authors

PHILIP BRIGGS & ARIADNE VAN ZANDBERGEN

Philip and Ariadne are based in Johannesburg and specialize in Africa. Philip has written travel guides to Uganda, Kenya, Tanzania, Malawi, Mozambique, and South Africa, and with Ariadne's pictures, they contribute regularly to several travel and wildlife magazines, including *Travel Africa* and *Wanderlust*.

FIONA DUNLOP

Fiona's taste for the tropics, ancient cultures and developing countries has been tested to the full while writing about southeast Asia, India and central America. Before her immersion in this peripatetic lifestyle, she spent 15 years in Paris working in and writing about the arts. Now based in London, her articles have appeared in the *Observer*, the *Sunday Times*, *The Times*, *Elle Decoration*, and *Homes & Gardens*.

WILLIAM GRAY

William is a travel writer and photographer based in Oxfordshire, England. His first book, *Coral Reefs & Islands— The Natural History of a Threatened Paradise*, was commended in the 1993 Conservation Book Prize. His articles and photographs regularly appear in several publications, including *National Geographic Traveler*, the *Sunday Times*, *Sunday Telegraph*, *The Times*, and *Wanderlust*.

PAUL GROGAN

Paul is a travel writer and photographer, and was Deputy Editor of *Global Adventure* magazine from its its launch to 2000. His work has appeared in *The Times* and *Condé Nast Traveller*, and he is the co-author of *The Action Guide Europe*. His expe- ditions include the first British descent of Peru's Cotahuasi River by raft.

CARRIE HAMPTON

Carrie was born in London, England but never felt truly at home there. At 19 she set off to explore America and has been four times around the globe over the following 20 years. However, it was not until she set foot in Cape Town that Carrie felt she had 'arrived'. Her articles and photographs on southern Africa appear in international travel journals, magazines, newspapers, and across the internet.

CHRIS MCINTYRE

Chris taught for three years at a rural school in Zimbabwe before writing guidebooks on Namibia, Botswana and Zambia. Now based in the U.K., he runs a tour operation that specializes in this region, whilst writing and photographing for books and articles. His work regularly appears in *BBC Wildlife*, *Wanderlust*, *Travel Africa* and *The Times*.

GUY MARKS

Guy first caught the travel bug in the early 1980s when he drove from England to Cape Town. He lives in England and is a well known travel writer and photographer for national and international publications. He is author of *This is Egypt* (New Holland 1998), and *Travel Writing and Photography* (Traveller's Press 1997).

RICHARD WHITAKER

Richard teaches Classics at the University of Cape Town and has travelled extensively and enthusiastically in the U.S.A. Europe, Australia and throughout southern Africa. He is widely published on a number of topics, including his travels.

MICHAEL WOODS

Michael has worked for the past 12 years as a writer and photographer concentrating on adventure and wildlife travel. He has tried a wide range of outdoor activities since his youth, although these days he focuses on climbing and cycling.

How to Use this Book

The book is divided into three distinct sections:

SECTION 1   PAGES 6–17

This comprises the introductory material and some general practical advice to guide you on your travels. We have included an introduction to the writing team. Our authors come from all walks of life and cover a wide age range. What they do all have in common, though, is a spirit of adventure, boundless enthusiasm, and a wealth of travel experience.

The map on pages 10–11 is colour-coded to show the area covered and highlight the regional divides.

Pages 12–17 contains practical advice from an experienced traveller, which is complemented by information given later.

The seasonal calendar in the inside front cover gives a guide to the optimum time to visit the areas covered in the adventures. However, there are of course many factors affecting when you might like to go, and greater details of climate patterns and their effect on activities are given at the end of each chapter. When arranging your trip always seek advice about the conditions you are likely to encounter from a tour operator or the tourist information office in the relevant country.

SECTION 2   PAGES 18–256

The main section of the book contains 25 adventures, chosen to give you a taste of a wide range of activities in a variety of places—some familiar, others not. The first page of each adventure carries a practical information box that gives you an idea of what to expect, plus a grade, numbered according to the relative difficulty of the activity or the level of skill required.

Going it Alone—Each adventure ends with a page of dedicated practical advice for planning that specific adventure yourself. This information should be used in conjunction with the "Blue Pages" at the end of the book (see below).

Any prices mentioned in the book are given in US dollars and were the approximate prices current at the time of the trip. Due to variations in inflation and exchange rates these are only meant as guidelines to give an idea of comparative cost.

 Challenge Rating: If you have even thought about booking the trip, you will manage

 Not too difficult but you may need some basic skills

 You will need to be fit, with lots of stamina and may need specialist qualifications

 You need to be fit and determined—not for the faint-hearted*

 This is for the serious adventurer—physically and mentally challenging!*

Sometimes only part of the trip is very hard and there may be an easier option

 Comfort rating: Indicates the degree of hardship you can expect, where 3 is comfortable and 1 is uncomfortable. This category not only covers accommodations, but also factors such as climate and other conditions that may affect your journey.

 Specialist equipment: Advice on any equipment needed for the journey, covering specialist items like diving gear, and also clothing and photographic gear.

SECTION 3   PAGES 257–320

"Blue Pages"—*Contacts* and *A–Z of Activities*—begin with selected contacts specific to the 25 main adventures. Here you'll find names referred to in the main stories, including tour operators, with addresses and contact numbers.

The A–Z lists a wide range of the best activities available in the region, with general information and full contact details of the outfits and organizations able to help you plan your journey. Finally, the book ends with a comprehensive index and gazetteer.

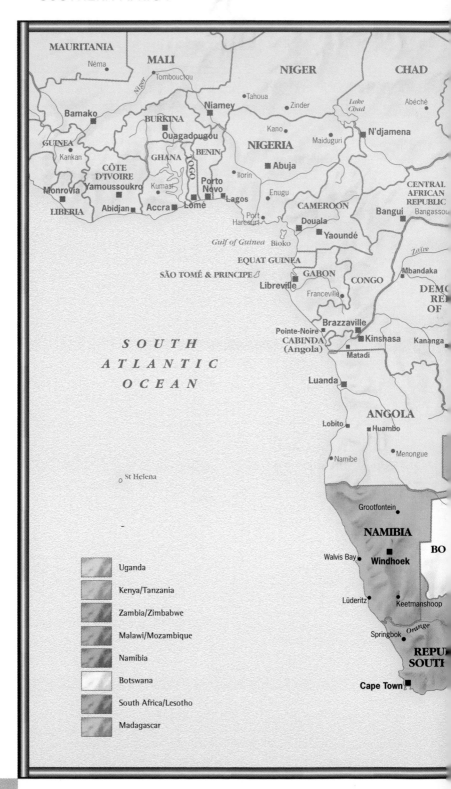

MAURITANIA
Néma

MALI
Tombouctou

NIGER

CHAD
Abéché

Bamako
Niamey
Tahoua
Zinder
Lake Chad

BURKINA
Ouagadougou

Kano
NIGERIA
Maiduguri
N'djamena

GUINEA
Kankan

GHANA
BENIN

CÔTE D'IVOIRE
Yamoussoukro
Kumasi
Porto Novo
Ilorin
Abuja

Monrovia
Abidjan
Accra
Lomé
Lagos
Enugu

CENTRAL AFRICAN REPUBLIC

LIBERIA
Port Harcourt
CAMEROON
Bangui
Bangassou

Douala

Gulf of Guinea Bioko
Yaoundé

EQUAT GUINEA
SÃO TOMÉ & PRINCIPE
GABON
Libreville
Franceville
CONGO
Mbandaka

Zaire

DEMO RE OF

Brazzaville
Pointe-Noire
CABINDA (Angola)
Kinshasa
Kananga

Matadi

S O U T H
A T L A N T I C
O C E A N

Luanda

ANGOLA
Lobito
Huambo

Namibe
Menongue

○ St Helena

Grootfontein

NAMIBIA
BO
Walvis Bay
Windhoek

■ Uganda

■ Kenya/Tanzania
Lüderitz
Keetmanshoop

■ Zambia/Zimbabwe

■ Malawi/Mozambique
Springbok
Orange

■ Namibia
REPU SOUTH

■ Botswana
Cape Town

■ South Africa/Lesotho

■ Madagascar

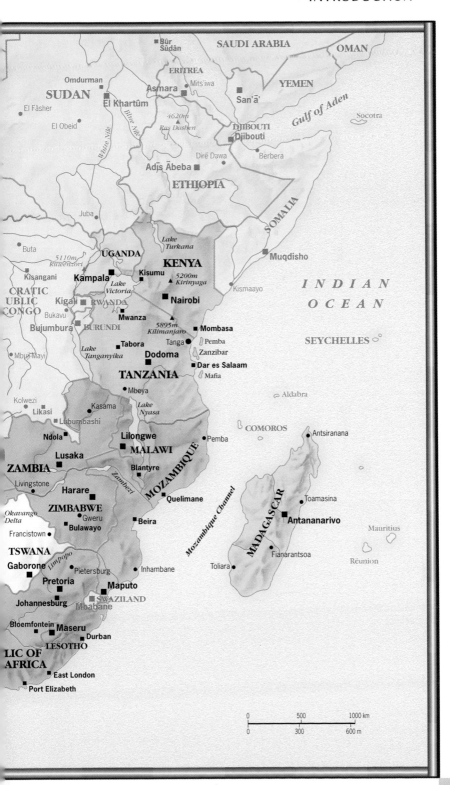

Practical Matters

TRAVEL DOCUMENTS

Although a passport is the first thing to be packed by most travellers, it is worth checking to ensure that it is valid for much longer than your stay, and there are enough blank pages left for visa stamps. Many immigration officials are reluctant to stamp previously used pages, no matter how much space is left on it. It is also important to carry several copies of the passport, especially the front cover, personal details page and those pages containing any essential visas. These copies can speed up a new passport should it be lost or stolen. It is also worth leaving copies at home with friends or relatives, in case you lose everything.

Check at least a couple of months before you leave about the visa requirements for the countries you are visiting. Obtaining visas has become much easier in the last decade or so as governments have realized that tourism numbers increase with a reduction in red tape. Many countries now allow tourist visas to be issued on entry, especially if you arrive by air, whilst others still require you to obtain a visa before travelling. If possible, get a visa for the longest duration possible and certainly for longer than you intend to be there. This allows you to stay on if you like it too much to leave, and provides leeway for any problems with delays departing the country, such as cancelled flights or illness.

HEALTH MATTERS

Nothing can make such a difference to your enjoyment of an adventure as your health, so it is worth taking as many precautions as possible to maintain it. Necessary vaccinations vary with the country you are visiting and even which region of the country you go to, but ensuring your protection against tetanus is current is important wherever you go. Give yourself plenty of time, at least six weeks, to get all the necessary vaccinations, as some require more than one visit to the doctor. Even if you think you already have a full complement of inoculations it is still worth checking with a

66	LANGUAGE
Botswana	English and Setwana
Kenya	Swahili and English
Lesotho	Sesotho and English
Madagascar	Malagasy and French
Malawi	English
Mozambique	Portuguese
Namibia	English
South Africa	Afrikaans and English
Tanzania	Swahili and English
Uganda	English
Zambia	English
Zimbabwe	English

LOCAL CURRENCY

It is reasonably straightforward to exchange any major European or North American currency in the region, though US dollars are always a very safe bet. It is best to carry the majority of your money in the form of traveller's cheques and on a major credit card, such as Visa, Mastercard or American Express.

Botswana	Pula = 100 thebes
Kenya	Kenyan Shilling = 100 cents
Lesotho	Loti = 100 lisente
Madagascar	Malagasy Franc = 100 centimes
Malawi	Kwacha = 100 tambala
Mozambique	Mozambique Metical = 100 centavos
Namibia	South African Rand = 100 cents
South Africa	Rand = 100 cents
Tanzania	Tanzanian Shilling = 100 cents
Uganda	Ugandan Shilling = 100 cents
Zambia	Kwacha = 100 ngwee
Zimbabwe	Zimbabwe Dollar = 100 cents

doctor before travelling as situations change regularly and there can be sudden outbreaks of diseases. Record your vaccinations on an International Health Certificate and carry it with you.

Don't ignore the dentist, either, in preparation for a trip. Get your teeth checked out at home as it can cost a surprisingly large amount of money to get dental work done in other countries; costs that may not be covered by your travel insurance. It's particularly important to have your teeth in good working order when visiting very cold places, as the temperature can cause problems with fillings. A comprehensive travel insurance policy that covers substantial medical costs is essential on any trip.

INSURANCE

Unless you are fabulously wealthy or a big time gambler then comprehensive travel insurance is essential. It may seem to cost a lot for something you are unlikely to use, but if things do go wrong then it could not only save your holiday but, it could save you going bankrupt too. If you aren't convinced, then consider the cost of being airlifted from a mountain environment with a serious injury, then being transferrred to a suitable hospital. Think in tens of thousands of US dollars and suddenly the insurance fee seems a bargain. If you want to ensure the best care then take out a good policy, including cover for personal accident, medical and air ambulance, personal liability, legal

 VACCINATIONS

Check with your doctor for the latest information but the following vaccinations are recommended for travel to any of the countries in southern Africa: yellow fever (if coming from an infected area), typhoid, polio, cholera, tetanus and hepatitis A. You should also follow an anti-malarial tablet regime.

CUSTOMS/ENTRY REQUIREMENTS

In addition to the necessary visas, entry to the following countries is normally dependent on you having a passport with at least six months validity remaining, sufficient funds for your stay and a return air ticket or proof of onward travel.

Botswana Visas are not required for stays of up to 90 days for nationals of most Commonwealth countries, most European countries and the U.S.A.

Kenya Many visitors do not require visas to enter Kenya, including visitors from the United Kingdom and some other European countries. Time limits depend on your nationality, with U.K. nationals being allowed to stay for up to 30 days and other nationals for up to three months. Visas should be applied for before travelling.

Lesotho For stays of up to 30 days nationals of the U.K., Canada, Australia, Japan, other E.U. countries and several other countries do not need visas. Nationals of the U.S.A. do require visas. Single entry visas last for up to three months and multiple entry ones for six months.

Madagascar All visitors require a visa and they are valid for up to 90 days and must be used within six months of date of issue. It is essential to get a visa before arriving in the country.

Malawi Nationals of the U.K., U.S.A., Canada and Australia and some other E.U. countries do not need visas for stays of up to three months.

Mozambique All foreign nationals require visas and they last for one month from date of entry on single entry visas or 90 days on multiple entry visas. It is essential to obtain the visa before entering the country.

Namibia Nationals of the U.S.A., Canada, Japan, Australia, New Zealand and all E.U. countries (except Greece) do not require visas for stays of up to three months.

South Africa Holders of passports from the U.K., other E.U. countries, U.S.A., Canada, Australia and Japan do not require visas for stays up to 90 days.

Tanzania Visas are required by most foreign nationals and should be acquired before arriving in the country. Single entry tourist visas are usually valid for three months. It is best to obtain one before arriving in the country, but they are also available at the major air and land entry points.

Uganda Most foreign nationals do require visas to enter Uganda and single entry visas last for up to three months from date of issue. They should be acquired before entering the country.

Zambia Visas are required by U.K. nationals (unless you are travelling in a recognized organized tour), E.U. nationals (except Ireland), and U.S.A. nationals. They are valid for 90 days.

Zimbabwe Visas are not required by nationals of the U.K., Canada, Ireland and Sweden, whilst U.S.A. and other E.U. nationals can obtain one on arrival. They are valid for three months from date of issue.

expenses, cancellation, personal baggage and loss of passport. Make sure the policy covers 'adventure' activities, which are usually excluded in ordinary policies. With the baggage cover, check the single item limits, as expensive items, such as cameras, can fall outside this. If you're lucky enough to travel a few times a year, consider an annual policy. They can be cheaper than several individual policies.

Keep receipts for anything you buy to go away, or instead take a photograph of all your gear laid out. With more fraudulent claims taking place every year, insurance companies are even keener to prove ownership. Each insur-

🕐 TIME DIFFERENCES

	London, noon G.M.T.	New York, noon E.S.T.	San Franicisco, noon P.S.T.
Botswana, Lesotho, Malawi	+2	+7	+10
Mozambique, Namibia, South Africa	+2	+7	+10
Zambia, Zimbabwe	+2	+7	+10
Kenya, Madagascar	+3	+8	+11
Tanzania, Uganda	+3	+8	+11

ance company has differing requirements for lodging a claim but the very least you will need to do for theft cases is obtain a signed local police report detailing the incident and every item that was taken.

MONEY

There are several useful ways of getting access to money while travelling that reduce the risk of loss through theft. A very popular option is to take traveller's cheques, which can be converted into local currency at banks and larger hotels or even used to pay directly for goods and services. The most globally accepted traveller's cheques are Thomas Cook, American Express and Visa in US dollars. Be aware though that on top of the commission fees most issuers charge to issue the cheques, you are often charged another commission fee to use them, which can result in significant loss of value (3 percent or more). They are easy to replace, though, if you keep good records.

With the spread of automatic bank teller machines (A.T.M.s) to even remote areas, an easy way to get money is via a credit or debit card. If you have a Personal Identification Number (P.I.N.) and a card that is linked to one of the international transaction systems, such as Link or Cirrus, you can withdraw local currency up to your daily limit. Many machines detect the nationality of your card and provide instructions in your own language, just to make things even

easier. This is a very safe way of carrying money and can be very cost effective on debit cards. However, credit card companies treat foreign currency withdrawals as cash advances and usually charge a commission fee and interest from the day of withdrawal. Wherever you travel, carry some cash with you, but not so much that losing it could spoil your trip. The more remote the area you are visiting, the more important it is to carry smaller denominations, as change for large notes can be hard to come by if you are only buying a snack.

There is no completely safe method of carrying your money, but a travel money belt or neck pouch are especially popular as both are concealed under your clothing and are big enough to carry a passport too. It is wise to carry a small wallet with a little money in that is easily accessible, so that you do not have to rummage under your clothes to buy small things. It can also be a useful decoy if thieves accost you. Giving up your lightly filled wallet may be enough to make them happy! Avoid revealing your main stash of cash in crowded places, such as markets. Do not leave money hanging around in hotel rooms, no matter how exclusive a place it is. We all bow to temptation some time, so avoid tempting room cleaners and hotel staff with wallets or expensive equipment. Use the hotel safe deposit box, making sure you get a full receipt. Many insurance policies don't cover valuables stolen from a room if a box is available.

Travelling Safe

WHAT TO TAKE

While the majority of things you take with you when you are travelling are specific to each country, there is a core of travel gear that can be considered important on all trips.

BAG IT UP

Although travellers can be seen using all sorts of luggage carriers, some are just suckers for suffering. Unless every single aspect of your trip is sorted beforehand and you are doing everything from a base then forget about taking a hard suitcase. They are unwieldy and generally not suited to more adventurous trips. Holdall bags, available from outdoor stores, are large, robust, have good carrying handle options and some even have tuck-away backpack straps for short hikes to hotels or stations. However, if you plan on doing any lengthier walks with your luggage, then it is worth buying a suitcase-style travel backpack. Most have excellent harnesses for carrying heavy loads over a reasonable distance. The straps all pack away to make the luggage look smarter in hotels and prevent straps snagging on conveyor belts. The main compartment opens up fully like a suitcase, so it is easier to keep clothes neat, and they have numerous extra pockets and storage areas for organizing your luggage. Top-loading backpacks, or expedition-style packs, are only really necessary if you envisage doing long hikes where you need to carry a lot of equipment.

In addition to your main baggage, a daypack is invaluable for use as hand luggage on aircraft and for carrying around towns or on day trips. If you can avoid taking more than two bags, then you will find things a lot easier when taking public transport. Make sure you have some way of securing all bags, such as a lock or a strap.

CLOTHING

Clothing requirements will very much depend on what you intend doing and where you intend doing it. For flexibility in varying climate conditions, it is better to take a number of thin layers rather than one or two thick layers. Most trips require a lightweight waterproof jacket and a warm layer, such as a fleece jacket, to keep the chills at bay on cool evenings. Footwear is heavy and bulky. Seasoned travellers will take just one pair of shoes and maybe lightweight sandals or sand-shoes for relaxing times and visits to the beach. There is plenty of good travel footwear available these days, with shoes or boots that are okay for light hiking but still smart enough to wear out to a bar.

ACCESORIZE

Useful accessories include a universal sink plug (you'll be amazed how many hotels do not have sink plugs!), a lightweight travel towel, a pocket knife and some duck tape, which can be used for backpack repairs. A basic first aid kit is essential too.

FILM

For photographers it is wise to take as much film as you think you'll need for the entire trip (overestimate rather than run out of film when things get exciting). Film is generally available in major cities around the world but it is hard to ensure quality of storage conditions in some places, so play safe and take it with you. Keep the film in your hand luggage for all air travel and, except in airports in developed countries with 'film safe' X-ray machines, insist on having it hand searched at X-ray machines. This is usually agreed to with little fuss. X-ray effects build up on film with each pass through a machine, so avoid taking left-over film from previous trips.

WHAT TO AVOID

A few simple precautions can make your trip a lot safer.

DRUGS AND OTHER TRAPS

It may seem obvious, but using or carrying illegal drugs of any kind whilst travelling is asking for trouble. If you're caught then it may not just be a fine or the drugs that you lose, but your freedom too, possibly for years. In countries that still operate the death penalty, drug smuggling is often one of the qualifying crimes.

Perhaps the easiest trap to fall into is purchasing souvenirs made from parts of endangered animals. Check your own country's customs regulations before travelling to ensure that you do not unwittingly contravene the law. Penalties for smuggling endangered animals, dead or alive, can be as severe as those for drug smuggling in some countries. Never carry anything for anyone else through customs, no matter how friendly they may seem or how much they offer to pay.

PERSONAL SAFETY

Whilst staying safe is very important on your travels, there is little point in becoming so obsessed with it that it spoils your holiday. Using the common sense that comes naturally to most people when visiting any big cities is really all you need on adventures in remote regions too. A healthy level of scepticism will help prevent you falling foul of the various tricks and scams that travellers encounter.

TRAVELLERS TIPS

• Treat any stranger that approaches you with caution. The more eager the person, the more caution is necessary.

• Learn to say no with some conviction.

• Stay as calm and clear-headed as possible, though this can be hard in stressful, crowded situations.

• Take a second or two before answering any question from a stranger.

AT NIGHT

Talk to friendly locals that you have met, such as hotel owners and tour guides, and ask about safe and unsafe areas to visit. It is very much in their interest that you remain safe for the sake of the tourism business. If possible, when you arrive somewhere, take time to get to know the place before heading out for a big night of partying, and don't drink too much. Avoiding getting very drunk is a major factor in staying safe.

Avoid wearing any signs of wealth. Even if your watch and jewellery are not that expensive in your own country, they are relatively valuable in many other countries where incomes are much lower. The majority of impromptu attacks are money related, so keeping your valuables out of sight is a good idea. Use a money belt or pouch that fits under your clothing and avoid accessing it in public areas. When going out around town, leave any large sums of money in your hotel safe deposit box.

DRESS SENSE

Dress conservatively. Flashy or revealing clothes all attract the wrong sort of attention. For women, it is sensible not to expose too much of your body no matter how strongly you feel that your personal rights should allow you to wear whatever you want. This is particularly important in countries where it is culturally insensitive to wear such clothing.

BE HONEST

On active adventures there is often an inherent but usually small risk of personal injury or worse involved. Be very honest with tour operators about your own abilities. There are often easier options available. Halfway down a big, wild rapid in a raft is not the time to divulge that you cannot swim. Take responsibility for your own actions, think on your feet rather than being led like a sheep, and voice concerns over any safety issues that you are not happy or comfortable with. Good operators won't take offence at such questions.

UGANDA

Uganda is as exciting as it is inviting. Characterized by swathes of lush, green land, rolling hills and mountain forests, it boasts unique attractions, including the source of the world's longest river, the Nile, and the home of the earth's last remaining population of mountain gorillas. The raging white-water rapids of the Nile provide a perfect antidote to the serene tranquillity of the gorillas' natural habitat, and both are easily accessible to any visitor with a sense of adventure. But the real beauty of Uganda lies in its people, who are as warm and welcoming as any in Africa. In a land where anarchy once ruled, there exists a spirit of goodwill that is humbling in its intensity. After a decade of recovery and reform, the country known as the Pearl of Africa is shining brighter than ever.

Lake Bunyonyi nestles in a rich farming community near Kabale, stretching out to the Virungu Mountains in the north and the gentle hills of Rwanda to the south

1 Rafting the Source of the Nile

by Paul Grogan

The source of the Nile still has one or two surprises in store for the unsuspecting traveller. As it begins its epic journey to the sea, it provides not only perfect conditions for rafting, but also one of the most spectacular and tortuous waterfalls in the world.

I don't think I have ever been so terrified. Gripping my paddle with one hand and my camera box with the other, I feel completely out of control. The first rapid on the river is fast-approaching, and the noise is deafening. Just when I think I'm sure to take a tumble, my driver screeches to a halt, reaches out a hand and says "Two thousand shillings, please." I am, of course, sitting on the back of a suicidal scooter.

These scooters—or *boda-bodas*, as they are called—are every bit as scary as any rapid you're likely to raft. For scarcely more than a few pennies, you can jump on the amply padded seat of any passing scooter, and travel wherever you want to go, with the minimum of fuss.

Although I chose to travel by public transport, it's easier to get to the river's source with individual raft companies, who usually provide transport from Kampala to the put-in point. I arranged my river trip through Adrift, who made the first descent of this section of the Nile in 1996. They pick up punters from almost anywhere in Kampala, and the 90-minute journey to Jinja is an essential part of the day's experience.

GETTING TO THE SOURCE

After the briefest of briefings, a few introductions, and some spectacularly corny jokes from the day's raft leader, the bus makes a breakfast stop at the "in-your-face chicken place." Before you have time to wind down your window, the verge is swarming with vendors, selling everything from chicken-on-a-stick to roast banana, or *gonja*. Roadside food is an integral part of travel in Uganda, and despite the risks to body and soul, it's an experience not to be missed.

Once stocked, the bus continues on its way to Jinja, a town on the banks of Lake Victoria. As you enter Jinja, the road from Kampala crosses Owen Falls Dam, which marks the present source of the Nile. Before the dam was built, this was the site of Ripon Falls, where the Nile began its 6,437km (4,000-mile) journey to the Mediterranean Sea. The "discovery" of the falls in 1862 is commemorated by a plaque to John Hanning Speke and James Augustus Grant, the first European explorers to set eyes on the source.

 No experience is necessary, although it helps to be comfortable with water. Apart from a few intense periods of paddling, rafting is rarely strenuous. To keep energy levels up, have a hearty breakfast and lunch.

 If you want all the comforts of home, you probably need $100 per night. However, if you're happy with clean, comfortable accommodation in smaller hotels and lodges, you'll be paying less than $10 per night. Eating out is excellent value for money wherever you are, and Kampala boasts some fantastic restaurants. Outside major towns and cities, food is generally simple but substantial.

 No specialist equipment is required for rafting. Wear waterproof sunscreen, and only wear sunglasses if you have something to hold them in place. Food and drink are provided, and if you want to take a camera, waterproof boxes are available. For Murchison Falls, sturdy shoes or boots are a must, as are bottles of mineral water—it can get extremely hot in the bush.

The start of Adrift's one- and two-day rafting trips is marked by Bugugali Falls, an immense and impressive rapid on a broad sweep of the river downstream of the dam. The campsite overlooking the falls has an expansive view upstream, and is a great place to stay if you want to fall asleep to the therapeutic thunder of the rapids below.

As I'm squeezing into my helmet and buoyancy aid, however, therapy is the last thing on my mind. Colin, our raft leader for the day, gets us kitted out, while Adrift's photographer Dave keeps everyone smiling for the camera. On closer inspection, our fixed grins are revealed as nervous grimaces: the sights and sounds of the first rapid are beckoning.

As Colin checks everyone's equipment, Piley, who will be paddling the safety raft, asks if I would like to kayak instead, as there is one too many for the raft. I have been kayaking for almost seven years, but nothing I have paddled even resembles what I can see from the bank. Undeterred, Piley passes me a paddle, and I find myself jelly-legged at the brink of Bugugali Falls, waiting for the first raft to come down.

BUGUGALI FALLS

Bugugali Falls is the most accessible of the rapids on this section of the Nile, and you're almost guaranteed a gathering of spectators to wave you on your way.

The falls are, in reality, more of a sloping ramp than a definite drop, over which the Nile pours with awesome power. To the left of this tongue of glassy-green water is an exploding diagonal wave, curling over every few seconds, like a breaker collapsing on a beach. To the right, at the bottom of the ramp, is an enormous stopper, or keeper, where water folds back on itself to form a hole of white water. The trick, I am told, is to paddle just to the right of the diagonal wave, and then just to the left of the hole. The problem is that the entire force of the world's greatest river is doing the exact opposite. Still, I console myself, at least

A RIVER WITH TWO SOURCES

The precise location of the source of the Nile was the last unsolved mystery of the exploration age, complicated by the fact that it actually has two sources. The much shorter Blue Nile was traced to its source on Lake Tana, in Ethiopia, as early as the 1770s, by explorer James Bruce. It was almost another 100 years before the Nile's true source (being furthest from the sea) was seen by a European for the first time.

I'll have a chance to see how it's done before it's my turn.

After a half-hour crash-course in rafting, Colin's team is ready to tackle the falls. Expertly and confidently, he guides the raft towards the lip, before urging poised paddles into action. The raft sneaks past the diagonal wave, but an imbalance in power spins it, side-on to the stopper. Before you can say "Forward HARD!" the raft is vertical, balancing on its left tube like a car on two wheels. Arms, legs and paddles flail as gravity begins to take over. Remarkably, the raft rights itself as quickly as it was wronged, and bodies are tossed back inside, like fish into a boat.

Having seen most of the action unfolding in the viewfinder of my camera, I still have no idea what *not* to do. As I turn, untidily, into the pounding current, the rafts below wait expectantly for my demise in the eddy. They are not disappointed. I sneak past the top obstacle, but this leaves me too far right, and too far gone to escape the white jaws of the stopper. I am punched by a wall of water, flipped upside down, and pummelled for what seems like forever, but is probably barely more than a second. Suddenly, I'm floating ignominiously beside my boat, with cheers ringing in my ears.

In terms of international grading, the source of the Nile is second to none. Of the 11 major rapids tackled on the first

day, four are classed as grade V, the highest grade that can legally be rafted by a commercial company. Its rapids and falls demand constant respect and vigilance; but its profile makes it as safe as any grade V in the world. Unlike most rivers of a similar grade, the Nile is wide and deep, with very few rocks to obstruct its powerful flow. The result is big waves and even bigger stoppers, but without the holding power of similar drops on more rocky rivers. In short, even if you take a spanking, you'll bob out at the bottom without a bruise—as I did.

Below Bugugali Falls, two more rapids follow in quick succession. A feeling of invincibility, instilled by my earlier suc-

cess, allows me to pay more attention to the rafts, and to watch their progress from below each rapid. Easy Rider is a relatively straightforward, V-shaped wave that the 5m (18ft) rafts sail over with disdain. Further on is Total Gunga, the first of the grade V rapids, with vast 4.5m (15ft) standing waves and big holes, left and right, to catch any wayward rafts. A standing wave is one that peaks continuously in the same place, rather than travelling downstream with the current, and is usually formed by some disturbance, such as a rock, or a change of depth below the surface. In some cases, a wave train is created, with each peak higher than the last. Gunga means "full

Left: *Punching through the waves of the intimidating Big Brother rapid at the source of the River Nile*
Inset: *Getting "geared-up" with the raft company before challenging the pounding current is a good distraction for pre-rapid nerves*

river" in Swahili, or "run the guts" in the local language, and here the rafts are dwarfed by the swollen water.

BIG BROTHER

For sheer anticipation, nothing beats the funnelled force of Big Brother. As the river rounds a bend to the left, it narrows and drops over a long shelf, producing a smooth slide into a succession of enormous standing waves at the bottom.

Safely installed in the eddy below, I watch Piley ease the safety raft over the brink of the drop. I follow its progress, snapping away with my camera on motor-drive, until it's through the first big wave. Then I bring the camera down to my side,

just in time to see the final wave collapse on Piley's boat and flip him like a paddling-pool dinghy. With the weight of an extra five paddlers, Colin's raft is heavier in the water, and punches through the waves without any problems.

THE BAD PLACE

Two more, smaller rapids lead to Lunch Island, where a substantial buffet is laid out. I'm still feeling fragile about what's in store, and struggle to eat more than a sandwich or two. The local safety kayakers, Moses and Charles, have no such reservations, piling their bread high with a cocktail of salami, peanut butter, jam and mayonnaise!

UGANDA

The hardest rapid of the day comes after lunch, but not before a stretch of flat water. There are no crocodiles on this section of the Nile, so the emerald-green pools provide the perfect opportunity to go for a swim, or soak up the sun after lunch. Then it's back down to business. Overtime is the second grade V of the day and, although not as intimidating as some of the earlier rapids, it is more technically demanding. Rocks near the top force the raft left; it then has to work its way right again to avoid a huge hole formed by the first obvious drop. From here, it's essential to power back across to the left to avoid the second drop—a vertical waterfall with a very rocky bottom.

Arriving ahead of the rafts, I get out above the rapid, and ask Moses to show me the route down. It's an unwritten law among paddlers that the longer you look at a rapid, the bigger it gets, so rather than watch Moses from the bank, I follow him like a lemming, trusting his line and emerging, exhilarated, in the pool at the

bottom. Still grinning with relief, I clamber out of my boat and claw my way up a rock in the middle of the river to take some photographs, just in time to miss both rafts arriving, upright, at the bottom of the rapid.

Finally, at the end of a perfect day's paddling, we face the biggest rapid of them all. In fact, Itanda is so big that we have to carry our boats around the top section, and put back onto the river for its final drop. Hundreds of metres long, and barraged by raft-eating stoppers, Itanda is a bad place to be, for all but the most experienced paddler. When it was first kayaked, by an adrenalin-fuelled New Zealander called Troy Bentley in 1996, he was rinsed in one of the holes for almost a minute, before emerging, dazed but coherent: "Dude, that's bad." Ever since, the final hole of Itanda has been known as The Bad Place.

The bottom section of Itanda is little more than a single stopper, but it's one of the biggest of the day, and provides a fitting finale. Once again, I watch as Colin's raft begins to drift sideways into the maw, and—whether by design or accident— the raft flips in an instant, tossing its occupants into the water, to be fished out in the eddy below. Five hours after the first rapid of the day, the river has had the last laugh; but for us, the grimaces have all become grins.

MURCHISON FALLS

The Nile, however, is by no means spent. Three hundred kilometres (180 miles) downstream, near its confluence with Lake Albert and the headwaters of the Blue Nile, the world's greatest river is forced into a gap barely 7m (24ft) wide. Combined with a vertical drop of some 25m (80ft), this constriction produces one of the most spectacular cataracts on earth: Murchison Falls.

Reaching the falls is all but impossible by public transport, so I hire a four-by-four in Kampala. Inside the national parks, the roads and dirt tracks can become treacherous after a thunder-

---

RIVER GRADING

International grading of white water uses the following approximate guidelines. The rapids at the source of the Nile are graded from III to V, although the depth of the water and the absence of rocks makes it much safer than the grade would suggest.

I Relatively flat water, with a few added ripples for fun

II One or two obvious obstacles to negotiate, and just that little bit more bouncy

III Bigger waves with more obstacles, through which an obvious line can be negotiated

IV More powerful and continuous, with big waves and less obvious obstacles

V As for IV, but more technically demanding, through which there may not be an obvious line

VI The limit of possibility—generally only negotiable at particular water levels

storm, and even outside, there are very few surfaced roads.

Murchison Falls are not the only treasure waiting to be discovered. Covering over 1,500sq. km (600sq. m), the national park is the largest faunal reserve in Uganda, featuring tropical savannah and woodlands, deciduous forest, evergreen forest and permanent swamps.

A PLAGUE OF FLIES

We leave Kampala early in the afternoon, in the hope of making it to Masindi by nightfall. The signpost to the park isn't obvious, even when you're looking out for it: count on it taking a couple of hours to get to the turning, and a further hour to get to Masindi. Arriving just before dusk, we filled up with petrol and bought provisions before settling into a local hotel.

The next morning, we plan for an early start, but a torrential storm keeps us at bay until 8am. Afternoon thunderstorms have become an almost daily ritual during our stay in Uganda, but they're usually short-lived, and leave the lush vegetation glowing with colour. This time the rain packs down the dirt on the road, making it much more manageable, and the drive less dusty. On our way to the falls, we pass through the Bugungu Game Reserve, where we are greeted by troops of baboons, lining the road as if paying their respects.

The dirt track deteriorates as it begins to wind down to the banks of the Nile, revealing a landscape of gently undulating bush. Driving through one of the hollows, I wind down my window for a better look at a monkey dancing about in the tree-tops. Before we know what's happening, our jeep is inundated with tsetse flies. Not much bigger than the common housefly, these flies have a nasty bite. In parts of Africa, they carry the sleeping sickness virus *trypanosomiasis*, which can be serious in humans if left untreated. At present, however, there is no sleeping sickness in Uganda. I later learn that tsetse flies are irresistibly drawn to large moving objects, such as

---

DRIVING IN UGANDA

Before you head off into the bush in your jeep:

❑ Check all the important functions of the vehicle before you leave, particularly lights and indicators

❑ Make sure that all the doors lock, and that a spare tyre and jack are included

❑ Buy a good map from one of the big bookshops in Kampala

❑ Plan your route before you go, and if in doubt, ask

❑ Fill up where and when you can, especially in Murchison Falls National Park

❑ Carry plenty of water and food

❑ Drive carefully on dirt roads, particularly in the wet season.

---

cattle, or safari vehicles—and have a penchant for colours like dark green. After a period of frenzied insecticide, I'm dreading the moment of disembarkation, but when we stop under an acacia tree, a stone's throw from the falls, the flies lose interest and disappear.

A SERPENT WITH SEVEN TONGUES

We are warmly welcomed to the falls by Stephen Asiimwe, a park warden, whose surname means "Thanks to God" in Bantu dialect. He tells us, with some pride, that it takes a year to train as a park warden, and competition for posts is fierce.

Long before you see the falls, you can hear their thunder, underscored by a continuous, resonant boom. Upstream, as far as the eye can see, the Nile races past with unimaginable speed and power, producing monstrous standing waves and churning holes. Only when you near the very lip of the drop, and the 7m (24ft) constriction below, can you fully appreciate the river's potential power. Even then,

U G A N D A

it's hard to take everything in: the jet of water corkscrews through the narrow gorge, exploding first against one wall, then the other. The noise makes it difficult to talk, and the spray creates two distinct rainbows. Legend has it that the rainbow is a serpent with seven tongues, and is a sign that the gods are angry.

Leading us up a short path, Stephen shows us the second fall, on the other side of the river, a pillow of white just visible over the lush canopy of the forest. These falls were formed as recently as 1962, when a flash flood punched a second gorge through the rock, and washed away an existing bridge that had spanned the main falls. A rectangular concrete pillar is still visible on the very edge of the drop, and in low water it's possible to crouch on top of the pillar, only metres from the cascading chaos.

Murchison Falls has never been paddled. Stephen tells us that, in 1997, an American team applied for permission to raft the falls, but the national park authorities refused to take responsibility for the consequences. Your first view of the falls will be enough to convince you of the wisdom of their decision. After its tortuous descent, the Nile loses much of its youthful energy, and from here as far

Above: White water on the lip of Murchison Falls
Right: A basking crocodile best viewed from the top deck of a river launch

as Lake Albert, some 28km (18 miles) downstream, it flows undisturbed. The calm waters and verdant banks are a haven for wildlife. In order to see it all closer to hand, we book a launch trip from the national park headquarters in Paraa, an hour's drive from the falls.

THE FALLS FROM BELOW

If you've never been boating on a river full of hippos, the launch trip is a must. Soaking up the mid-afternoon sun on the top deck of the launch, we spy crocodiles, buffaloes, giraffes, waterbucks, and hippos, not to mention dozens of species of bird, including grey herons, pied kingfishers and the rare giant kingfisher. As we drift, we pass a sandstone cliff. It is punctuated with holes, swarming with tiny white-fronted bee-eaters, which lay their eggs in the cliff, and, despite the confusion, always know which hole to return to.

As we round the corner and moor up to an island, we can see the falls in their entirety for the first time. The sight silences the entire group. Here, the Nile that I challenged and paddled only a few days before has the last word.

GOING IT ALONE

INTERNAL TRAVEL

Getting to the source of the Nile is easy. Adrift collect clients from the Sheraton Hotel in Kampala and the Red Chilli Hideaway on the outskirts of town. If you're in a group, you can probably arrange to be picked up anywhere in Kampala; even if you're not, it's relatively easy to get to any of the pick-up points by taxi or *matatu* (white minibus). Adrift also arrange transport back to Kampala after the rafting, with complimentary beer and soft drinks to help while away the journey. If you've not had enough of the Nile, you can arrange to be dropped at the campsite overlooking Bugugali Falls. The following morning it's easy to get a *boda-boda* (scooter) to the bus station in Jinja, and from here you can catch one of the regular buses back to Kampala.

Getting to Murchison Falls is more difficult. You'll need your own transport, although hiring a jeep in Uganda is by no means cheap. There are dozens of rental agencies to choose from in Kampala, and it's worth shopping around to see who can offer the best deal (see the Contacts section at the back of the book). There is no public transport inside the park gates, so the only way to get into the park is in a private vehicle.

WHEN TO GO

Because the Nile is dam-regulated, the water levels remain more or less constant throughout the year, making rafting possible year-round. The best time to travel to Murchison Falls is from June to September, as these are the driest months of the year; even then, it's worth being prepared for wet weather, as afternoon thunderstorms are common. During the rainy season, many of the unsurfaced roads become impassable, making it difficult and potentially dangerous to get around. From June to September temperatures average a comfortable 25°C (80°F).

PLANNING YOUR TRIP

No special arrangements are needed for rafting: Adrift take care of everything for you. If you go to Murchison Falls, you can pre-book accommodation and game drives through the Uganda Tourist Board in Kampala before you go, or arrange everything when you arrive at the park. Game drives can be booked at the park headquarters in Paraa, as can morning and afternoon launch cruises. A visit to the falls themselves does not need to be booked in advance—simply turn up and take the tour.

HEALTH MATTERS

Comprehensive travel insurance is essential. Hepatitis, meningitis, polio, typhoid and yellow fever inoculations are all recommended, as are malaria tablets. Consult your doctor at least six weeks before you go. In the event of cuts and scrapes, particularly on the river, clean the affected area with one or two drops of iodine, and cover with an absorbent dressing to prevent infection. Untreated tap water is best avoided—bottled water is readily available. Roadside food is an experience not to be missed, but make sure it's freshly cooked and piping hot before purchasing.

WHAT TO TAKE

Although no technical equipment is required for rafting, Murchison Falls provides the perfect opportunity for game-viewing and photography. It's worth packing a pair of pocket binoculars to spot birds and animals on the river. If you're interested in preserving your memories on celluloid, a good zoom lens—300mm or longer—and a tripod could make all the difference.

2 Gorilla-tracking in the Impenetrable Forest

by Paul Grogan

Home to one of the world's last remaining groups of mountain gorillas, Uganda's Impenetrable Forest is more like a prehistoric world than a national park. After a visit to this "planet of the apes," nearby Lake Bunyonyi is the perfect place to unwind.

Perched on the end of a sheet of corrugated iron, I must be at least a metre (3ft) from the apparent safety of the pick-up truck's flatbed, my feet dangling over the speeding road. It is the first day of my journey after Bwindi National Park, and until now things have been going quite smoothly. I grip the edge of the sheet with white-knuckle fists, until a whispered word from a fellow dangler convinces me that if I want to keep my fingers, I should hang on to something else. For the remainder of the journey I tether my fingers to the straps of my holdall, safe in the knowledge that if I should fall, at least my bag will come with me.

It can take up to six hours to find the gorillas, although two or three hours is more likely. If in doubt, be prepared: take plenty of bottled mineral water (available at the park entrance) and a full packed lunch, and don't be afraid to rest when you need to.

In Uganda accommodation is either ridiculously cheap or horrendously expensive—many of the cheaper options offer excellent value for money and are usually clean and comfortable, particularly in the national parks.

No specialist equipment is required for gorilla-tracking, but you'd be well advised to bring sun screen and a hat, and a waterproof jacket, in case of a thunderstorm. Sturdy shoes or boots are also a must. If you're interested in photography, take more film than you think you might need. It can be extremely dark in the shade of the forest, even on bright days, so fast film (ASA 400 or 800) is essential. If you plan to take a lot of photographic equipment, check the insurance small print to ensure that it's covered.

POST BUS TO KABALE

Our adventure had started in Kampala. Getting around in Uganda, as in most East African countries, is as much of an adventure as the adventures themselves. Booking through a tour operator or renting your own vehicle are by far the easiest ways to arrange a gorilla trek, but getting to Bwindi from Kampala is relatively straightforward, and arguably more entertaining, by public transport.

My girlfriend, Emma, and I decide to take the post bus from Kampala, a comfortable and convenient means of getting around. We arrive at the city centre depot at 7am to ensure a seat for the 8am departure. The Post Office only sells as many tickets as there are seats on the bus, so we're guaranteed some comfort for the six-hour journey to Kabale, the town at the end of the line. The bus wastes no time getting to its destination. Unless nature calls, there's no need to get off, and at some villages the mail is simply flung from the bus door. While the ruthless driving delivers us on time, I can't help but feel robbed as we cross the equator: I long to jump off with my makeshift plug-hole (a bottle of mineral water), to see which way the water whirls.

BWINDI BOUND

We reach Kabale in the early afternoon, and try to find a *matatu*, or public minibus, to take us to Bwindi, the home of the mountain gorillas. Uncertain of local prices, and unable to find a regular bus, we eventually book a taxi at the national

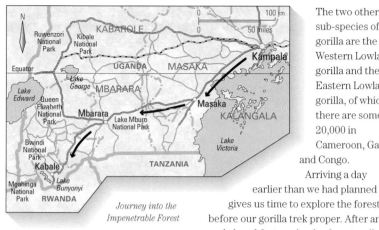

Journey into the Impenetrable Forest

The two other sub-species of gorilla are the Western Lowland gorilla and the Eastern Lowland gorilla, of which there are some 20,000 in Cameroon, Gabon and Congo.

Arriving a day earlier than we had planned gives us time to explore the forest before our gorilla trek proper. After an early breakfast, we book a forest walk at

park information centre, and are whisked right up to the gates of the national park for $50. Initially, I am indignant at the high price, but by the end of the journey I'm ready to sell the driver my soul. The road winds up into the mountains of the Rift Valley, and, as it deteriorates, the bottom of the car takes a pounding from rocks and stones. It takes almost four hours to make the journey, and by the time we arrive it's too dark for the driver to go back. To compound my admiration, a sticker on the car's dashboard reads: "May God bless my hands to drive you more safely." Grateful to have made the journey in a day, Emma and I check into one of the thatched huts by lantern-light, and wait for the dawn.

Bwindi was designated a national park in 1991, in an attempt to protect one of the last remaining habitats of mountain gorillas on earth. In fact, Bwindi is home to half the world's gorilla population, boasting an estimated 300 individuals. The only other place in the world where mountain gorillas are found is Mgahinga National Park, some 40km (25 miles) south of Bwindi. In the far southwest corner of the country, Mgahinga is contiguous with the Parc Nacional de Volcans, in Rwanda, and the Parc National des Virungas, in the Congo. It is possible to see the gorillas there, but political problems in the Congo make tracking them across borders impractical.

the park headquarters, next to the campsite. Medad, our guide, leads us into the forest for the first time, and we are joined by Chris, a personal fitness trainer from New Zealand. A number of forest tracks start at the park headquarters; with a whole day to kill, we opt for the Waterfall Trail, a moderate walk that takes three to four hours at an easy pace. Under cover of the canopy, it's much cooler in the forest, and although it's by no means dry, the humidity never feels oppressive.

A few minutes' walk into the forest, Medad introduces us to the kind of wildlife we might expect to see. In addition to gorillas, chimpanzees and baboons, black-and-white colobus monkeys are typical. Less common are duiker, bush pigs and elephant—although they can be seen higher up the mountains. The forest also boasts hundreds of bird, butterfly and plant species. Fig trees grow in abundance, providing food for gorillas in the form of leaves, fruit and even bark; Medad tells us that gorillas are easily tracked by trails of fig trees stripped of their bark.

We eat lunch at the foot of Munyaga Falls, a wispy, 30m (100ft) cascade, in a tiny, sunlit clearing. The smells and sounds of the forest provide a welcome contrast from the rigours endured the previous day. Back at the lodge that afternoon, the sky is bruised black and blue by a threatening thunderstorm,

which, we soon realize, is a daily ritual in the mountains.

BACK ON TRACK

Eight o'clock isn't an early start in the tropics, but the shutters in the thatched huts block out almost all light, and it's very difficult to get up in time for breakfast at 7am. Eating at this time of the day is important, though, as it can take many hours' walking to find the gorillas, and, even in the relative shade of the forest, energy reserves are quickly depleted.

It's less than a minute's walk to the park headquarters, where we sign for our permits and meet the other members of our group. Susanna and Bodu are both journalists from Germany; David is an electrical engineer from America, and Kathy, David's wife, is a computer programmer. Only when we all pile out of the pick-up truck at the trailhead do I appreciate the full extent of our entourage. In

Above: A safari tent can be a warm welcome for a weary trekker in Bwindi National Park
Inset: Reassuring presence of an armed guard accompanying a group tracking gorillas
Right: Trails of fig trees stripped of their leaves provide a clue to the whereabouts of gorilla families

addition to our guide, we are accompanied by three more trackers, and three guards. In fact, everywhere we go in Bwindi National Park, we are seldom far from the watchful gaze of our armed sentinels. Following the kidnapping of foreign tourists in April 1999, the national park authorities recruited and trained what amounted to a small army to ensure that it would never happen again. Throughout our stay in the park, troops are drilled on a daily basis, from sun-up to sunset, watching over the camp day and night. While their presence now is

reassuring, the kidnapping did leave its legacy: the overnight drop in tourism was catastrophic. People from all over Uganda were affected by this lone act of aggression, from tour operators to roadside bakers. Uganda's recovering economy has relied heavily on the tourist dollar, and the subsequent loss of investment has been keenly felt. Gradually, though, the tourists have returned, to find a country desperate to please, and hell-bent on protecting its interests.

Before we set off, our guide, Stephen, introduces himself, and briefs us on the ground rules. If any of us has a cough or a cold, now is the time to turn back: if Stephen or any of the trackers suspects that one of us is covering up an infection after this point, they can forbid us from seeing the gorillas. Although human beings possess antibodies to fight infection, the gorillas are unlikely to have developed any such immunity, and they could be severely affected, particularly if the strain is highly contagious. Similarly, all human waste has to be carefully buried and all rubbish diligently carried out of the park. Once we find the gorillas, caution is our watchword: where possible, we must stay at least 5m (16ft) away, and it's important to avoid sudden sounds or movements that might make them nervous. Flash photography is forbidden, as it frightens the animals and can make them agitated and aggressive. Unless provoked, gorillas are peaceful animals, despite their impressive size: males can weigh up to 180kg (400lb).

Once he is sure we have all understood, Stephen tells us a little about the national park and the animals. In the interests of the gorillas, permits to the park are deliberately limited to a dozen per day, split between two groups. The group we are hoping to see is called the M (or Mubare) group; the H (or Habinyanja) group is further away, and less accessible. (One of the problems of tracking gorillas is that they move around in search of food, and sometimes walk deep into the forest, away from appreciative eyes.)

OTHER NATIONAL PARKS

There are nine national parks in Uganda, many within a day's drive of Bwindi. Mgahinga, in the southeastern corner of Uganda, is another gorilla sanctuary. To the north of Bwindi is Queen Elizabeth, which has birds and hippos and sometimes buffaloes, elephants and lions. Bordering Queen Elizabeth is Kibale, home to the highest density of primates in the world. Less well-known, but well worth a visit, is Lake Mburo to the east, which can be explored on foot or by canoe. At the time of writing, Ruwenzori is closed, but it's worth trying to visit if the political situation in the Congo improves.

Time with the gorillas is strictly limited to one hour a day, to prevent excessive contact and overhabituation. Although the Ugandan Wildlife Authority (UWA) could quite easily cash in on its monopoly, it works hard to preserve a natural resource that is as valued for its rarity as for the revenue it generates.

OUT IN THE MIDDAY SUN

At first our walk is relatively easy going, but the path soon steepens as we head higher into the hills. We're not yet in the forest, and the mid-morning sun is merciless, but the views are fantastic. The landscape is lush and green all the way across the border with the Congo, and along the way we pass dozens of smallholdings and terraces being worked by local farmers. Plantain—or *matooke*—is the staple food in Uganda, and it's not uncommon to see bicycles buckling under what looks like a hundredweight of raw bananas. Cheap and cheerful, *matooke* is prepared as an accompaniment to meat, fish and vegetables. The texture is not dissimilar to squash or pumpkin, but it's definitely something of an acquired taste.

After an hour's walking, the trail reaches the forest edge. On the previous day, the M group was found not far from here, and it makes sense to pick up their trail and follow the signs of their migration. Gorillas roam only as far as they need to for food, stopping at night to build nests of branches and leaves, either in a clearing or up in the trees. In the event, it's only a few minutes before we hear the first rustlings ahead. We still can't see the gorillas, but the discovery gives us a chance to regroup and prepare cameras and tripods for our imminent encounter. Treading carefully and quietly through the dark forest undergrowth, we're almost on top of the group before we see them.

Gradually, outlines begin to emerge from the shadows. Ahead is a pair of playing adolescents; to the left, a languishing silverback, and, to our right, a female on the move. Stephen explains that these gorillas live in small groups, which are fairly stable, and remain together for years. Each group of females and their offspring is led by a dominant silverback male. On reaching maturity, the males leave the family group to start their own harem, while females move on to join another group.

With the exception of the silverback—who is not about to be disturbed from his siesta—it's all we can do to keep track of our group. Within a few minutes of our arrival, the female breaks rank and saunters over as if to say hello. Seen through the zoom lens of my camera, she seems to be getting a little too close for comfort, but just when I think things are going to get embarrassingly intimate, she changes her mind and strolls past. Apparently, it's not unusual for habituated gorillas to be as curious about us as we are about them. Only the day before our visit, one of the babies took a female trekker by the hand as if they were walking in Central Park.

Despite the sobriety of the occasion the guards start laughing—but not nearly as much as they do when the silverback decides to rouse himself for a romantic encounter with the female. It's by no means a quiet congress, with a great deal of grunting and groaning on the male's part, but the female might as well be buffing her nails throughout the whole episode for all the interest she shows.

Before you can say "change of film", your time is up, and you wonder where it all went. Chances are, a great deal of this precious hour will be spent trying to capture a cartwheel on camera, but unless you know exactly what you're doing, you're better off buying a brimming collection of perfectly exposed postcards. It's hardly surprising to learn that the word *bwindi* means "dark place" in Swahili; as a consequence, photography in the rainforest is notoriously difficult. If you are intent on taking the perfect shot on your first visit, you're likely to miss the experience completely. If you go without any distractions, it's a meeting that will stay with you for the rest of your life.

PAYING THE PRICE

Many travellers would have you believe that tracking gorillas has become prohibitively expensive. However, when you consider that most foreign visitors will have paid four or five times the amount just to fly to Uganda, it's difficult to justify their complaints. By limiting the number of permits to 12 per day, the Ugandan Wildlife Authority is fighting to secure the fate of the gorillas for future generations: the only way to maintain this status quo is to channel funds back into Uganda's once beleaguered economy. The difference it makes to the lives of local Ugandans is enormous, while most foreign visitors will hardly notice the blip in their bank balance.

LAKELAND PARADISE

Reluctant to join the road-race back to Kampala, Emma and I decide to spend a few days relaxing on Lake Bunyonyi, a small haven of secluded islands and warm

UGANDA

Below: *An early morning fisherman glides across the serene waters of Lake Bunyonyi*
Left: *The islands dotted across the lake are easily accessible by dugout canoes*
Right: *at the Buhoma Campsite in the Bwindi National Park*

UGANDA

water in Uganda's southwestern corner. Getting there is simply a matter of making our way by taxi back to Kabale, and then finding a pick-up truck with enough corrugated iron in the back to carry one extra passenger… and his bag.

Emma is riding shot-gun, standing right behind the cab and craning her neck for the first view of the lake. As we crest the pass, the pick-up truck stops to unload its cargo and (luckily for me) some of the passengers. Below us, the lake stretches out to meet the Virungu Mountains of the Congo to the north, and the rolling hills of Rwanda to the south. The lake is dotted with islands and crisscrossed by the wakes of dugout canoes. Five minutes later, we, too, are plying across the water to Bushara Island, our home for the next few days.

RELAXING AMONG THE ISLANDS

As we paddle out to our lake-side paradise, our guide—another Stephen—gives us a tour. Of the lake's 39 islands, many are completely uninhabited, although some are cultivated and one or two are even permanently occupied. There are campsites and lodges on Bushara and Jasper's, and nearby Bwama Island used to be a leper colony, but is now home to a primary and secondary school. Between Bushara and Bwama is a

lone island with a single tree. Legend has it that when the local young girls became pregnant out of wedlock, they were banished to this island to starve to death. Whether this is just a superstitious native legend or a myth propagated by visiting missionaries, Stephen admits, is difficult to determine.

At the far end of the lake lies Rwanda and the impressive Kyevu Market, where it's possible to visit the local pygmy community. The round trip takes about nine hours by canoe, but only five by motorboat, and is well worth the journey if you want to visit Rwanda and experience a local village market for an afternoon.

Ours is a more relaxing agenda. Landing at Bushara Island, we meet two friends: Joe, an economic adviser to Uganda's Minister of Finance, and his girlfriend, Jarina, who works for a charity in Kampala. We have the island to ourselves, and for two whole days we swim in the lake, eat at the island's restaurant and drink lake-chilled beers on the jetty. By day we watch for the dozens of bird species that frequent the lake year-round, and by night we stay in luxury safari tents, with views across the lake. We even brave an open crossing in our own canoe to buy some beer from one of the neighbouring islands. We return in the moonlight. In Uganda, even the simple act of going out for a drink can be an unforgettable experience.

PUBLIC TRANSPORT

Because private transport is a luxury in Uganda, public transport is correspondingly efficient: wherever you want to go, you can always find someone to take you there. In towns and cities, taxis and *matatus* (minibuses) are perhaps the most convenient way to get around, although for short distances you might be better off on a *boda-boda*, or scooter. Lethal or exhilarating, depending on your point of view, *boda-bodas* come into their own in heavy traffic and will take you anywhere in the city for a handful of change. In smaller towns, scooters are replaced by bicycles with padded seats, providing a far more sedate and civilized way to travel. For longer journeys, coaches are more common, but by no means less exciting: known as carpet-bombers, they fly along the potholed roads with disdain, leaving cyclists and pedestrians spluttering in a tumultuous wake of smoke and sand.

GOING IT ALONE

INTERNAL TRAVEL

Getting to Bwindi is an adventure in its own right, and you're likely to see more of the country and its people if you use public transport. There are regular bus services connecting all the major towns in the south east, and *matatus* (minibuses) and taxis serve local routes. Alternatively, Kampala's General Post Office operates a bus service to all important administrative centres three times a week. Tickets are sold on a first-come, first-served basis, so it's advisable to get there an hour or so early. From Kabale, it's another three hours' drive to Bwindi by taxi. You might be able to arrange a lift at the national park office in Kabale for a small fee.

Without your own vehicle, the only way to get back to Kabale from Bwindi is to arrange a taxi at the park headquarters. It's only a short taxi-ride from Kabale to Lake Bunyonyi, where a flotilla of dugout canoes is waiting to take you anywhere on the lake.

WHEN TO GO

The best times to go to Uganda are January and February, and between June and September, as these are the driest months of the year. During the rainy season, many roads become impassable, making it difficult to get around. Even in the dry season, it pays to be prepared for wet weather, as afternoon thunderstorms are not uncommon. From June to September temperatures average a comfortable 25°C (80°F), rising to 27°C (85°F) in January and February.

PLANNING A TREK

There are dozens of tour operators to choose from in Uganda, offering a huge variety of adventure tours, from a day's rafting on the source of the Nile to a two-week tour of Uganda's national parks. Prices usually include transport, accommodation, food, park entry fees and guides, and often work out to be no more expensive than going it alone. It is possible to arrange everything independently, but you have to be more flexible, particularly when it comes to tracking gorillas. The number of permits is strictly limited to 12 per day, most of which are snapped up by tour operators, but it is possible to book treks through the Uganda Wildlife Authority in Kampala (see Contacts or A–Z). If you have no luck there, and are determined to do things the hard way, it's worth going to Bwindi on the off-chance: you usually won't have to wait for more than a day or two.

HEALTH MATTERS

Comprehensive medical insurance is essential. Vaccinations against hepatitis, meningitis, polio, typhoid and yellow fever are recommended, as are malaria tablets—check with your doctor at least six weeks before departure. Take care what you eat, but don't be too timid—trying new foods and flavours is all part of the experience. Reliable bottled water is readily available everywhere in Uganda.

WHAT TO TAKE

❑ An umbrella—you'll be thankful for some shelter in the event of an unexpected thunderstorm.

❑ A pocket torch—most accommodation will have electricity or a lantern, but a torch will come in handy for walking back and forth after dark.

❑ A warm fleece or coat—even in the dry season the evenings can get cold.

❑ A long-sleeved shirt and trousers to protect against mosquitoes, particularly at dusk.

❑ A pair of pocket binoculars—Lake Bunyonyi is a haven for dozens of spectacular bird species.

❑ An inflatable travel pillow—getting from place to place means a lot of travelling, and potholes are not conducive to an afternoon snooze.

TRAVELLERS' TIPS

❑ At the time of writing, visas can be obtained on arrival at Entebbe for $30, but it's best to check with your nearest Ugandan Embassy before departure.

❑ Take traveller's cheques in US dollars. If you do take cash, make sure the notes are less than five years old or you may have trouble exchanging money or paying for park permits.

❑ When paying for public transport or roadside food, try and check to see what everyone else is paying. If you're in any doubt, ask one of your fellow passengers.

❑ In national parks, it's worth tipping more than you would back home. The very fact that you're in Uganda probably means that you won't miss the money, but the wardens, guides and guards are outstanding and worth every penny.

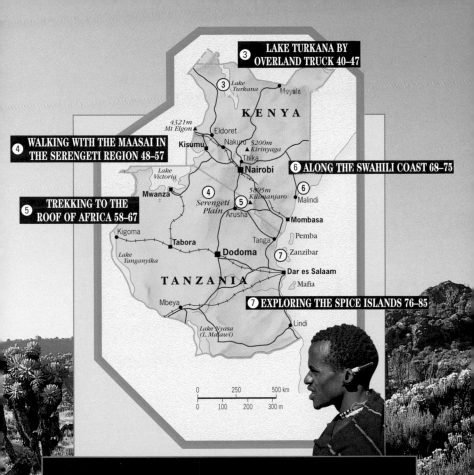

LAKE TURKANA BY OVERLAND TRUCK 40–47

③ Lake Turkana

Moyala

K E N Y A

4321m Mt Elgon ▲

Eldoret

WALKING WITH THE MAASAI IN THE SERENGETI REGION 48–57

Nakuru

5200m ▲ Kirinyaga

Kisumu

Thika

Nairobi

Lake Victoria

ALONG THE SWAHILI COAST 68–75

Mwanza

⑥ Malindi

5895m Kilimanjaro ▲

TREKKING TO THE ROOF OF AFRICA 58–67

④ Serengeti Plain

⑤ Arusha

Kigoma

■ **Mombasa**

Tabora

Tanga

Pemba

Lake Tanganyika

Dodoma

⑦ Zanzibar

■ **Dar es Salaam**

T A N Z A N I A

Mafia

Mbeya

EXPLORING THE SPICE ISLANDS 76–85

Lindi

Lake Nyasa (L. Malawi)

0 — 250 — 500 km
0 — 100 — 200 — 300 m

KENYA • TANZANIA

From the snow-capped summit of Kilimanjaro, Africa's highest mountain, to the coral reefs of Zanzibar Island and Malindi, the East African countries of Kenya and Tanzania offer a kaleidoscope of adventure opportunities. Some of Africa's most famous wildlife reserves lie against the spectacular backdrop of the Great Rift Valley, stretching through both countries in a rugged mosaic of escarpments, volcanoes, lakes and rolling savannah. They include the Serengeti and Maasai Mara, home of the legendary wildebeest migration and of the proud Maasai people. After viewing wildlife on foot or from a hot-air balloon, travellers can reach new heights by scaling Kilimanjaro, or take to the depths by scuba-diving off the reef-fringed coast. The region's culture and history is equally diverse, particularly on the offshore islands of Lamu and Zanzibar. Here, centuries of trade with the Middle East and beyond have left a rich legacy of fascinating traditions, lifestyles and architecture.

Impressive giant groundsel on the trail up Kilimanjaro

KENYA

3 Lake Turkana by Overland Truck

by Philip Briggs

Lake Turkana, the largest desert lake in the world, is something of a legend in East Africa: a place everybody means to visit but few ever do. An eight-day round trip took me through some of Africa's wildest terrain, with diversions to the game-rich Samburu National Reserve and montane forest of Marsabit National Park.

The arid badlands of northern Kenya remain as they have always been, a land apart, thinly populated by semi-nomadic pastoralists, whose colourful, traditional attire and ascetic lifestyle seem thrillingly anachronistic in a country that otherwise ranks as one of the most modern and economically buoyant in Africa.

The moonscapes of northern Kenya seem an improbable setting for the 11th largest natural freshwater body in the world: Lake Turkana, a 250km (155-mile) long sliver of green water, hemmed in by the walls of the Great Rift Valley. This remote and inhospitable region, which covers an area similar to that of Great Britain, was among the last parts of Africa to attract European explorers. Lake Turkana was "discovered" by the Hungarian adventurer Count Teliki in 1888, more than two decades after all the other great lakes of the Rift Valley had been made known to the outside world.

A WET BEGINNING

Leaden skies and drizzle envelop Nairobi on the day we board the overland truck to Lake Turkana. It has been pouring down over Kenya's capital city for the past week. The rain persists throughout most of our first day in the truck, which involves crossing the fertile central highlands immediately north of Nairobi. In more flattering weather, this landscape of rolling green hills, small subsistence farms and remnant patches of evergreen forest has a lush beauty all its own, particularly when the snowy peak of Mount Kenya—at 5,199m (17,000ft), Africa's second highest mountain—emerges from its customary cloudy shroud. The desert beckons.

The long drive provides a good opportunity to get to know our fellow passengers. In addition to my South African self and Belgian wife, the group consists of a young, bronzed English couple who've been backpacking in East Africa for several months; three 18-year-old Kenyan students; a trio of well-travelled Danish doctors in their 30s and 40s; and a pair of 20-something Israelis draped with cameras and

 Practically no physical effort is required on the overland truck trip. If you suffer from back problems, however, the rough roads could inflict some serious damage.

 You will camp most nights in a reasonably spacious tent provided by the operator. Normally you have to set up your own tent. Foam mattresses are provided, and you can hire a sleeping bag if you don't have your own. By day the combination of dust, heat and rough roads can be rather taxing. This is not a trip suitable for travellers expecting anything approaching luxury, but the level of comfort is comparable to a well-organized camping safari.

 Binoculars will enhance your enjoyment of game drives, allowing you to get a better look at distant animals and colourful birds. Dust can damage sensitive camera equipment. Carry your camera in a dustproof cover and avoid removing or putting in a new film in the open.

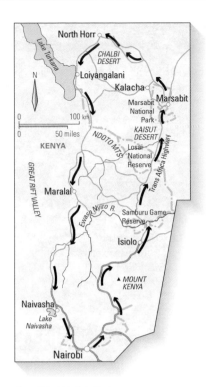

From Nairobi to Lake Turkana

camcorders. There is no public transport to the lake, while driving up in a rented four-by-four is both costly and logistically daunting: the target market for this overland truck trip is pretty much anybody who wants to see Lake Turkana.

CREATURES GREAT AND SMALL

Our goal for the night is Samburu Game Reserve, an unfenced expanse of dry, hilly scrub, bisected by the Ewaso Nyiro River and a ribbon of woodland. In the late afternoon we descend from the central highlands to Isiolo, the gateway town to the north. The transition from grassy meadow to dusty acacia woodland is as abrupt as it is welcome. We finally get blue skies, and the last stretch of surfaced road we will see for a while recedes in a cloud of dust.

Towards dusk we arrive at the semipermanent camp that will be our home for the next two nights. Set in a grove of

tall fig and acacia trees no more than 100m (304ft) from the river bank, the camp has a quintessential African bush atmosphere, enhanced by a steady through traffic of small animals. Unstriped ground squirrels scamper between their burrows; a troop of scrounging vervet monkeys lurks in the trees; a diminutive Guenther's dik-dik grazes nervously in the nearby bush. After nightfall, we are introduced to the undoubted star of the camp: a semiresident small-spotted genet, whose fearless behaviour indicates that she hasn't read the field guides describing this beautifully marked nocturnal carnivore as "shy and elusive."

After an early night, we awake at 6am for a game drive along a track following the north bank of the river, where we encounter most of the common herbivores: reticulated giraffe, plains zebra, Grevy's zebra, African elephant and several different types of antelope. The game is less prolific to the south of the river, where we spend the afternoon, but what its lacks in quantity is made up for in quality. A personal highlight of the afternoon game drive is my first sighting of a striped hyena, rarer and more localized than the ubiquitous spotted hyena. This is matched by a long look at a female leopard and two sub-adults drinking at the river. Big cats are not especially common in Samburu, and leopards—notoriously elusive throughout their range—are perhaps the most sought-after animal on any East African safari.

We visit a Samburu village on the fringe of the game reserve. The village consists of perhaps a dozen low, circular thatched huts, built by plastering mud over a skeletal wooden frame, and it is home to an extended Samburu family, presided over by a patriarchal chief. To the Samburu, cattle and wealth are all but synonymous; at the core of any Samburu village, positioned where it can most easily be defended, lies the cattle stockade or *boma*, effectively the communal piggy bank. The village we visit derives much of

its income from entertaining tourists, and our short tour is followed by demonstrations of traditional crafts such as spear making, then an energetic dance routine performed by traditionally dressed Samburu warriors. In less remote parts of East Africa, one might be tempted to question the authenticity of it all, but in Samburuland most people still dress tradionally: we see dozens of practically identical villages along the roadside.

A HIGHWAY AND A TOURIST LODGE

The long, lonely road that runs northward from Isiolo to the Ethiopian border is marked on some maps as the Trans-Africa Highway. This is, indeed, the most viable land route between Kenya and Ethiopia—but a *highway*? We are talking

about a spine-jarring ribbon of corrugated sand, baked hard by the relentless sun, and pockmarked with all manner of outrageous gulleys and potholes. On the third day, we spend eight hours experiencing the topographical idiosyncracies of the Trans-Africa Highway. At first, the scenery outweighs the brutal physicality of the 250km (155-mile) stretch of road that links Samburu to Marsabit: wide, open plains studded with tall mountains and jagged rocky monoliths that jut out like gigantic shark teeth. The wildlife, too, provides welcome distraction: we pick out the a herd of Grant's gazelles and a few dik-dik, grazing on the low, dry scrub; a pale chanting goshawk perches on the naked branch of an umbrella thorn tree; and a pair of Harlaub's bustards scurry hysterically into the yellowing grass. In the middle of these empty badlands, there is something strange and deeply stirring about the occasional sight of a solitary Samburu warrior draped in customary red blanket, herding his precious cattle along the road.

My back is in agony by the time we ascend to the cool highlands around Marsabit, and frankly it would take more than the sight of blanketed warrior to stir me (a signpost reading "massage parlour" might do the trick!). Still, it is comforting to know that the most grinding drive of the trip is behind us, and my spirits rise further when Michael announces that, before setting up camp, we will be dropped off at the national park's tourist lodge for a drink.

Marsabit Lodge is, indeed, deserted of tourists, but it does boast a superb location, on the edge of a crater lake encircled by lushly forested cliffs. It's a real treat to spend a couple of hours here, sipping beers (no fridge, alas) and watching the passing parade. A pair of fish eagles circle overhead, while the grey herons, African

Above Left: *Ethiopian painting in a church in Kalacha*
Left: *Turkana woman fetching spring water at Loiyangalani,clad in the traditional colourful clothes of her tribe*
Above: *Elephant strolling in Samburu Game Reserve, an unfenced expanse of dry, hilly scrub*

DRY COUNTRY ANIMALS

Samburu Game Reserve hosts many of Africa's typical plains animals, but it is arguably of greatest interest for those species which are restricted to the belt of arid land separating the moist highlands of southern Kenya from central Ethiopia. Samburu, for example, is practically the only accessible reserve in Africa to harbour the rare and localized Grevy's zebra. The reticulated giraffe is another Samburu "special," similar in size to other giraffes, but with more beautiful markings. The most striking of Samburu's mammals is perhaps the gerenuk: in Swahili this remarkable gazelle antelope is called *swala twiga* (literally "giraffe antelope"), an apt name for a creature that feeds off high branches by standing on its hind legs, extending its long neck and burrowing between the thorns with its small head.

spoonbills and yellow-billed storks that line the lake shore are interrupted several times by the pugnacious swoopings of a peregrine falcon. Over the course of the afternoon, seven elephants emerge from the forest on the opposite shore of the lake, and make their way ponderously to a salt lick immediately below the lodge. As the sun sets behind us, we sit in awed silence, sipping sundowners, less than 5m (16ft) away from these massive beasts.

The elephants move off and so do we: to set up camp in a splended patch of forest on the edge of the national park. As we cluster around the fire after another delicious dinner, Michael urges us not to worry about any bumps we might hear above our heads tonight, explaining that the baboons in this campsite habitually defecate all over the tents.

A CRACKED DESERT

The next 48 hours have a surreal quality, as we cut westwards from Marsabit to cross the remote Chalbi Desert. Over the two days we spend driving through this fantastically empty landscape, we pass only two other vehicles. Occasionally, a family of Somali ostrich or a herd of Grant's gazelles breaks into a run at the approach of our truck. We stop for a picnic lunch beneath an approximation of a shady tree. A solitary old man appears, as if from nowhere. He watches us for 10 minutes or so, then wanders back to wherever he came from.

We spend the night at a mission campsite in Kalacha. This oasis of palm and acacia trees, fed by underground springs, has supported a human community for millennia. Several circular cairns outside the town are said to be the work of giants who lived here in the distant past—a folk memory substantiated by the discovery of several 2m (6ft) tall human skeletons below the cairns (few modern Kenyans attain that sort of height). Kalacha is the largest town for 100km (60 miles) in any direction—yet, aside from the church, the mission, and perhaps a dozen other brick buildings, it essentially consists of a sprawl of about 100 traditional Gabbra huts. These domed constructions of wood, mud and cloth are unlike any other traditional huts I have seen in East Africa; but, oddly, they are almost identical in design to the homes built by unrelated desert nomads elsewhere in Africa (for instance, the Nama of Namibia and the Taureg of Mali).

The heart of the Chalbi lies to the west of Kalacha, and supports no permanent settlement, with the exception of the small town of North Horr, a palm-lined oasis built around ancient freshwater springs. This is a landscape as empty as any in Africa, lacking even the gigantic dunes that give form to the Namib and Sahara. Essentially a large pan, the Chalbi is transformed into a vast, shallow lake after heavy rain, but most of the time it is bone dry: a flat, cracked expanse of baked mud, punctuated by dazzling patches of white salt and a taunting mirage that hovers permanently on the horizon.

After a few hours, the featureless pan gives way to a series of rocky rises. Silence descends over the truck every time we bump and grind our way to the top of a ridge, willing *this* to be the big one. Finally, we hit the jackpot, and everybody tumbles out of the truck to soak in the scene. We have reached the eastern escarpment of the Great Rift Valley, that immense geological scar which cuts through Africa all the way from the Red Sea to the Zambezi. Perhaps 50km (31 miles) distant, the mountainous western escarpment shimmers purple in the hazy, midday heat. Far below us lies the Rift Valley floor, almost entirely bereft of vegetation. In the middle of all this austerity, just as green and inviting as its alternative name, the Jade Sea, would suggest, lies the goal of our journey: Lake Turkana.

DESERT LAKE

We spend the next two days based at Gametrackers' private camp, a line of domed reed huts that mimic the homes of the Turkana people. The camp is rustic in the extreme, but all the more attractive for it—not to mention a welcome change from sleeping under canvas. Much of Turkana's scenic intensity derives from the contrast between the dried lava flows and patchy clumps of spiky grass that characterize the bleak shore, and the rich, green hue of the lake. Swimming is virtually irresistible, despite the soapiness of the alkaline water, and the mild unease induced by the thought of the 22,000 Nile crocodiles said to inhabit the lake. Fortunately, they are not believed to frequent this particular stretch of shore.

Nearby is the largest town on the entire eastern shore of Turkana: Loiyangalani—little more than an overgrown village. Ariadne spends a wonderful afternoon photographing Turkana women in what increasingly becomes a party atmosphere. I communicate with the women using a combination of broken Swahili and gesticulation. Meanwhile, the older women take visible delight in removing the goatee-like beaded decorations that hang from below their lips, to reveal a pierced hole, which they use as a sort of spittle cannon.

Next morning, we take a boat trip to Elmolo Island, named for the tribe of fishermen who live there. The Elmolo are reputedly the world's smallest tribe, numbering about 300, and their island is

---

DESERT NOMADS

Northern Kenya is home to several different ethnic groups, practically all of whom are pastoralists, retaining to a greater or lesser degree the nomadic lifestyle of their forebears. This constantly changing human landscape is perhaps the most fascinating aspect of the trip to Turkana, especially as there is no other part of East Africa where traditional culture remains so little affected by modernization. The Samburu are cattle-herding people. They speak the same language as the Maasai, and share a common ancestry, having migrated to their present homeland from Ethiopia about 300 years ago. They are characteristically draped in red blankets, decorated with elaborately beaded jewellery, and have ochred hair. The Rendille people of Marsabit dress similarly, but their language and appearance suggest origins somewhere in Somalia. The Rendille generally herd camels rather than cattle, as do their western neighbours, the Gabbra of the Chalbi Desert. Perhaps the most distinctive people of all northern Kenya, however, are the Turkana themselves. Many older people in this area still dress in animal cloths; the women wear beaded jewellery and ochred mohican-styled hair, and have pierced chins and handsome, almost masculine features.

KENYA

Above: The relentless sun offers no respite when you are building a new home
Right: Elaborately beaded Samburu Girl

correspondingly tiny. This is our one truly contrived and unedifying cultural encounter, marred by a guide whose every conversational gambit amounts to a hint for a further payment. On the way back from the island, we follow the shore closely and eventually come across a genuinely impressive crocodile—one of the biggest I've ever seen.

VILLAGE DANCING

As evening falls, we discover that the camp is ideally positioned to catch the richly coloured sunsets for which Turkana is famous. Then, after a dinner of fresh fish, we head out to a nearby village to watch local dancers. This, in direct contrast to our earlier experience at Elmolo, is a winningly informal and authentic affair. We are invited to join the inhabitants of a small village as they leap up and down, chant, and bang drums, without any attempt at explanation or formal choreography. Aside from the fact that we pay, it is difficult to imagine an encounter of this sort that could be less contrived or "touristy." The villagers were merrily bouncing up and down when we arrived; I have little doubt that they will still be at it an hour after we leave.

The two-day return trip was a long,

bumpy drive. Yet, curiously, it is only as we return to relatively familiar surroundings that the full impact of our time in the desert sinks in. On the way up to Turkana I might have described the vegetation around South Horr as arid woodland; on the return trip it seems indecently lush and cluttered. Turkana recedes almost into the realms of fantasy, as we ascend towards Maralal through grassy meadows, dotted with small herds of zebra, patches of montane forest draped in wispy strands of lichen and moss, and orderly plantations of exotic pine trees. At Maralal, we head straight for the bar to drink chilled beer and nibble on crisps and roasted peanuts. It's only a prosaic room with a few tables and chairs and a fridge, but it still feels gloriously sophisticated!

The following night, Ariadne and I dine in one of Nairobi's many excellent Indian restaurants, and reflect on one of the most strange and memorable trips we have ever undertaken in Africa. We are left with the sense of having travelled not merely through space, but also through time—to an older, purer, emptier Africa.

GOING IT ALONE

GETTING THERE

Jomo Kenyatta Airport, outside Nairobi, is one of the busiest on the continent, and there are regular flights there from most major cities in Europe and elsewhere in the world.

INTERNAL TRAVEL

Most visitors to Kenya arrive at Nairobi, which is also where the Turkana truck sets off. There is no need to use any other internal transport for the truck trip. Independent travellers will find that most of the country is covered by reasonably swift and efficient bus services, as well as overcrowded and accident-prone *matatus* (a name applied to practically any form of public transport that isn't a bus).

WHEN TO GO

Trips run throughout the year. Assuming that you combine a Turkana trip with other travels in Kenya, seasonal factors elsewhere in the country will be a greater determining factor in your timing than those in the north.

OFF ON YOUR OWN

Short of kitting out your own vehicle, or hiring one (in which case you should ideally travel in convoy), an overland truck is the only reliable way of reaching Turkana. Nevertheless, adventurous travellers might consider trying to reach eastern Turkana using a combination of public transport and hitching. The best option is to take a bus from Nairobi to Maralal, where you should find some sort of public transport to Baragoi or South Horr. There is no public transport north of South Horr, but if you don't mind waiting for a few nights, you should eventually find a lift.

The western shore of the lake is accessible using public transport. Take a bus from Nairobi to Kitale to Lodwar, then pick up a *matatu* to Kalekol, within walking distance of the lake shore when water levels are high. Turkana has been receding for many years, and visiting Kalekol has been a pointless excercise; but the water level rose after the El Niño rains of 1997/8. Check the situation before heading this way.

If you are thinking of going to Turkana on public transport, carry a current guidebook to Kenya for detailed transport information and accommodation recommendations.

HEALTH AND SAFETY

❑ Malaria is the most important concern for travellers to Kenya. Take prophylactic drugs, and cover up between dusk and dawn, applying insect repellent to any exposed skin. People travelling to remote destinations (such as Turkana) should carry a cure for malaria in case of emergency.
❑ The desert sun is relentless. Bring a hat and sunblock.
❑ Don't drink the water in villages and other out-of-the-way places. Carry plenty of bottled mineral water with you.

❑ Northern Kenya has experienced spasmodic outbreaks of banditry. The overland trucks won't go there if there is any cause for concern. Ask for current advice if you plan to travel independently.

TRAVELLERS' TIPS

❑ Bring plenty of light clothing, and a jumper for the chilly desert nights.
❑ The dust may affect people who wear contact lenses; it is worth carrying a pair of glasses as a back-up.
❑ Always wear solid footwear after dark—scorpions and snakes are common in dry climates.
❑ The colourful tribespeople of northern Kenya often refuse to let travellers photograph them, or expect a payment or gift in return. Never photograph people without first asking permission.
❑ Stock up on bottled water in Nairobi. On the rare occasions when you can locate it along the road, it will be at a grossly inflated price.
❑ Carry plenty of small change. Few locals ever have enough money to give change for large bills.

4 Walking with the Maasai in the Serengeti Region

by Paul Grogan

The Serengeti is one of Africa's most famous savannah regions. I combined a walking safari in the game controlled area, accompanied by Maasai tribesmen, with a more traditional vehicle safari in the national park. Together, these different approaches give a unique perspective on the land, its wildlife and its people.

Mogea drew a long knife from the leather sheath tied around his waist. He ran the blade down the edge of his spear, sharpening one weapon against the other. There were vultures circling overhead and the Maasai were cautious. Something, somewhere, had made a kill.

It was the first morning of my three-day trek in the remote and little-visited Loliondo game controlled area, in the Serengeti region of Tanzania. Bordered by the Serengeti National Park to the west and the Ngorongoro Conservation Area to the south, Loliondo has no physical boundaries: only arbitrary lines drawn on maps. There are no fences, and the wildlife, left free to roam, is as abundant here as in the designated park area. There was every chance of stumbling across a lion lurking in the long grass.

3 Each day you can expect to walk for five or six hours. This is over rough ground and can be quite hard-going and tiring, so you need to be reasonably fit. You are usually at a shady spot for an extended lunch period, but temperatures could be extremely high.

★★ This trip uses a variety of accommodation, from luxury lodges to temporary camps on the walk. However, you will be comfortable at all times and will never be without hot showers, good food and warm beds.

You need a good pair of walking boots. A water bottle is essential. Binoculars are a great benefit for wildlife-spotting, especially on the walk. There are excellent opportunities for wildlife photography, but beware of trying to carry too much heavy equipment.

We were a small trekking group of just six visitors accompanied by three local Maasai: Mogea, Saltiel, an elder from the local village, and Kiguana. Both Saltiel and Kiguana carried bows and arrows to add to Mogea's armoury. The arrows were tipped with a deadly poison made from the sap of a plant known as the desert rose. If one of these were fired into an animal and the wound didn't kill it, the poison would soon render it unconscious. At least, that was what Saltiel told us; I'd really rather not put it to the test.

A HALFWAY HOUSE

It had taken me two days to get to this part of Tanzania. I had flown in from London to Dar es Salaam, and then on to Kilimanjaro airport. I was met there by Freddie, who was going to be my driver for the next few days, and who would also be my guide when I wasn't walking with the Maasai.

The airport is not far from Arusha, a large town where most safari companies have their local offices. There are plenty of hotels there, too, but I had no real need to stop. Like many people who visit the area, I headed straight out to a safari lodge for my first night.

It took about an hour and a half to cover the 88km (55 miles) from Arusha to Makuyuni; there, the surfaced road runs out, and the final 30km (19 miles) or so of dirt track to get to Kirurumu Lodge took another hour and a half. By the time I arrived it was already dark, so I had to

THE BIG FIVE

In the days when trophy-hunting was the norm in colonial Africa, there were five big trophies that the hunters prized most. These great creatures—elephant, rhinoceros, lion, buffalo and leopard—made grotesque souvenirs. Thankfully most visitors nowadays only want to shoot things with their cameras, but the challenge of seeing the big five is as exciting as it ever was.

wait until the following morning to enjoy the fantastic, expansive view across the Great Rift Valley.

This was an ideal place to start a safari: only 20 minutes from Lake Manyara National Park, and an hour and a half from Tarangire. To the north, the Ngorongoro Crater is also an hour and a half's drive, and the lodge is about half way between Arusha and the Serengeti. Kirurumu is perched on the edge of the Great Rift Valley escarpment, overlooking Lake Manyara.

As the dawn mist cleared I could see a patchwork of fields on the valley floor, drifts of pink flamingoes on the lake, forests of acacia and distant bushland fading into an endless African landscape.

AN INTERRUPTED JOURNEY

The drive from Kirurumu to Serengeti was a safari in itself. The road climbed steeply via the village of Karatu to the very edge of the Ngorongoro Crater. From a viewpoint on the crater rim the land dropped sharply away to the floor some 600m (1,960ft) below. A lake formed the centrepiece to grassland and areas of thick forest. Even from above I could see that the open spaces were crammed with wildlife. The steep volcanic walls encircling this 23km (14-mile)-wide crater were bathed in cloud. As it drifted, the view changed and blocks of shade danced across the crater

floor before it disappeared completely, as the mist engulfed us.

Our journey continued on the outer slopes of the crater wall through the Ngorongoro Conservation Area. We passed several small Maasai dwellings and, once we reached the open savannah, saw Maasai walking with their cattle, grazing alongside herds of zebras, gazelles and other plains animals. They appeared to be in perfect harmony with each other, the Maasai and their cattle posing no threat to the wildlife. I was to learn a lot more about the Maasai people's harmonious relationship with their environment as they guided me on the walk over the next few days.

It was supposedly only about four hours from Kirurumu to the Serengeti area, but we were in no hurry. We stopped for supplies in Karatu, and were obliged to stop for bureaucratic paperwork as our road passed through the Ngorongoro Conservation Area. Once down on the savannah floor, we enjoyed a bit of casual game-watching from the jeep, and even stopped in a Maasai village to learn a little of the traditional way of life. Evening was drawing in by the time we were close to our camp, but the day was still not over. Günter, our safari organizer, had gone ahead to set up our camp. Whilst watching out for our arrival, he had spotted five cheetahs on a kill and, as we approached the camp, he led us off to watch this unscheduled highlight.

LOOKING FOR TROUBLE

As it turned out, these were not the only cheetahs in the area. When we left our camp in the early morning, with our Maasai and their sharpened weapons, we headed towards a group of circling airborne scavengers. It was that special time of day when it is still cloudy, the air is still cool, and the animals are at their most active. I was understandably keen to see game—but I didn't relish the idea of meeting a lion at close quarters.

We didn't need to go far to discover what the vultures had spotted. Saltiel

Above: *Our knowledgeable Maasai guides and the close physical contact maintained with the environment made our walking safari a most rewarding way of experiencing the country*

Inset: *Examining the imprint of an elephant's footprint made when the soil was still soft, just before the dry season—a valuable detail for trackers*

Right: *A Maasai meeting at the village of Olbalbal in Ngorongoro*

found the remains of an impala. It had been killed in the night by cheetahs and there was now very little left. We all breathed a sigh of relief that the predator hadn't been a lion but a cheetah—slightly less dangerous. In any case, the big cats had moved on and we were in no immediate danger.

Our focus now turned from the harsh world of prey and predator to more gentle subjects. In a tree close by, two vibrantly coloured green and orange lovebirds were feeding their young through a small hole in a tree trunk. As we moved on we saw a family of warthogs running through the bush, hartebeest quietly grazing, and giraffes delicately stretching for leaves in the tops of tall flat-topped acacias.

A CLOSE ENCOUNTER

Suddenly, the Maasai brought us to an abrupt halt, stooped and peered through the trees. I couldn't see a thing at first, but they pointed out four buffaloes standing in the shadows. Buffaloes are probably more dangerous than lions. If surprised, they have a nasty tendency to charge, and there is nothing that will stop them. We could have walked right into them, but luckily the Maasai spotted them while we were still about 80m (260ft) away. It was time enough for the animals to get our scent and to walk away, rather than challenge us.

This demonstration of the Maasai's skills made me feel a whole lot better about the situation. I had expected to be accompanied by a ranger with a rifle, and yet having only the Maasai at our sides made me feel quite safe. Their skills and their knowledge were far more impressive than a guy with a gun. They were our guards and our guides in their own land; they respected the bush, but were not threatened by it.

READING THE SIGNS

This trip was only possible with a licence granted by the Loliondo District Council, which, in turn, was dependent on an agreement between the safari company and Saltiel's village. Günter, who had made these agreements, seemed to have a special rapport with the locals. As well as being an experienced safari leader he was an expert linguist and conversed fluently in the local dialect. The Maasai were men of few words, but when they did explain something Günter was quick to pass on their comments in perfectly clear English.

"*Tembo*" said Kiguana, pointing to a patch on the ground. The word means elephant—but this looked like any other patch of ground to me. Günter stooped to show us a large, round, shallow depression in the soil. This was an imprint made by an elephant's foot a few weeks ago: it had passed that way when the soil was still soft, just before the dry season.

Further ahead there were more recent signs of elephant. The trees, which the Maasai called *osilale*, were battered and limb-torn. *Osilale* is a favourite of the *tembo*, being a softer thorn tree than the more common acacia. Soon we passed recent footprints, only a couple of days old, judging by the damaged vegetation. The elephants had torn up aloe plants

and casually strewn them about and, in doing so, they had left their cannon-ball-sized calling cards. We could see where they had passed the trees, stripping the bark; and we could see where the bark had passed through them.

PRECIOUS WATER

When the early morning cloud burned off each day the fierce African sun desiccated everything, including us. It soon became clear, as we drank from our water bottles, how important a water source would be in this harsh environment. There was only one waterhole in this area, frequented by most animals in the dry season and particularly significant to the Maasai. When the Serengeti National Park was created, it included this part of Loliondo, and the Maasai lost their rights to use the land. However, they were able to show that it was the only source of

---

MIGRATIONS

The Serengeti is home to a migratory population of around 2 million wildebeest and 300,000 zebras, plus gazelles, elands and topis, and the predators that follow them. The migration follows the availability of grass which is dependent on the rains. The usual pattern is:

September to November—the herds are in the Maasai Mara, Kenya

December—move south along Loliondo/Ngorongoro/Serengeti borders to the short grass plains in the south

January—zebras foal

February—wildebeest calve

March—heavy rains

April—herds move west to central Serengeti

May to July—move into the western corridor of the Serengeti

July and August—move north to the Maasai Mara

year-round water for miles and that they relied on it for their cattle; they won their claim and, in the early 1960s, the park border was altered. It is clearly visible on the maps as a v-shaped diversion in to the water source and back out again.

We visited this water hole several times over the next three days of our walking safari. It was a haven for yellow-billed and Marabou storks during the day, but the majority of wildlife activity was at night. We saw fresh footprints each morning: the waterhole was being visited by lions and at least two hippos.

LIVING THE SAFARI LIFESTYLE

Each day we walked for miles, through a range of different vegetation. The Serengeti is famous for its vast open grassland plains, but that is only part of what the area has to offer. In this small section of Loliondo we passed from grassland to thick thorn bush and light forest. We walked on the flat plains, through hidden valleys and up rocky hills. The best lookout points were *kopjes*, prominent rocky outcrops that look as though they have just been dumped on the landscape. From the top we could sit and rest, have some water and a snack, and plan the next part of our walk. We had pre-arranged meeting points for lunch, where we would rendezvous with a jeep from the camp. As a result, we didn't have to carry too much food and water, but we did have to keep to a schedule.

After a long and leisurely lunch break there was more walking for anyone who still felt up to it, although two or three of the less keen walkers headed back to camp with the jeep. The afternoons seemed very short, as lunch tended to stretch until 3pm or later. In this part of the world it gets dark at about 6pm and, being on foot, it was important that we returned while it was still light. The guides allowed for unexpected delays, so we were generally back by about 5pm. By this time there was hot water ready for the shower, which we took turns to use.

> ## BUSH WALKING
>
> ❑ Be prepared for long, hot walks. Once you are out on the walk it is impossible to return without the rest of the group, the guides and the guards.
> ❑ Wear good, strong walking boots to protect you from thorns.
> ❑ Watch where you are walking: there are unexpected holes to trip you up.
> ❑ Wear long trousers or the thorn bushes will make their mark.
> ❑ Always carry plenty of water.
> ❑ Don't leave your first-aid kit back at camp—you are unlikely to hurt yourself whilst in your tent.
> ❑ Try not to make too much noise, as you will reduce your chance of spotting game.

The cook was busy preparing salads and soups, roast meat and chicken dishes. Somehow the camp staff had managed to bring enough ice with them to last the three days, and there was no shortage of chilled beers. The walks were tiring, but it's amazing what a hot shower, a cold beer and idle chat around a blazing campfire can do to revive the spirit.

SPEARS AND ARROWS

On one particular night we had a lot to talk about. It had been a long, hard walk, and we had stopped as usual on a *kopje* to take a rest and view the surroundings. Out in the bush, not far from us, Kiguana noticed two hyenas. They were striped hyenas, which are quite uncommon and much bigger than the usual spotted ones, abundant in the Serengeti. One ran away when they noticed us, but the other bounded towards the rocks and stood quite boldly at the base, looking up at us. He was a big beast, ferocious and uncannily confident. He sniffed the air and snarled, standing proud as if to challenge us. We were safe up on the rocks, though, and finally he retreated back to the bush.

Left: *A Serengeti big cat lounging in the shade. Despite their size, lions are quite easy to overlook as they are perfectly camouflaged to lie in the short yellow grass*
Right: *A wildebeest moving across the plains looking for fresh grass. The animals seemed indifferent to our jeep, which allowed us to get some wonderful close-up views*
Below: *Zebras palpably enjoy cooling off in waterholes, a precious part of the harsh environment*

Our path was to take us past that bush, and we weren't sure if he would still be there, or what his reaction would be. Mogea and Kiguana forged ahead, their weapons at the ready. As we approached the bush, the hyena sprang out of nowhere. The Maasai were prepared: Mogea ran at him, wielding his spear over his shoulder. The hyena ran a few paces, then turned and stood his ground: stalemate. Mogea stood fast, threatening the animal with quick, sudden movements as if about to charge. Kiguana had an arrow drawn, his bow taut and ready to fire. But the Maasai were bluffing. They had no desire to harm the animal—just to ward him off. For a moment it seemed that this confident beast would attack, but eventually he accepted defeat. He didn't run away: he just crept off and watched us from a distance. We didn't run either: we walked on. Kiguana put the arrow back in its quiver, and Mogea relaxed. He ran the blade of his knife down the edge of his spear, sharpening one weapon against the other, just as he had done on the first

morning. That night, the Maasai laughed about the episode, around the campfire, but even they admitted that they had rarely seen such a big and bold hyena. If they hadn't been armed, things could have turned out very differently.

INTO THE SERENGETI NATIONAL PARK

Our next close encounters were to be from the safety of a vehicle. For the final two days of the adventure we headed into the Serengeti National Park for some conventional game-viewing. Nobody is allowed out of the vehicle while it is in the park, and it was odd to think that we had been walking openly in this terrain beyond the border.

With a jeep we could cover far greater distances than we ever could on foot. We were able to go looking for particular species, moving quickly from one habitat to another, or following a tip-off from the guides in other passing vehicles. We devoted our first game drive to tracking down lions, and found some within a short distance of our camp. Their camouflage was perfect. The grass didn't begin to cover these big animals, yet their colour was a perfect match and, laying low within it, they had mastered the art of invisibility.

We had to move on: there were 1,320sq. km (510sq. miles) of Serengeti for us to explore and a host of other animals that would unwittingly take centre stage that day. Serengeti means "endless plains"—and herds of zebras and wildebeest were on the move across those plains, making their way to greener grass. In the jeep we could position ourselves very close to the game, which seemed untroubled by our presence. Wherever we stopped, a pride of lions was never far away. At one waterhole the migrating zebra were tense and whinnying: they could sense the lions' presence. Sure enough, two big cats lay in wait right by their path.

TAKING A WALK ON THE WILD SIDE

We saw more game in Serengeti from the jeep than I would have thought possible, moving quickly to find the action. Yet it was the walking safari that provided the truly enthralling experience. Seeing the country on foot and making physical contact with the environment was a very rewarding way to go game-spotting. We covered a relatively small area, and didn't get particularly close to the animals; but we came to understand their movements by revisiting the same spots, seeing new prints and new signs of grazing damage on the trees and plants. In a sense, we felt even closer to the animals. We had the chance to see the bush the way the Maasai do, as a part of it, rather than just looking at it through a lens on a casual drive past. By the time we left the park and headed back for a last night at Kirurumu, I had definitely walked on the wild side, on an adventure that showed me the world of the bush in an entirely new light.

SERENGETI LIONS

There are around 3,000 lions in the Serengeti, so there is a very good chance of seeing some. Their population suffered a setback when it was seriously affected by an outbreak of canine distemper in the 1990s, with 90 percent of the lions exposed to the virus and many dying. A programme of vaccinating dogs in the surrounding villages seems to have brought the disease under control and the lions have succeeded in making a dramatic comeback. Populations are still being monitored, not just for the disease, but also for a number of behavioural studies. You sometimes come across lionesses sporting the very latest design of radio collar, and nursing young cubs. Obviously these fashion accessories are attracting all the right males.

GOING IT ALONE

INTERNAL TRAVEL

Local flights connect Dar es Salaam with Arusha or Kilimanjaro airports, where the safaris usually begin. Several bus companies also operate between Dar es Salaam and Arusha, taking about eight hours to complete the journey. There is no public transport system to get you to Kirurumu or the Serengeti, and you would be unable to go walking in Liliondo without the backup and services of a safari company. Transport is therefore part of the safari arrangement, starting from Arusha.

PLANNING

Choose the time of year that fits in with the local weather patterns and accessibility to the area. If you want to go at a different time of year, there are other places in northern Tanzania where you can walk. Most nationalities require a visa to enter Tanzania. This can take several days and is quite expensive. Make sure you leave enough time to obtain this before your scheduled departure date. If you have limited time and want to arrange your safari for a specific date it is best to pre-book from your country of residence. You are unlikely to be able to walk into a tour company office in Arusha and find a walking safari that sets off the next day.

WHEN TO GO

Northern Tanzania has two rainy seasons. The long rains fall from March/April to early June and the short rains are around November. The best time to see large numbers of wildebeest is either during the northern migration in June or again in February when the herds are calving in the Serengeti. The Loliondo area is accessible from early May but the tracks could be muddy until a little later. The dry months, from June to the start of the short rains, are a good time for trekking to see resident game in Loliondo and to concentrate on ethnobotany and culture, rather than on massive herds of plains animals. The area is still accessible during the short rains but you can expect heavy showers.

HEALTH MATTERS

If you are entering Tanzania from a country where yellow fever occurs you will need to show your vaccination certificate against yellow fever when you enter the country. If your trip included a visit to Zanzibar, a yellow fever certificate is required, regardless of your starting point.

Malaria is prevalent in Tanzania. Take precautions to avoid getting bitten by malaria-carrying mosquitoes, such as wearing long-sleeved shirts and long trousers in the evenings, when the mosquitoes are at their most active. You should also take plenty of insect repellent. Seek medical advice about malaria prophylactics.

Make sure that all drinking water has been purified. Boiled or bottled water should always be available on an organized safari.

WHAT TO TAKE

❑ Avoid taking heavy hard suitcases. Everything you take has to be loaded onto vehicles with limited space.
❑ You need long trousers to protect yourself in the bush, but you should avoid overheating. Lightweight cotton trousers are ideal.
❑ You need a good pair of walking boots and an adequate supply of socks—there will be no facilities for washing clothes whilst away from the lodges.
❑ Take warm clothes for chilly evenings and long-sleeved shirts to keep off biting insects.
❑ A daypack is ideal for carrying your water bottle and the clothes that are peeled off as the day warms up.
❑ Take plenty of film and spare batteries and as much camera equipment as you can manage—but don't try to carry too much of it with you on the walks.

CHOOSING A SAFARI COMPANY

❑ Avoid companies with beaten up old vehicles—you don't want to spend your time broken down on the tracks.
❑ Make sure that the company has adequate backup, should you get into trouble.
❑ Choose a reputable company that has a proven track-record of walking safaris.
❑ Make sure you know what is included in the price (such as park entrance fees).
❑ Find out about the company's environmental policy.
❑ Walking trips can usually only operate with special permits and local co-operation: check that the safari company has these permits and that locals such as Maasai guides and guards get a fair wage for their services.

5 Trekking to the Roof of Africa

by William Gray

Kilimanjaro, Africa's highest mountain, towers above the plains, its snow-capped summit rising to 5,896m (19,457ft). Many of the 20,000 trekkers a year who come here set out simply to conquer the "Roof of Africa," but as I discovered on a six-day guided hike, the mountain's true appeal lies in its landscapes and natural history.

There are few clues to Kilimanjaro's looming presence. If you arrive, as I did, when the dormant volcano is obscured by thick cloud, you could easily drive straight past it none the wiser. There are no lines of rugged foothills or plunging valleys to suggest that you are approaching a mighty peak. It rises abruptly from the dusty savannah of northern Tanzania, rearing 4,800m (15,840ft) above the Great Rift Valley. Only 40km (25 miles) at its widest point, it is one of the world's highest free-standing mountains.

The Chagga people, who farm the rich, volcanic soils around the base of Kilimanjaro, have long revered the mountain. Local chiefs once claimed that anyone who tried to reach the summit would be struck down by evil spirits.

Nowadays, there are several well-marked trails to the summit. None requires mountaineering skills, but the trek is still physically demanding and around half of those who set out to climb Kilimanjaro turn back before they reach the top. My wife, Sally, and I opted for the popular 64km (40-mile) Marangu Route.

From Kilimanjaro International Airport, 80km (50 miles) away, it was a short taxi ride east via the bustling town of Moshi before we reached Marangu village, nestling in coffee and banana plantations on the lower slopes of the mountain. The gardens of Marangu Hotel were ablaze with flowering bottlebrush and hibiscus shrubs, and in one corner a large jacaranda tree had carpeted the lawn with mauve petals. "When it's clear you can glimpse the snows of Kilimanjaro through the branches of that tree," the director of the hotel told us as we unloaded our backpacks from the taxi. But the cloud remained thick and stubborn for the remainder of the day, obscuring any tantalizing views.

Instead we focused on the final preparations for our trek. The staff at Marangu Hotel went to great lengths to ensure that we were suitably equipped for the extreme cold and harsh conditions we

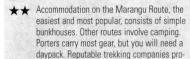
All routes involve walking between five and seven hours most days. The gradient is fairly gentle to start with, but the final ascent to the summit is extremely steep. Licensed guides are compulsory and their local knowledge will enhance your experience. You should be reasonably fit and fully aware of the effects of high altitude. For less taxing trekking, look to the Crater Highlands region west of Kilimanjaro.

★★ Accommodation on the Marangu Route, the easiest and most popular, consists of simple bunkhouses. Other routes involve camping. Porters carry most gear, but you will need a daypack. Reputable trekking companies provide excellent and plentiful food.

See What to Take for a full list of clothing and equipment. All trekking routes are non-technical—you can walk to the summit without ropes or mountaineering experience.

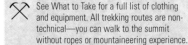
Right: *Trekking through the moss and lichen-clad cloud forest on the slopes of Kilimanjaro, a dormant volcano. The forest is where you are most likely to glimpse the local wildlife*

would encounter high on the mountain. Like soldiers at a military inspection, we laid out our clothing ready for appraisal, confident that the thermal underwear, fleece jackets, gloves, woollen hats and windproof coats we had brought with us would be more than adequate. But five minutes later there was a gentle knock at the door and a woman walked in laden with balaclavas, extra gloves and fleece pullovers.

TEAMWORK

Early the following morning we met our trekking team. Nelson, our head guide, was only 29, but he had already accumulated 10 years of experience on Kilimanjaro, reaching the summit more than 50 times. His assistant, Matthew, and four porters, Isaac, Raphael, Joseph and John, who would carry food and cooking equipment, comprised the rest of the group. All six were Chagga, the local people who settled the lower slopes of

---

CHOOSING A ROUTE

Of the six official trekking routes, the following are the most popular:

Marangu Route Over 80 percent of trekkers choose this trail, linking three bunkhouses and covering a total distance of 64km (40 miles), including the descent. A minimum of five days is required, although six would help with acclimatization.

Umbwe Route A steep and direct route involving a spectacular final approach to the summit via the Western Breach. It requires at least five days and is recommended for experienced trekkers only. Accommodation is in tents.

Machame Route At least six days' camping is needed for this scenic 61km (38-mile) route, which ascends gradually to the Shira Plateau before approaching the summit from the west. The descent is via the Mweka or Marangu trails.

Kilimanjaro around 400 years ago.

We shook hands with each man before bundling all our gear into a van and driving the few kilometres to Marangu Gate, where our trek would begin. A fine rain hazed the windows of the vehicle as we climbed steadily through densely populated farmland. Roadside stalls brimming with fresh fruit and vegetables bore testimony to the well-watered and highly fertile volcanic soils.

Several other trekking groups (mostly couples or small groups) had already arrived, and their porters were busy making final adjustments to their loads. To ensure no porter carries more than 18kg (40lb), all loads are weighed and evenly distributed amongst each team.

Formalities at Marangu Gate included paying national park fees. Everything above 2,700m (9,000ft), as well as a corridor either side of the trail below this altitude, lies within Kilimanjaro National Park. We also registered our planned schedule in case a mountain rescue (a rare event) would become necessary.

INTO THE WOODS

While the porters marched ahead, Sally and I shouldered our daypacks, containing drinking water and extra clothing, and followed Nelson and Matthew into a monochrome forest, suffused with mist and dripping with beards of moss. The trail was wide and the gradient gentle, but Nelson encouraged us to walk slowly. "If you find you have to breathe through your mouth, slow down," he advised us. "*Pole, pole,*" Swahili for "slowly, slowly," would become a familiar chant in the days ahead.

Guides are compulsory for treks on Kilimanjaro (and porters are highly recommended), and Nelson immediately captivated us with his knowledge of the mountain's natural history. He knew the names of all the trailside flowers, from the sweetly scented begonia to the delicate, bugle-shaped blooms of *Impatiens kilimanjari*, which is found nowhere else in the world. From the impenetrable tangle of trees and ferns he identified the high-pitched calls of sunbirds and the occasional raucous cry of a brightly coloured Hartlaub's turaco bird.

The forest zone through which we were walking is where most of Kilimanjaro's resident animals are found. Kilimanjaro's forest animals are shy and elusive, and the most you are likely to glimpse, as we did, is a troop of blue monkeys crashing about in the canopy above.

The luxuriant forest owes its existence to the high rainfall, which can reach 2,000mm (80in) a year on the southern slopes where most of the trails (including the Marangu Route) begin. Soon our boots were caked in thick, ochre-red mud.

After three hours of easy walking, we paused for lunch by a stream where giant tree ferns raised a parasol of fronds 5m (15ft) above the ground. The first of several groups of trekkers descending the

mountain began to pass us. Their hands and faces were heavily tanned and they all looked utterly worn out. Some tramped past without a check in their stride; others paused and smiled wearily at us. "Beautiful, amazing, fantastic—and exhausting," was one Australian's verdict of his trek. Others offered us cryptic advice, like "Just watch the feet of the person in front," or "The worst thing you can do is look up."

When we resumed our leisurely ascent, Nelson began pointing out subtle changes in the forest. Plants that we had seen growing in wild profusion lower down now formed smaller clumps. One species began to predominate—a giant 3m (10ft)-tall heather festooned with long hairy growths of lichen. Gradually, almost imperceptibly, the montane forest was succumbing to the altitude; plants that could not tolerate the drier, colder conditions higher up were giving way to those that could.

ALTITUDE SICKNESS

The summit of Kilimanjaro lies 500m (1,650ft) higher than Everest Base Camp in the Nepal Himalaya, which most trekkers take two weeks to reach. Although many people do reach the top of Africa's highest mountain, many more do not as a result of suffering from the effects of high altitude. It is important to understand the symptoms of altitude sickness and how to prevent and treat it.

Acute mountain sickness (AMS) usually develops at altitudes above 3,000m (9,900ft). If you begin to experience mild symptoms, such as headache, loss of appetite, nausea, sleeplessness and fatigue, stop your ascent and rest. If the symptoms worsen, descend until they have fully abated. You may then be able to resume your ascent.

Ignoring the mild symptoms of AMS and pushing yourself higher may lead to much more serious conditions. Pulmonary oedema (fluid on the lungs) and cerebral oedema

(swelling of the brain) can be fatal.

Good trekking companies provide guides who are trained in dealing with altitude sickness. You can increase your chances of avoiding AMS by following some simple guidelines for acclimatization: ascend slowly, spend an extra night between 3,000m and 4,000m (9,900 and 13,200ft), avoid alcohol and eat high-carbohydrate meals. Drink plenty of fluids. Avoid dehydration, which can exacerbate AMS or lead to heat exhaustion. Adding extra salt to your meals helps replace what is lost in your sweat, but it is absolutely crucial to drink at least 5l (8.8 pints) of water every day.

AMS can affect the fittest trekker and even those who have previously climbed to high altitude. Tragically, a handful of people die every year on the mountain, having ignored or failed to recognize the warning signs of AMS, and pushed themselves towards the summit.

TANZANIA

ABOVE THE CLOUDS

Five hours after setting out, we reached Mandara Hut, a cluster of small triangular wooden cabins scattered across a clearing, near the upper limit of the forest at 2,743m (9,051ft). Matthew led me and Sally on a short excursion to Maundi Crater. Pock-marking the slopes of Kilimanjaro are dozens of these small "parasitic cones." Within half an hour we emerged above the forest into a meadow of tussocky grasses, from where it was an easy climb to the edge of Maundi Crater. Below us spread a spectacular blanket of clouds, rucked up against the forest through which we had climbed during the day. Occasionally a small window would open in the clouds, revealing the tawny haze of African savannah far below.

But it was to the north that our eyes were irresistibly drawn. Burnished gold by the setting sun, the craggy spires of Mawenzi (one of the three sister peaks of Kilimanjaro) raked the sky. To the west, the smoother and taller, ice-covered dome of Kibo glinted from behind a ridge. The summit seemed distant and surreal, its bright glaciers jolting the senses after the muted greens of the forest.

SNOWS OF KILIMANJARO

Kilimanjaro was born from the immense tectonic forces that have shaped Africa's Great Rift Valley. About 750,000 years ago, it began erupting through a fracture in the earth's crust, spewing lava across the plains from three volcanic cones.

Shira, furthest to the west, was the first of these to expire and now forms the lowest and most eroded of Kilimanjaro's peaks at 3,962m (13,075ft). Next to die was Mawenzi, 5,149m (16,992ft), lying to the east, but Kibo did not cease major activity until around 350,000

years ago and may even have erupted within the last few centuries. Although glaciers, landslides and weathering have taken their toll, Kibo's cone shaped summit still rises supreme, snow-topped and gleaming between Shira and Mawenzi, reaching 5,896m (19,457ft) at Uhuru Peak—the highest point of the crater rim.

FOOD FOR THOUGHT

Back at Mandara Hut, Nelson had prepared a feast of warm popcorn, flasks of

tea and coffee, fresh papaya and a main dish of fried chicken, pasta and vegetables, followed by tinned peaches.

We ate as much as we could, knowing that as we trekked higher our appetites would wane. The effects of high altitude on the human body are not to be underestimated. Loss of appetite is one thing, but acute mountain sickness (AMS, see panel, p. 61), commonly known as altitude sickness, can lead to serious or even fatal conditions.

INTO THIN AIR

Nelson woke us at 6am with sweet tea and a bright smile. During the night the cloud base had settled lower on Kilimanjaro, and Mandara Hut was bathed in early morning sunshine. Tendrils of mist rose like steam from the

Left: *Kibo Peak: the summit of Kilimanjaro looms above the rock cairns*
Above: *No matter how clean they start off, hiking boots soon become coated in yellow-red dust*

TANZANIA

surrounding forest and there was a cacophony of bird calls.

Although, as on the previous day, the gradient was gentle, we began to feel the harsh edge of high altitude. With clear skies and no tree cover, the sun's heat was intense and we were soon donning hats and dousing ourselves with sunblock. But we immediately felt chilled whenever a wisp of cloud chased up from the forest below and obscured the sun.

Above 3,000m (9,900ft), we began to notice the air becoming thinner as its oxygen level dropped. Our steps became ever shorter and slower in order to keep our breathing under control and we paused more and more often to rest and gulp water.

The moorland was a complete contrast to the forest. Wide vistas suddenly opened around us and the flanks of the mountain were pimpled with minor cones. As we followed the undulating trail across shallow valleys and ridges created by ancient lava flows, gradually climbing higher and higher, there were more glimpses of Mawenzi and Kibo looming nearer.

Despite the harsher growing conditions, the moorland zone supports a wide variety of plants, including some of Kilimanjaro's most distinctive species. The giant lobelia is easily identified by its rosette-like spiral of leaves, which close at night over the delicate central bud to protect it from frost.

Without doubt the most impressive plant you will encounter here is the giant groundsel. Growing to 5m (16ft) high, its woody trunk is crowned with large, thick leaves and an insulating skirt of dead leaves around its base.

As we walked slowly through this strange world of giants, we began to notice a variety of small birds. An iridescent flash of green heralded the presence of scarlet-tufted malachite sunbirds. By contrast, small flocks of alpine chats compensated for their drab plumage with shrill outbursts of their whirring, piping song.

LOWER TRAILS

For those would like to experience some of Kilimanjaro's spectacular landscapes and unique ecology without attempting to reach the summit, a good idea is to base yourself at Mandara Hut, from where nature trails wind through the montane forest and moorland. There are also plans to introduce other lower routes on the mountain.

THE TRANSIT CENTRE

We took over seven hours to reach Horombo Hut, our next overnight stop at 3,720m (12,276ft). Horombo is Kilimanjaro's transit centre. Many trekkers, like us, spend an extra night here on the ascent to assist with altitude acclimatization, and trekkers also spend a night here on their way down. The centre is an unlikely village of wooden huts perched on a small plateau, bustling with trekkers, porters and guides.

That evening the large dining hut was packed with a hundred or more trekkers of all nationalities escaping the brutal cold that followed sunset. Despite the variety of languages, the hut seemed to reverberate with two distinct tones of voice: the relief and elation of those heading down and the quieter, more anxious murmurs of those yet to challenge the summit. Sally and I managed to consume another of Nelson's huge meals, but the cold, thin air conspired against sleep.

There was a thick frost the following morning, sparkling on the clumps of tussock grass and the brittle blooms of the everlasting flowers that grew in a nearby gully. The stream had frozen overnight and we had barely finished using the small dish of warm washing water that Nelson had brought us before an alpine chat hopped in for a bath!

We spent the day exploring the gully, climbing above Horombo Hut before slowly making our way back down again.

The point of an acclimatization day is not to put your feet up, but to take a short walk above the altitude you will sleep at.

LAST WATER

There are two routes leading from Horombo Hut: a lower and an upper one. Your aching legs and straining lungs may tell you otherwise, but it is well worth taking the latter for its stupendous views.

To begin with, the trail climbed steeply and we were forced to pause every 20 minutes or so to rest. Any diversion became a welcome opportunity to stop. A pair of augur buzzards pirouetted overhead and later we glimpsed a rare lammergeier, or bearded vulture.

A wooden sign beside the path gave a more urgent reason to halt. Carved in bold letters across the weathered board were the words "LAST WATER." Nelson advised us that our trekking team would now have to carry all the water it needed until we returned to Horombo in two nights' time. The porters marching ahead of us would already have refilled several large water containers, but Sally and I still replenished our own bottles from the ice-cold stream gurgling below the sign.

As we walked higher into the dry, dusty realm beyond the last spring, Mawenzi reared to our right, its rugged cliffs as stark and forbidding as a medieval fortress. After several deceptive rises, we emerged on a broad ridge scattered with cairns left by previous travellers. Hidden until that moment, the sudden appearance of Kibo was at once magnificent and shocking.

With our backs to Mawenzi, we gazed across The Saddle, a barren alpine desert sweeping to the very foot of the enormous volcanic cone. A sliver of ice was visible on the crater rim, glinting like a bone from the grey, scarred hide of the mountain. Far across The Saddle, etched into the flank of Kibo, was an unmistakable path: a series of tight switchbacks clawing its way to the top of the crater.

ACROSS THE SADDLE

It was a draining three-hour slog across The Saddle at 4,400m (14,520ft). Cloud bubbled up either side of the boulder-strewn desert, while a cruel wind hissed through the last, hardy clumps of grasses. By late afternoon we reached Kibo Hut, 4,700m (15,510ft) up, cowering at the foot of the great cone. There was little sign of activity. The atmosphere inside was quiet and sombre. Everyone had seen all too clearly what lay ahead.

BID FOR THE TOP

To reach the crater rim in time for sunrise and tackle the steep trail when its loose gravel surface is still frozen, most trekkers aim to leave Kibo Hut at 1am or earlier. With this in mind, we tried to get an early night. By 6pm we were cocooned in our sleeping bags, motionless and wide awake. Few people manage to sleep in the cold, oxygen-deprived air of Kibo.

At midnight, the first sounds of movement could be heard. Nelson brought us tea and biscuits while we squeezed into every item of clothing we had brought with us. Outside the summit reared black and massive against a star-washed sky. Nelson arranged us in single file, between him and Matthew, as we walked slowly away from the frail sanctuary of Kibo Hut.

High above us on the trail, I could make out tiny pinpricks of torchlight from trekking groups already on their way. Immediately, the path began to climb and we settled into a steady rhythm: left foot, breathe in; right foot, breathe out. Apart from the crunch and rattle of loose stones from our footsteps, there was silence.

I hardly remember when things started to go wrong. We were well beyond 5,000m (16,500ft), approaching the final, steepest section. A well of nausea formed in the pit of my stomach and I began to have trouble controlling my breathing. I tried to focus on walking 50 pigeon steps between each rest, but I'd hardly start before stumbling off the path. Every few minutes, Sally or Nelson would ask if I was OK, but my positive responses were

Above: *The open moorland of the The Saddle*
Right: *Giant lobelia*
Far right: *An ominous warning sign*

becoming increasingly incoherent. My head began to pound.

Five hours after setting out from Kibo and a few hundred metres short of Gillman's Point (where the trail reaches the crater rim), I slumped onto a large boulder and stared out across The Saddle to Mawenzi. I was vaguely aware of an earnest discussion taking place between Sally and Nelson. A bitter wind ushered in the first scarlet hint of dawn behind Mawenzi, blushing the crests of the "cloud sea" far below.

Having come so far, I obstinately denied that I was showing worrying signs of altitude sickness. After a rest and some tea, I said I would be fine and ready to continue. But my headache grew steadily worse and no sooner had I swallowed the tea than I was retching it up again. Nelson firmly took my arm and, followed by Sally and Matthew, we swiftly descended to Kibo Hut. Almost instantly my symptoms began to abate, and by the time the first rays of sunlight hit Kilimanjaro's summit I felt well enough to enjoy the spectacle from a ledge outside the hut.

Out of the 15 or so trekkers who had set out that morning, only seven made it to the summit. As I watched them return, exhausted yet elated, I couldn't help wondering what views they must have witnessed from the Roof of Africa.

I thought the disappointment would strike me during the two-day descent to Marangu Gate. But instead I felt a strong, personal sense of achievement. Despite not making it to the top, we had experienced one of the greatest adventures Africa has to offer.

GOING IT ALONE

WHEN TO GO

Although trekking is possible throughout the year, the best times are during the dry seasons from late June to early October and late December to early March. In the wet seasons, trails through the forest are slippery and the final section to the summit may be blocked by snow. At any time of the year, be prepared for rain. Temperatures can range from 15 to 20°C (59–68°F) on the lower slopes to less than 5°C (41°F) above 4,000m (13,200ft). Icy winds can plunge temperatures to well below freezing.

ARRANGING A TREK

Independent trekking on Kilimanjaro is not allowed. All treks must be booked through a tour company, of which there are dozens in nearby Arusha, Moshi and Marangu, catering for all budgets. Be wary, however, of companies offering "bargain deals," as these may compromise on food, equipment or the quality of guiding. Make sure you are dealing with a licensed operator and that your trek package includes the services of a guide (obligatory), porters (highly recommended), food, all hut and camping fees, national park fees and transport to and from trailheads.

INTERNAL TRAVEL

Most trekkers base themselves either in Arusha, Moshi or Marangu. If you are arriving by air at Kilimanjaro International Airport, between Moshi and Arusha, there is a shuttle bus operated by Air Tanzania to Moshi. Taxis also run from the airport, but at 10 times the expense. There are scheduled flights from Dar es Salaam, Mombasa, Nairobi and Unguja. There are also regular shuttle bus services to Moshi from Nairobi and Mombasa. There are several minibuses a day between Arusha and Moshi and on to Marangu. The trailhead for the Marangu Route lies 5km (3 miles) beyond Marangu village.

HEALTH MATTERS

It's important to be reasonably fit before undertaking this trek. The best preparation is regular walking.

Inoculations against yellow fever, polio, tetanus, hepatitis A and meningococcal meningitis are recommended. Protection against malaria is also highly advisable and you should aim to take weekly malaria pills at the beginning or end of your trek.

Although the mountain streams look clear, it is wise to treat all drinking water, using either iodine tablets or a water filter. You should bring a small first-aid kit that includes paracetamol, a knee-support bandage, throat lozenges, a blister care kit and an oral rehydration treatment.

In the unlikely event of an emergency, park rangers operate a mountain rescue service on the Marangu Route.

OTHER TREKS

Kilimanjaro tends to overshadow Tanzania's other superb trekking locations. These include Mount Meru, the country's second highest peak at 4,566m (15,068ft), in Arusha National Park. Four days are recommended for the hike to the summit of this beautiful volcano.

TREKKERS' TIPS

❑ Carry a water bottle that can be slipped inside your jacket for the final early morning ascent, otherwise its contents will freeze.

❑ During the descent, a trekking pole will help take the strain off your knees.

❑ Lightweight binoculars enable spectacular close-up views of both the birdlife and surrounding peaks.

❑ Walk slowly; breathe through your nose, not your mouth.

❑ Aim to drink 5l (8.8 pints) of fluid each day.

❑ Be prepared for climatic extremes—from rain in the forest to intense sun on The Saddle and freezing temperatures at the summit.

❑ Pick up all litter, resist any temptation to pick the flowers and keep to trails to avoid erosion.

6 Along the Swahili Coast

by Philip Briggs

Renowned for its perfect beaches, the north coast of Kenya also offers unexpected possibilities for active travel and exploration. These range from offshore coral reefs to mysterious medieval ruins; and from steaming tropical jungles to the time-warped Swahili towns of the Lamu Archipelago.

Do beaches get any better than Turtle Bay? Situated below the resort town of Watamu on the north coast of Kenya, this vista of cool white sand and tall coconut palms is travel brochure perfection, splendidly subverted by a series of eccentrically eroded coral outcrops, which sprout upwards from the inviting turquoise waters of the Indian Ocean like oversized mushrooms. True, Turtle Bay might be a little crowded by Kenyan standards, but that only means that you might, at any given moment, count 20 or so tourists scattered along a mile of sand.

Watamu was our second stop along the coast. My wife, Ariadne, and I had arrived at Mombasa the previous day, using the overnight train from Nairobi, and hopped straight on to a local bus heading northwards to the ancient port of Malindi. Once an important medieval gold-trading centre, Malindi today bears few signs of antiquity. In the space of an hour, we were able to wander along the beach to the obelisk erected in 1499 by the Portuguese navigator Vasco Da Gama, then return to the town centre to check out a pair of 19th-century Islamic pillar tombs. With its slightly seedy air of a fading beach resort, Malindi has to be classed as a minor disappointment.

You could, if you chose, explore the north coast following a strictly prescribed itinerary. But if any one phrase sums up the mood of this part of Kenya, it is: blissfully laid back. The best plan is to improvise. So it was that, after a night in Malindi, we headed 16km (10 miles) south to Watamu and Turtle Bay.

CARNIVAL TIME

Turtle Bay and its environs forms the core of Kenya's oldest marine national park. As soon we had settled into a hotel room overlooking the bay, we arranged to take a glass-bottomed boat out to the Coral Gardens about 1.6km (1 mile) offshore. Here, we saw for ourselves why the reefs off the east coast of Africa are rated among the top three diving sites in the world. Snorkelling through the translucent green water of the Coral Garden, we were surrounded by hundreds upon hundreds of fish, large shoals that swerve and circle through the open water in mysterious unison, and hardy loners foraging between the cracks in the coral.

Butterflyfish, angelfish, parrotfish—the vernacular names attached to these

Unless you want it that way, little physical effort is required to explore the coast. Public transport can be physically taxing due to the combination of heat, humidity, overcrowding and—north of Malindi—rough roads.

At the right budget, the coast can be explored in unqualified luxury, since all the main tourist boards have at least one hotel or lodge conforming to the highest international standards. Even those on a tight budget will find local guesthouses and restaurants above average comfort levels by East African standards.

Binoculars would be useful for those with a specific interest in birdwatching. All underwater and watersports equipment can be rented on the spot, thought it's not always of the highest quality. If possible, unless you're travelling light, take your own snorkelling equipment.

denizens of the reefs give some indication of the Coral Garden's psychedelic carnival of improbable shapes and iridescent colours. It is a mind-expanding spectacle, like floating at the centre of a gigantic aquatic kaleidoscope, with every colour of the rainbow represented—and a few more besides.

Something of a carnival atmosphere also pervades the small village of Watamu, which I had visited before in 1986. Back then, this humble fishing village of a few dozen mud-and-thatch huts was practically indistinguishable from any number of similar coastal settlements. Somewhere along the line, however, tourism has brought a dramatic transformation. The mud huts now rub shoulders with mock German beer halls, trendy curio shops and grimly functional concrete guesthouses. The Swahili fishing community, meanwhile, has been boosted by photogenically strutting Maasai and Samburu warriors from upcountry, dolled-up "bar girls" from the cities, and stoned Rastafarians from wherever.

THE LOST CITY

Early the next morning we escaped Watamu for the serenity of the nearby Arabuko-Sokoke Forest. The only substantial patch of indigenous coastal forest left in Kenya, Arabuko-Sokoke covers roughly 518sq. km (200sq. miles) and harbours several endemic animal species. Birdwatchers visit the forest to see the Sokoke scops owl, Sokoke pipit, east coast akalat, Amani sunbird and Clark's weaver. For most visitors, however, these attractions are outweighed by the brooding presence of the Gedi ruins.

Gedi is an enigma. A 45ha (111-acre) walled city, established in the 13th century and abandoned in the 17th, it must once have been among the most prosperous settlements along the coast. Yet its original name is buried in the mists of time, and although it lay barely 16km (10 miles) from Malindi, no corresponding settlement is mentioned in the 15th-century Malindi Chronicles, or indeed

anywhere else. Stranger still, the city was built deep in the jungle, far from the ocean. Even if Gedi's founders had good reason to choose such an obscure site, the city's wealth implies that it must have been too active in trade to have languished in anonymity.

Gedi is the archetypal lost city: a conglomeration of cracked ruins that feel like an extension of the tangled coastal jungle that threatens to engulf them. Local people avoid the place, believing it to be haunted. James Kirkman, the archaeologist who first investigated Gedi, felt "that something or someone was looking out from behind the walls, neither hostile nor friendly but waiting for what he knew was going to happen."

We poked around the large and reasonably well-preserved mosque and palace, as well as examining the rest of the town. We then followed a forest path to the outer walls of the old city, on the lookout for the golden-rumped elephant shrews that inhabit the forest. Three times we heard something heavy crash into the undergrowth. An elephant shrew, or just a small antelope? At Gedi, there seem to be more questions than answers.

THE LIVING CITY

The next morning we flew to Lamu over a practically uninhabited coastline of endless white beaches, sparkling lagoons, tall dunes and meandering rivers. From the light aircraft, we could see how the numerous small, flat, mangrove-lined islands of the Lamu Archipelago started life as part of a river delta. After landing at the airstrip on Manda Island, we crossed by *dhow* to Lamu, the name not only of the archipelago but also of its most populated island and largest town.

In common with pretty much every other traveller who has made it to Lamu, we fell in love with the place. Lamu has never been the most important of the old Swahili ports that line the coast of East Africa, but it is the only one to have survived into the modern era without significantly changing shape over the

centuries. Yet Lamu is more than a slice of living history: the old town really comes across as a melting pot of the ancient and the modern, the African and the Arabic, the traditional and the exotic.

There are only three motorized vehicles on Lamu. Time is measured at the pace of a human step, and the days slip by almost shapelessly. We spent much of our time getting lost in the maze of back alleys that climb uphill from the waterfront, enjoying the unique open-plan architecture of the multi-storey houses and admiring the craftsmanship that has gone into carving the heavy wooden doors that characterize the town. Every so often, we would escape to a breezy rooftop, and watch the Swahili women glide through the town below, inscrutable behind their black *bui-bui* veils.

In the heat of the day, and in the evenings, we would visit one of the string of restaurants along the waterfront, host to a lively and endlessly mutating community of travellers and locals. The menus here combine traditional Swahili dishes and seafood with firm backpacker favourites such as pancakes, garlic toast and fresh "juice" made by blending whole fruit with ice. In contrast to a place like Watamu, Lamu has managed to embrace tourism without compromising its soul.

Left: *Shela Beach, 2.3km (½ mile) from Lamu Town, is the island's main swimming beach, adorned by the relaxed Peponi Hotel*
Above: *Swahili woman wearing a* bui-bui *veil standing in a traditional doorway*
Below: *The only form of public transport is the brightly painted* dhow—*also popular with the local children*

Understandably, many travellers stay in Lamu rather longer than they had intended. Many never explore much beyond the confines of the seductive old town, but the onward possibilities are manifold. We spent a couple of nights at Shela Beach, a 13km (8-mile) slice of white sand that lies within walking distance of Lamu Town. Shela exudes tropical languor, as does its main tourist focus, the Peponi Hotel. It is a place for those perfecting the art of doing nothing, shifting between bar and beach, watching the stately *dhows* sail past, and lolling around beneath the palms devouring paperbacks and soaking up sunblock.

ISLAND HOPPING

Time takes on a certain fluidity when you head far enough off the beaten track in Africa. Suddenly, you enter the realm of pure African time: a place where local people might sit uncomplainingly for days while they wait for a ferry to arrive, and where you can finish a couple of novels while waiting for a vehicle that is coming soon, whenever, some time.

After a few days on Lamu, I was itching to head off into the unknown. I persuaded Ariadne that instead of undertaking a conventional *dhow* trip to one of the nearby ruins or reefs, we should aim for the little-visited but historically fascinating island of Pate. Our enquires about getting to Pate were met with a predictable tangle of rumour and misinformation, but eventually we established that a motorized boat travels there daily following a schedule based around the tide and the captain's whim. On the morning we wanted to leave, we positioned ourselves at a restaurant close to the jetty; half a novel and several fruit juices later, we were collected by a crew member—and off we sailed!

It took two hours to reach the jetty 5km (3 miles) from Pate town, where we were braced for a hot walk in the midday sun. To our pleasant surprise, however, the boat was met by a car—or, more precisely, a spectacularly battered old safari

---

THE LUNATIC EXPRESS

The overnight train between Nairobi and Mombasa follows the line built in the 19th century as part of the colonial drive to "open up" the African interior to European commerce. In his minor classic, *The Lunatic Express*, Charles Miller unveils the story behind the construction of this line, an engineering marvel that resulted in untold loss of life—mostly through disease, but more notoriously at the jaws of the "man-eaters of Tsavo," a lion pride that claimed 50 lives before it was hunted down. Today, the Mombasa Train evokes travel in the grand style, with starched tablecloths, colonial silverware and impeccably attired porters. However, the train was twice derailed in the 1990s, resulting in hundreds of fatalities, and the buses that cover the road running parallel to the railway aren't a great deal safer. Aeroplanes, it must be said, are.

---

vehicle. The vehicle, we were told, would pass near Pate town before continuing on to Siyu, 8km (5 miles) further along the bumpy track that crosses the island. We hadn't intended to visit Siyu; but there was no point in stopping halfway! In the event, the vehicle spluttered to a halt somewhere between Pate and Siyu, so we ended up walking the last 30 minutes anyway.

The first thing we saw upon entering Siyu was a 19th-century fort, a testament to the town's former status as, in the words of one Victorian visitor, "the pulse of the whole district." Later, we were shown the crumbling walls of a grand old mosque and numerous ornate graves, semi-obscured by a tangle of matted vegetation. You mightn't think it today, but Siyu in her heyday was a renowned centre of Islamic scholarship and craft, with a population of more than 20,000.

The imposing fort has the presence of a stone Gulliver in a settlement of 100-odd Lilliputian dwellings. The mud-caked outer walls and thatched roofs of Siyu's quadrangular one-storey houses create the impression of a neat and orderly but otherwise unremarkable village. Yet the interiors have a clear Arabic influence, and the rear arched entries, which open into large bathrooms, place Siyu in an architectural lineage stretching back to the likes of Gedi. Whatever its pedigree, Siyu is indisputably a backwater today. There is no guesthouse, no electricity, and—the acid test of obscurity—not a Coca Cola bottle to be bought. Communal pride of place goes to the recently installed public telephone, shown off to us by at least three different people in the course of one afternoon ramble.

We slept in the house of the hospitable Auni Mohammed, who asked a fair fee for a comfortable room and a tasty meal of chicken, spaghetti and spiced tea. After dinner, we did the circuit of Auni's extended family. The next morning, we were taken to the cemetery to pay our respects to Auni's late parents. This is Africa at its most refreshingly unaffected, a facet of the continent that too few visitors will ever see.

THE FORGOTTEN CITY

Friday is the Islamic Sabbath. It is also the day of rest for the only vehicle on this devout island. We therefore walked the 90-minute path from Siyu to Pate town, passing through thick coastal bush rattling with birds (at one point a mighty bateleur eagle soared above us in search of prey). Lamu is often described as existing in a time-warp. Quite what that makes Pate, I don't know, since it is possibly the most bizarre urban anachronism in East Africa. Upon entering the town, the transition from open coconut plantation to closed alley is abrupt and unexpected. Built upwards, rather than outwards, Pate has the feel of the centre of a large, traditional city, and we were constantly getting lost within its disorientating maze of alleys. Yet, incredibly, Pate supports only 2,000 people and it consists of maybe 100 buildings.

More than anywhere else I have visited on the Swahili Coast, this half-forgotten town is a place where practically every strand of coastal history can be seen to intertwine. At one time Pate attracted large numbers of Arabic and Portuguese settlers, and this is made evident simply by the cosmopolitan character of its human faces. The chequered

THE HISTORICAL FRAMEWORK

Maritime trade has linked the coast of East Africa to the outside world from the time of the ancient Egyptians and Phoenicians and into the modern era. The Swahili people who inhabit the coast today are primarily descended from the Bantu-speakers who arrived from the African interior roughly 2,000 years ago, as well as from the Arabic traders who settled in the area from the 9th century A.D. onwards.

The Golden Age of Swahili culture was contempory with the European middle ages. Coastal trade was based around gold, mined deep in the southern African interior, trans-ported via the Zambezi Valley to the now-submerged port of Sofala, then carried by boat to Kilwa in southern Tanzania. At its height, the Swahili Coast was dotted with more than 30 different city-states. These were architecturally impressive settlements: Kilwa, with its sunken swimming pool, massive mosques and population of 10,000, was described by the medieval globetrotter Ibn Buttata as "one of the most beautiful and well constructed cities in the world."

The end of the Golden Age came in 1498 with the arrival of the Portuguese on the east coast of Africa. In trying to assert control over the ancient Indian Ocean trade routes, the Portuguese contrived to destroy them.

KENYA

economic history of the coast is reflected in the modern "old town," essentially an 18th-century entity built over the ruins of a more illustrious medieval predecessor. Most of the modern houses have literally been built from the rubble of the ruined city that sprawls across the tobacco fields on the edge of town. Although less well preserved today than Gedi, medieval Pate must have been far more extensive.

In Pate, we stayed with the eminently tranquil Abala Hassan, patriarch of the town's tallest building, where a couple of rooms are retained for the use of the rare passing traveller. After exploring the town, we watched the sun set brilliantly from the third-storey rooftop of Abala's house, before enjoying another excellent dinner washed down by the fresh, mineral-rich milk of young coconuts. Replete, we chatted quietly with Abala and his son, bathed in a gentle sea breeze that carried up the animated gossip and braying donkeys from the alleys below.

It was an evening which somehow embraced the romance of African travel. What more appropriate way to end our time on this historic coast than in one of its oldest and most peculiar settlements, far from the nearest electric light, staring at the night sky that guided ancient mariners across the Indian Ocean all those centuries ago?

Below: Banana and coconut plantations surround Pate town on the little-visited but historically fascinating island of the same name

GOING IT ALONE

INTERNAL TRANSPORT

Air Kenya flies daily between any combination of Nairobi, Mombasa, Malindi and Lamu. For the budget-conscious, a daily overnight train and numerous buses connect Nairobi to Mombasa, while plenty of public transport runs along the coast as far north as Watamu and Malindi. There is a strong case for flying between Malindi and Lamu: the road is long, hot and dusty, and vulnerable to spasmodic outbreaks of banditry.

The only public transport on the Lamu archipelago is the motorized *dhow,* which runs daily between Lamu town and Pate island at high tide. Private *dhow* trips to the coral reefs, and elsewhere on the archipelago can be negotiated on the waterfront.

WHEN TO GO

There is no truly bad time to explore the coast of Kenya. The wettest months, generally April to June, are best avoided, though rainfall generally comes in short dramatic storms. The driest months are January and February, but this is also when the sticky heat is most oppressive.

OFF ON YOUR OWN

Any reader who has backpacked elsewhere in the developing world will find travel in this region pretty straightforward. If cramped local buses and simple accommodation don't appeal, then you would definitely be better off setting things up through a tour operator.

TRAVELLERS' TIPS

- ❏ Bring plenty of light clothing. Sweaters are unlikely to be needed.
- ❏ You have to pay a substantial fee to photograph Swahili women in *bui-bui* veils.
- ❏ Carry plenty of small change, particularly to off-the-beaten-track areas.
- ❏ A hat, sunglasses and sunblock are essential. Don't use locally sold lemon grass oil as a substitute for sunblock: potentially irritating, it can cause pale skin to burn more!

HEALTH MATTERS

The coast of Kenya is a very high risk malaria area, with the likelihood of infection greatest during the rains. Take prophylactics, cover up at night, be generous with the insect repellent, always sleep under a net and—should you be travelling in remote areas—carry a cure just in case.

Tap water in the larger towns along the coast is generally regarded as safe to drink, though it can't hurt to stick to mineral water, which is widely available.

Without adequate protection from the sun, a very real risk of coming down with severe sunstroke is attached to spending a day out in a traditional *dhow.*

When snorkelling, always wear a tee-shirt to protect your back from the sun and—if flippers are not available—some form of footwear to protect against sharp coral cuts and stinging creatures. For the same reason, never touch coral with your hands.

CRIME AND SECURITY

It would be asking for trouble to wander around Mombasa or Malindi at night with anything more valuable on your person than a bit of spending money. Mugging is commonplace on certain beaches, particularly south of Mombasa, so ask local advice before you stray too far along deserted stretches of sand.

Be wary of strangers who offer to share their food or drink with you on public transport. In recent years along the coast, a number of travellers have been doped and relieved of their possessions in this manner.

7 Exploring the Spice Islands

by William Gray

Bathed by turquoise Indian Ocean waters, the Zanzibar archipelago, comprising Unguja (or Zanzibar island) and Pemba, have been enticing travellers for centuries. I spent five days delving into the myriad passageways of ancient Stone Town, diving on pristine coral reefs and sampling the island's legendary spices.

Many people visit the Zanzibar archipelago, lying about 40km (25 miles) off the coast of Tanzania, to relax after a dusty wildlife safari or a gruelling Kilimanjaro trek. There are certainly plenty of idyllic, sandy beaches on which to recuperate for a few days, but sooner or later the fascinating cultures, legendary history and superb marine life of these islands will prove an irresistible lure; and that is when your Zanzibar adventure will begin.

Unguja is less than 85km (53 miles) long and only 30km (19 miles) at its widest point. It is a low, flat island rising to a mere 120m (395ft) above startling azure seas. When the British explorer Richard Burton first laid eyes on Unguja in 1856, his journal waxed lyrical—

Although getting around Unguja independently is straightforward, a guide is invaluable for obtaining a more in-depth insight into the island's history and culture. Numerous excellent scuba diving sites.

Accommodation in Stone Town ranges from lavishly restored 19th-century residences to modest guesthouses. Along the coast you will find everything from luxury resorts to budget beach bungalows. Although the climate is hot and humid all the year round, temperatures are often moderated by the sea breeze. Take precautions against sunburn, particularly during boat trips or when snorkelling.

Dive companies rent all snorkelling and scuba equipment. Protect your feet by wearing hard-soled wet socks or amphibious sandals when wading to and from boats. Remember to pack modest, culturally sensitive clothing for walking around towns and villages.

"Earth, sea and sky all seemed wrapped in a soft and sensuous repose." But in 1866, David Livingstone wrote: "The stench… is quite horrible…. It might be called 'Stinkibar' rather than Zanzibar."

Livingstone was referring to Zanzibar town, the island's main settlement on the western coast and the first stop for most of today's visitors. Whatever your first impressions of Zanzibar town may be, one thing is certain—they will reflect the vivid and colourful atmosphere of more than 2,000 years of history.

FIRST IMPRESSIONS

The oldest and most fascinating part of Zanzibar town, known as Stone Town, is sandwiched between the seafront and Creek Road. My first foray into its labyrinth of narrow streets resulted in a fairly predictable outcome: within five minutes I was completely lost. If this happens to you, don't panic. Eventually you will regain your bearings by emerging at the seafront, and in the meantime you can absorb the ambience of one of the most picturesque and spectacularly chaotic places in Africa.

For several hours I wandered the streets, each one a narrow canyon hemmed in by tall, ancient buildings. Elaborately carved balconies jutted from their sand and lime-coated walls, now cracked and pitted with age. In places, entire buildings had collapsed into a jumble of white limestone rubble, dazzling in the sunlight that streamed through the gap in an otherwise unbroken canopy of corrugated rooftops.

The streets, usually no wider than 3m (10ft), were thronged with human traffic. Women dressed in traditional Muslim robes glided past, while children played marbles, noisily chasing them down the paved alleyways. Men hauled carts laden with local fruits and vegetables or pondered life in the shade of intricately chiselled wooden doorways. Others played chess or painted colourful Tanzanian Tingatinga designs to sell in one of the many curio shops.

I was quickly discovering that, in Stone Town, you should always be prepared for the unexpected. On one street corner I came across the latest scores from the English Premier Football League chalked on a wall. That evening, from the magical open-sided Tower Top Restaurant above Emerson's & Green Hotel, I spied satellite dishes that have sprouted from the rusted patchwork of Stone Town's rooftops. They seemed a perfectly natural progression of the complicated history and mêlée of cultures that have made Zanzibar what it is today. As I sat down, barefoot on Persian rugs and cushions, to a sumptuous meal of crab claws, fresh fish and coconut rice, the dulcet tones of a Pavarotti CD wafted from the restaurant, mingling with the "call to prayer" chant of half a dozen mosques in the streets below.

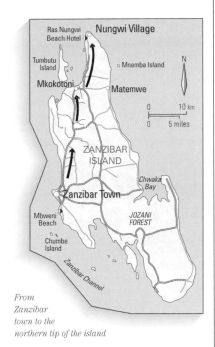

From Zanzibar town to the northern tip of the island

HISTORIC TOUR

The following morning, I employed the services of Hamisi, a registered guide from Ocean Tours. We began by walking to the Old Dhow Harbour.

Hamisi led me to the dockside, where 50 or more *dhows* were tied up, forming a huge raft bristling with masts and rigging. All were constructed entirely of wood, their bows often carved with swirls of Arabic or Swahili script. A large, triangular sail, which is knotted to a long spar and then hoisted up the short mast when the *dhow* is underway, lay crumpled across the deck of a recent arrival. A few *dhows* had nothing more than palm-thatched canopies for shelter. Hamisi

informed me that their design hadn't changed for hundreds of years—a chilling thought, when one looked down into the dark openings leading to their cargo holds, where Zanzibar's most infamous commodity was once packed. By the mid-19th century, up to 30,000 slaves were passing through Zanzibar each year.

The next stop on my walking tour was the Arab (or Old) Fort, easily identified

ELEPHANT-PROOF DOORS

While exploring Stone Town, you will notice that many of the carved wooden doors are studded with large brass spikes. This may be an adaptation of an ancient Indian practice that prevented doors being smashed in by war elephants. There are 560 carved doors in Zanzibar, the oldest of which dates back to 1694. Traditionally, the door was the first part of the house to be erected. The larger and more elaborately carved it was, the greater the wealth and social standing of its owner.

by its massive castellated walls, which rear up behind Forodhani Gardens (a popular evening spot for enjoying inexpensive street food). Having ousted the Portuguese, who had occupied Zanzibar for almost two centuries, the Omani Arabs constructed the fort in around 1700.

Next to the fort stands the even more prominent Beit el Ajaib, or House of Wonders. Framed by pillars and wide verandas, this multi-storey palace was constructed in 1883 by Sultan Barghash. Two huge wooden doors are surmounted by carvings of lions, vultures and snakes—symbols of power and royalty.

EXPLORERS AND CONCUBINES

Later that afternoon, Hamisi collected me in a minibus and we drove north past Livingstone House on the outskirts of town. Built in around 1860, this imposing building (now the main office of the Zanzibar Tourist Corporation) was used as a staging post by many European explorers, including Burton, Speke, Cameron and Stanley. Livingstone stayed here prior to his last expedition in 1866,

in search of the source of the Nile. A short distance beyond Livingstone House, we arrived at the ruins of Maruhubi Palace. Completed in 1882, the once elaborate structure was used to house Sultan Barghash's harem of 99 concubines. It was destroyed by fire in 1899. Some say it was an accident, but I couldn't help believing Hamisi's theory that the sultan's wife, consumed by jealousy, was driven to arson! All that remains are a few pillars of coral limestone, the Persian-style

Left: A freshly opened nutmeg fruit, showing the bright red strings of mace that enclose the actual nutmeg
Below: Clove buds are spread out to dry in the sun

bathhouse and the shells of several of the concubines' living quarters.

SPICE PLANTATIONS

No visit to Zanzibar would be complete without a guided tour of one of the spice plantations that have made the archipelago famous worldwide. We left Stone Town early the following morning and drove inland through dense stands of coconut palms. After cloves, coconuts are Zanzibar's most important crop. The coconut milk is widely used in Zanzibari cuisine, and the white, fleshy kernels are dried to produce copra, which is then processed into oil. Fibre from the outer husks of the coconuts, called coir, is woven into ropes and mats.

After passing through the almost regimental ranks of tall, straight coconut palms, the spice plantation we finally reached appeared wonderfully lush and unkempt—a riot of exotic plant growth. We walked on narrow footpaths through the cultivated jungle. Every few minutes Hamisi would dart into the undergrowth, reappearing clutching a different spice to challenge my senses of smell and taste.

For someone familiar only with the packaged, dried and shrivelled products that end up in supermarkets, these encounters with fresh spices "in the raw" were a revelation. Hamisi unearthed the vivid, yellow root of turmeric, which he said local women use to make their faces "shiny and nice." We unravelled vanilla vines, wrinkled our noses at lemongrass and split open yellow pods containing glistening scarlet and black nutmeg. Another random turn off the path revealed cardamom, peppercorns, ginger, cinnamon and, of course, cloves. By the latter half of the 19th century, the Zanzibar archipelago was producing over 90 percent of the world's cloves.

FISHING COMMUNITIES

With the sweet, pungent aroma of freshly plucked clove buds lingering in our nostrils, we returned to the minibus and began driving north. The island of Unguja

ON THE MENU

If you enjoy seafood, you'll experience culinary heaven in Zanzibar. Freshly caught lobster, prawns, kingfish, squid and crab are always available. Not surprisingly, many dishes are prepared in spicy sauces and served with coconut rice. In Stone Town, dinner at the wonderfully atmospheric Tower Top Restaurant, above Emerson's & Green Hotel, is not to be missed. For something cheaper and less formal, try the nightly food stalls in Forodhani Gardens (opposite the Arab Fort), where every type of seafood imaginable is cooked before your eyes.

has a population of around 600,000 and there were few moments when I couldn't glimpse a traditional clay and thatch building set back from the roadside. On several occasions we swerved to avoid huge swathes of cloves spread on the tarmac to dry in the sun.

Outside the handful of towns on Unguja, most people live off the land or the sea, by farming or fishing. When we arrived at the little-visited coastal village of Mkokotoni, trading at the local fish market was well underway. Men presented their fresh catches to the auctioneer and there followed a brief, frenzied outburst of talking and gesticulating as the fish was sold to the highest bidder. I watched as a procession of technicoloured parrotfish, spotted rays, sharks and giant tuna were slapped onto the bartering table, sold and then hacked to pieces—all in a matter of minutes. It was tempting to slip out a camera to capture this graphic scene on film, but as Hamisi gently reminded me, this was not a show for tourists and the fishermen might object to being photographed.

A short distance from Mkokotoni I gained another fascinating insight into the lives of the fishing community. For centuries, the *dhow*-builders of Nungwi Village, at the northern tip of Unguja, have passed their unique skills down through the generations. "There is no instruction book for this sort of thing," Hamisi told me as we watched one man shape the keel from a single piece of casuarina wood while another mixed kapok (a local cotton-like material) with oil to plug any gaps in the hull.

CORAL ISLAND SANCTUARY

For the adventurous traveller there are many opportunities to experience the wilder, more natural side of these islands. Apart from the Jozani Forest, about 35km (22 miles) southeast of Zanzibar town, most of Unguja has been transformed by centuries of cultivation, while many prime coastal locations are currently in the throes of development for new hotels.

Tiny 16ha (40-acre) Chumbe Island, lying 6km (4 miles) southwest of Stone Town, stands out as a rare, pristine jewel. Its virgin coral reef (formerly part of a restricted military area) was officially declared Tanzania's first marine national park in 1994. Together with the island, which is protected as a forest reserve, the whole area is known as the Chumbe Island Coral Park (CHICOP). All visits to this speck of paradise must be arranged through the CHICOP office or one of the tour operators in Zanzibar town.

As we began the 30-minute ride to Chumbe Island, the view back towards

Stone Town was timeless—a procession of *dhows* tacking out of the harbour, each bearing a single white sail taut before the stiff breeze.

As we tucked into the lee of the island, the sea became a smooth, glistening sheet of turquoise, so clear I could glimpse fish flickering through the coral, like pulses of electricity. The helmsman nudged the boat as far towards the island as he could. To minimize impact on the fragile reef environment, there is no jetty or other landing convenience at Chumbe, so I waded ashore in true castaway fashion.

If you were to become marooned on Chumbe, you would hardly complain. To help fund CHICOP's unique education programme (in which former fishermen are trained as park rangers and groups of schoolchildren are shown the beauty and importance of the reef and forest), seven stunning bungalows have been built at one end of the island for overnight visitors such as myself.

Constructed entirely of mangrove poles and thatch, each self-contained bungalow has solar-powered halogen lamps, composting toilets and a unique rain-catchment device. The only other constructions on the island are an education and dining area (resembling a miniature thatched version of the Sydney Opera House) and an old stone lighthouse built by the British in 1904.

Salim, one of Chumbe Island's new fishermen-turned-rangers, led me to the top of the historic tower for a bird's-eye

TOP DIVE SITES

Pange Reef Maximum depth 14m (46ft). Ideal site for beginners and night diving, with a chance of encountering turtles.

The Wreck Max depth 12m (40ft). Remains of the *Great Northern*, a British steel cable-laying ship that sank on New Year's Eve 1900.

Nyange Reef Max depth 30m (100ft). Black-tip reef sharks are occasionally sighted.

Tambare and Boribu Reefs Max depth 30m

(100ft). Renowned for whale shark and barracuda.

Nungwi/Leven Bank Off the northern tip of Unguja; the best site for drift dives.

Mnemba Reef Superb variety of fish, corals and sponges: everything from steep drop-offs to shallow beginners' dives. Visibility averages 25m (82ft).

Kisimkazi Resident pods of bottlenose dolphins.

TANZANIA

view of the island and its surrounding reef. From the blustery balcony surrounding the original lamp, the dense, unbroken canopy of Chumbe Island's forest provided a glimpse of what the entire Zanzibar archipelago must have been like before humans arrived. Over 60 species of bird have been recorded on the island.

Salim guided me along a trail through the so-called "rag forest" that flourishes on Chumbe's limestone foundation. The island is actually an ancient coral reef that was left high and dry when sea levels dropped about 10,000 years ago. Salim showed me startling evidence of this: the unmistakable shapes of giant clam shells and fossilized coral entwined with the roots of a strangler fig tree.

SNORKELLING SAFARI

Chumbe's living coral reef encircles the island like a precious necklace. It supports an astonishing 200 species of hard coral (90 percent of the total ever recorded in this part of the Indian Ocean), as well as 370 varieties of fish.

Equipped with snorkelling gear and special waterproof fish guides, Salim and

I took a boat ride to the reef crest, no more than 200m (660ft) offshore. Slipping over the side into the comfortable 28°C (82°F) water, we drifted with the current, peering through our masks at the reef 3m (10ft) below. Almost immediately, Salim spotted a small green turtle resting on the sandy seabed at the base of the reef. But I couldn't stare at one thing for long—my eyes constantly skipped from one dazzling sight to another. One moment we were hovering over the intricately sculpted dome of a huge brain coral, the next we were distracted by a flash of blue and yellow as an emperor angelfish paraded from cover. Huge shoals of nocturnal squirrelfish squirmed in the shade of overhanging plate corals, awaiting dusk before venturing further afield. By the time we lifted our heads above the surface, over an hour had passed and the tide was beginning to ebb.

Above: *Sailing off to explore the teeming reefs around Mnemba Island*
Right: *Homeward bound after a snorkelling expedition on Chumbe Island*
Inset: A *dazzling shoal of yellow-striped snappers gathered around an expanse of foliose coral*

TANZANIA

As we returned to shore, the setting sun laid an amber path across the still waters of Chumbe's coral lagoon. Each dusk the island is overrun by hordes of crustaceans. Emerging from their daytime burrows, thousands of land hermit crabs begin their nocturnal foraging. I tracked them down by torchlight, following their distinctive tank-like trails across the sand. They weren't difficult to find. More often than not, my encounters resulted from tripping over one.

DIVING THE REEFS

Returning to Unguja early the next morning, I took a taxi across to the northeast side of the island for my final two nights and a chance to scuba dive at one of Zanzibar's other renowned sites. Close offshore lies the sand island of Mnemba, set within its own coral reef. The exclusive resort on the island is extremely expensive, so most people stay on Unguja and take boat trips out to the reef.

I decided to base myself at Matemwe Bungalows, a line of 12 stone and thatch *bandas* set above a low cliff of weirdly eroded limestone. It was low tide when I arrived, and the lagoon was peppered with dozens of local villagers scouring the shallow waters for shellfish and other edible reef life. Several fishing *dhows* were hauled up on the nearby beach of powdery white sand, which is backed by a long line of flouncy coconut palms.

The atmosphere at Matemwe is very laid back. For romantics there is an information sheet pinned to the reception noticeboard listing useful phrases in Swahili, such as "You and me, let's sail away beyond that never-ending horizon."

Apart from Ras Nungwi Beach Hotel, further north, Matemwe Bungalows operates the only serious scuba diving centre on Unguja outside Zanzibar town. Greg, the resident instructor, can arrange anything from a "Discover Scuba Diving" try-dive for beginners to a four-day open water certification course.

As the tide began to flood the lagoon, I joined Greg and six others (a mixture of snorkellers and try-divers) for our first trip to Mnemba. We clambered aboard a traditional wooden *dhow*, specially adapted for diving, and set out on the leisurely 40-minute voyage.

A cluster of other boats were already moored at the dive site when we arrived, their anchors lodged harmlessly in a sandy area next to the fragile reef. An hour later, sitting amongst the happy, wet faces of the freshly returned novice divers, I was ready to take the plunge.

Somersaulting backwards off the side of the *dhow*, I joined Greg 6m (20ft) down on the seabed. Exchanging "OK" signals, we began to fin slowly towards the reef. Like at Chumbe, it was teeming with life, from great citadels of sea anemones bustling with clown fish to convoys of surgeon fish swooping through the corals. A colony of garden eels rose vertically from their burrows, like a crowd of exclamation marks, while goat fish ploughed the surrounding sand, feeling for morsels with their sensitive whiskers.

A little further on, we sank to our knees before a large coral outcrop, or "bommie." At its base, a trio of grey moray eels writhed next to a skulking lion fish. Gobies and blennies perched, wide-eyed, on coral ledges as a procession of butterflyfish, damsels, angelfish and parrotfish swam past.

Continuing our descent to 20m (66ft), we cruised over twisted pipes of blue sponges before reaching the climax of the dive—wide swathes of foliose corals, coating the reef like the petals of an enormous flower. Above them dense shoals of snappers parted briefly as we swam onwards, their yellow and blue flanks flickering inches from our faces.

Having gasped away my air supply in 40 minutes, I reluctantly surfaced and swam back to the *dhow*. With vivid images of the dive fizzing through my mind, I regretted that only a day remained of my visit to Zanzibar. Such is the extraordinary diversity of attractions around this tiny island that no matter how long you stay, it will never be long enough.

GOING IT ALONE

WHEN TO GO

Zanzibar has a tropical climate with average temperatures of around 27 to 29°C (80–84°F). It is possible to visit all year-round, but the coolest, driest months are June to October. When the northeast monsoon blows from November to February, the heat and humidity build prior to the main rainy season between March and May. Although the rain is heavy during this period, it is not constant, and travellers may benefit from good deals on accommodation and excursions. Keen divers should avoid these months, however, since the rain can lead to poor underwater visibility. Game-fishing is best from October to March.

INTERNAL TRAVEL

Travellers have several options for getting around on Unguja (Zanzibar island). The most convenient (and expensive) is to book all your tours and transfers through one of the many travel companies located in Zanzibar town. Popular guided tours include the spice plantations, Jozani Forest, Prison Island, Nungwi Village and Stone Town. Independent-minded visitors can rent cars and motorbikes (you'll need an international driving licence), or use public transport. *Dalla-dallas* (public transport vehicles, cheap and often crowded with locals) run between most towns on the island. There are also taxis at the airport and in Zanzibar town, but none have meters so you should agree a price with the driver before setting off.

PLANNING

With so much to see and do on Unguja it is worth spending some time planning ahead. Most travellers split their visit between Stone Town and one of the beach locations. You should allow an additional four to five days if you intend to complete an Open Water diver certification course. A few daylight hours spent wandering around Stone Town on your own is highly recommended, before taking a more structured guided tour. Be wary of employing the services of so-called guides who approach you in the street. These touts make their money from showing tourists around hotels and curio shops where the owners pay them commission.

Genuine guides from reputable travel companies are always registered with the Zanzibar Tourism Commission. The key sites to visit on a Stone Town tour include the House of Wonders, Palace Museum, Arab Fort, Anglican Cathedral, St Joseph's Cathedral, Hamami Persian Baths, Old Dhow Harbour, Old Dispensary and the market.

SAFETY

Unfortunately, robberies and related crimes are on the increase in Zanzibar town and along some beaches. Take sensible precautions: avoid displaying expensive cameras or flashing a thick wad of notes for every small purchase; walk in a group or take a taxi if venturing out at night, and leave all valuables in your hotel safe.

WHAT TO TAKE

❑ Mask, snorkel and fins.
❑ Thick-soled wet socks or amphibious sandals for wading in lagoons.
❑ Sunglasses, sun cream and wide-brimmed hat.
❑ Diver certification card (if qualified).
❑ Insect repellent.
❑ Water purification tablets or water filter.
❑ International driving licence.
❑ First-aid kit.

TRAVELLERS' TIPS

❑ Always ask permission before photographing people.
❑ When walking in the villages or Stone Town you should wear clothes that cover shoulders and thighs. During Ramadan, the annual 30-day Muslim fast, conservative dress is even more important, and you should also avoid eating or drinking in the street.
❑ Resist the temptation to purchase coral, shells or other reef curios. The coral reef ecosystem is very fragile; besides, it is often illegal to import these products into your home country.
❑ If you are new to scuba diving, take the time to practise your buoyancy skills before venturing near coral reefs. An accidental swipe of a fin or even the touch of a hand can kill corals that have taken decades to grow.

Map labels:

Lake Mweru
Mbala
Kasama
Lake Bangweulu
Solwezi
Mpika
Chingola
Kitwe
Ndola
Chipata
Liuwa Plain
Z A M B I A
Kabwe
Lusaka
Kafue
Monze
Lake Kariba
Victoria Falls
Livingstone
Harare
Hwange
Kadoma
Z I M B A B W E
Gweru
Bulawayo
Limpopo
Zambezi
Luangwa

⑧ A WALK ON THE WILD SIDE 88–95

⑨ CANOEING ON LAKE KARIBA AND THE LOWER ZAMBEZI 96–103

⑩ VICTORIA FALLS 104–113

Scale:
0 250 500 km
0 100 200 300 m

ZAMBIA•ZIMBABWE

Often referred to as "The Real Africa," Zambia conjures images of vast tracts of unspoilt wilderness and intrepid tales of early explorers. Over 30 percent of the country is protected in nature reserves, including the world-renowned South Luangwa National Park, where you can track big game on foot—the ultimate safari. In a landlocked country dominated by a dry, undulating plateau, Zambia's rivers provide a lifeline to its extraordinary variety of wildlife. None is larger or more impressive than the Zambezi River, which flows along the border between Zambia and Zimbabwe. From Victoria Falls to the calmer waters of Lake Kariba, the Zambezi is southern Africa's premier adventure destination, offering white-water rafting, microlighting, canoeing, bungee-jumping and a host of other activities. Further south lie the ancient ruins of Great Zimbabwe and the strange balancing rocks of Matobo National Park. In Zambia and Zimbabwe, you will discover spectacular landscapes, superb wildlife and some of Africa's remotest camps and best guides.

Victoria Falls: A chance to ride the highest-graded rapids in the world

8 A Walk on the Wild Side

by William Gray

With its large concentration of mammals and prolific birdlife, the South Luangwa National Park is renowned as one of Africa's foremost safari destinations. Setting out on a three-day guided walk, I discovered fascinating insights into bushlore and tracking, as well as the thrill of exploring an untamed African wilderness on foot.

Unfolding in a timeless mosaic of meandering rivers, shaded woodlands and seasonal lagoons, South Luangwa National Park in eastern Zambia covers an area of 9,050sq. km (3,500sq. miles)—over three times the size of Rhode Island and half the area of Wales. The park is sandwiched between the Luangwa River and Muchinga Escarpment, and is home to more than 50 species of mammal and some 400 varieties of bird. Although some national parks elsewhere in Africa can match this diversity of wildlife, few can provide the intimate wilderness experience that has become South Luangwa's trademark. South Luangwa's speciality, the walking safari, provides the ultimate brush with nature.

Pioneered in the 1930s by conservationist and author Norman Carr, walking safaris can range from a short ramble lasting a couple of hours to a week-long adventure, spending successive nights in remote and rustic bush camps. My wife, Sally, and I opted for Chilongozi's three-day walking safari from their magnificent Chibembe Tented Lodge in the north of the park.

JOURNEY TO LUANGWA

Although it is possible to travel overland to South Luangwa National Park, many visitors fly directly to the small town of Mfuwe, which is only a one- or two-hour transfer from most safari camps. The

2 Distances covered are generally no more than 6 or 7km (4 miles) each day. There is some scrambling up and down river banks, but most walking is over flat terrain following existing trails made by wildlife. Your main luggage is transported ahead to each night's camp, but you will need to carry a small pack containing items like water bottle and sun screen.

★★ The main camps and lodges at the start and end of walking safaris provide extremely high standards of accommodation. Bush camps along the trail are more rustic and basic, but you will still experience excellent food and a good night's sleep. Most walking is undertaken during the cooler early morning and later afternoon periods, when wildlife is also more active. However, you should be prepared for dusty conditions and a few insects.

 Essentials include a wide-brimmed hat for protection against the sun, dull khaki-coloured clothing and strong but lightweight walking shoes. See What to Take for more details.

FEET VERSUS WHEELS

To make the most of a visit to South Luangwa National Park, allow an extra day either side of your walking safari to explore a wider area of the park by vehicle. On game drives you can usually get much nearer to wildlife than by approaching it on foot. The South Luangwa National Park also permits night drives, allowing fascinating spotlit glimpses into the lives of nocturnal species, including the leopard, hyena, civet, various owls and the rarely seen aardvark. For obvious reasons, nighttime walking is not recommended.

ZAMBIA

ZAMBIA

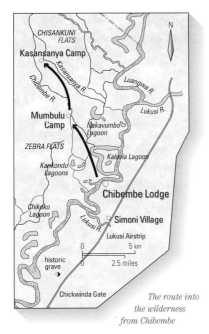

The route into the wilderness from Chibembe

grandiose title of the Mfuwe International Airport belies its small size and "frontier" atmosphere. When our Zambian Airways twin-propeller Beechcraft touched down after the one-hour flight from Lusaka, I couldn't see more than a handful of other aircraft—all tiny Cessnas, used by bush pilots to reach even more remote corners of eastern Zambia.

Inside the single-room terminal, we were met by Matthews, one of Chibembe's driver-guides. Bundling our bags into the back of a Land Rover, we began the two-hour drive north to Chibembe. The heat was intense—the kind that makes you gasp: it was like opening the door to a very hot oven. It sapped the moisture from our mouths and turned sweat to salt in a matter of seconds. We were visiting South Luangwa in late October, the hottest month, when temperatures soar to over 35°C (95°F), prior to the summer rains, when the park becomes flooded and inaccessible.

After stopping to buy fresh fruit and vegetables from a roadside stall on the outskirts of Mfuwe, we soon left the tarmac road and began bumping along a rough dirt track past villages of traditional clay and thatch huts.

We reached Chibembe at nightfall, just as a full moon, tinged orange by the fading sunset, was rising above the camp. Simon Bicknell, our walking guide, welcomed us with chilled drinks and we settled into a semicircle of wicker chairs overlooking the Luangwa River. A small campfire sent shadows dancing through the grove of mahogany trees in which Chibembe's seven luxurious walk-in tents were pitched. There were sounds of animals everywhere. The distant "whoop" of a hyena, the ratchet-clicks of frogs and the trilling of a pearl-spotted owl all merged into the strange percussion of an African night.

THE SMALL FIVE

Most people are familiar with the "big five" (elephant, lion, rhino, buffalo and leopard), but on a walking safari the smaller things often make the greatest impression. The smooth, conical pits dotted around sandy clearings are traps of the voracious ant lion. This tiny creature (the larval stage of a dragonfly-like insect) lurks at the bottom of the pit with jaws open, waiting for an unwary ant to stumble in. The termite is another insect which is seldom seen, but which builds a conspicuous home. Vast colonies construct mounds, or termataria, which are often taller than a human. Look under piles of elephant or buffalo droppings and you may find dung beetles, industrious insects which collect balls of dung, on which the female lays her eggs. As dusk falls over the Luangwa Valley you are sure to hear the tinkling chorus of tree frogs, which can sometimes be seen clinging to tent posts and other man-made objects using the suction pads on their feet. Agama lizards are more often glimpsed during the day, when they bask on tree trunks.

ZAMBIA

A NEW PERSPECTIVE

Early the following morning, Simon introduced us to Koffie and Mackson, who would comprise the rest of our walking team. As scout, Koffie would take the lead, a hefty Winchester 458 rifle slung over his shoulder. Simon, armed only with binoculars and bird guide, would be next, followed by Sally and myself. Mackson, the intriguingly titled "tea-bearer," would bring up the rear carrying everything he needed to make the perfect "bush brew"—from fire sticks to a teapot!

As we prepared to leave, Simon reeled off the three golden rules of a walking safari: always walk in single file; never get ahead of the scout, and, if an animal charges, don't run. We nodded gravely at each one, then made our way down to the river, where a small skiff was waiting to ferry us to the opposite side. As the boatman paddled us across the silt-laden waters of the Luangwa, several pairs of eyes were watching us. The Luangwa has one of the densest hippo populations of any African river and, in the days ahead, they would never be far away.

Chibembe Tented Lodge is named

Left: *Pellets give an intriguing insight to the diet and whereabouts of animals—these leopard droppings show fur and indigestible puku fawn hooves*
Below: *A walking safari provides the ultimate brush with nature*

after the tributary that flows into the
Luangwa River directly opposite the
camp. This would be the watercourse
that we followed on our first day's walk.
Scrambling up the loose sand of the river
bank, we looked briefly back at the white
canvas tents half-hidden in the mahogany
trees before turning around and walking
silently into the African bush.

Almost immediately, my senses went
into overdrive. On foot, every sound,
sight and smell registers with an intense

*Below: A giraffe sampling one of the fruits of the
sausage tree*

clarity. You rapidly develop a vivid awareness of your surroundings, acutely aware
that you are now part of the food chain.

SMALL WONDERS

By 7am the heat was already building and
we kept to the patchy shade of woodland
growing beside the Chibcmbe River.
Small herds of impala and puku (two of
the most common antelopes in South
Luangwa) froze at our approach, staring
intently before losing their nerve and
wheeling away in a skittish dance of
spindly legs. We also glimpsed waterbucks and zebras, but generally the larger
mammals are much harder to approach
on foot than they would be on a more
traditional vehicle safari.

Instead, Simon focused on small wonders. Widely regarded as one of Zambia's
most knowledgeable guides, he paused
every few minutes to reveal a nugget of
bushlore or to identify a bird from the
chattering cacophony of calls in the surrounding trees. The chaos of animal
prints around a waterhole were as clear
to Simon as entries in a visitors' book. But
even after 15 years of guiding, there was
still an eager edge to his voice. "Every
walk reveals something new," he told me.

To illustrate his point, he led us to a
succession of trees, shrubs and herbs,
each with its own range of medical or
practical applications. We sniffed brittle
sprigs of bush lavender, which can be
crushed to make a decongestant, a mosquito repellent or a mellow tea. We also
nibbled tentatively at the tart fruit of the
tamarind tree (a favourite of baboons and
elephants), wary of the fact that it makes
a strong laxative. The kabonga bush, on
the other hand, yielded an aphrodisiac,
while the inner bark of the mahogany
could be used to induce vomiting. Cut the
bark of the lilac tree, however, and its red
sap is thought to unleash evil spirits.

One of the most distinctive trees
found near rivers in South Luangwa is the
sausage tree, so-called because of the
enormous pendulous fruits that hang
from its branches. A salve produced from

GOOD SHIT

Delving into animal droppings is a favourite pastime of all walking safari guides. Studying their size, shape, distribution, warmth and contents can reveal not only what species they came from, but also clues to the animal's diet and how recently it was in the area. Most striking are the chalky-white hyena droppings, with their high content of crushed bone. For ultimate intrigue, however, the civet (a nocturnal cat-like creature with a spotted coat and varied diet) produces the most challenging offerings. In one civet midden we identified ebony seeds, snake scales, feathers and scrub hare fur.

these extraordinary fruits has been found to be effective in treating eczema.

TEA BREAK

By mid-morning, sweat had plastered the shirts to our backs and a persistent swarm of tiny, stingless mopane bees flickered around our arms and faces in search of moisture. Nearby, a Cape turtle dove chided us with its harsh, repetitive call: "Work harder, work harder…"

We sought refuge in the shade of a large tamarind tree that had sprouted from a termite mound beside the Chibembe River. Less than 10m (30ft) away, a baboon rocked back on its haunches and regarded me with frank curiosity, while a flock of Lillian's lovebirds gathered by the river for a drink. Apart from a noisy pod of hippos grunting and blowing bubbles, there was a sense of heat-stunned calm.

None of us saw the crocodile stalking the shallows. Just as I was leaning back against the trunk of the tamarind tree, there was an explosion of water as the reptile lunged at the lovebirds. They scattered in panic, their bright green and orange plumage flashing like shards of broken glass as the crocodile slipped

slowly beneath the surface again.

Throughout this commotion, Mackson had been quietly gathering twigs and dried elephant dung to make a small fire for our cup of tea. Proud of his traditional fire-making skills, Mackson has little use for matches. He placed his favourite piece of mahogany, dimpled with small holes, on the ground and added a little sand to one of the holes to provide friction. Then came the clever part. By turning a long stem of strawberry bush rapidly between his palms while one end was lodged in the hole, he generated enough heat to form a tiny, glowing ember. Judging the moment to perfection, Mackson neatly flicked this onto his carefully prepared tinder and nurtured it until the first flame bloomed.

A few minutes later, all five of us were sipping tea from cups and saucers—a strange and indulgent experience in the depths of the African wilderness, but an extremely refreshing one nonetheless!

BUSH CAMP

Daily walking distances are rarely more than 6 or 7km (4 miles) on this type of safari. The emphasis is on appreciating the subtleties of the environment. After our tea we continued walking for only an hour or so before reaching Mumbulu Camp. Constructed entirely of natural materials (and rebuilt every season when the floodwaters subside), Mumbulu was an eco-masterpiece. "You won't find a single nail here," said Simon, showing us around the cluster of huts overlooking a bend in the Chibembe River.

Each building consisted of a thatched roof and reed walls lashed to a frame of mopane branches using strips of bark from the monkey bread tree. Behind the sleeping huts were open-air bush showers (a water container with a shower head in one end) and composting toilets, all cleverly concealed in reed and thatch.

We laid low through the hottest part of the day, relaxing in the dining shelter, which also served as an excellent wildlife hide. In the distance a lone bull elephant sloshed across the Chibembe River using his trunk to sweep fountains of cooling water across his back. Below us, the river was clogged with broken ebony trees—the victims of the previous season's flood. Each dead branch and twig protruding above the surface seemed to be adorned with bee-eaters and kingfishers. From these convenient hunting perches, giant, brown-headed, malachite and pied kingfishers dived for fish. Standing out, even from this resplendent collection of birds, were the carmine bee-eaters. Each September and October, large colonies of these magenta and turquoise-coloured gems dig nesting burrows in the sandy river banks of the Luangwa Valley.

ON THE TRAIL OF A KILL

Less than 20 minutes after leaving Mumbulu Camp for our late afternoon walk, Simon spotted several vultures drifting in lazy circles to the west. Usually that meant only one thing: the vultures had spotted a dead or dying animal.

We began walking stealthily in their direction until Koffie stopped abruptly and pointed at the sandy game trail we were following. There, half filled by

SAFARI SNIPPETS

- ❏ Instead of building nests, palm swifts stick their eggs directly to palm fronds, using their saliva.
- ❏ The go-away bird often perches on treetops, calling out its name.
- ❏ The mopane tree is named after its butterfly-shaped leaves.
- ❏ The flowers of the sausage tree open at night to attract pollinating bats.
- ❏ The leaves of the sensitive plant, a variety of mimosa, immediately fold up when touched.
- ❏ Male hippos have lower canine teeth up to 45cm (18in) in length.
- ❏ An adult bull elephant weighs an average of 5,000kg (11,000lb).

shadow from the low sun, was the perfect paw print of a lion. Simon and Koffie studied the spoor and soon determined that it had been made by a large male heading in the same direction. Judging by its clarity, the print might have been less than a day old. Casting about for more clues, Koffie soon picked out the tracks of other lions. A pride had recently passed this way and the vultures suggested that they had made a kill. The big question was: when?

Simon slowly scanned the area ahead with binoculars. We crept forwards, using a straggly line of bushes for cover. I was half expecting a lioness to charge at any moment, but when we finally came across the carcass of a buffalo it became clear that it was already perhaps three days old. The lions had moved on. All that remained of their kill was skin and bones—the final pickings, for vultures and hyenas to squabble over.

THE HUNTERS AND THE HUNTED

The following morning, we discovered more evidence of South Luangwa's thriving big cat population. Slashed across the base of a tree were the claw marks of a leopard. A short distance away, Simon found one of the cat's pellets—a bundle of fur, from which he teased out the tiny undigested hooves of a puku fawn, the leopard's last meal.

There was no let-up in the heat during our second day's walk. We followed the dry streambed of one of the Chibembe's tributaries until we emerged in a large clearing of hard sun-cracked mud. When the rains finally broke, the swollen rivers would flood areas like this to form a patchwork of streams and shallow lagoons. For now, however, all that remained were clues to a watery past—the broken shells of freshwater mussels and the trail made by a lone hippo when it abandoned its shrinking waterhole. At the centre of the dried-up lagoon, a family of warthogs wallowed in the last puddle of soft mud, while nearby a fish eagle fed on a large stranded catfish.

APPROACHING RAINS

No matter how desiccating the dry season, the larger rivers of the South Luangwa always endure. This, along with its diversity of habitats, is why the valley is such a magnet to wildlife.

From our second camp, Kasansanya (literally "flooding water"), we watched a spectacular herd of over 70 zebras make its way to the river to assuage its thirst. They were soon joined by puku, impala,

Above: *A pod of hippos in the Chibembe River*

bushbucks and baboons. Vast flocks of tiny red-billed queleas pulsed from riverside trees to the water's edge and back, while a pod of hippos, perhaps 100 strong, began a chorus of snorts and bellows.

That night, the incessant trilling of the frogs seemed louder than ever, almost as if they could sense that the long-awaited rains were finally approaching. Once or twice, we glimpsed lightning flare in the belly of distant clouds, and by dawn there was a loamy, moist tinge to the wind.

As we began our final walk back to Chibembe, ominous clouds were bubbling up behind us. It seemed that we would be leaving just in time; but had it not been for the impending rains, I could easily have spent another week roaming the Luangwa Valley. Our three-day walking safari had provided a rare glimpse into one of Africa's last pristine wildernesses. Witnessing it on foot had added a unique perspective and a change of pace and rhythm that in today's busy, crowded world is hard to find.

TOP TEN MAMMALS AND BIRDS

Baboon	Carmine bee-eater
Cape buffalo	Crowned crane
Elephant	African fish eagle
Thornicroft's giraffe	Guineafowl
Hippo	Ground hornbill
Impala	Pied kingfisher
Leopard	Lillian's lovebird
Lion	Red-billed oxpecker
Warthog	Saddlebilled stork
Burchell's zebra	Red-billed quelea

GOING IT ALONE

WHEN TO GO

Walking in South Luangwa National Park is only possible during the dry season, from June to the end of October. The summer rains, which usually arrive by the end of November, swell the rivers and flood surrounding land. For this reason, many of the camps in the park are seasonal and have to be reconstructed every April or May, when the floodwaters have receded enough to allow access. Daytime temperatures are most pleasant from June to August, averaging 24°C (75°F). The heat steadily builds throughout the dry season, occasionally soaring to 45°C (113°F) by the end of October—often referred to as the "suicide month." Wildlife viewing can be particularly rewarding in the latter half of the dry season, when birds and animals concentrate around the last remaining areas of water.

INTERNAL TRAVEL

The easiest and quickest way to reach South Luangwa National Park is to fly there. Zambian Airways and Proflight offer daily one-hour scheduled flights between Lusaka and Mfuwe, with occasional connecting flights to and from Livingstone (near Victoria Falls). You can also fly to Mfuwe from Lilongwe in Malawi. It is a two-hour transfer by road from Mfuwe Airport to most of the camps and lodges in and around the park. An alternative, but more expensive option for reaching Chibembe Tented Lodge is to charter a light aircraft from Lusaka to Lukuzi airstrip (two-hour flight), followed by a 15-minute drive. If you are planning to travel overland to South Luangwa you will require a four-wheel drive vehicle and should seek local advice on road conditions before setting off.

CAMPS AND LODGES

There are several camps and lodges in South Luangwa National Park and along its eastern and southern boundaries, many of which offer walking safaris in addition to more traditional game and night drives. The majority are expensive, which is not surprising, considering the very high standards of accommodation, food and guiding, as well as the logistics of operating a seasonal camp in such a remote location. Most companies have offices in either Mfuwe or Lusaka and many are promoted by specialist safari travel agents in the United States, Britain and elsewhere. The most straightforward way to arrange a safari is to contact either the operators or their agents. Operators offering walking safaris include Chilongozi, Chinzombo Safaris, Kapani Safari Lodge, Robin Pope Safaris, Kafunta River Lodge and The Wildlife Camp (cheaper, self-catering camping).

HEALTH MATTERS

❑ Take precautions against malaria by sleeping under a net, using insect repellent and starting a course of preventative pills before you leave home.
❑ Inoculations against yellow fever, polio, tetanus, hepatitis A and meningococcal meningitis are recommended.
❑ Be sure to drink plenty of fluids, particularly if you are walking in the hottest months of September and October. Heat exhaustion through dehydration can be extremely serious.

WHAT TO TAKE

❑ Lightweight, loose-fitting cotton clothing in "earthy" colours.
❑ Wide-brimmed sun hat, sunglasses and high factor sun cream and lip salve.
❑ Insect repellent.
❑ Comfortable lightweight walking boots.
❑ Water bottle, torch and daypack.
❑ Binoculars, camera, lens-cleaning cloth and plenty of film.
❑ Field guides to birds, mammals, plants and tracks and signs (although most camps usually have a good selection).
❑ Small first-aid kit with insect bite and sting relief cream, plasters and a blister care kit.

TRAVELLERS' TIPS

❑ A walking safari is a multi-sensory experience with plenty of time to discover the sights, smells, sounds and even tastes of the African wilderness. The slower you walk the more will be revealed.
❑ Remember that this is an environment inhabited by large predators and other potentially dangerous animals. Never wander off on your own or get in front of the armed scout.
❑ In the unlikely event of being charged, don't run but follow your guide's instructions.
❑ Keen birdwatchers will want to bring a good pair of binoculars.

9 Canoeing on Lake Kariba and the Lower Zambezi

by Michael Woods

Zimbabwe lies in the middle of southern Africa. It boasts a wonderful climate, landscapes ranging from mountains to agricultural plains, the south bank of one of the largest man-made lakes in the world and magnificent game parks; and flowing along its northern border is the mighty Zambezi River.

Having flown from London to Zimbabwe's capital, Harare, I climbed aboard a five-seater charter aircraft to fly noisily up to Mana Pools National Park. The park lies on the south bank of the lower Zambezi, between Lake Kariba and the border with Mozambique, and it was here that I was met by James, our guide, and Tafara, his assistant. They were going to be taking care of our group for the next four nights, as we canoed down the lower Zambezi. I was joined by Australians Cath and Shawn; Julia and Mark from California, and Robbie and Gigs, South Africans.

While our luggage was being loaded into an open, four-wheel-drive safari truck, I took the opportunity to change

Some canoeing experience would be an advantage but is not essential as the boats are very stable and the current is of great assistance in carrying you from camp to camp. Regular stops in the shade mean that this is not a marathon. The morning walks in Matusadona National Park can become very hot towards the end of the walk as the sun lifts increasingly overhead. Light boots are useful for both adventures.

On the canoeing section, the tents are spacious and provided with comfortable beds and many other thoughtful facilities while the food is of a very high standard. Once on Lake Kariba, the lodges are of a generally high standard.

You may want to take your own small dry bag which is handy for cameras and other valuables. Binoculars for every member of the party are a boon.

from my travelling trousers into a pair of shorts and find my binoculars. Then James drove us through part of Mana Pools National Park to Vundu Camp, where lunch was already laid out and waiting for us. After our meal, the vehicle took us a few miles up the river to where our canoes were ready to launch.

James gave us a short but comprehensive safety talk, the most important part of which was our conduct in the vicinity of hippos. Although these animals have become accustomed to seeing canoeists on the river and remain relaxed in their presence, an occasional rogue hippo may take umbrage and upset a canoe—or even munch through the plastic hull. In this situation the drill is to abandon ship and, contrary to standard canoeing practice, swim away from the boat, in case the hippo comes back for another bite.

ON THE RIVER

We set off with two or three people in each boat. I shared a canoe with James on that first afternoon and, along with the dry bag he had provided for my camera, boots and other things, we had a cool box, first-aid kit and James's rifle. We propelled the canoes with single-bladed paddles, steering from the back seat—an art which takes a little practice. Although a broad expanse of water, the Zambezi is surprisingly swift and, even without paddling, we found that we were covering the ground quickly. On the far side of the river, in Zambia, a range of hazy mountains provided a peach-coloured backdrop for the forest, while on the Zimbabwean side stood the national park and its tall mahogany and acacia trees.

Until the 1950s the river was more seasonal, and torrents of water would pour down in the rains, occasionally over-spilling the banks and flooding the forests. More often it would remain within the river's course but tear great lumps from the cliffs, sometimes ripping out trees and destroying termite mounds. At the same time it would deposit vast sand banks and even develop new islands. Since the completion of the dam at Kariba in 1958 the extremes of water level have been moderated, and now the river rises and falls more erratically, in response to demands for electricity and variations in the water level of Lake Kariba. There are still floods after heavy rainfall but, although it was the driest part of the year, the river rose by 300mm (12in) during our three-day voyage as the engineers at Kariba released a large quantity of water.

We stopped first at one of the earth cliffs to enjoy the spectacle of a carmine bee-eater colony. These birds, magnificent with their rose-coloured plumage, excavate high-rise tunnels in which to lay their eggs in September and October.

REVENGE OF THE RIVER GOD

Nyami Nyami is the name of the river god believed by the local Batonga people to inhabit the Zambezi and to have been seriously angered by the construction of the Kariba Dam and the attempts to impede the flow of water. Various calamities overtook the construction of this major civil engineering project—a massive flood early in the scheme ruined months of work, the road bridge to Zambia was later blown away and various accidents took their toll of dam workers, thus confirming the Batonga's predictions.

When we arrived, most of the birds vacated their holes and perched in a row on the the bank, adorning a dead tree like some exquisite table decoration.

We continued downstream, avoiding stumps and logs concealed just beneath the water ready to upset an unwary canoeist, and only visible because of a slight rippling on the surface. Small groups of waterbucks and buffaloes grazed on the extensive green flood plains which lay beyond the banks and, as the afternoon cooled, baboons wandered nonchalantly down to drink and to feed on succulent water hyacinths.

This time of day also suited the elephants, who came down to the river to feed, drink and bathe. Small groups of bulls were ripping up aquatic grasses, skilfully biting off the roots and chewing up the green shoots and stems. More than once we beached the bows of the canoes almost at the feet of these giants, which looked enormous to us from our low, sitting positions. They were almost within the touching distance of an extended trunk, but they did not turn a hair and ate on unperturbed by the presence of their human observers. Bull elephants tend to be safer and more predictable than cows with calves in this situation and, like many animals, appear not to perceive danger from water. As a canoeist the secret is to keep quiet, move slowly, remain seated and wear dull green or khaki clothing so that you do not attract attention to yourself.

As the sun sank towards the mountains, we rafted up for what James called "leg over time." The four canoes came together in parallel, linked by the draped legs of those in the adjacent boats. Then Tafara opened one of the cold boxes and passed around cool drinks. With those in the outermost canoes paddling gently, we drifted languidly, beers in hand, towards our campsite at Vundu. While some people went to wash, the rest of us sat around the camp fire sipping beers and listening to the growing volume of night sounds. Loud frogs were joined by the

soft calls of a scops owl and the deep grunting laughs of hippos.

When it was my turn for a shower, I found myself in a canvas cubicle, under a bucket with a tap and a shower rose, looking up at hundreds of millions of stars. Refreshed and kitted out with long sleeves and long trousers to protect against biting insects, I returned to the fire and to a three-course dinner with wine. In the distance, we could hear the occasional high-pitched giggle of a spotted hyena and, once, the straining groans of a lion from across the river.

THE MORNING AFTER

My wake-up call the following morning was a soft "Hello" and the sound of dirty water from the wash basin being thrown to the ground and replaced with fresh, warm water. We drank tea and coffee by the river before setting off for an early walk. Mana Pools is an unusual national park: it's the only one of Zimbabwe's parks (and one of a very few on the entire continent) that contains dangerous animals and allows the public to walk there unaccompanied. However, we had our guide, James, who led us in single file into the open woodland with his rifle slung over his shoulder. Signs of the previous night's events were everywhere. Here, a spotted hyena had paced down the track, leaving large footprints from its powerful front legs and smaller ones from the weaker hind feet. There, a zebra had rolled, smoothing out the dust and leaving pony footprints in the sand.

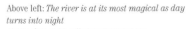

Above left: *The river is at its most magical as day turns into night*
Above: *Our guide offering instructions*
Right: *Lunch on a submerged sandbank*

Scratch marks made by long quills showed where a porcupine had shuffled down the path.

We returned to camp for breakfast and then set off in the canoes once more. This was to be a very different kind of day. A fresh east wind had sprung up in the night and was blowing up-river, kicking the surface into bouncing, glinting wavelets which occasionally splashed against the canoe. This added to the excitement of the first stretch of river, where we encountered the only rapid on the voyage. It was more wetting than dangerous and gave none of us any problems.

While the wind meant that the second day was more tiring than the first, it did

ZIMBABWE

have two advantages. The haze that had blurred the Zambian mountains had blown away, leaving them clearly etched against the blue sky; and we were kept cool, so we could paddle in relative comfort. The temperature was deceptive, though: the sun was just as fierce and was reflected by the water, making it essential to use a high factor sunblock on exposed skin. A broad-brimmed hat, sunglasses and lip salve were also vital. Even though I wear shorts as much as possible and tan easily, I found that, in the afternoons, those areas not used to direct sunlight, such as my upper legs, began to burn. A small towel draped over them for a couple of hours was enough protection.

We had not been paddling for more than an hour when James pointed out a nyala, a spiral-horned antelope that is a speciality of Mana, and spends most of its time skulking in thick scrub. I once spent three days in the park searching for nyala without success. We paddled swiftly to the spot but the animal had disappeared up the bank. James leapt out, barefoot, and set off to try and track it. The rest of us were rather slower, cramming our feet into sandals (it was hardly worth putting boots on, as this was not likely to be a long or protracted walk). At the top of the bank we found ourselves bent double, ducking under low, arching twigs, trying not to step on dry sticks and looking ahead all the while for the shaggy grey coat and spiral horns.

We worked our way round in a large circle, finally finding its tracks and glimpsing it once as it stood, perfectly still, in the bush. At last it lost its nerve and bolted, with head low and horns laid along its shoulders. This was its home ground and there was little chance of our seeing it again. We made our way back to the canoes, took a drink and paddled on.

The rest of the morning was uneventful. Whenever we could, we left the main river to the hippos and took off down smaller side channels. These were less troubled by the wind, so we were able to drift down them. They were a paradise for

water birds and I had my binoculars constantly at the ready round my neck. We saw African jacanas using their long toes to walk over water plants without sinking. Grey, black-headed and Goliath herons, along with great egrets and little egrets, fished by the water's edge, occasionally catching their writhing prey and wrestling to rotate the fish and ensure that it went down head first. Pied kingfishers hovered overhead, then plunged under the surface to catch their lunch.

From time to time we would stop at the bank for a drink, a stretch and a chance to look at this skull or that flowering bush. But lunches were always eaten on a submerged sandbank in the middle of the river. The water was shallow enough here, at 300mm (12in), for us to get thoroughly soaked without fear of crocodiles, while James and Tafara prepared the food. We sat on stools to eat fresh quiche, baked in camp only that morning. The combination of the cooling river and regular drinks meant that we could continue canoeing through the heat of the afternoon.

FOLLOWING THE TRAILS

Generally, as the temperature fell, we would go for a longer walk. Wearing light boots, we could explore Mana Pools at its best. With no giraffes to browse the high branches, there were long, shimmering views under the trees into the far distance, which were given a faintly blue tinge by the famous Mana haze. From time to time James would kick up a cloud of dust to check which way the wind was blowing. Mammals rely heavily on scent so we had to approach downwind.

It was also important to keep a look out for any animals which might be antagonistic. Lions generally hide up in cover, so we were always cautious when going through long grass. James was always conscious of the whereabouts of elephants, and in which direction they were going. They would only be a problem if we surprised them and, as we rarely made any secret of our presence, this was unlikely. On one day we came across a large, scattered herd of eland, Africa's largest antelope and one of its most timid. They all kept their distance—even a very large bull, whose curled horns were adorned with great clumps of green grass.

Camp was very welcome on the second night. The staff had taken our tents from Vundu and driven them down to Chessa. We began to settle into a routine of camp life and the dining area and camp fire were always in a magnificent location overlooking the river. The moon was waxing throughout our trip; by the last night, it was casting a glittering silver path across the surface of the river.

Before we reached camp, though, we had an episode of real excitement. We were within reach of the spot where the canoes were to be lifted out for the last time when the alarm call of a baboon attracted our attention. In the distance, across a flood plain on our right, three impala were standing stock still, staring away from us towards the river bank, and a large cloud of dust indicated that something dramatic was happening.

James was extremely keen to see what was going on and took us at full speed to the bank. We pulled our boots on as quickly as we could. In the distance we could already hear a continuous growling and snarling and we set off, almost at a trot, in the direction of the noise. We had reckoned without three deep drainage channels, which lay between us and our destination. There was no choice. Off came the boots and in we plunged, sinking up to our thighs in fetid, black mud.

There was no time to pull our boots back on: we crossed the grass to the next channel in bare feet. At last we arrived at a low bank and a termite mound. Slightly below us and across another channel, five young lions and four lionesses were grouped around the body of an undefinable animal, squabbling and fighting, ripping at the carcass and swallowing rapidly as each tried to get as much as possible. It was a thrilling climax to a wonderful trip.

LAKE KARIBA

The following day, James took us to the airstrip to wait for our various planes. I was booked on a charter flying up Lake Kariba to Matusadona Water Lodge. After taking off, it headed up river, flying low enough for us to spot hippos lazing in the water and the occasional herd of elephants wandering through the trees. Approaching the lake, the river narrowed until it ran through a gorge that cut through a cleft in the hills, neatly plugged by the curving wall of Kariba Dam. The plane banked over the enormous expanse of water and landed at Kariba.

My next plane left half an hour later, and the flight down the southern shore of the lake took only about 20 minutes. I was met by Shasha, the camp manager, and driven to a wooden pier, where a powerful speedboat whisked me out on to the lake. We bumped over the waves towards the lodge. Lake Kariba began to fill in 1958, when the dam was completed, and is now the size of an inland sea, 300km (180 miles) long and 35km (21 miles) wide, with 5,000km (3,000 miles) of shoreline.

DETERMINED KILLERS

Spotted hyenas are frequently portrayed as scavengers, picking up scraps from the table of the king of beasts. In fact hyenas are more efficient killers than lions. They use their remarkable reserves of stamina to run their prey down and, having done so, may burst into fits of giggles which attract other hyenas and often lions too. The big cats drive the hyenas off the kill so that, at first light, visitors often see a pride of lions feeding and circling hyenas apparently waiting to scavenge some food. In fact the lions are more likely to be the scavengers in this scene and the hyenas are simply waiting to get their kill back.

ZIMBABWE

In a matter of minutes the boat slowed and began to thread its way between the gaunt, grey skeletons of trees drowned during the creation of this great reservoir. We rounded a corner into a bay and there was "the mother ship," the sitting, dining and bar area of the Water Lodge, securely moored to several of these old trees.

I had arrived for my two-night stay in time for brunch. It was very much hotter than on the lower Zambezi, partly because Kariba sits in a sheltered bowl and partly because of the humidity generated by the lake. Consequently, siestas were the order of the day, and I took one of the canoes, moored outside the mother ship, and paddled to my room, tied up in a private spot some distance into the bay, where my luggage had already arrived.

The mornings here are taken up with long walks in the adjacent Matusadona National Park. The two that I joined each lasted almost five hours, and the heat had become uncomfortable by the time we returned the lodge. We tracked rhino without success, but came upon the droppings of a lion. We also spotted a herd of buffaloes, a waterbuck and a bushbuck. The game in Matusadona is not as prolific as it is in Mana Pools. The elephant-stunted bush is also much hotter to walk through than the tall, shady trees. However, it's the challenge of tracking black rhino that is one of the main incentives for walking here.

In the afternoons we set off in the boat with Craig, our guide. Both trips were very similar. On the first we landed about 1.6km (1 mile) away on a beach near to a point where we had spotted an elephant drinking. Craig, barefoot, led us into the mopane scrub. After half an hour he spotted the bull ambling through the bush. He carefully calculated the route he expected the elephant to take and sat us on some logs beside the path. With the silence of a burglar, the animal padded through the trees and strolled past within 15m (50ft) of us, without realizing that we were there.

As the sun finally sank into the waters of the lake, we set off for the lodge. The colours drained from the landscape and behind us the sky and water blended into one, so that our wake appeared to come from nowhere as we parted the air, now warm, now cool, but always smelling of the dust of Africa.

Below: *Elephants are generally undisturbed by human observers*
Right: *A carmine bee-eater perched on a suitable vantage point from which to swoop on passing insects*

GOING IT ALONE

It is almost impossible and extremely inadvisable to canoe on the lower Zambezi without the help of a reputable operator and the services of a professional guide. In the first place, getting hold of a canoe is difficult; secondly, canoeing is only allowed by permit, and almost every slot is taken up by the main operators. Even if it were possible to find and launch a canoe, the Zambezi is a powerful river, full of obstacles, crocodile-infested and containing unpredictable hippos. There should always be a minimum of two canoes and a guide is essential. Consequently the only recommended way to canoe this river is with an organized group, which can be booked in Harare, probably Victoria Falls or, best of all, in your home country. It is unlikely that you could book a trip in Kariba.

MANA POOLS NATIONAL PARK

By contrast, it is possible to visit Mana Pools National Park independently, and both walk and game drive in this beautiful area. The road into the park from the main Harare– Lusaka road is very poor, and should only be tackled in a four wheel drive vehicle, which you can hire in the capital for the 400km (240-mile) drive to the park. You will only be allowed to enter the park if you have booked accommodation or a campsite in advance: catching a bus up the main road and hitching (illegally) into the park is a non-starter. In the peak season, sites in the park are hard to get and are allotted in a draw, and the park is closed between November and April.

It is perfectly possible to walk without a rifle as long as you take care and maintain your concentration. If you keep away from thickets and dense grass, you are unlikely to surprise any of the animals which might turn on you (buffalo and lion are the most likely). There are no longer thought to be rhinoceroses here; leopards are generally too timid and, as long as you treat elephants with respect (especially cows with calves), you should have no problems. It is better to go later in the dry season, when the vegetation has died down, than shortly after the rains, when the grass will still be thick and high.

MATUSADONA NATIONAL PARK

Once again you will need the services of a professional guide if you are going to walk in Matusadona National Park. Most of the camps and lodges along the Zimbabwean shore provide this opportunity and you can travel to those closest to Kariba by speedboat, rather than by flying in. Some camps are larger and a bit more impersonal but less costly. As is the case everywhere else, the more exclusive, the more expensive. Some of them offer the chance of going on game drives, as well as boat trips and walking safaris.

An independent alternative to staying in a lodge is to rent a houseboat, which comes complete with skipper, chef and deckhand. All you have to do is supply the food and drink. If you also hire a professional guide, you can land and walk in the national park.

Otherwise, you can still cruise the shoreline in the small motorboat which comes with the main craft, looking for mammals and birdwatching. Crucially, this means that you can also enjoy sunset drinks on the lake, which is always a magical experience at Kariba.

TRAVELLERS' TIPS

- ❑ Always be aware of the direction of the wind.
- ❑ Take plenty of water and wear sunblock, a broad-brimmed hat and khaki or green cool cotton clothing (not white).
- ❑ Go out early or late to avoid the heat of the day, and keep track of where you are, with a compass if necessary, to avoid getting lost.
- ❑ It is useful to carry both a torch and a box of matches.
- ❑ Every one in the party should have their own pair of binoculars to enjoy their safari experience to the full. These are also very useful for spotting danger from a distance.

ZIMBABWE

10 Victoria Falls

by Michael Woods

Victoria Falls is surely the adventure capital of Africa. On Zimbabwe's northern border, the rapidly expanding town's main attraction is the falls themselves, where the Zambezi River plunges 110m (360ft), at the rate of 750 million litres (165 million gallons) every minute.

A wall of water rose above us, towering over our heads as the blue raft was borne upwards. Then it all started to go horribly wrong. The last thing I heard was a brief expletive from Artwell, our steersman, and the Muncher (as Rapid Eight is fondly known) gave a sudden surge, which tipped all eight of us into the raging waters of the Zambezi. Only Artwell stayed aboard. I was one of the first to be hauled back into the raft, and I turned to help my fellow rafters. Grabbing them by the shoulders of their tight-fitting life jackets, I pushed them down briefly, giving them an extra boost from the buoyancy so that, as I lifted them up, they were already popping out of the water like corks, and I could haul them into the raft.

I had been picked up by the rafting truck from the Victoria Falls Hotel at 8am, going out into the world with no more than I stood up in—leaving behind anything likely to be lost in the river or ruined by water. I drank tea with my fellow rafters: two parties of young overland truckers, most from Australia, New Zealand and the United Kingdom, with a smattering of other Europeans. We were all preparing ourselves for the raft ride of a lifetime, along the narrow gorge of the Victoria Falls.

Once you have run the gauntlet of the peddlers on the approach to the entrance to Victoria Falls National Park, you can stroll along the very edge of the gorge, looking across to the water opposite— one of the most spectacular views of any waterfall in the world. The greatest volume of water will be tumbling over in March, April and May and, while this sounds a dramatic sight, the density of spray is so great that it often obscures the Falls themselves. (At the end of the dry season, in October, the Falls can be disappointing, often shrinking to about half the width of the river.) An umbrella is a useful accessory at any time, especially if you want to take pictures, as the spray can fall like a heavy storm.

Victoria Falls town buzzes with activity, its streets thronged with overland trucks, open safari vehicles, lorries carrying canoes, stores and rafters to and from the river. There is always some new and daring activity on offer—an abseiling day (which includes a gorge crossing), tandem microlighting over the Falls, tandem kayaking and body-boarding down the rapids… if there is an adrenaline rush to be had, someone will have tried it and thought of a way of selling it to others. During my own visit I sampled an elephant-back safari, canoed the Zambezi above the Falls, took a helicopter flight

3 While you do not need to be particularly fit for any of the adventures at Victoria Falls, you do need to be prepared to face the challenge of the highest-graded commercial rapids in the world. Being able to swim also helps.

★★
★ Most of the accommodation in Victoria Falls is of a good standard, with plenty of choice, and there is no need to rough it here.

Your own dry sack for the canoeing and a compact waterproof camera for the rafting trip are both worthwhile, although not essential.

over the Falls and visited an African village, staying overnight in a mud hut. But before all that, I had to survive my journey along the gorge.

PREPARING FOR THE GORGE

Artwell gave us a safety talk, showed us the equipment (helmet, life vest and paddle), had us sign the inevitable indemnity form, and told us about our options. These were to paddle, or to sit in a rowed boat with an oarsman. The rowed boat is more powerful, and passengers can cling onto the safety rope around the edge of the raft. Theoretically they fall overboard less frequently than paddlers, who, on the other hand, are said to have more control over their fate. Only by paddling hard can you get enough momentum to allow the steersman to direct the raft. But generally speaking a paddler is too busy paddling to hold onto the safety line until the situation is beyond redemption. Of our groups, 22 people chose to paddle and two to go in a rowed boat.

The lorry took us to the rim of the gorge. I joined the others, full of unspoken trepidation, as we climbed down the steep path to the river. In the dark pool of a back water, the four rafts were waiting for us, along with six boats from other companies. We were joining the river above Rapid Six, The Devil's Toilet Bowl, rather than higher up. Once aboard, our crew of eight practised following Artwell's instructions for turning and for holding on at difficult moments. Our sandals were tied to the back of the raft, the first-aid kit was lashed in place, our life jackets and helmets were given a final tweak—and we were off.

ON TO THE RAPIDS

The pattern at the first rapid was generally repeated throughout the trip. We paddled down-river between the soaring basalt walls of the gorge, until a roaring sound and the sight of foaming, boiling water in the distance indicated a rapid ahead. At most of the big rapids, the drop down to the beginning of the white water

was invisible until we were completely committed. In the beguilingly still pool above the rapid, Artwell gave us our instructions. "Paddle until I say stop," he told us. "We are going down the right side to avoid the big whirlpool on the left." It was not called The Devil's Toilet Bowl for nothing. And if we fell out? "If you fall into the whirlpool, hold the shoulder straps of your life jacket, bring your knees up to your chest and, after about 10 seconds, you will come up to the surface. Then lie back, point your feet downstream and wait to be picked up." With four rafts and three or four safety canoes, this usually happens fairly quickly.

"Paddle!" We reached the lip. Ahead, a dark V of water disappeared under two great tubes of white foam rolling in from either side, and became a series of tall, standing waves. Then we were right into it: a chaos of noise, bucking movement and a maelstrom of foam. A big wave washed down the left of the boat and four people, including Artwell, were gone. We were going sideways through the rapid. The raft threatened to flip over. Then, suddenly, the water was much smoother. Artwell surfaced and clambered aboard. The other three finally came up and were hauled in. Nick, who had rafted this river a few weeks before, was delighted to find that theory worked in practice, and that he had survived the whirlpool. Michelle, on the other hand, thought she had taken her last breath and came back into the raft a bit shaken. But she was soon ready to face the next ordeal.

We set off downstream towards Gulliver's Travels, a complex rapid with several technical difficulties that merged into a single wet blur once we were in it. Halfway through, a rock loomed on the left. The paddlers on that side, fearing the worst, dropped into the bottom of the boat and held on. Those of us on the right followed their example and, for a moment, the raft was without an engine. When we finally emerged unscathed, Artwell roundly berated us for not obeying his instructions.

The river exacted its own punishment at Rapid Eight, where we all went overboard. As we took our places again, Greg's wife noticed that Greg was missing. We all anxiously scoured the raging torrent for a red helmet and Artwell wolf-whistled to the other rafts and held his arms wide, questioning. Then his experienced eye spotted that one raft had a crew of nine, instead of eight. Greg had been picked up.

We portaged around Rapid Nine and ran Rapid 10, a low-grade rapid without even a name. It was lunch time. Our picnic spot lay on a heap of boulders on the outside of a bend, and the food was ready when we arrived. During lunch everyone discussed the rapids to come and Rapid 18, Oblivion, took on a satanic reputation: an evil place, it was said, where hardly any rafts survived upright at this time of the year. When we rejoined the rafts, it was without those who had come for only half a day. A few day rafters also decided that being tossed into a raging torrent was not their idea of fun, and had taken the opportunity to leave before Oblivion.

We now faced the Overland Truck Eater (11), the Three Ugly Sisters (12a, b and c) and the Mother (13). Artwell had taken over one of the rescue canoes, a

Above: Strolling along the very edge of the gorge, reminiscing on running the gauntlet
Right: Vertiginous view of the dramatic Falls; there are often rainbows caught in the spray

much more enjoyable experience for these regular rapid-runners than piloting a raft, and in his place we had Morgan, a cool customer who took us through the big rapids without loss. (Anyone falling out at 12a is unlikely to be picked up until after 13.) Easier rapids followed and several stretches of calm water, during which we strung ourselves behind one of the rowed rafts to save energy. The gorge was very beautiful, with towering slabs of dark grey rock punctuated here and there with small bushes and fig trees. These still channels provided chances for a swim and more than once we all voluntarily left the boat to splash around in the river.

Oblivion was coming. We ran the Terminator (Rapid 16) and Rapid 17, before gathering in the pool above 18. Rafting suddenly became a spectator sport, as we stood on the inflated tubes and watched the other two paddled rafts flip over in its tumult. Now it was our turn. Expressing more confidence in our ability to sail through than any of us genuinely felt, we paddled over the gleaming lip. There are three giant waves to

Oblivion. You paddle the first two and then cower in the bottom of the boat and hang on for the third and biggest. We navigated one and two perfectly.

As for three, one moment I was in the bottom of the boat and the next I was almost underneath it, with the Zambezi water sluicing powerfully up my nose, intent on flushing out my brain. Somehow I clung on. I came up to find the rest of the crew still aboard, cheering and punching the air. I had been the only one to take an early bath! John hauled me on board and we paddled on. Full of bravado, we ran the last, unnamed rapids with paddles reversed and the raft sideways and still, somehow, emerged intact. And then it was time to get out.

It was a long, hot climb to the trucks, but water was supplied on the way and we took it at a steady pace, the beer and dry shirts at the top providing ample incentives. Back at the Kandahar offices, we agreed to meet in the pub later to view the video and the photographs of our exploits taken by the company's photographers, and I went back to my hotel for another, safer dousing—in the shower.

ELEPHANT-BACK SAFARI

My companions on the next Victoria Falls adventure were Miz Ellie, Jock, Jack and Jumbo—all elephants who live just outside Victoria Falls at Elephant Camp, in the middle of a large wildlife estate, through which they carry their human cargoes every day.

I had been collected from my hotel and driven the 25km (15 miles) to the camp, passing herds of impala and small groups of kudu on the way. After a cup of tea, we met the elephants and watched them enjoy a short training session. This training is stimulating for the animals and helps to ensure the clients' safety—for you ride an elephant only on its terms.

With the saddles in place we climbed aboard, sitting astride the elephants behind their handlers. Then, following an armed guide, we set off along old game trails into the bush. As they paced along

the elephants snatched trunkfuls of the path side vegetation and, unless pressed by their handlers, they were happy to stop and browse. An elephant's digestive system is primitive and inefficient, so they need to eat large quantities of food throughout the day. These elephants tend to get a better diet than their wild counterparts—but old habits die hard!

As Miz Ellie walked gently forward, her shock-absorbing, cushioned feet sent up silent puffs of dust. We moved through the bush with the firm, rocking movement that only an elephant can achieve. Like cliffs, elephants look much bigger from the top down than from the bottom up: the ground looked very hard and a very long way away. But, without any sudden movements from my steed, I quickly began to relax into her rhythm.

This was the way to see Africa. Up here, I had the advantage of a high viewpoint without the noise and smell of a vehicle. Better still, we could fit down the narrowest of paths; and to most of the other animals, we looked and smelled like elephants, rather than humans. Although elephants do not deliberately creep up on other animals, they make so little noise that it is easy to approach without causing alarm to the creatures you have come to see.

When we came across it, game seemed hardly bothered by the approaching elephants. It was the guide on the ground who created most disturbance, and, if he blended among the elephants, we could approach animals such as impala. The main problem with elephants as safari vehicles, though, is that they fidget, rarely standing still long enough to allow you to get good photographs.

Back at the camp, we watched them at their waterhole, drinking and playing before lunch. I spent a whole day at the Elephant Camp, but usually the options are to meet and ride the elephants, either for a morning or an afternoon and early evening, to stay at Elephant Lodge for one or more nights and get to know the them better, or to go on a one-night elephant-back safari, camping out with the elephants sleeping near by. Whichever option you choose, you will almost certainly find, as I did, that the most special part of an elephant-back safari is the opportunity to spend time near these intelligent animals, enjoying the privilege of their company.

CANOEING THE UPPER ZAMBEZI

Above Victoria Falls, the river feels young and exuberant; the islands are rocky, the area is open and there are rapids to run. While these are not the dramatic grade IV and V rapids encountered in the Zambezi Gorge, but grade I and II rapids are quite fierce enough in a small canoe. From Victoria Falls, my fellow paddler, Steve, and I were driven westwards towards the Botswana border, before turning right through Zambezi National Park to the river.

Our guides, Ndoga and William, inflated the two canoes and we climbed aboard. These rubber boats are unwieldy craft, difficult to steer and sluggish to drive forward, but remarkably stable and almost unsinkable. We propelled them with double-bladed kayak paddles, which gave us more control through the rapids. We had about 18km (11 miles) to travel downstream to Victoria Falls, and the river was doing its best to help us.

Very quickly we came upon the first of many elephants we were to spot during the day. A lone male had come down to drink on a sandy beach. We canoed up to a fallen tree and held on against the current to watch it at close quarters. After a while he picked up a couple of handfuls of dust with his trunk, tossed them casually over his back and wandered off.

Our first rapid lay just around the corner. The river was in constant ferment, with great boiling upwellings of black water, as if the water were simmering in a giant cauldron. Once at the rapid, it turned from black to white and from smooth to decidedly choppy. There were two obvious lines (routes) here: one down to the right, through practically smooth water, and one in the middle, where the waves were largest. We took the centre line, and by the time the bouncing canoe had been expelled at the far end, there was almost as much water in the boat as outside it.

Downstream, there were many faster sections, where the surface of the now shallow river was more broken, but the rapids were evenly spread out. On the Zambian bank there is no national park and, among the trees, we could see lodges, farms and beautifully situated riverside houses. On the Zimbabwe side, beyond the large trees that thrive on the river's moisture, the park vegetation was

BRIDGING THE GORGE

Mose-oa-Tunya ("The Smoke that Thunders"), as Victoria Falls is called in the local tongue, was "discovered" by David Livingstone in 1855 and renamed after his queen. This dramatic waterfall, which, at its peak, casts a cloud of spray up to 0.5km (0.3 miles) into the air, creating a rainforest as a result, was bound to become a tourist attraction. A railway line reached Victoria Falls in 1904 and the Victoria Falls Hotel was strategically located next to the station, with lawns running down towards the waterfall. The railway was continued across the Zambezi Gorge, just a few metres downstream of the Falls, and deliberately located so that the spray lands on passing carriages. Spanning a gaping chasm 110m (360ft) deep, with a single arch of steel, the cantilevered bridge was designed by Sir Douglas Fox and prefabricated in Britain but, once in Africa, the final piece refused to slot into place at the first attempt. The engineers tried again in the cool of the early morning—and it fitted perfectly.

mainly bush, well trimmed by elephants. Just before lunch we were overtaken by a motorboat flying downstream. It was a Sunday and, as many people had the day off, there were a number of fishermen on the bank and in the river.

We landed on an island, where Ndoga and William upturned a canoe to make a convenient table on which to spread our lunch. Although we were in the shade, it was very warm and our inflatables made excellent sofas so, after we had eaten, we napped for a short while before pressing on downriver. Only one more rapid required us to stop and empty the boats, and then we were into deeper, wider stretches of Zambezi—hippo country.

We generally managed to keep clear of these large and potentially lethal mammals, although on one occasion Ndoga and I actually paddled right over the top of one as it loitered under the water. Only when we were some distance past did the flat head break the surface and the nostril flaps open with a snort, sending jets of spray high into the air. By now we were

Above: Canoeing in the young and exuberant waters above Victoria Falls
Above right: Perhaps the ultimate place to try bungee jumping?
Below right: The best way to explore the bush is on elephant back; you not only have a marvellous view, but can approach wildlife closely

quite close to the town and passed cruisers and a burbling diesel pontoon boat full of diners. We pulled our canoes out of the water beside the old landing stage, where tourists would disembark from the flying boats in the 1940s and 50s, at what was known as Jungle Junction. The canoes were deflated and loaded on to the truck, having taken us through a few of the river's many different characters in the space of one short day.

SONGWE POINT VILLAGE

Makuni Village lies on the Zambian side of the border but you can only arrange to visit the village, and stay at nearby Songwe Point, from Victoria Falls. Makuni is a traditional African village, almost a town, and home to 8,000 people, most of whom live in mud huts thatched with grasses. Its British-educated chief is the 19th in line, and lives in a palace in the village itself. As part of the Songwe Point experience, we spent an afternoon wandering around the village, watching women crush maize, care for children, wash their pots and begin to prepare food for the evening.

Although the earth paths running between the houses were often littered with peelings and bits of wood, feathers, rags and scraps of polythene, each family compound was beautifully neat and tidy. Inside the millet stalk fences we found two or three rooms: bedrooms, a washing room and a store with an outdoor kitchen. Invariably the ground was

ZIMBABWE

swept clean and in some there were even flower beds, decoratively surrounded by empty bottles. Under a tiny shelter near the edge of the village, a wizened black-smith pumped bellows with his feet and hammered metal for tools while, near by, a group of carvers wittled away at wood so impossibly hard that a single carving can take a week to make.

Following our visit to the carvers' market, we drove past Songwe village to Songwe Point, a replica African village on the very lip of the Zambezi Gorge. Here, mud huts have been built as bedrooms and a dining area. There are many concessions to European tastes and sensitivities. Each double room is equipped with a mosquito net and an *en-suite* flush toilet and wash basin, for example, and there are four bathrooms for the eight huts, each over-looking the Gorge so that it is possible to stand in the double shower or lie back in the large bath and enjoy the fabulous view.

After a last drink around the fire, we settled down to *ntsima*, a traditional maize porridge, accompanied by beef stew, chicken stew, sweet potatoes, pumpkin and rice—a banquet, by village standards. Later the staff regaled us with songs and dances before we retired to our rooms. In the silence of the African night I could hear the roar of the Zambezi far below.

HELICOPTER FLIGHT

I had experienced the river at its most turbulent and its gentlest; I had seen Victoria Falls from the clifftop, from the water and from a mud hut. My final adventure gave me a bird's-eye view—from the rear passenger compartment of a helicopter. We sped, nose downwards, over the sprawling town of Victoria Falls, spread out below us, and easily made out the Victoria Falls Hotel and the station, the golf club, Victoria Falls Safari Lodge and, unmistakably, the Falls themselves.

After we had flown over them a couple of times, the pilot tilted the aircraft at what seemed to be an impossible angle. It felt as though we would slip sideways and plummet earthwards at any moment, the rotating blades losing the purchase needed to lift the machine. We made a tight circle over the waterfall, the rotors beating the air noisily, and then the pilot turned and repeated the manoeuvre for those sitting on the other side. I was sharing the compartment with an Austrian woman, who appeared to spend the entire flight staring at the floor and praying. She missed a spectacular view of the water. After a final circuit we flew upriver for a short distance and then turned to the left to land at the heliport from behind, facing into the wind. It had been one of the fastest, and one of the most remarkable 15 minutes of my life.

GO INTO YOUR DANCE

The Craft Village is the location of tribal dancing, which takes place in the evenings. Several tribes put on a range of different dances to celebrate a variety of events, from war preparation to circumcision. The costumes alone are worth seeing. Elaborate masks play a big part in these dances, as does fancy dress, including tight, beaded bodices and wide, hooped skirts. Animals are often represented. In one witty dance a crocodile chases a man who is out trapping fish. Acrobatic feats are also important: one man dances at the top of two flimsy poles about 10m (30ft) high, while, in another display, a dancer picks up a section of railway track with his teeth! Go to Songwe Point prepared with a simple but universal story, dance, mime or similar short entertainment, as joining in is part of the fun and it enables you to pay a little back to the villagers.

GOING IT ALONE

INTERNAL TRAVEL

It is very easy to get to Victoria Falls. There are scheduled flights from within Zimbabwe and international flights from other countries, such as Namibia and South Africa. Buses and trains run from Bulawayo, or you can hire a vehicle and drive from within Zimbabwe or from outside, coming through Namibia's Caprivi Strip (not recommended at the time of writing), or north from Gaborone in Botswana.

PLANNING

Once in the town you can book all sorts of adventures. There are several agents in the middle of town, all of whom have sandwich boards outside, advertising their wares and enticing you inside. Although one-day activities can generally be booked once you arrive in the Falls, it is often better to book beforehand, to ensure that you are dealing with a reputable operator. In any case, if you are hoping to do anything that involves an overnight stay—a rafting trip lasting several days, a two- or three-day canoeing trip, a short safari or an overnight at the Elephant Camp—then it is essential to book from your home country to avoid disappointment. Some trips may be full while others may not run for lack of numbers.

TRAVELLERS' TIPS

Cheapest is not always best. There are a number of cowboy operations running in the Falls area, and it is worth checking the prices against some of the major operators in town to see if what you are being offered

is well below the market price. If it is, you should be suspicious; there are rafters who are not members of RAZZ (Rafting Association of Zimbabwe and Zambia), either because they are not up to standard or because they are saving by not paying the fees. In either case, avoid them.

While Victoria Falls is not a particularly dangerous place, it has lots of potentially innocent westerners to target, and attracts its fair share of tricksters and petty criminals. One favourite scam is to offer to change money on the black market, using forgeries or currency from another African country such as Zambia. Use banks for currency dealings.

OFF ON YOUR OWN

While you can readily find operators on the spot to enable you to feed your desire for an adrenalin rush, it is much more difficult to undertake any of the activities entirely independently, for instance by hiring a canoe and paddling it down river yourself. Nearly all of these adventures entail far too much risk for all but the most experienced to try independently. It is strongly advisable to go with a guide—and, in any case, there is rarely the option of entirely independent adventure. About the only thing you can enjoy totally unaided is hiring a car and taking a game drive into Hwange National Park (check that the hirer will let you do this). Here you may be able to rent national park accommodation, depending on its availability, so that all you need to provide is your own food.

WHERE TO STAY AND EAT

Victoria Falls offers a wide variety of accommodation, ranging from the colonial splendour of the Victoria Falls Hotel and modern upmarket hotels such as Victoria Falls Safari Lodge, to comparatively inexpensive but comfortable hotels such as Sprayview, to camping in the town itself. There is also a host of eating experiences. The Victoria Falls Hotel has a smart dining room (jacket and tie are required, but the hotel keeps a supply of both for guests to wear), or the more casual Jungle Junction restaurant. The Boma Restaurant at the Victoria Falls Safari Lodge offers the opportunity to try a range of game meats (ostrich, crocodile and a variety of antelope as well as domestic animals) and many of the local foods, including caterpillars. The carnivore restaurant at the Crocodile Farm has a fixed-price eat-as-much-as-you-want menu, which is also very popular.

WATER HORSES

The hippopotamus is reputed to be the most dangerous mammal in Africa. Hippos feel safest in water deep enough for them to sink out of sight if danger threatens, and most attacks come about because a hippo feels trapped either in shallows or away from water entirely. These great water horses spend their days wallowing and resting. At night, though, hippos leave the water to graze on nearby land, returning to water by the morning. They defecate in the water, naturally transporting nutrients from the land to feed fish and other creatures, which, in turn, will become food for other animals.

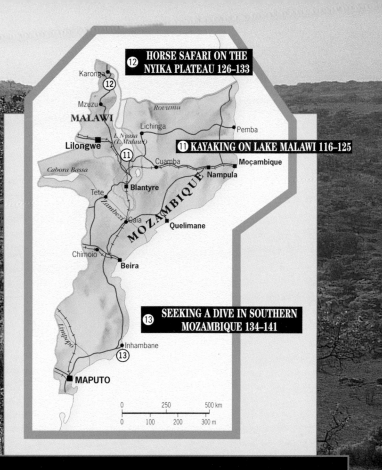

Karonga
⑫
Mzuzu
MALAWI
Lichinga
Rovuma
Pemba
L. Nyasa (L. Malawi)
Lilongwe
⑪
Cuamba
Moçambique
Cabora Bassa
Nampula
Tete
Blantyre
Zambezi
Caia
Quelimane
MOZAMBIQUE
Chimoio
Beira
Limpopo
Inhambane
⑬
MAPUTO

0   250   500 km
0   100   200   300 m

MALAWI•MOZAMBIQUE

Malawi and Mozambique may share the shores of Lake Malawi, but there the similarity ends. Malawi is a very manageable strip of country tucked into the the Rift Valley, where mountain plateaux descend to the lake shores and south into tropical lowlands. There's abundant wildlife here, as well as traditional villages and sandy beaches, so this is the place to combine safaris with relaxing lakeside stays. Mozambique, on the other hand, is a country that only recently emerged from a devastating civil war. As a result, the seemingly endless coastline bordering the Indian Ocean harbours a fledgling infrastructure. Yet the unique character of its former Portuguese capital, Maputo, the pioneering nature of its beach hotels, its rich underwater world and the echoes of history make this a poignant and unforgettable destination.

The Nyika plateau is perfect horse-riding terrain, offering fantastic opportunities to see wildlife and remote areas that would otherwise be inaccessible

MALAWI

11 Kayaking on Lake Malawi

by Fiona Dunlop

One of the greatest attractions of the tiny country of Malawi is its vast and immensely beautiful lake. Here you can soak up the atmosphere of an African village, before striking out in a kayak to explore uninhabited islands, to snorkel among exotic fish and to join the wildlife that has made this "Lake of Stars" its home.

Lake Malawi, Africa's third largest lake and the 11th largest in the world, occupies a good chunk of the eastern half of this friendly little country. Its huge, 580km (360-mile)-long expanse is classed as an inland sea; far from being a tranquil stretch of calm water, it has unpredictable storms, waves and winds, and changes in water level. Fish and fishermen, dugouts and steamships, distant shores and sandy beaches are all reflected in a huge sky that inspired David Livingstone's epithet, "Lake of Stars." For some, it makes the perfect place to relax after gruelling overland journeys or safaris; for me, it was a destination in itself: a place to skim over the waves in a kayak, to snorkel among *mbuna* fish, to hike around desert

Kayaking does not require any previous experience and, like snorkelling, is an easy activity to pick up. The Klepper sea-kayaks are both lightweight and stable. Some fitness is necessary, however, both for kayaking and for the boulder-strewn hikes on the islands.

In Chembe itself, hotels are fairly basic. On the islands you will be fly-camping, so don't expect great comfort, and the absence of electricity or generators means that hurricane-lamps and torchlight are the evening norm. Be prepared for the hot climate, mosquitoes and flies.

For the kayak trip it is best to take only a small pack or bag with minimal equipment. Waterproof or trekking sandals are ideal, plus loose cotton clothes, a light sweater for the evening, swimsuit, towel, broad-brimmed hat or cap, suncreen, torch (preferably a head-torch) and binoculars.

islands, to watch monkeys, birds and lizards, and to observe the life of Malawi's largest traditional fishing village, Chembe.

CHEMBE VILLAGE

Livingstone's ghost still hovers at Chembe: in 1875 he set up his first mission here, at Cape McLear, on the Nakumba Peninsula. The mission moved on due to a high incidence of malaria, but the village survives, together with its mission school. Chembe straggles over 4km (2 miles) along the lake shore, against a dramatic backdrop of rocky hills that veer from a tawny brown in the dry season to luminous green during the rains. Rising above it all are mighty baobab trees, their gnarled, centuries-old trunks completely dwarfing their surroundings. Outside, women sweep or weave rush baskets, men repair fences or palm-thatch and hordes of children gravitate between it all, a constant reminder that nearly half Malawi's population is under the age of 15. The pace is slow, occasionally interrupted by the arrival of a *matola*, a pick-up truck that carries packed groups of villagers along the appalling road from the nearest services town at Monkey Bay. This remoteness is accentuated by the absence of electricity and the on-off telephone lines. One day I watched a succession of optimists loitering around the only public phone; they would pick up the receiver, listen, replace it, wait, then start again. Time is not an issue here.

From dawn till dusk, the beach is the

focus of village life, as fishing is its economic mainstay and the lake provides fresh water. Surprisingly, considering the extensive human activity near by, hippopotami still wallow in shallow reedbeds that form part of the shore, occasionally making underwater attacks on boats, while herons, egrets and ibises swoop through the air. Studding the horizon are the silhouettes of nine islands, all part of Lake Malawi National Park; and in the foreground, countless fishing dugouts glide through the waves in search of *utaka*, a tiny, silvery fish, and above all *chambo*, the lake's delicacy.

TURBULENT PAST

The lake and its environs were once an important source of trade for Africa's east coast, furnishing gold, ivory and ambergris to traders who even supplied Chinese junks. Later, the slave traders took over: the Portuguese, in neighbouring Mozambique, and the stronger Yao, from the northern end of the lake, who became middlemen for Omani traders in Zanzibar. The terror of 19th-century slave raids was further exacerbated by the Ngoni, relatives of the Zulus, who swept up from the south, pillaging and massacring everything and everyone they encountered, until their power was diluted by their leader's death in 1845.

Lake Malawi's slave trade finally ended in 1895. In 1902 Nyasaland (the colonial name for Malawi) became a separate territory and, 60 years later, an independent nation. Yet despite colonialism and the subsequent 30-year dictatorship of Life President Banda, local government has changed little. Any issue in Chembe is first discussed with the village Chief who, if necessary, will consult the Chief of Cape McLear or, above him, the District Commissioner.

Today, although the days of the slave trade are thankfully long gone, the Chewa people of Chembe are still up against a wall of human suffering produced by malaria, bilharzia and AIDS, all of which are rife. Yet as I strolled along the beach

THE BAOBAB

Chembe village and Domwe Island both harbour wonderful specimens of the baobab, or monkey-bread tree, one of the most massive flowering plants, whose trunk can exceed 30m (100ft) in circumference. This semi-succulent tree thrives in hot, dry climates as it is able to store water in its trunk, and is remarkably tough. It's been known to survive for 2,000 years—even when the inner trunk has become hollow and rotten. Its curious shape has inspired countless myths and legends, one of which is that God planted the baobab upside down, as it only produces leaves during the wet season and these are limited in number.

watching fishermen mending their pink *chilimira* nets, children scrubbing pots in the sand and women in boldly patterned *kikoi* (sarongs) fetching water to carry on their heads in stately style, this was all hard to believe. People are exceptionally friendly, and you rarely walk alone. The day I set off to cover the 6km (4 miles) to Otter Point from my hotel at the opposite end of the bay, I had no fewer than five lengthy conversations on the trot.

TO OTTER POINT

The national park boundary lies about 1km (0.6 miles) west of the village. I followed a sandy path through aloes, savannah, eucalyptus trees, euphorbias and doum palms to the Environmental Centre, an educational project that stands next to the original site of the Livingstonia mission, of which nothing remains. Immediately beyond lie the peeling walls of Cape McLear's first hotel, a short-lived relic of the British colonial era. After opening in 1948 to greet visitors arriving by flying boat from

Johannesburg, its heyday lasted three years, but it now functions again, in low-key style. In front, on one of the most beautiful beaches in Cape McLear, I was confronted with a large and fearless family of yellow baboons, who bounded around the rocks,

Above: The pace of life in the traditional fishing village of Chembe is relaxed
Left: With people in the foreground, the immense size of the baobab tree becomes apparent

babies clinging to the backs of the females, and approached me with eye-rolling requests for food.

As I continued along the deserted, rocky trail, now accompanied by the loquacious Patrick, I had a surprise encounter with a rock hyrax, or dassie. This small, guinea-pig-like creature flew across my path to land on the branches of a nearby tree. A popular myth has it that the hyrax is the elephant's closest relatives—hard to credit when you see these furry, tree-climbing, rabbit-sized creatures. In fact, although they originated from a common stock, they have been separate for over 50 million years.

At Otter Point itself, huge grey boulders create a pathway out into the lake, making a perfect lookout for observing spotted-neck otters ducking in and out of the water in search of fish. The day was cloudy, but the oyster greys of the metallic lake, vast sky and granite foreground had a subtle beauty. It provided Patrick with the perfect opportunity to extract from his threadbare pack a succession of bracelets, necklaces and beautifully carved wooden Bao boards (a fast and strategic local boardgame vaguely resembling backgammon and played with round seed pods). Commerce remains king on Lake Malawi.

MALAWI

KAYAKING TO DOMWE ISLAND

However enjoyable the lake shore, the islands were beckoning and I was impatient to embark on my four-day kayak trip. Paddling with Francis, the cook, to my first port of call, Domwe Island, proved quite painless. There was little wind; clouds screened the sun's fierce rays; the two-seater sea kayak was lightweight, and we had only 4km (2 miles) to cover. As we paddled, Francis following my rhythm from the back seat, we discussed Chembe, the lake and his family.

When we finally landed in front of a couple of discreet huts on a sandy beach, it was hard to believe that this was actually an island, as Ilala Gap, the narrow channel that separates Domwe Island from the cape, had been barely visible. Nor was there much evidence of a camp. My kayak guides were completely in tune with the atmosphere of these wild islands, and had done their utmost to keep structures on Domwe and Mumbo, my next stop, to an absolute minimum, blending them harmoniously with the vegetation. On Domwe, the only imprints of civilization were five double tents scattered up the slope among the trees, a lakeside kitchen hut, an open-air dining shelter, septic toilet huts, a bucket shower, a solar panel which enabled radio communication, and a couple of hammocks. That was all we needed.

The gentle-mannered camp caretaker, Mr Bizness, and more jocular Francis made up the staff, while Morne, a young South African diving instructor, was my appointed guide. We were joined by Knut, a Norwegian following Morne's divemaster's course. Later that afternoon, as the sun was setting, two more members of the team kayaked in to stay overnight: the dynamic Marzi and her partner, Jurie, both South Africans, and the brains of the operation in Chembe. We all gathered on a huge boulder to toast the sunset, which gradually erupted into a blaze of salmon pinks. For the next three days I was to be the only outsider apart from the regular

CICHLIDS AND ADAPTIVE RADIATION

The *mbuna* cichlids (rock fish), whose name derived from the Tonga people of Nkhata Bay to the north of the lake, are now cited as a classic example of adaptive radiation. This theory, first put forward by Dr Geoffrey Fryer in the 1950s, maintains that a species can "radiate" into numerous closely related species, due to modifications in their lifestyle or habitat. Most changes occur in their feeding mechanisms and, as the majority never venture away from their elected rocks (the source of algae), new species can be extremely localized; so the *mbuna* around Domwe are very different from those around Mumbo.

team, baboons, birds, jewel-like lizards, butterflies and, less enjoyably, clouds of flies. Leopards, cerval (spotted, feline animals) and blue monkeys have also been spotted in this wild environment.

INTO THE TREES

On Domwe, the largest of the lake islands, with a circumference of 10km (6 miles), the savannah is dominated by African mahogany trees, baobabs, pampas grass and, further up the hill, wild rock figs, whose long roots engulf the huge granite boulders, sometimes splitting them open. Morne took me on an afternoon hike here, and immediately we were rewarded with the back view of a francolin partridge scuttling into the undergrowth. Soon afterwards, a large family of yellow baboons proved as curious about us as we were about them. We had climbed on to one of the monumental boulders to gain a better view of them, and found ourselves opposite a pair of baboons gazing intently at us from another rock, with a companion equally transfixed in a nearby tree.

The staring game could have continued indefinitely, but we had to move on.

We followed a steep trail winding up to the summit of Domwe. The path over rocks and through scrub is well defined, but Morne had a machete in hand for errant growth and any unfortunate encounters. Among the lurking hazards we could have encountered were the green mamba snake, tree snakes, scorpions and centipedes. Something else to watch out for here is the *chitedze*, or buffalo bean, a hairy seed pod that, if touched, causes severe irritation and burning. Luckily, we met nothing more alarming than the orchestra of cicadas which, at the zenith of the mid-afternoon heat, reached its deafening climax. After a hot, strenuous climb we finally reached the summit, where we were rewarded with superb views over the lake, Cape McLear and even distant Chembe village. Morne pointed out a hump on the horizon of this seemingly infinite aquatic expanse: this was Mumbo, my next island destination. It looked far, far away.

UNDERWATER

Before setting off the next morning, I went snorkelling off the end of Domwe's beach, favoured by sculptural rocks and clear water, giving excellent visibility. The extraordinary cichlid fish dominates here. No one is exactly sure how many cichlid species exist in Lake Malawi: estimates vary from 500 (more than Europe and North America's combined total of freshwater species) to 1,000. Snorkelling is like swimming in an aquarium: you see endless variations of rare and unknown fish, from tiny, silvery *utaka*, nibbling at plankton, to larger, predatory tilapia or brilliantly coloured *mbuna* feeding on algae, or small catfish—one of the few non-cichlid groups.

I kayaked the 8km (5 miles) to Mumbo with Knut in little more than one and a half hours, a respectable time considering that the wind had moved to the west and the waves were against us. As the choppy water kept rippling towards us, there were moments when I thought we were not making any headway. However, we finally neared the little island and paddled towards the cove, and I saw that this was not one but two islands. The smaller island was the site of the camp.

MUMBO MAGIC

Domwe's installations may have been discreet, but Mumbo's were completely invisible. The mound of rocks and vegetation that was to be our islet home lay about 10m (30ft) across thigh-deep water from the landing beach. From there a very vague path led up across boulders and tree roots to level ground at the top, where the camp was installed. I was glad that I was not the one to be carrying supplies, drinking water and iceboxes up this obstacle-strewn trail.

I opted for the most isolated tent, precariously perched on the narrow point of the islet to face sunrise. This not only ensured dawn awakenings but also, I was to discover, a heightened awareness of the winds. As they howled through the night, buffeting my little canvas home and knocking branches against the awning, it felt at times as though the tent was going to take off and fly over the lake with me inside.

SCUBA-DIVING

The crystal-clear waters and endless varieties of fish surrounding Cape McLear provide an exceptional setting for scuba-diving. Several dive operators in Chembe village offer four- or five-day open-water courses leading to a PADI certificate that are arguably the cheapest in the world. Basic accommodation is sometimes included, and equipment is generally of a high standard. This is one of the reasons for Chembe's status as a backpackers' mecca in the early 1990s, but with the growing popularity of Nkhata Bay, to the north, this business has quietened down.

MALAWI

RHYTHMS OF DARKNESS

The sun had set by 6pm, and we spent the long evenings around the sheltered dining area, next to a permanent camp-fire with water constantly on the boil and hammocks slung between the trees. We chatted, played Bao or read books by the hurricane lamps until Francis, the cook, produced our gourmet dinner from his kitchen. Time after time this was a feat of imagination and healthy fare, as a large stock of fresh ingredients had been brought by motorboat, and Morne would occasionally harpoon some fresh *chambo*. Fresh egg-bread was baked on the fire, and cool drinks were always available from the icebox. By 9 or 10pm we were usually ready for bed, and I would pick my way by torchlight along the rocky trail that led to my tent. The vivid dreams I had there may have been induced by anti-malarial drugs; or perhaps they were part of the Mumbo magic.

Our sense of total isolation was dis-turbed only by the engines of night fishing boats, which cruised around Mumbo before anchoring to fish illegally. Some 20,000 people make their living from the lake, and the tonnes of fish that are netted provide about 70 percent of Malawi's protein. Its illegality is a prickly issue.

Above: *Pulling ashore on Mumbo island*
Below: *A lone fisherman drifting through the crystal clear water around Mumbo island*

MUMBO'S WILD SIDE

Mumbo was named Elephant Island by British settlers who, in 1876, found a lone male elephant there. How it got there remains a mystery: it's a long swim from the shore. Unsurprisingly for those days, it was shot, and the island's name reverted to Mumbo. This means "bat," of which there are many. Nevertheless, when Knut, Morne and I set off on a morning hike around the island, we saw no bats—but we did see a wealth of birdlife, including a nest of African fish-eagles, whose high-pitched yelp was already a familiar sound around the islet; white-breasted cormorants, reed cormorants, giant kingfishers, pied kingfishers, half-collared kingfishers, black kites and yellow-billed kites. The mocking chat was another highly audible bird, and at one point the brilliant yellow plumage of the lesser masked weaver flashed through the foliage.

HUMAN INTRUSIONS

The trail varied in difficulty. Sometimes we walked comfortably across flat rock surfaces; sometimes we had to cut our way through, scratched by the undergrowth, tripping over roots or clambering over huge boulders. At one point Morne decided to find a particular lookout point that he had seen from the water and, after various false turnings, we finally emerged from the dry forest onto a huge rocky shelf jutting high above an idyllic cove. Below us was a fisherman and his dugout, in front the glittering blue expanse of the lake, and to the side the canopy of trees with their incredible birds.

Continuing our hike, we saw smoke rising through the trees and soon

MALAWI

LAKE MALAWI NATIONAL PARK

Declared a World Heritage Site in 1980, this was the world's first underwater, freshwater national park. Although smaller than Lake Victoria and Lake Tanganyika, its sister lakes to the north in the Western Rift Valley, Lake Malawi is the fourth deepest in the world, reaching depths of up to 700m (2,300ft). Each of these three gigantic lakes contains more species of fish than any other lake in the world, and almost all these fish are endemic to each lake.

stumbled upon an encampment of fishermen. Dozens of *chambo* were laid out on drying racks, and the firewood probably came from the African mahogany trees, whose charred stumps we had passed earlier. Rather than waste energy felling a tree, the locals simply set fire to the base until it topples over. Clutching their machetes, Morne and Knut looked sufficiently bush-friendly to inspire respect and, admonishments made, we continued back towards the islet.

REPTILIAN LIFESTYLE

Just as we were nearing the landing-beach, we heard a rustling in the undergrowth. A stripe-bellied sand snake had just pounced on a lizard and was grappling with it beneath a bush. We watched, fascinated, as the 1m (3ft)-long, yellow-bellied snake slowly strangled the lizard by wrapping itself tightly around it. Relieved to have escaped its attention ourselves, we waded across the narrow channel to climb back up to our islet haven.

Here, a shimmering of different colours and patterns, slipping rapidly over the rocks, turned out to be the rainbow skink, a beautifully coloured, smooth-skinned lizard that favours granite outcrops. Breeding males turn copper colour with orange tails, while females sport blue and white stripes ending in an electric blue tail. Far larger in scale was the resident rock monitor lizard, that skulked around the bucket-shower shelter before noisily scuttling away when any human approached.

The days on Mumbo flowed by. We kayaked, watched fish eagles swoop artfully onto their prey, Morne and Knut dived, and I became an obsessive snorkeller. When the morning of departure came, winds had sprung up and the lake looked distinctly choppy under a menacing grey sky, so any idea of kayaking the 10km (6 miles) was abandoned. Chugging back in the motorboat to Chembe, with Mumbo receding into the distance, I felt distinctly nostalgic. But when I lay in my tent hotel that night and heard drums beating in the village, I knew that, in Africa, there's always a new experience around the next corner.

DR LIVINGSTONE, I PRESUME?

Dr David Livingstone, a Scottish missionary of the London Missionary School, first heard of the existence of Lake Malawi in 1856, when he reached Tete, in Mozambique, becoming the first European to cross Africa from west to east by following the Zambezi river from Angola. Determined to put an end to the barbaric slave trade, his solution was to bring the three "C"s—Christianity, commerce and colonialism—to the interior. In order to do this, he needed to find a navigable channel. Thwarted by the Kebrabasa Rapids on the Zambezi, just west of Tete, he turned to a tributary, the Shire River. This eventually lead him to Lake Nyasa (Lake Malawi), but not without endless disasters and tragedies. However it was only after Livingstone's death in 1874, in Zambia, that the iniquitous slave trade was finally destroyed.

GOING IT ALONE

WHEN TO GO

Intermittent showers start in November, but the wet season is above all in December to March, with the last downpours in early April. This period is when temperatures rise to an average 29°C (78°F). That does not make it a bad season to visit, as sometimes rain occurs only at night and even in the daytime it is always followed by dazzlingly clear skies. The dry season lasts from May to October, with the lowest average temperatures of 21°C (69°F) in July. Water temperatures remain a pleasant and constant 25°C (75°F) near the surface.

INTERNAL TRAVEL

The easiest way to get to Cape McLear is by plane from Lilongwe to the airstrip at Club Makokola. This weekly flight (Sundays) also connects with Blantyre. From Club Makokola you need to arrange a transfer with a Chembe operator or, more economically and more painfully, take a local bus (*matola*) to Monkey Bay, about 40km (25 miles) to the north, and there pick up another one to Chembe. The road is in very bad condition, and even in a four-by-four it takes about one and a half hours to cover the distance from Club Makokola to Chembe, so allow a lot more time by pick-up truck.

A far more leisurely and memorable way to arrive in Monkey Bay is by the lake ferry, if possible with the most modern one, *Ilala II*. This makes a weekly tour of the lake, usually stopping at Mbamba Bay in Tanzania, Nkhata Bay, Likoma Island and Monkey Bay, as well as numerous smaller villages. For information on timetables, call the Malawi Lakes Services office in Monkey Bay (tel: 265 587311 fax: 265 587359), bearing in mind that these are extremely notional.

PLANNING

If you are prepared for the discomforts of the local bus and basic accommodation, it is quite possible just to turn up at Chembe without booking. For slightly more comfort, make a reservation for hotel and road transfer a few weeks in advance. The kayak safari runs permanently, but as space in the wilderness camps is limited, advance booking is advisable. Similarly, the flight to Club Makokola is only by a 12-seater plane, so needs advance booking.

HEALTH AND SAFETY MATTERS

Cape McLear and Lake Malawi in general is a high-risk malarial zone, above all during the wet season, so prophylactics are essential. Also make sure your tetanus, polio and typhoid vaccinations are up to date. Vaccination against hepatitis A is also strongly advisable. The other hazard to watch out for here is bilharzia (schistosomiasis), a parasitical worm that lives in stagnant waters used by humans for washing and urinating, and that can work its way through your skin. There is little you can do to avoid catching bilharzia other than keeping clear of reedy areas and the lake near villages. Swimming and diving in open water and off the islands should be relatively risk-free. If you do catch this disease (easily confirmed by a blood test at least six weeks after exposure), the treatment is simple and effective.

There have been cases of muggings in Chembe, so try not to offer thieves any obvious temptations. It is not advisable to walk alone or for long distances at night.

WHAT TO TAKE

- ❏ Light cotton clothes and a light sweater for evenings.
- ❏ Good waterproof trekking sandals, swimsuit, towel.
- ❏ Broad-brimmed hat or cap, sunscreen.
- ❏ Torch, camera, film and batteries, optional binoculars, books.
- ❏ There is no bank at Chembe so you need to have enough Malawi kwacha with you for your needs, although US dollars and SA rands are accepted by the kayaking operation and dive-shops.

OTHER ATTRACTIONS

The Shire River, that drains into the southern end of Lake Malawi, eventually leads to Liwonde National Park, bordering the banks of Lake Malombe. Riverine swamp, deciduous woodland, open savannah and stretches of mopane woodland on higher ground are home to a fantastic variety of birds as well as hippopotami, crocodiles, elephants, leopards and the recently introduced black rhino. This park can become unpleasantly hot and humid during the wet season, and is most comfortable between June and August, although game and birdwatching are better in October and November.

12 A Horse Safari on the Nyika Plateau

by Fiona Dunlop

The remote grasslands of Nyika plateau in northern Malawi make perfect horse-riding terrain, as well as offering a good sample of Central Africa's wildlife, diverse vegetation that changes with the altitude, and vivid wildflowers carpeting the hills. All this is laid out in endless panoramas, blending into spectacular African skies.

There it crouched on the track in front of us, brilliantly lit by the spotlight from the open roof of the Landcruiser: a live leopard. Apparently untroubled by this interruption of its nocturnal prowl, it slunk along slowly for a while, before bounding away through the bracken. David, our safari guide, thought we could probably track it down again after turning round and returning along the same track. Sure enough, we did, and were able to watch it for a few enthralled minutes more before, yet again, it opted for the obscurity of the African night.

NYIKA'S DRAW

A wide range of animals and vegetation takes advantage of Nyika's unusual habitats. At times, it hardly seems like Africa, lulling visitors into impressions of the bleak Scottish highlands, with the scent of pine trees and cool evenings spent in front of log fires sipping whisky. But the lodge walls are decorated with bows and arrows, spears, and handmade flintlock rifles—all confiscated from local poachers.

About 5,000 years ago these undulating grasslands were densely forested, but a drier climate and devastating bush fires have produced seemingly infinite vistas, where the horizon recedes north to Tanzania and west to Zambia. Nyika lies along the African Rift Valley, and seismic movements, combined with heavy rainfall, have led to landslides and shifts in the landscape. But this is still perfect country for riding, a method of transport that offers fantastic opportunities to see wildlife in remote areas that would otherwise be inaccessible.

LILONGWE—CAPITAL CITY

Our horse safari group formed in Lilongwe, the modest Malawian capital, that looks more like two crossroads in the bush. Everything seems to have been designed for notional future expansion, with the airport 25km (15 miles) away across the scrub, and wide avenues and landscaped roundabouts awaiting something more than a handful of minibuses, trucks and cattle. You can do the rounds in little more than an hour, taking a minibus to cover the 5km (3 miles) between the old town and the new Capital City, founded in 1975. At the old town crossroads, a handicrafts market packed with hardwood chairs and carved spoons shows off Malawian artistry

 Although beginners are catered for at Chelinda Camp's stables, anyone embarking on a horse safari should have reasonable riding experience.

★★ Accommodation at the main lodge is more than adequate, and the stand-up safari tents are comfortable. However be prepared for low night temperatures and rudimentary washing facilities. Excellent food is the compensation.

 You will need jodhpurs or loose cotton trousers, half-chaps, riding boots and/or walking shoes, a broad-brimmed hat or cap, riding gloves, a fleece, sunscreen and binoculars.

among the second-hand footballs, pad-
locks and new kitchen mops. It was here,
in a hotel next to the old town's only landmark, the post office, that most of our
group had met up.

Three riders had flown in from
London, another from Germany, and I had
come from the south; the sixth member, a
South African, was already at Nyika.
Spirits were high as our 12-seater Cessna
bumped along the airstrip: the days ahead
were to be spent on horseback, the nights
in a mobile camp. Not an experienced
horse rider, I wasn't as confident as my
companions, who all had years of practice. But I had been reassured that the
Nyika horses would give me no problems.

EQUESTRIAN INTRODUCTIONS

That afternoon we were taken to the
stables and introduced to our horses. I

*Above: Nyika's mountain air is cool and fresh, and
its vast expanse is home to an amazing range of
plant and animal species—a rider's paradise*

was grateful to be given Mwezi (meaning
"moon"). According to Eve, the eternally
patient Canadian in charge of the stables,
Mwezi was a great all-rounder and, above
all, a relaxed and steady walker. However,
the day we stopped to look more closely
at a hyena kill being devoured by vultures, when a hyena returned to watch us
from 100m (300ft) away, neither Mwezi
nor any of the other horses felt relaxed.
Nor did we. Bucking, neighing and pulling
at their reins, the horses were instinc-
tively aware of the potential danger, in
high contrast to the cool approach of our
leader, David Foot. He later related a
breath-taking story of charging a hyena
on horseback, then being followed back

MALAWI

to camp with it snapping at his heels.

That first afternoon I soon discovered that Mwezi was not too keen on other horses coming too close. She suddenly kicked one culprit and reared. I managed to cling on, and, as the days went by, we arrived at a mutual understanding.

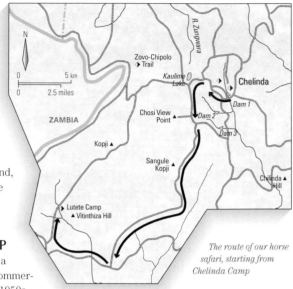

The route of our horse safari, starting from Chelinda Camp

CHELINDA CAMP

Beside the airstrip lies a pine-forest, part of a commercial experiment of the 1950s, before the area was declared a national park. This is home to the national park office and workers' compound. There are about 40 staff, including armed rangers, whose job it is to track down poachers. Close by, Chelinda Camp itself includes a campsite, self-catering chalets, lodge rooms and the latest addition—a cluster of luxury log chalets, high on the hillside. Between them lies a small artificial lake, rich in water birds.

Not everyone comes to Nyika to ride. The cool climate, fresh mountain air and vast rolling expanse entice hikers from the hotter lowlands, and wildlife-lovers come to enjoy a wealth of different animals and plants. Malawi is the meeting-place for east African and south African animal species and vegetation, and Nyika encompasses most of them. Elephants roam around its northern reaches, while zebras, warthogs, honey badgers, hyenas, jackals, cerval and no fewer than 10 species of antelope are frequently spotted. Lions have not been seen since the mid-1960s, probably due to the shortness of the grass, their favourite cover, but, as a result, Nyika is thought to harbour Central Africa's highest density of leopard—the alternative predator.

SADDLING UP

Back in our comfortable saddles, we rode sedately in single file or in a less regimented cluster, descending to cross

NYIKA PEOPLE

Nyika's geological history may recede into the shadows of the Rift Valley origins, but relics of man's presence show that hunter-gatherers were present over 3,000 years ago. Malawi's earliest evidence of Stone Age man lies at a site 70km (43 miles) to the north of the park. Five rock shelters have been found within the park, pointing to early hunting expeditions made from the lowlands. There are also later iron-ore pit mines. However, it is thought that Nyika saw no permanent inhabitants until the mid-19th century, when refugees came here to escape the Ngoni, a branch of the Zulus, who were attacking fom the south. The name "Nyika" is derived from a Swahili word meaning "wilderness."

streams either on foot or with heel-kick-
ing encouragement to the horses, trotting
through the shady, fragrant pine forest or
cantering across the blissfully wide open
spaces. Our first ride was led by Eve,
backed up by one of the grooms, and on
subsequent days by David, an accomplished horseman with a keen eye and
extensive knowledge of the wildlife and
nature of Nyika.

Our first morning ride immediately
gave us wonderful views of reedbucks
and roebucks leaping gracefully away as
we approached. A family of five Burchell's
zebras tottered up a hill with their
ungainly, toy-like movements. Later we
rode within 10m (30ft) of a large group of
roan antelopes, one of which had just
been born and was suckling its mother.
David explained that their lack of fear
was due to our being on horseback; had
we been on foot, they would have taken
off long before.

This ride also gave us a preliminary
taste of the large variety of birds of prey
in Nyika. At the hyena kill, we saw the
largest of the park's five vulture species,
the lappet-faced vulture, backed up by
white-headed and white-backed versions.
A group of ravens wheeled through the
sky above a jackal, and augur buzzards
were a constant presence. Hundreds of
magnificent butterflies floated past, their
luminous colouring in keeping with the
wildflowers that were bursting into bloom
at ground-level. Wild gladioli, lilies, irises
and terrestrial orchids pushed up greed-
ily through the grass near the dambos,
seasonally boggy watercourses between
the hills that offer rich wildlife pickings.

HYENA-WATCHING

Late that afternoon, as the sun was setting, David took us on a walk to see a
hyena den. This was when I became
sorely aware of the altitude. At 2,200m
(7,217ft), I was panting breathlessly as
we ascended a minor slope through the
pine forest.

In front of us the beauty of this unique
region unfolded, bands of horizontal
colour receding to the horizon. Suddenly,
David signalled to us to be quiet: he had
spotted the den. We walked on sound-
lessly in single file, crouched and
eventually sat down to watch these
dark-brown creatures with their sloping
backs and massive heads. Down in the
valley we could clearly see an adult and
three cubs prowling around a dark hole in
the ground—their den. The mother
raised her head, sniffed the air, then
looked steadily in our direction. By now,
binoculars had been whipped out and the
staring game continued in close-up. The
cubs, meanwhile, were oblivious to us,
not having yet acquired their mother's
sharpened sensitivity.

NIGHT SAFARI

Our vigil continued for another half hour,
by which time the sun had set, the air was
decidedly cool and a thumbnail sliver of
moon hung in the sky. Shivering now, we
climbed back up the hill to find the jeep
and thermoses of hot coffee and tea
spiked with whisky being offered by
Thomas, a Welsh student who was
temporarily working at Chelinda. It was
just what we needed to regain our
strength for the next episode: the
night drive.

With David at the wheel and Thomas
standing in the open roof, powerful
searchlight in hand, we slowly drove
around the perimeter of the pine forest.
This is known as a favourite sheltering
ground for bushbucks, elands, roans and
leopards, but sightings can of course
never be guaranteed. First we saw a
mountain nightjar, frozen by the beam
of the light on the track ahead, then a
fleeting vision of a group of reedbucks
and several scrub hares leaping through
the bracken. At one point a sound slowed
us down to scan the trees: there in the
foliage sat a spotted eagle owl, on the
lookout for rodents. But the climax
was undoubtedly our sighting of the
young leopard. After that, everyone felt
justified in returning to the creature
comforts of Chelinda.

MALAWI

HEADING SOUTHWEST

The horse safari proper started on the third day when we headed for Lutete Camp, one of three camping areas used for mobile camps. This one lay in the lee of Vitinthiza Hill, about 35km (22 miles) southwest of Chelinda towards the Zambian border. As a less experienced rider, I was urged to miss the morning ride and join the group at lunchtime. Somewhat saddle-sore from the previous two days, I agreed. It would also give me

the opportunity to soak up the views without having to worry about the potential antics of Mwezi, my not always so trusty mount.

As the jeep bounced along, grinding in and out of four-wheel drive, Robyn, David's wife, filled me in on the radically changing vegetation. We were descending and soon the savannah gave way to *Brachystegia*, the dominant tree of Nyika. This semi-deciduous, broad-leafed woodland plays an important part in

water conservation, as the roots prevent the erosion of the plateau escarpments and any subsequent silting-up of rivers. In drier areas, trees are few and far between, and at higher altitudes the growth is stunted, but here, as we descended to about 1,700m (5,557ft), the *Brachystegia* multiplied. At certain

Right: *Classic African landscape: a lone acacia tree silhouetted against the blue sky*
Below: *Negotiating a seasonal boggy watercourse*

points, we passed charred and blackened ground—the result of a local practice designed to keep bush fires at bay. Despite this desolation, brilliant green shoots and wildflowers of all colours were bravely pushing through.

More uplifting was the multiplication of stark, granite outcrops and finally, that archetypal African tree, the *Acacia abysinnica*. Its dramatic, flat-topped, parasol crown often stood in splendid isolation on a ridge, or perfectly silhouetted against an area of low *Protea* bushes. As we rounded another rocky outcrop, the valley opened up before us with the flattened summit of Vitinthiza Hill in the background.

DE LUXE CAMPING

Thomas and four assistants had been hard at work all morning, and five tents were already in place, leaving only the final touches to complete. As I entered the "canteen" tent I realized that the horse safari did not mean hard living by any means. A full bar was set up on a side-table opposite a long dining-table already laid for lunch, and the tent design enabled flaps to open at eye-level on a 360-degree panorama. Over the next few days, hot water would appear miraculously whenever necessary—but it was often a race to the shower before night, and the temperatures, fell.

Our rhythms soon fell into place. The day kicked off with staggeringly beautiful sunrises accompanying pre-breakfast rides. We were on horseback during the day, taking walks in the late afternoon, and the long evenings ended around a camp-fire beneath spectacular night skies. These activities were punctuated by a succession of copious meals, from cooked breakfasts to three-course dinners. Lunch was often a sandwich on the ride, usually at strategic lookout points with sweeping views. Everyone slotted into the routine with ease, and the small group of riders, all of whom were in their 30s, got on well.

UNADULTERATED NATURE

The environs of Lutete camp proved quite different from the high plateau, and wildlife followed suit. Here, the russet-coloured *Brachystegia* woods, dotted with vermilion-coloured coral trees and the eternal umbrella-like acacia, were a complete contrast to the rolling grass-lands. As we rode past a lake, we spotted a pair of beautiful red-and-green Schaw's louries and we were constantly chased by the whistling of the southern boubou and the whoop of hoopoes. Frogs, too, were highly audible in this water-rich area, roan antelope grazed, as did huge herds of the much larger eland. Wildflowers

grew in psychedelic abundance; we even dismounted one day to look more closely at a spectacular fireball lily.

Perhaps the greatest and most constant element was the awe-inspiring sky. At dawn and at dusk it would light up the dazzlingly patterned cloud formations in mauves, greys, pinks, oranges and purples, behind the silhouette of Vitinthiza Hill. During the clear, star-studded evenings shooting stars plummeted to the horizon. On the day of my departure, as the tents were dismantled and the others rode over the brow on to their next camp, I meditated on the charred remains of our campfire. No horses, no tents, no riding companions… only the sky remained.

GOING IT ALONE

WHEN TO GO

Elevation and rains are the key factors to bear in mind for Nyika, as they vary considerably throughout the park. In winter, between June and August, the high plateau where Chelinda is located sees frosts, and day temperatures rarely exceed 15°C (56°F). At this time, animals such as elands, roan antelopes and zebras head down to the lower woodlands, where it is several degrees warmer. During the Malawian summer, from January to March, there is heavy rainfall, making access roads impassable except by four-by-four vehicles. Hiking and the odd short ride are still possible, as there are brilliant sunny intervals between showers, with clear views opening up towards Lake Tanganyika. The best periods to visit are towards the end of the rainy season, when everything is lush green in late April and May, and late in the dry season, in September–October, although night temperatures are still cool.

INTERNAL TRAVEL

Air Malawi flies twice a week (Sunday and Thursday at the time of writing) between Lilongwe and Chelinda, stopping at Mzuzu on one of these days. The horse safaris are geared to this timetable. An alternative is to travel by road which, outside the rainy season, is a tough but feasible journey even in an ordinary car. From Lilongwe to Mzuzu is 367km (228 miles), a four-

hour drive on a good surfaced road. From Mzuzu continue north to Rumphi, then embark on 59km (36 miles) of unsealed road to the park entrance, followed by a further 56km (34 miles) of dirt road to Chelinda. Altogether allow at least five hours for the Mzuzu–Chelinda journey. The road transfer from Mzuzu can also be arranged with the Nyika Safari Company.

PLANNING

Both the horse safari and the internal flights need to be booked at least two or three months in advance, as space on these trips is limited. Make sure your inoculations are up to date; if you are travelling to other parts of Malawi, start your malarial treatment two weeks before leaving. Keep your luggage to a minimum, although you can always leave a bag at the lodge while on safari.

HEATH MATTERS

Nyika Plateau is a non-malarial zone, so prophylactics are not necessary here. However, as you cannot avoid going through Lilongwe on your journey, it is advisable to take precautions while you are there by using repellents and mosquito coils. Drinking water is quite acceptable. Make sure you are inoculated against typhoid, tetanus, polio and hepatitis A.

WHAT TO TAKE

❏ Jodhpurs and/or loose cotton trousers.
❏ Half-chaps.
❏ Riding gloves.

❏ Long-sleeved cotton shirts.
❏ Fleece.
❏ Warm, waterproof jacket.
❏ Comfortable, warm clothes for the evenings.
❏ Broad-brimmed hat or baseball cap.
❏ Swimsuit (for braving cold water rivers).
❏ riding boots and/or good walking-boots.
❏ Camera, film and batteries.
❏ Binoculars.
❏ Sunglasses.
❏ Sunscreen.
❏ Torch.

OTHER NEARBY ATTRACTIONS

A complete contrast to Nyika Plateau lies immediately to the southwest at Vwaza Marsh Game Reserve. These flood plains of the South Rukuru river offer a wetter, marshier terrain that attracts herds of elephants, zebras, buffaloes, impala, hippos and Lichtenstein's hartebeest. Monkeys, storks, herons and birds of prey are also present. Jeep transfers can be arranged from Chelinda, or directly from Mzuzu to Kazuni Camp, where budget and more luxury accommodation is available.

If all you want to do after the horse safari is dive straight into Lake Malawi, then head for Mzuzu and east to Nkhata Bay. This burgeoning lakeside resort offers a good choice of non-luxury accommodation and a whole array of watersports off its rocky coves and sandy beaches. Just south of Nkatha Bay is Chintheche, lakeside home to a comfortable lodge in a more peaceful setting.

13 Seeking a Dive in Southern Mozambique

by Fiona Dunlop

The word has been out for some time that Mozambique's 2,500km (1,553-mile) coastline offers some of the world's best diving. Blighted by civil war and devastating flooding, the public image seems a world away from the islands and powdery white beaches, where palms nod lazily, and casuarinas sway.

With our compass set for Inhambane, we thundered 470km (292 miles) north from Maputo along the EN1, Mozambique's best surfaced road. We passed circular thatched mud huts, children holding out live chickens or bags of charcoal for sale, and women balancing huge bundles of firewood on their heads. Beside the road lay skeletal, rusting caracasses of buses and trucks, alternating with the roofless shells of derelict, gutted houses. Both were stark reminders of the civil war that ended in 1992, after some 30 years of suffering and bloodshed. Tourism is still embryonic in Mozambique, despite an increasing influx of South Africans in campers and jeeps, who head north over the border in search of paradise.

MAPUTO AWAKES

When I arrived in Maputo, the sprawling, once glorious "Beirut of Africa,"

that became the "aid capital of the world," I was confronted by a medley of paradoxes. A smiling teenager does his best to sell model bicycles ingeniously made out of wire. Others unfurl rolls of batik paintings or wave wooden sculptures from across the boulevard, while the less entrepreneurial simply squat beside platters of peanuts or cigarettes. Behind them, a brand-new billboard proclaims the wonders of a washing powder.

On Saturdays a crafts market materializes on the Praça 25 de Junho. Beautiful marquetry boxes, finely carved combs, Makonde sculptures, masks from Zaire are all laid out in the dust.

Beyond the market stands a modest, 19th-century Portuguese fort, the red brick walls studded

 Diving operations and horse-riding are well run here and cater for all levels. Sportfishing is not for everyone, and surfers will need experience to conquer the breakers.

 ★★★ There is a good choice of accommodation in the Inhambane area, ranging from basic backpacker lodges to more comfortable, though reasonably priced hotels and self-catering chalets.

 Take waterproof sandals, sunscreen, a wide-brimmed hat or cap and a swimsuit. Snorkelling and diving equipment can be rented. If horse riding, make sure you have a pair of closed walking shoes.

with cannons, its interior home to government archives and cultural events. When I wandered into the grassy courtyard, a jazz band was setting up. so I headed for one of several shady pavement cafés on Avenida de 25 septembre.

MAPUTO'S MULTIPLE PERSONALITY

Maputo grows on you. Much is said about its resemblance to Lisbon or Barcelona, but this could not be further from the truth. As I continued my exploration, past crumbling buildings and Soviet-style apartment blocks, down potholed side streets and past seedy bars, a potent and unique atmosphere took shape. Between the peeling façades, jacaranda, flame and acacia trees, stood a pre-fabricated, iron-plated house designed by Gustave Eiffel, still pristine and surrounded by a lush,

Above: *Tourism is still embryonic in Mozambique— you will more than likely find you have the beach to yourself; the water is perfect for surfing* Left: *Woman doing her washing in Lake Nhyameavali*

tropical garden. A few blocks further on, an ornately stuccoed mosque stood next to a 1930s hotel.

Central Maputo's most obvious monument is a blindingly white, brutalist cathedral whose lofty spire dominates the Praça da Independencia. This arose in 1944, apparently built by young girls taken into forced labour by Portugal's oppressive regime. Maputo mesmerizes by its many contradictions.

NOCTURNAL PURSUITS

When Nick, my guide to Mozambique, appeared, remarkably fresh after a six-hour drive from Johannesburg, I was watching the light fade over Maputo's beautiful harbour from my hotel balcony. A band had set up in the square below and was belting out African rock.

Nick suggested that we sample the city's after-hours scene. Maputo's nightlife managed to resist the 18 years of civil war; the population still drank beer and rum and still danced through the night; prostitutes still plied their trade.

MOZAMBIQUE

This was my chance to discover yet another aspect of the capital: that of seaside bars and family seafood restaurants along the beachfront. The steamy bars thronged with a bewildering mix of nationalities and, at the Feira Popular, we sampled the succulent giant prawns that had made the gastronomic reputation of Lourenço Marques (Maputo) in pre-war days. Next door, a Chinese restaurant flashed its lanterns at a well-dressed group of aid-workers. We were in a cosmopolitan whirlpool where anything is possible, legal and illegal alike.

HEADING NORTH

Next morning, as we headed out through the outskirts to reach the main coastal highway, the road suddenly deteriorated into an unsurfaced stretch. We passed a ramshackle market, a vast rubbish tip being picked over by the desperate and, further on, a police roadblock. We were waved through without any demand for money being made—a sign of economic progress, according to Nick.

For the next six hours we rarely saw another private car. The road was ours, apart from the occasional minibus or long-distance bus that would veer crazily in our direction. Disappointingly, the coast remained out of sight, just a few kilometres to the east, but gradually the flat, characterless savannah gave way to a more undulating landscape dotted with trees and scrub. Mango trees, coconut palms and cashew-nut trees multiplied

and women squatted in their shade behind mountains of fruit and vegetables. After crossing the Limpopo river at Xai Xai, we turned off at Chidenguele to see the beautiful Lake Nhyameavali. At the end of a tough stretch of sandy track, I had my first sight of the idyllic Mozambiquean coast, unfolding behind white sand dunes.

FISHY BUSINESS

This coast is prime territory for deep-sea fishing, a trade exploited by Russian and Japanese trawlers. On Tofo beach, where I stayed before moving on to Barra, pairs of local fishermen would set off in the golden flush of dawn in colourful little skiffs that bounce through the waves to reach calmer waters barely 100m (300ft) out. From here they scatter to reel in a steady catch throughout the morning before returning around midday to sell kingfish, marlin, dourado, sailfish, tuna or shark to clients who come directly to the beach. It is quite usual to see a massive, 3m (9ft)-long fish—too large to transport or even too much in quantity and price for local customers—being hacked into manageable portions at the water's edge.

Not surprisingly, this sea of plenty has attracted several sportfishing operators, most of whom double up as hoteliers or restaurant owners. Allen, who has been running deep-sea fishing at Tofo since the mid-1990s, explained that one of this area's advantages is the absence of big rivers unleashing polluted water.

LOURENÇO MARQUES

Maputo—or Lourenço Marques, as it was formerly known, in honour of the 16th-century Portuguese navigator—only became the capital of Mozambique in 1907. This marked a shift in the focus of Portuguese commercial interests from the Ilha de Moçambique, in the north, to this generous harbour close to the South African border, and connected by rail to the mines of the Transvaal. Before that, the settlement in Delagoa Bay (which appeared on maps as early as 1502) had seen a constant stream of trade from the interior in the form of gold, ivory, ambergris, rhinoceros hooves and slaves. As well as the Portuguese, the British and Dutch were also sporadically present there, using the bay as a stopover on the long haul back from the East Indies.

DIVERS' PARADISE

The diving fraternity can fly in directly from Johannesburg to Inhambane to plunge into depths of up to 35m (115ft) off Barra. Seven dive sites have so far been identified, all within easy reach of the shore, while Tofo's potential is only now being investigated by two new diving schools. Sightings have included manta rays, one of the most other-wordly underwater sights, moray eels, octopus, king fish, devil rays, rock cod, turtles, barracuda, and carpet and ham-merhead sharks. Add to this dolphins and humpback whales, which gather in these warm waters from July to October, and you have an enticing agenda.

RIDING THE WAVES

Nick, an accomplished surfer, first came to Tofo in the early 1990s, later setting up a surfers' lodge. One afternoon, when the waves had reached promising heights, I accompanied him and two young Dutch surfers to the furthest beach to see some action. For the next hour or two they bobbed around offshore, waiting for the big ones. Nick rode the crests, but the currents proved tricky for Jan and Johannes, who had both just started their surfing life in South Africa.

Leaving them to their foamy fate, I walked back the 4km (2 miles) along a scenic cliff path. A smiling fishermen sauntered past and we exchanged a "Bom dia,"; he was followed by a gracefully erect lady in a colourful sarong, with a basin of fish on her head.

BACK TO TOWN

Inhambane, the local market town that looks across the bay at the more industri-alized Maxixe, has a charming, slow-paced atmosphere, heightened by the presence of sea on two sides. Established by the Portuguese in 1534, it is one of the southern hemisphere's oldest settlements, and was the southern-most point for Arab traders as far back as the 10th century. This long history is rep-resented by a few elegant old colonial buildings, some with wild fig trees pic-turesquely splitting their walls and others immaculately restored. A mosque, still in use, dates from 1840, but the 200-year-old cathedral overlooking the harbour is now derelict. If you are courageous and believe in the durability of four rusty iron ladders (I didn't), you can climb up into the bell tower for panoramic views of the town, the bay and the sea of coconut palms, said to be Africa's largest palm grove. A few steps beyond, overlooked by the freshly renovated telecommunica-tions centre, is the site of the old slave market. A wall plaque dating from 1988 spells out the tragedy of this human traffic, stating that the last slaves were transported in the early 20th century, while a graphic mural gently flakes away in the hot sunshine.

INDEPENDENCE AND CIVIL WAR

Mozambique's history as a Portuguese colony ended in 1975, the result of over 10 years of guerrilla conflict to gain indepen-dence. This achievement in turn triggered off a new confrontation between the hard-line Marxist government, Frelimo, and its Rhodesia- and South Africa-backed opposi-tion, Renamo. Russians moved in to reap the rewards from their new protégé, inflation soared, and by the 1980s the government had staggered from economic disaster to a semi-permanent state of bloodshed. Maputo was relatively unscathed, as the tragic toll of atrocities was concentrated mainly in rural areas. Today, tens of thousands of landmines are still buried in Mozambique's soil.

So I found myself wading out to join the motorboat bobbing in Tofo's waves and then speeding across the sea, scanning the horizon for whales. This was the end of the season, but a distant spout proved that at least one remained. Behind the wheel, Jan looked anxiously at the sky. Grey clouds were gathering menacingly and it did not look promising for either snorkelling or diving. We soon rounded the headland, with its landmark lighthouse, and closed in on the Praia da Barra, a blissful strip of palm-fringed white sand. Jan made a quick turn, then accelerated towards the beach, where we landed with a welcoming thud.

In the bay, the ragged sails of anchored *dhows* fluttered as they waited to fill with passengers, who are carried through the shallows on the shoulders of boatmen. (This adds considerably to the length of the crossing to Maxixe that can take anything from 20 to 45 minutes, depending on the wind.) Near by, children were looking for crabs in the mudflats beside a few rusting wrecks resembling beached-up whales. Over at the Mercado Central, brilliant colour returned in the form of glistening piles of seafood, mountains of mangoes, papayas and a wealth of vegetables.

LOCAL LOGISTICS
Tofo lies 23km (14 miles) east of Inhambane. The last 6km (4 miles) are along a sandy track, just about practicable in a normal car. The turn-off to Barra, however, soon leads to deep sand that can only be tackled by four-wheel drive. When I shifted base from Tofo to Barra, I jumped at the chance of a more direct and painless route—by sea. A group of backpackers had organized a motorboat to take them across Inhambane Bay to Linga Linga to snorkel and, hopefully, catch sight of the elusive dugongs that live there. These herbivorous mammals, now an endangered species, are notoriously difficult to see, despite their ancient reputation of being mistaken for mermaids by the mariners of old.

UNDERWATER FORAY
When I at last dived into the deep blue to observe the marine life of the Indian Ocean, I felt that I had reached another dimension. Above, below, and beside me, the shadowy bodies and fluorescent fins of other divers glided by; from us all there rose a steady stream of mercurial bubbles. We were 10m (32ft) below the surface at a dive site dubbed Anchor Bay, a mere five minutes from the beach, where we hoped to have close encounters with manta or stingrays, eels, and a colourful host of tropical reef fish. I had had ear-pressure trouble on the way down, but the South African dive instructor, Ron, was always close at hand to encourage me to take it slowly.

Finally I joined the more experienced divers, who were already exploring the underwater coral jungle. Within minutes, Ron made the "come and look" sign, pointing out in a crevice beneath an overhang the spiny pink form of a devil

Above: *Launching the dive boat into the sea*
Right: *A colourful array of local boats drawn up on the beach at Tofo*

firefish. This was one of several creatures he had warned us not to touch, as its feather-like dorsal protruberances can be fatal. Next to appear was an eel, curled beneath a rock, followed by countless stonefish, which, despite being immobile, possess venomous dorsal spines.

DANGERS AND BEAUTIES

Suddenly I was surrounded by flashes of silver, turquoise and yellow, all swimming in formation; this turned out to be a shoal of blue-banded snappers. Then a work of art swam past my mask, its broad diagonal bands of black and white contrasting with a slim yellow tail. This was the schooling coachman, a member of the highly visual butterflyfish family. It was soon rivalled by a brilliantly coloured emperor angelfish and, on a larger scale, a marbled leopard grouper, whose colour changes according to its surroundings: in this case, it was a mottled pink with deep blue fins. Over the rather colourless coral—owing to the bleaching effect of El Niño—sprawled dozens of huge starfish, while between the overhangs nestled spikey black sea-urchins— another marine creature to avoid, although it is merely annoying and painful, as opposed to fatal.

Ron had given us a pre-dive lecture on the subject of sharks, of which there are many in the area. They were not to be feared, as local specimens were mainly of the black-tip and white-tip variety—generally not considered dangerous and certainly not known to attack divers . However, before diving, we had to sign a disclaimer form that spelled out the potential danger of diving with sharks— adding a certain spice to the whole experience.

RIDING HIGH

On my last morning, still under a glowering grey sky, I set off on horseback with Birgit, the riding instructor, to see more of the area. Happily astride Marlin, a well-behaved seven-year-old, I followed her from the stables straight over the dunes to the water's edge. We walked and cantered along the deserted beach, before ascending a steep path through casuarinas to the lighthouse, where, beside the roofless shell of an abandoned restaurant, views opened up along the endless beach. So far, the only living creatures we'd seen had been the lighthouse keeper's chickens, but now a group of vervet monkeys bounded past and, as we descended to the lagoon, the odd goat emerged from the bushes.

At the top of the next hill, crowned by a radio mast, we were greeted with a fantastic 360-degree panorama that swept over Barra, Tofo, mangroves, palm trees and distant lagoons. With thunder cracking on the horizon, we trotted back through immaculate village compounds, passing a small boy doing his drum practice on jerrycans, then across parched mangrove swamps back to Barra Lodge. A few hours later, as the tropical downpour teemed down and the 10-seater plane sped along Inhambane's wet runway, I could see a stout woman walking tall and proud through a field, under a maroon umbrella. It was my last sight of the new Mozambique.

DIVING RESORTS

The adjoining beaches of Barra and Tofo offer the most wide-ranging facilities and levels of accommodation, as well as being classed among Mozambique's top three diving spots. There is luxury at the much-touted Bazaruto Islands but despite excellent hotels, fishing and diving in coral reefs, drawbacks include unpleasant razor clams on one coast and extremely shallow water on the other, leaving swimmers, surfers and body-surfers frustrated. The third alternative is Inhaca island, 34km (21 miles) from Maputo, where there are spectacular coral reefs but shallower waters. The less developed north of Mozambique will soon rival these well-trodden resorts.

GOING IT ALONE

WHEN TO GO

The tropical climate of Mozambique assures sun throughout most of the year, with rains occurring from November to March. From April to September, temperatures are slightly cooler and it is generally dry. Be wary of the South African school holidays, when the few hotels are booked out and beaches plagued by jeeps and campers. The main holidays are from December to early January, in April and in July. The rest of the year, Mozambique remains a calm and relaxing destination.

INTERNAL TRAVEL

For the moment, no domestic flights run between Maputo and Inhambane. There are, however, direct flights from Johannesburg with Eagle Air and with a charter plane operating with Barra Lodge packages. A more economical option is to take a long-distance bus. These run daily between Maputo and Inhambane, taking about eight hours. The tragic floods that occurred in 2000 left the main road badly damaged, and until repairs are finished, this journey is likely to be a lot longer. Unless you have arranged to be picked up, you will need to take a *chapa* (pick-up truck) from Inhambane to Tofo.

PLANNING

All visitors need visas, obtainable through their local Mozambique embassy or consulate. These can take a week to process. To get one, you will need your passport (valid for at least 6 months), three photos and a photocopy of your ticket or travel agent's confirmation. If travelling via South Africa, charter flights to Inhambane can be booked through Mozambique Connection or Barra Lodge.

HEALTH MATTERS

Anti-malarial prophylactics (mefloquine) are strongly advised as this is a high-risk area, and the course of treatment should be started two weeks before arrival in Mozambique. Inoculations against hepatitis A, polio, tetanus and typhoid should also be up-to-date. Tap water is not drinkable, but bottled water is widely available.

SAFETY TIPS

Be extra vigilant while visiting Maputo, as foreigners are easy targets for muggers or pickpockets. Don't carry large amounts of money, display any jewellery or even cameras. In smaller places such as Inhambane it is generally much safer, but do not tempt fate by walking long distances on your own or after dark, especially on the beach.

Be careful with your belongings on Mozambique's beaches, as impoverished locals may remove anything left lying around—even a towel. Only have the absolute minimum with you.

Driving after dark is not advisable for personal safety reasons and because some vehicles do not have lights.

If venturing off the beaten track in rural areas, be aware of the danger of landmines. Most mined areas are well marked with skull and crossbones danger signs, but accidents still happen.

WHAT TO TAKE

❑ Light cotton clothing and a light sweater for evenings.
❑ Waterproof sandals, a wide-brimmed hat or cap, a swimsuit, sunscreen and sunglasses.
❑ Insect repellent.
❑ Torch.
❑ Books, camera, film and batteries.

OTHER ATTRACTIONS

The archipelago of the Bazaruto Islands and its network of sandbars, channels and coral reefs, lies just off the coast at Vilanculos, 780km (485 miles) from Maputo. International and domestic flights arrive at Vilanculos's smartly renovated airport from Maputo, Beira, Harare and Johannesburg. The four idyllic islands of Bazaruto, Beguerra, Magaruque and Santa Carolina were all declared a national park in 1971 to protect their abundant marine life, birds and butterflies. From Vilanculos you can hire a *dhow* or a motorboat to explore the islands, stay at one of the luxurious though sympathetically designed hotels, at campsites on Bazaruto and Benguerra or in one of an expanding number of lodges on Vilanculos beach itself.

If you want to stay closer to Maputo, are entranced by the name Limpopo and intent on luxury accommodation, a good hideaway exists at Zangoene, right on the river mouth. This lies 250km (155 miles) north of Maputo, 36km (22 miles) off the EN1, and offers good snorkelling, fishing, microlighting, and diving.

Map labels: Ondangwe, Rundu, Etosha Pan, Tsumeb, Outjo, Grootfontein, 2621m Brandberg, **14**, Okahandja, Swakopmund, Gobabis, **Windhoek**, Walvis Bay, **15**, Rehoboth, Lüderitz, Keetmanshoop, Karasburg, **16**, Orange, Namib, Desert, Fish

0   250   500 km

0   100   200   300 m

NAMIBIA

N amibia is startling. Its landscape varies dramatically: the windswept Skeleton Coast; the classic, sweeping curves of the central Namib's apricot dunes; the mountains and canyons of the central highlands; the rolling, vegetated sand of the Kalahari; the verdant waterways of the Caprivi Strip; the vast Etosha salt pan. It never fails to amaze. Much of Namibia's magic lies in its enormous wilderness areas, home to very few people but plenty of wildlife. Exploring these on foot and by vehicle, you'll discover fascinating endemic species, as well as plenty of big game—thriving both in the national parks and outside, due to the success of community conservation projects. On a practical level, Namibia's infrastructure is excellent. The phones work; smooth, well-signposted roads make self-drive trips easy, and a low population density, coupled with a warm, dry climate, make this a healthy, as well as a beautiful country to visit.

The sweeping sand dunes of the Namib are everyone's idea of what a desert should be like; this is one of the driest places on earth

14 Driving the Skeleton Coast and Damaraland

by Chris McIntyre

Where the Namib Desert meets the Atlantic, in northwestern Namibia, lie the Skeleton Coast and the wilderness of Damaraland. These form a vast region crossed by few roads. We joined a small expedition from Swakopmund to explore the area with one of Namibia's top guides, Bruno Nebe.

Early one October morning, during the height of Namibia's hot season, we left Swakopmund in a chilling fog. During a few relaxing days there we'd eaten good seafood and explored a little of the surrounding desert in our small hired car. We'd also become used to the fog blanketing the coast in the morning. "It's due to the Benguela current," Bruno said, cryptically, when he met us. "Comes straight from the Antarctic—makes the ocean cold and accounts for the desert." He packed my friend Purba's bag into the back of his Land Rover, and tied my rucksack to the roof rack. We set off along the coast road with our new companions, Jean and Peter England.They'd been to Africa before but

had never seen giraffes, an omission they hoped Bruno could remedy.

The emerging scenery, as the mist broke up, was desolate. On the left, the gravel sloped down to a wide beach and the ocean. On the right, it stretched away to the horizon. Our smooth, fast road followed a straight line north.

WLOTZKASBAKEN

About 30km (19 miles) of flatness from Swakopmund, the scene was interrupted by a small settlement. "That's Wlotzkasbaken," said Bruno, turning off. We drove around its deserted streets, where each house was overshadowed by a long-legged water tower. It looked like a colony on the moon. Bruno explained it had been named after Paul Wlotzka, the keen fisherman who first built a hut here. Having begun as a place to fish, it grew into a small resort town where wealthy Namibians came in October and at Christmas to escape the heat inland.

DESERT COLOURS

Back on the road, the gravel plains blurred into a watercolour landscape, varying from black to muted yellows and subtle reds. As we drove along, Bruno explained that the earth's rotation determines the coast's southwesterly winds. He told us that the ocean's cold current limits evaporation and cloud formation, so there is little rain; however, moisture is present in the morning fogs, caused when the hot desert air meets the cold sea air.

Although the area covered is very remote and potentially very difficult, visiting it with a good local guide takes all the worry out of the visit.

This is a camping trip—but it's a camping trip with style. The tents, mattresses and duvets are very comfortable and the guide takes care of most of the cooking, so the food is good. You will use a spade to dig your own toilet, though a civilized "throne" is carried, in case you're unhappy squatting. There's a solar shower to hang under a tree. Rhino-tracking can become arduous; early morning starts are essential to minimize exposure to the heat.

Binoculars are important, especially if you're keen on the wildlife. A camera is essential. Daytime light levels are very high, so bring lots of slow film and a polarizing filter. Make sure that all your optical equipment is stored in dust-proof bags.

Within an hour, we reached Henties Bay, the first (and only) real town north of Swakopmund. It stands at the mouth of the Omaruru River, which now so seldom flows to the ocean that they've built a golf course in its sandy riverbed.

We stretched our legs and took a cold drink from one of the cool boxes. The hot sun dazzled, but the southwesterly wind blew cool. Bruno detoured around town before leaving. Many of its original houses had been built from driftwood from the nearby shore and large packing crates, and painted with bright colours and designs. Only a few of these remained, but even their replacements were bright and idiosyncratic.

LICHEN FIELDS

Continuing beside the ocean, we passed wide, flat salt pans, where the salt was several metres deep. Then, on a slight rise in the middle of nowhere, a sign appeared beside the road to Cape Cross Seal Reserve. We turned left, as directed, before unexpectedly pulling off the road, which continued across a rolling, black gravel plain. Bruno located a small bottle of water and wandered off over the gravel, beckoning us to follow. Crouching, he picked up a piece of rock. We looked closely, and saw that it was covered in shrivelled, dry lichens, like the rest of the gravel around. He'd already told us that the Namib's lichens survive on just the moisture in the fog plains, and are so fragile that a single tyre track would scar the landscape for decades. Now he poured water over the rock, simulating a heavy fog. Gradually the lichens unfurled and their colours rekindled in bright oranges and reds.

CAPE CROSS

Shortly, we drew up at Cape Cross's small national parks office, paid our entry fees, glanced at the huge whale jawbone on display, and continued to the end of a rocky promontory. This was one of the few rock outcrops on Namibia's sandy and largely featureless coast. Getting out of the vehicle invited a full-scale assault on our senses. The sea breeze chilled us, and we were surrounded by the noise of crying and whining. Then the smell, the overpowering stench, hit us—the heavy odour of rotten fish. Over a waist-high wall, tens of thousands of Cape fur seals covered the rocks beside the sea. They moved, called and squashed into all the available space. Beyond, the high surf bobbed with hundreds of black, shiny heads.

We wandered along, absorbed by the spectacle. Gradually we forgot the shock of the cold, the noise and the smell. We could have touched the closest seals, but they scarcely noticed as we stared, pointed and clicked away with our cameras. Soon the first bulls would arrive, and fight for territories; the pregnant females would give birth to pups, before mating with the dominant bulls.

INTO THE WILDS

Driving back to the main road, we paused at a small shop near the parks office for a drink. There was a display of the area's seal-hunting history, which also sold a selection of seal-skin shoes—a fine and waterproof leather, we were assured. We rejoined the main road and settled down, numbed by the warm air and gentle, rocking motion. Bruno slowed down and took an unsigned track inland across the yellow-brown plain. There we entered the wilderness, surrounded by desert and silver pools of mirages. Mountains rose up, hazy blue in the uncertain distance. Our progress slowed—but there was no rush.

MARVELLOUS WELWITSCHIAS

Continuing east, towards the mountains, the track was often vague. Bruno had driven this track a month ago—and his was probably the last vehicle to have passed. On the plains around us, low-growing plants started to appear. In one area they seemed to be growing particularly well, so we stopped. The largest was a tangle of light green, leathery leaves

Above: *Where underground water percolates through to the surface it can support lush vegetation, an extremely rare sight in Damaraland; the dry, muted scrubland beyond is more typical of the region*

Left: Welwitschia mirabilis: *endemic to Namib's gravel plains, this unique species can live up to 2,000 years*

perhaps 45cm (18in) tall and several metres across. This was Namibia's most famous plant species: *Welwitschia mirabilis*. This extraordinary plant of the Namib's gravel plains has fascinated scientists since it was first described by Austrian botanist Friedrich Welwitsch in 1859. Despite all the foliage, each of these large plants had just two, long, shredded leaves, which grow continuously from a stubby wooden base. This unique species is thought to be most closely related to the conifer family. It gets moisture from the condensed fog; a waxy coating on the leaves minimizes water loss. Each plant could probably live for around 2,000 years—and this landscape wouldn't have changed much since they germinated.

MESSUM CRATER

Resuming our journey, Bruno dug out a map. He traced a circle of desert with his finger, showing us where an ancient volcano had once stood. Now, there was nothing left of it but concentric circles of mountains, forming an amphitheatre 22km (14 miles) across: Messum Crater.

We followed the track up and over the rim, and spotted tufts of tall, yellow grass beside *Welwitschia* plants. Inside the crater was a golden-yellow plain. Its forbidding sides were scarred by black dolerite dykes—a few prickly *Euphorbia virosa* succulents clung to the steeper parts, their stems sporting vicious thorns. It was an unforgiving place in the heat. Yet there was something magical about such a dry landscape, largely untouched by people, animals and even plants.

Climbing out at the other side of the crater, we spotted six zebras in the far distance, and stopped to steady our binoculars. "Hartmann's mountain zebras—they've been hammered by hunters around here for years, so they're very skittish," said Bruno, as the zebras fled over a distant ridge.

THE LONG OASIS

We hadn't passed another vehicle since the coast road. Finally we entered a hilly area and juddered down a narrow track into a small settlement. This was the Save the Rhino village. Bruno chatted in Afrikaans, paying our camping fees, planning the following day and listening for news—which wasn't all good. Elephants had recently been seen around here, one with an injured leg. Some thought this had been caused by a shotgun; all feared that the elephants would be aggressive.

We could have camped by the village, but finding a quiet spot was more appealing, so we headed into the adjacent Ugab valley. Its steep rocky walls were a few hundred metres apart, and between them lay a flat, sandy bed dotted with thick stands of ana trees and false ebonies. It was immediately refreshing to be amongst such lush vegetation. Like many of Namibia's rivers, the Ugab seldom flows over the ground, but its waters constantly percolate beneath the sand, supporting lush vegetation. Dig deep enough and you always find water here—as the elephants know.

TEMPORARY RESIDENTS

Our Land Rover progressed downstream, crawling slowly and zig-zagging while we looked for the elephant herd. It was nerve-wracking. A hidden herd of elephants may sound unlikely, but in Africa it's easy. Eventually Bruno's sharp eyes picked out part of a head, downstream, peering from behind some trees. We stopped to watch, engine running. In this deep sand the Land Rover couldn't outrun them. The head watched us, probably with equal trepidation. But ears gently flapping, it soon went back to feeding. This herd is part of a small population of desert-adapted elephants that were rescued from extinction in the late 1980s by community conservation initiatives. Now many of Damaraland's river valleys have resident herds, though conflicts with humans remain a problem.

Eventually we turned around, satisfied that the elephants weren't too annoyed. Halfway back towards the village, we stopped at a bend where the river was wide. We thought about camping under trees in the centre, to allow elephants to pass either side of us, but chose instead to camp next to the outside wall, leaving more space on the bends inside for the herd to pass. It had been a long, hot day. Gin and tonics were handed round and, as as the light faded, Peter and I collected dead wood for the fire while Bruno cooked dinner.

Over barbecued fish, salad, and a glass of wine we learned some basic bush safety tips, including a caution against wandering out of our tents at night. There seemed little chance of this, as after 10 minutes of gazing at the sky through the tents' open mesh windows, we were all fast asleep.

OUT OF THE VALLEY

We woke at 5.30am, just after first light, breakfasted quickly and drove down to the village. Two trackers hopped in the back and introduced themselves as Furai and Johannes. An hour later we'd left the main Ugab Valley and were tentatively edging our way up a steep, V-shaped tributary. Huge slabs of slippery shale lay around, calling for extra concentration from Bruno at the wheel. The sun was already brightening the tops of the valley walls when we emerged onto an impressive, open plain. In the distance stood a range of cone-shaped mountains. The foreground was flat, with occasional low trees and sparse vegetation, dominated by distinctive blue-green *Euphorbia damarana* bushes. Endemic to Damaraland and highly poisonous to most creatures, this is the favourite food of the area's rhino.

TRACKING

Soon we stopped and the trackers climbed on to the Land Rover's roof, from where they could see the ground more easily. Within half an hour they found rhino spoor, and we all got out. Furai, Johannes and Bruno wandered around, scanning the ground. They'd found the evidence, but suspected that it was almost a day old. So we drove on, searching for fresher signs.

The scenery was stunning: a grand, open landscape with grasses, low bushes and the odd tree, backed by distant rocky mountains. At one stage Furai shouted that we should stop and look. A rhino! We peered and saw nothing. Using our binoculars, he changed his mind. It was a gemsbok. We could see it only when it moved. At around 10.30am Johannes spotted more spoor—made that morning, he assured us, by Inyanga, a 23–4-year-old cow in prime condition. As he and Furai came down from the roof, Bruno explained that they knew every rhino in the area—their names, their territories, their tracks and their temperaments.

Again the trackers ranged across the bush, talking to each other as they went. The rocky land made tracking difficult: only occasional spoor could be seen. The trackers' routine became familiar. They'd follow the trail together, talking and pointing at spoor as they went. Then, periodically, they would lose it and split

up, wandering around, scanning for a displaced stone here, a nibbled twig there, or the faint impression of a footfall. Once back on the track, they'd converge for a discussion and, having agreed on their strategy, continue to follow it together. Meanwhile, we stayed in the Land Rover; the sun was now high and the heat was sweltering.

Bruno had prepared us with a safety chat, as black rhino are one of Africa's most temperamental and dangerous animals. Nobody carried a gun—a deliberate policy to avoid gung-ho guides and rhino deaths. The standard rhino-avoidance technique—climbing a tree—was useless, as there were no tall trees near by. It would be essential to stay still and quiet, and to lie flat on the ground if necessary.

Inyanga's spoor headed parallel to our vehicle's track at first, then doubled back. Bruno turned the Land Rover around and followed Furai and Johannes, who were tracking near the vehicle. Eventually Furai signalled. The spoor was diverting away, so it was time for us to walk. Twenty baking minutes later we passed a few tiny, muddy puddles that still held water. Inyanga had been here recently. There were clear, fresh tracks in the mud. I caught up with Furai, but he told us to get back, and to stay at least 100m (30ft) behind him, so that we would have us some protection if they did surprise an animal by mistake.

WAITING AND WATCHING

After an hour's walk the temperature was well above 40°C (98°F). There was no shade. We were hot and tired, but the adrenalin and anticipation kept us alert. Furai and Johannes were ahead, entering a slight dip—a drainage line, dotted with a few low bushes. Suddenly they turned and gestured at us to keep still. Inyanga was about 50m (164ft) up the valley. Keeping quiet and low, Bruno led us in a wide circle, downwind, before edging closer. She was sleeping under a small bush and we stopped about 30m (100ft) from her—close enough for a good view

on. Had the wind shifted? Could she smell us? There was nowhere to run, nowhere to hide and nothing to climb. We were three seconds' sprint from one of the planet's most dangerous females—and nothing we could do would stop her. Safety depended on stillness.

Our heightened senses slowed time. Her ears twitched. She cocked her head to listen, sniffed the air and turned quickly, as if startled, to stare at us. I was transfixed by a

with our binoculars, and for an occasional snort to reach our ears.

The five of us crouched down with Furai and Johannes on either side of us. We could just see the top of Inyanga's back and her twitching ears. Bruno whispered that rhinos have to get up and change position every 30 minutes or so, to turn the stomach and aid digestion. We would just watch and wait.

My pulse raced as she stood up. Nobody moved. She turned around, side

mixture of awe and terror. It seemed an age, but without further fuss, she lay down and went back to sleep. I breathed again. We rose and crept away slowly, keeping a low profile. Only from a distance did we raise our voices to a normal

Above: The White Lady frieze at Brandberg
Below: Elephants are generally safe to approach—unless you stumble on a mother and her calf
Right: Negotiating the huge granite boulders in the Tsisab Ravine

level, thrilled by the encounter. "Better than giraffe, Peter?" ventured Purba.

BRANDBERG BADLANDS

The following morning we approached the dusty-blue Brandberg, across rolling badlands of red-brown shales, interrupted by occasional shrubs or *Welwitschia* plants. The remains of an old road stretched like a ghost across the landscape. It felt like a long day.

BRANDBERG SKIES

A little before sunset we identified a good place to camp, then drove to the top of a hill for a sundowner drink, while watching the light fade over the Ugab Valley.

I slept soundly, woke before dawn and dressed quickly to climb up the massif. There I could watch the dawn creep over the great mountain's fawn rocks, turning them red and gold. Shortly Purba and Peter joined me; then we all scrambled down for breakfast.

Later we parked at the Tsisab Ravine, a steep valley on the northeastern side of the mountain. Brandberg, and this ravine in particular, is famous for its artefacts and rock paintings left by the Bushmen, who inhabited the area for about 7,000 years. It was already hot and the path wound gradually, but relentlessly, upwards. All around stood rounded, granite boulders, and poking up between them, like giant, upturned broomsticks, were Brandberg acacias.

HOT FRIEZES

It took about an hour for us to walk up to the mountain's most famous set of paintings: the White Lady frieze. This shelters under a rock overhang, in a shady passageway between two huge boulders. We entered the darkness and escaped the heat, and gradually our eyes became accustomed to the dark. The paintings were behind thick metal protective bars, but despite this, and the fact that elements had faded and were difficult to see, the skill of the artists shone through. The animals depicted were easy to identify;

their movement was brilliantly represented. However, one particular figure has caught the imagination of the outside world: the White Lady. Unlike most other figures, this one is white from below the chest—a colour and style reminiscent of early Mediterranean paintings. Almost Venetian in style, it has prompted speculation that the Bushmen had come into contact with people from the Mediterranean. More recently, less Eurocentric scholars have concluded that the lady is actually a boy, and that the white colouring is make-up for a hunting ritual or an initiation ceremony.

Eager for more, we climbed further up the mountain. There may be as many as 60,000 paintings on this mountain, many still undiscovered, and Bruno was the perfect guide, having spent two months exploring here while researching the life of an eccentric German, who devoted his last years to Brandberg's rock art. In another hour we found more paintings, cool caves sculpted into sensuous shapes, and even more heat. At one cave Bruno announced: "I promised to show you some giraffe. Well, what do you think?" He pointed to several beautifully painted animals with long, graceful necks.

Finally, hot and exhausted, we tramped down to the vehicle and clamoured for the fridge before making the 116km (72 miles) back to the coast and Swakopmund.

The sea was reflecting the last afternoon light when we arrived back at Swakopmund, ready for a shower and more seafood. First we dropped Jean and Peter back at their hotel. Purba and I would soon be on a plane home, but they were only half way through their trip. "You'll see plenty of giraffes in Etosha," promised Bruno, as we left them in the doorway. A few minutes later we clambered out, unloaded our bags and said our farewells. As the Land Rover disappeared between the palm trees, we felt the first stirrings of a chill mist blow in from the ocean.

GOING IT ALONE

WHEN TO GO

Namibia's coastal climate varies much less than that of the interior, and is generally fine all year. The climate in Damaraland varies more, with occasional frosts in August, whilst October is the hottest month. Isolated late-afternoon thunderstorms may bring rain between December and March. The rivers depend on the rainfall on Namibia's Central Highlands, further inland: they can flow anytime between December and April–May, and often will only flow for a day or two. Flash floods are a major hazard: do not camp in any river bed during this period. The best time for this trip would be the dry season, between April and November.

HOW TO TRAVEL

You can easily drive yourself from Swakopmund to Wlotzkasbaken, Henties Bay, Cape Cross and the Tsisab Ravine area of Brandberg—and for this a normal two-wheel drive saloon car is fine. However, to go cross country, visiting Messum Crater and the Ugab River, or to go offroad in Damaraland, you need to go with a local

guide who knows the area, and has some back-up lined up in case of a problem. It would be highly dangerous to venture there alone, as there are no roads, and nobody is likely to pass by to help you if you run into difficulties.

WHAT TO TAKE

❑ Torch.
❑ Personal medical kit (the guide carries a larger one).
❑ Camera with a zoom lens and binoculars.
❑ Personal water bottle.
❑ Sunblock, sun-hat and sunglasses.
❑ A map of the stars in the southern hemisphere.

PLACES TO VISIT

Henties Bay is a windswept town on the coast about 76km from Swakopmund. Namibians flock here in December and January on their annual holidays, to escape the interior's heat and to go fishing. Do fill up with fuel in Henties Bay if you're heading north. Henties Bay also has a supermarket and a few general shops, including a paint and hardware store that will rent out basic camping gear and fishing equipment. Most are centred on the

Eagle Complex in the centre of town.

All along the Namibian coast there are seal colonies, though the one at Cape Cross is probably the easiest to reach. Here, there are usually between 200,000 and 340,000 animals. The large males, or bulls, arrive from mid- to late October, when they stake their territorial claims. Shortly afterwards, in late November or early December, the females give birth to pups, which remain in the colony and continue suckling for the next 10 or 11 months. Shortly after giving birth, the females mate with the males who control their harems, and the cycle continues. At any time of year, the amazing sight of tens of thousands of heads bobbing on land and in the water is only matched by the overpowering stench of the colony that greets you. In the last few months of the year, the scene can be quite disturbing, with many pups squashed by the weighty adults, or killed by the area's resident jackals and brown hyenas.

The Skeleton Coast National Park is in a remote area so the Ministry of Environment and Tourism has strict regulations about entry permits here. If you are just passing through you can buy your entry permit at either gate: the Ugab River gate on the C34, or the Springbokwasser gate on the D3245. You must reach your gate of entry before 3.00pm to be allowed into the park—otherwise you will simply be turned away. If you plan to stay at Torra or Terrace Bay, this must be prebooked, via the Ministry of Environment and Tourism in Windhoek.

GENERAL TIPS

❑ Don't sleep outside your tent unless advised that it's safe by someone who knows the area very well.

❑ Climbing Brandberg is a serious expedition, and a number of the routes up it are technically difficult. Don't attempt this without a knowledgeable local guide.

❑ For photography, the first and last hours of the day are the best. The sunlight is very strong, so make sure you have a polarizing filter with you.

15 The Heart of the Namib

by Chris McIntyre

Beside the western coast of Southern Africa is the Namib—probably the world's oldest desert. We hired a car to drive ourselves across it, staying on arid farms and remote camps on the way. Amongst the desert's captivating scenery we found friendliness, remarkable wildlife and some of the tallest sand dunes in the world.

In some ways, Namibia is Africa for beginners. Wild game roams through its vast, open landscapes, yet it's free from many of the problems of African travel. Namibia's phones work; its roads are reliable, and it's generally safe and easy to explore. Because distances are large and public transport scarce, my friend Purba and I hired a car to drive into the Namib, staying at remote lodges, camps and guest farms along the way.

We arrived in Namibia early one October morning, at the height of the dry season, emerging through the dark clouds over Botswana into the clear air that covered central Namibia. We'd organized our hire car in advance, picked it up at the small, neat airport and were soon speeding towards central Windhoek. The tar road was wide, empty and smooth; bliss, after London's traffic jams. The air felt clear and sharp, with only a hint of the cool night air remaining. From a cloudless sky above, the sun lit jagged edges on the Aus Mountains to our left. The day was just beginning to warm up.

1 Provided that you can read a road map and drive carefully, Namibia is easy to visit, and makes a good first African trip. Having an air-conditioned car is worthwhile, especially if you're sensitive to heat. Climbing high on the sand dunes can be taxing, so start early and, if you're not feeling energetic, take the balloon ride instead.

★★ If you're on a moderately generous budget, Namibia's guest farms and lodges vary from comfortable to luxurious. You won't find any that are dirty or unpleasant, and the catering varies from acceptable to excellent. Camping is cheaper but more basic: bring all your equipment with you. The campsites are usually clean and well run, with toilets and showers often in very good condition.

Binoculars are important, especially if you're keen on the wildlife. A camera is essential. Light levels are high, so bring lots of slow film and a polarizing filter. Make sure that all your optical equipment is stored in dust-proof bags.

WINDHOEK

Windhoek was to be a short stop. It's a pleasant and safe capital, but we wanted to escape from the city and get straight into the bush. Much of Windhoek was deserted—it was a Sunday—but our essential stop, a large, out-of-town super-market, was heaving with people. We stocked up on crisps and snacks, and bought a small cool box to fill with cold drinks. Namibia's heat is deceptively dry, so maintaining your body's fluid reserves is essential. Finally we added six large bottles of mineral water, to keep in the car for emergencies.

Back on the open road, we cruised south through Namibia's central high-lands along the B1, the country's tar backbone. Beside the road, thin strands of wire fenced the wide verges from the bush beyond. Although it was cattle-ranching territory, nothing stirred. The scattered trees and bushes were parched; tufts of grass had turned to straw and much of the ground was bare.

REHOBOTH

In an hour we reached Rehoboth, the cen-tre of the Baster people, one of Namibia's many distinct cultural groups. Their ancestors were children of mixed-race parentage in the Cape, who, as outcasts, banded together and fled north from the expanding Cape Colony. By the 1870s they had reached Rehoboth, and founded their own town. We drove along the main street, where the houses all differed in

Below: *Vast, smooth red dunes surround the arid pan of Sossusvlei, which is filled with water for only a few weeks a year*

NAMIBIA

style and construction. Some were pastel blue or pink, others white, like small villas. All were separated by expanses of dry, orange earth, where goats had devoured everything green. Minutes later we left town through the sandy bed of the Oanab River, past muddy pools and old camelthorn trees.

GRAVE GRAVEL

A few kilometres further, we turned southwest from the main road and onto a gravel road: the C47. We'd been warned of the accident rate on Namibia's gravel roads—not a result of poor roads; on the contrary, the roads are generally excellent. However, gravel is deceptive and perspective can become confused in Namibia's huge landscapes. So every year a few drive too fast, lose control and skid. Remembering this, we slowed to a safe 70kph (45mph), and continued with an eye on the speedometer.

The hilly landscape of the central highlands rolled on. Every half-hour or so we'd meet another car, slowing until we'd emerged safely from the attendant dust cloud behind it. Several towns had large dots on our map—Kobos, Klein Aub, Rietoog—but all were easy to miss: just cattle posts with a handful of houses. Around us, the natural landscape was vast. Some of the hills were strewn with huge boulders, like pebbles piled up by an untidy giant. Others were shaped from neatly folded strata. Namibia's low rainfall means minimal erosion and sparse vegetation, so its geology is often visible, just waiting to be picked up. Once we stopped

to take a picture, stepping into the silent heat, squinting in the brightness at the mica, which glinted like diamonds in rocks beside the road.

Beside a gap in a range of brown, folded mountains we found Ballsport, a remote farm marked by a dot on the map. We wandered around whilst the car was filled with petrol from a squeaky, hand-cranked pump. A small swimming pool suggested that this was a guest farm, and this was confirmed by Ernst, the owner. Serious hikers use it as a base for the Naukluft Mountains and his wife, Joanna, had recently started horse trails.

With a full tank we turned from the high mountains into a small valley, where cliffs overlooked a dry, pebble-and-sand river on both sides. About three hours out of Windhoek, we reached Zebra River Lodge, where Rob and Marianne, the owners, wandered out to welcome us.

DRINKS ON THE ROCKS

Later, Rob drove up a mountainside in his four-wheel drive so we could greet our first Namibian sunset in style—with a gin and tonic and a spectacular view. Desiccated shrubs and a few low trees dotted the folded rocks of the Tsaris Mountains. This had once been a typical Namibian farm, a sheep ranch covering about 100sq. km (61sq. miles), but poor rainfall and rough terrain made it a difficult living. Rob and Marianne had bought the farm in the early 1990s, leaving their urban careers to renovate the farmhouse. They had always lived in Africa and loved the bush; this was their dream home.

DRIVING ON GRAVEL ROADS

❑ Never drive at night
❑ Always keep below 80kph (50mph) and treat bends with great caution.
❑ Stay in a slightly lower gear on gravel roads, as it gives you more control. Use third rather than fourth.

❑ When meeting oncoming traffic, slow down and put your headlights on. This will make you more visible to oncoming traffic in the dust cloud that you enter.
❑ Try to travel early in the day, arriving at your destination before 3pm. That way, if you have a problem on the road, another vehicle will find you before nightfall.

Rob's engineering know-how looked after the generator, whilst Marianne's cooking attracted guests from around the world.

Next morning we were up early, hiking boots on, to follow Rob's directions down an indistinct path into the mountains. With more walking trails than rooms here, we had this whole canyon to ourselves. The still air was stirred only by our footfall and the low drone of insects. Occasionally a bird broke from cover, and once a troop of baboons, high on the cliff, called out in alarm. After a few hours the path ended with a steep slope up to a natural pool, shaded by trees. It was 10am and already hot. Sitting back, we gulped from our bottles and tucked into snacks, watching flights of rosy-faced lovebirds arrive, drink and depart from this little oasis. Above floated the dark outlines of black eagles.

SOCIABLE BIRDS

We could have hiked there for days, but that afternoon we left for Sesriem. At first the Naukluft Mountains bounded our road, but gradually we left them behind, and were surrounded by spectacular plains of wispy golden grass. Rising above this, the highest things around were a few old camelthorn trees. Most of these housed at least one colony of sociable weavers—tiny birds that thatch their nests into an enormous structure, so heavy that often the branches break under its weight.

We planned to spend the next two nights in this area, at a lodge on the edge of the desert, Wilderness Sossusvlei Camp. Following the signs, we found their thatched gatehouse, left our car in a shaded parking spot, and bumped along a four-wheel drive track to camp.

IMMORTAL TREES

A genteel afternoon tea was served at 4pm, after which Chris, our guide, drove us into the lodge's small reserve. We sat back in the four-wheel drive, but were soon out looking at the smooth, curled trunk of a dwarf tree, just 15cm (6in)

high. So harsh and dry was the stony slope it seemed amazing that anything grew there, Chris told us that this was a rock commiphora—a member of the myrrh family. Its Afrikaans name was *kanniedood*, literally meaning "cannot die." He explained that these plants could survive for years without water, springing leaves and flowers for just a few months when it finally rains.

As we continued, we learned that this area had been farmland since the 1950s. Originally karakul had been farmed here—a central Asian sheep whose pelts make Persian lamb fur. Later, goats had been tried, but erratic rainfall and overgrazing exhausted the land. Our camp was relatively new, and its owners had bought up several neighbouring farms. The dividing fences had been torn down throughout and a tiny pool of water created below the camp to encourage the desert animals. Gradually, more antelope were being seen. Right on cue, Chris's practised eyes spotted three ostriches, strutting away from us in the distance.

After dinner, wandering outside onto the wide wooden balcony, we gazed up at the clearest sky that we'd ever seen. Minimal moisture or pollution and no town lights for hundreds of kilometres meant amazing visibility. Fortunately the moon had not yet risen, so the Milky Way and constellations shone bright. Seeing us there, Chris wandered over and ushered us to the telescope: "Have you ever seen the moons of Jupiter?"

BALLOONING

The moon was cool and bright when the alarm clock woke us. We'd decided to go ballooning, which starts at sunrise from Kulala, a lodge further west. We breakfasted swiftly but drove slowly. Our pilot, Eric, was a jovial Belgian who'd spent years in central Africa before coming to Namibia with a dream of ballooning over the dunes. We met at his small lodge, hopping on the back of a large lorry under a canvas shade with a party of eight French visitors and a German couple.

A short drive away, we stopped beside a rock outcrop to find a flaccid balloon lying on its side. Already, hot air was being fanned into it, as the crew walked into its billowing silk. Soon Eric called for us all to get into the basket, which had been divided into compartments and laid on its side for safety. The sun was rising over the Naukluft Mountains as the balloon strained to lift us. Gas heaters blasted scalp-tingling flames: one, two, three, four … until, quite suddenly, with a scrape and bump, we lifted off.

The messy mechanics of getting into the air were replaced by the amazing lightness of flight. The trucks and crew remained earthbound and scrabbled to guess our movements and follow us, but we were now weightless, suspended in the wind. We'd taken off between two hills, with the Naukluft Massif in the distance. Now we wondered where the wind would take us. Its direction, and therefore our direction, changed as we gradually rose. More of the landscape unfolded beneath us, and the back-up crew shrank down into insignificance. Eventually Eric levelled off, and barked a few instructions through the crackles of his walkie-talkie. We were heading northeast; he directed the ground crew to meet us.

Everyone whispered in awe. Eric pointed to dark maroon dunes ahead, which rose like mountain ranges—the first dunes of the desert. Meanwhile, the Tsauchab River's dry bed snaked westwards beneath us. Silently we crossed it into the Namib-Naukluft National Park. Later, we would follow this river bed, but for now we just watched as it floated by, not understanding its significance.

Above: *A balloon trip at sunrise is the best way to see the changing colours of the desert*
Below: *The scale of the dunes becomes apparent when people walk across them*

A murmur of wonder ran through the group as the first rays of the sun turned the highest, sinuous dune crests to a burning ochre. Quickly the colour spread to those in the distance, flowing down like patches of liquid amber. Geometric sections of deep, black shade seemed to recede between the dunes, as the cloudless sky remained an unwavering, cobalt blue. As the brightness spread, so its impact faded, turning the dunes bright apricot.

Never have I witnessed a sunrise so spectacular, or watched its progress so clearly. We were transfixed. Even the quiet whirring of video cameras and Eric's informative trilingual commentary couldn't disturb the peace.

As smoothly as it had risen, the balloon dropped at Eric's command. Our view narrowed and the back-up crew once again loomed large, arriving on a nearby track with the vehicle and trailer. Finally, as a *pièce de résistance*, the balloon hovered a few metres above a dune crest, playing for time while the crew manoeuvred the basket close by, grabbing the ropes of the hovering craft.

Just an hour after sunrise, we landed. It felt as if we'd been aloft for only minutes. When everything was finally loaded up, we drove out of the national park, stopping in the Tsauchab's sandy valley for brunch, before returning to Kulala to leave Eric with his other visitors.

ALONG THE TSAUCHAB

Back at camp, a sumptuous lunch lay on the table. We showered, relaxed and had only a small bite of a delicious salad. At camps like this, overindulgence seemed the greatest health risk. Later that afternoon we ventured out again, this time heading into the heart of the dunes.

We stopped at Sesriem, the gate into this part of the Namib-Naukluft National Park, one of Africa's largest parks. While Chris bought a permit, we wandered into the small shop next door, where even the shelves seemed sparsely stocked. On the road again, our destination lay 60km (37 miles) west, in the centre of the Namib's great dune sea. On either side of us the flat gravel plain was dotted with mirages and reflections. Beyond them rose mountains—some of rock, others of sand. We were just a tiny dot in a huge landscape.

Meandering along the plain beside us was a vague line of green camelthorn trees, marking the Tsauchab River. This is one of Namibia's many rivers flowing west from the high central plateau towards the Atlantic. Like most, its channel is filled with sand. Only rarely does its water flow over the ground here—perhaps for just a few days in each year. Normally it percolates underground, through the sand, and so keeps the line of deep-rooted camelthorns alive. However, the Tsauchab is unusual because it never reaches the ocean. Instead it flows into the centre of the Namib where, over the millennia, its sporadic flows have swept a flat path through the dunes. This lay around us, but its scale was difficult to judge. Were those dunes a few hundred metres, or tens of kilometres from the road? The trees gave some clue, and through the binoculars we could see large nests. "Lappetfaced vultures," said Chris, "Africa's largest vultures. They're under threat in many areas, but come here to nest. They don't like to be disturbed, and nobody ever goes near those trees."

THE PANS

Gradually, as we continued, the towering dunes began to converge, moving closer to the road. Increasingly, steep slopes of sand hemmed us in on either side. Finally, straight ahead in the distance, we saw more dunes, threatening to block our progress. These formed a sandbar—the beginning of the end of the Tsauchab's progress through the Namib Desert, and the start of an area loosely termed the Sossusvlei. When the river reaches this point, it spreads to form a series of lakes between the dunes: Nara Vlei, Dead Vlei, Hidden Vlei and, most famously, Sossusvlei, the valley furthest into the dunes. Being Namibia, these lakes fill for

only a few days in a decade—when high floods in wet years swell the river, giving it the strength to push this far west. The rest of the time, they remain silver-grey pans dotted with occasional trees and bushes, surrounded by some of the world's highest dunes.

In front of the sandbar were scattered feathery camelthorn trees, and here various normal cars had parked. With the luxury of a four-wheel drive, we skirted around this first pan and continued on a track of deep sand. It rapidly split into a plethora of deep tracks across the band of low, red dunes. For 10 minutes Chris expertly steered as the tracks veered around, over and between smaller dunes on the floor of the pan. Finally, we stopped. "This is as far as the vehicle can go," he said with a grin. "Now we walk!"

GEMSTONE DUNES

Despite the menacingly dark clouds that had, unexpectedly, gathered, it was still unbearably hot outside. Hats and sun block on, sleeves down, we left the vehicle with a bottle of water each. Although Sossusvlei is the pan that everybody knows, Chris suggested that we visit Dead Vlei, promising fewer visitors and a starker beauty.

We set off, walking across the clay pan and onto the dunes. Before long we stopped to watch two wedge-snouted desert lizards fighting. Between short, frenetic bouts, they chased each other around a bush and scent-marked patches of sand.

Sinking down half a step for every one taken, we plodded up a sand ridge, captivated by the different colours of the dunes. Tiny garnets, shining red, were among the grains which made up some of the crests.

ROARING DUNES AT DEAD VLEI

After half-an-hour's walk, we stood high on a ridge overlooking Dead Vlei: a huge, silvery pan, dotted with bleached skeletons of dead camelthorn trees and surrounded by dunes towering up to 250m (850ft) high. "They're over 500 years old," Chris commented, explaining that the trees had once flourished here, before the Tsauchab's course had moved slightly north, feeding into Sossusvlei and Nara Vlei instead.

Leaving our guide we ran down to explore the pan's surface. Once thick mud, it was cracked into solid crazy-paving slabs with a very fine grain. This pan was enormous. Sadly the cloudy sky cast a flat light, which was poor for photography, so my plans for prize-winning abstract pictures were foiled. Purba, though, was transfixed. Climbing up the slip-face of a big dune she had noticed that every movement made a noise that reverberated throughout the whole dune. Once, when we had attained a little height and slid down, it seemed to roar with a low, pulsating hum. Chris had told us about this, one of Namibia's "roaring dunes," but we had to hear it to believe it.

Exhausted, we wandered back. The sun was sinking fast, and we had to leave the park gate before sunset. Walking back on the high ridge, we stopped briefly to rest, and watched as the sun dipped beneath the clouds, bathing the pans in a gorgeous, ethereal yellow light. Far in the distance, we saw a small group of gemsboks, Namibia's largest and most graceful antelope. The lead animal climbed onto the crest of a dune and stopped for a moment, tilting its head—perhaps listening, or just surveying the scene; then, with a toss of its head, it disappeared. We left the pans and the park swiftly, for dinner and a deep sleep.

THE LIVING DUNES OF SOSSUSVLEI

Next morning we packed early and left camp at sunrise, determined to see the pans again before leaving the area. The sun was already warm when we stopped at the first pan and started walking. This time we just wandered around, gazing in awe as the light changed on the sensuous

curves of the dunes. Keeping quiet and staying alert, we saw a surprising amount of wildlife.

Aside from the many shady camelthorn trees, huge, strangely named !nara [sic] bushes had grown around mounds of sand, protecting their few succulent melon fruits with a tangle of leafless, spiky branches. Amongst these, large, black tenebrionid beetles scurried by on slender legs, avoiding passing lizards; dune larks flitted between trees. Again, stopping and sitting was the best way to observe. The less we moved, the more we saw. First we glimpsed groups of springboks feeding, then gemsboks. Occasionally we'd see another person or a vehicle in the distance, but the pans are big and people tend to disappear in the landscape. Finally, with amazing luck, we glimpsed an African wildcat: an unusual sighting even in wetter parks, so very unexpected here.

Above: *The blighted landscape of Dead Vlei looks ominous under the glowering sky*
Right: *A gemsbok looks over enquiringly*

GRAND CANYONS

The temperature was rising fast as we returned to the car, grateful for the soft drinks waiting in our cool box. Before leaving the area, we stopped briefly at Sesriem Canyon, five minutes' drive south of the park's entrance. We walked down into a water-sculpted fissure in the rocky landscape, where the Tsauchab River trickled along. Its periodic floods had not only filled Sossusvlei, but had also eroded fantastic curves, holes and donut shapes into the walls of the canyon. It was good to see water in this river at last.

About halfway to Swakopmund the road passed through two canyons: one created by the Gaub River, the second by the Kuiseb. As the road twisted and turned, dropping to the level of the river, we were reminded that we were still travelling on a rocky plateau. At the bottom of each river we'd cross over the dry, sandy bed on a simple concrete bridge. Then, on the other side, we'd bend and corkscrew up between the rounded mountains.

SENTINELS OF THE DESERT

North of the Kuiseb River, the desert changed again. No longer were there huge dunes: instead, we now drove through flat gravel plains. Amid these huge expanses of flatness, we saw rocky outcrops in the distance, known as inselbergs—from the German words for "island" and "mountain." These isolated massifs of rock were scattered around the plains, like giant worm casts on a lawn. They collect moisture from the Namib's morning fogs and each supports a unique community of flora and fauna. We sped past into the sinking sun, anxious to reach Swakopmund before nightfall.

We covered the last 160km (100 miles) to the coast in two and a half hours. Walvis Bay's wide streets and traffic lights were a shock, and its regimented grid seemed cramped, with so much space on the edge of the town. We turned north, to Swakopmund, seeking a good seafood dinner at the end of our adventure. The trip had taken us four days: we were hot and dusty and needed a shower. But we'd accomplished what the Tsauchab River had failed to do for millennia: we'd come from the mountains, made it through the dunes and finally reached the Atlantic.

GOING IT ALONE

WHEN TO GO

There are no bad times to visit Namibia, so decide what's important to you and choose accordingly. Namibia has a subtropical desert climate, which often shows huge local variations. Rainfall generally occurs from December to March, which is a fascinating time to visit. The birdlife is prolific and many animals have their young, although spotting them amidst the greenery can be difficult. The dry season, between April and September, is generally pleasant, clear and dry. April, May and June are beautiful months. This is the best time for photography, as the dust has been washed out of the air, the vegetation is still green, and the sky is clear blue with a few wispy white clouds.

Nights during July and August can be cold, with frost possible in the higher areas and the deserts. This is the best time for hikers, as then daytime temperatures are at their lowest. September, October and November are dry, as temperatures gradually rise. The later months of the dry season are the best time to see big game in Etosha. Then the small bush pools dry up, the green vegetation shrivels and the animals stay nearer to the water holes.

Namibia is never crowded and always seems deserted, but it does become busier around Easter and from late July to early September, when advance booking is essential.

HIRING A VEHICLE

Make sure that you hire a high-quality vehicle from a reliable company. It's usually best to reserve it in advance, before arriving. Before you sign for any car hire, read the fine print of the hire agreement, especially the insurance and the Collision Damage Waiver (CDW) clauses. These should explain what you pay if you damage the car. Cheap cars often come with minimal insurance, especially for accidents caused by negligence on gravel roads, where no other vehicles are involved.

Although it doesn't fit people's rugged preconceptions, a normal two-wheel-drive saloon car is fine for virtually all of Namibia's main attractions. As a rule, if you need a four-wheel drive to get you somewhere off-road, then you shouldn't be there without a knowledgeable local guide. The main exception to this rule is Sossusvlei, where a four-wheel drive will save you a couple of kilometres' walk. However, they can be hired at the gates, just for a day, from Sossusvlei 4x4 Car Rental, tel: 064 500142 or 063 293250; fax: 064 500941. A cheaper option is their shuttles, which run between the two-wheel-drive car park and Nara Vlei. For driving trips around the country, the best companies are: Avis (P.O. Box 2057, Eros Airport, Windhoek; tel: 061 233166; fax: 061 223072); Budget (P.O. Box 1754, Windhoek Airport, Windhoek; tel: 061 228720; fax: 061 227665), and Imperial (P.O. Box 1387, Eros Airport, Windhoek; tel: 061 227103; fax: 061 777721). Check out the deals offered by overseas operators, as arranging flights, car and accommodation overseas can often be cheaper than booking them all separately.

ACCOMMODATION

If you plan to camp, there are a number of sites where you can just turn up. Make sure that you buy all your food and camping equipment in Windhoek, as only basics are available away from the main towns. Note that the closest campsite within the Namib-Naukluft National Park for visiting Sossusvlei is Sesriem. It has only a few pitches and often fills up, so it should also be booked in advance.

If you prefer the comfort of guest farms and lodges, book them well in advance and plan your route carefully. Most are very small, and can be booked up months in advance during the busier seasons.

WHAT TO TAKE

- ❏ Torch.
- ❏ Medical kit.
- ❏ Camera with a zoom lens.
- ❏ Binoculars.
- ❏ Sunblock, sun hat and sunglasses.
- ❏ A small cool box—buy one in Windhoek when you arrive.

16 Sand, Sky and Water— Hiking the Fish River Canyon

by Richard Whitaker

The Fish River Canyon in southern Namibia is one of the world's natural wonders. With a group of friends I took up the canyon's unique challenge—an 85km (53-mile) hiking trail, over spectacularly rugged terrain.

"One of my boyfriends' mother was eaten by a lion." Only in Africa could idle conversation around the campfire produce a statement like this. The rest of us stared into the flames and said nothing. Struck though we were by the comment, our thoughts were elsewhere—on the long, unfamiliar trail that faced us the next day. Earlier, at sunset, I had driven the 10km (6 miles) from our campsite at Hobas to the edge of the canyon to take a look. I could report that no pictures gave any sense of the scale of the canyon: it was enormous, magnificent—and daunting.

At sunrise a local driver took us to the start of the trail. We were a party of five, ranging in age from the early 40s to 60: myself; my wife, Jennie, a radio producer; her cousin, Julia, a pediatrician; and our friends Gill, a librarian (she who had lost the potential mother-in-law); and her chemical engineer husband, Mike. From the starting point I looked over the edge, down into a wilderness of gullies, broken rock and towering buttresses, catching, far below, a glint of water.

From here the descent seemed impossibly precipitous. Yet once we were under way it was no more than a steep downhill slog, with chains providing a handhold on the trickier bits. Two hours later we reached the floor of the canyon and the beginning of the trail proper.

GETTING THERE

Weeks of planning and preparation had brought us to this point. We had appointed Mike our trail leader. A long-standing member of the Mountain Club of South Africa, Mike had been going off into the wilderness for weeks at a time since he was a young boy. Under his supervision we went on a few training hikes in the mountains around our home in Cape Town, and assembled the gear and provisions we would need. For firsthand advice I also contacted an old Fish River hand, Siggi Öhler, who has been guiding groups through the canyon for many years (see Contacts). He lent me a useful detailed map of the canyon, and gave advice about shortcuts. I remember thinking at the time: "I'm not interested in shortcuts. I want to experience every bit of the trail." Which shows how wrong you can be.

WEST COAST FLOWERS

Our route here took us north from Cape Town, through the wheat-growing areas

Any reasonably fit person can do this trail, but inexperienced hikers should join an organized tour (see Going It Alone). Expect to walk across rugged terrain for five to eight hours a day, over four to five days.

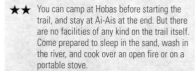
You can camp at Hobas before starting the trail, and stay at Ai-Ais at the end. But there are no facilities of any kind on the trail itself. Come prepared to sleep in the sand, wash in the river, and cook over an open fire or on a portable stove.

A long walking staff is essential to keep your balance when crossing the river and hiking over boulders; puttees (see box, p. 168) are also a must.

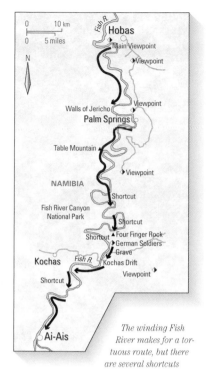

The winding Fish River makes for a tortuous route, but there are several shortcuts

of some white succulent flowers and bushes of brilliant yellow blossoms.

Later, as we walked the canyon, I saw single yellow flowers appearing out of what looked like bone-dry desert sand. It seemed impossible that they could last more than a few hours in this parching heat.

INTO THE CANYON

The first hour's walking on the canyon floor took us over brown beach sand, and then across long stretches of football-sized rocks, smoothed and rounded by the scouring action of the river. This was to be the pattern of each day's hiking: a walk through sand until our legs longed for the firmness of rock underfoot, then over rocks until they longed again for the softness of sand. It is the variety of surfaces—boulders, rocks, desert sand, dust, gravel—that, more than anything else, makes the canyon a tough challenge. But it was mainly on the first two days that the going was slow and difficult. By day three the canyon had widened out, more of the going was over firm gravel paths, and we could get further, faster.

All around there was evidence of the awesome forces that had created these huge boulders, masses of scree and sheer cliffs. For anyone who likes rocks and geological formations, the canyon is a dream. Round every corner we found something new: granites green with copper or pink with manganese, black

around Malmesbury, and across the desolate plains either side of Vanrhynsdorp. After passing through Namaqualand, we crossed the Orange River into Namibia at Vioolsdrif. Just before the border, quiver trees began to appear, starkly outlined against the blue sky. Another two hours' driving, about half of it on gravel, brought us to the campsite at Hobas.

On the way to and from Cape Town I looked forward to one of the most spectacular sights in South Africa: the flowers of the West Coast and Namaqualand. Each year, after the spring rains, from late August till the end of September, the parched countryside up the West Coast explodes with orange and white daisies, and the brilliant red and purple flowers of the succulent plants. But though it was early September when we drove through, the weather remained stubbornly overcast and rainy both ways between Cape Town and the Orange River. Without the heat of the sun the flowers stayed closed, refusing to show off their colours to us. We were at least rewarded with the sight

---

BEATING THE HEAT

It can get burning hot in the canyon, even in midwinter, so it's essential to keep yourself cool. Take frequent drinks of water, preferably with energy supplements—I was getting through 4–5 litres (7–9 pints) a day. Make sure your hat is made of absorbent cloth. That way you can keep dipping it in the river to cool your head down. A wet bandana or handkerchief to go round your neck is also a good idea.

dolerite dykes bursting through the layers of shale and sandstone, fantastic swirling lines of white silica in black quartzite, rocks that have been shaped by the elements into modern sculptures. In many places the sand glitters gold with fragments of iron pyrites.

The canyon can be very unpredictable. The trail had been closed a month earlier after a flash flood, and we saw the traces round about us. Driftwood had caught on boulders metres up the sides of the canyon, and a thick layer of chocolate-brown mud covered the rocks, cracking and curling like pieces of broken Easter egg.

MAKING CAMP

After a refreshing lunchtime swim we pressed on, hoping to stay overnight at Palm Springs. In mid-afternoon we came upon the extraordinary sight of a motor-scooter parked on the rocks to our left,

Above: A dip in the river is the perfect way to cool down in the middle of the day
Left: The kokerboom tree, known in English as the quiver tree because it is used by bushmen to make arrow quivers, grows in the most inhospitable places
Inset: Yellow Namaqualand daisies make a splash of brilliant colour among the rocks

the lone survivor of a crazy quixotic adventure (see box, p. 169). After another hour we saw our first large fauna: three klipspringers drinking from the river; and as evening drew in we heard baboons barking angrily at us from the cliffs. Although we had covered only 14km (9 miles), much of it had been boulder-hopping, so we were utterly exhausted. We gratefully abandoned our original goal and set up camp below the Walls of Jericho.

On this first evening a routine established itself which we were to follow every day. We unstrapped the groundsheets and spread them out to make a workspace on the sand, then unpacked the rucksacks, put the food on the groundsheets and hung our clothes in the "cupboards"—the scrubby tamarisk trees which somehow manage to grow in the sand. Some of us collected firewood, while others went down to the river to fill all the bottles so that there would be enough water for the evening.

On previous trails I had made the mistake of carrying too much food and too little drink, but not this time. I revived myself with water, laced with whisky from one of the many tot-sized plastic sachets in my pack. Dinner was a kedgeree of tinned salmon and rice. Delicious—but we were unable to scour the aura of fish out of the tin billycans and plastic cups, so for the next two days we drank salmon-flavoured tea and coffee.

After dinner I carefully smoothed the sand flat to form a bed, scooped out hollows for hip and shoulder, laid down my thin mattress, and climbed into my sleeping bag. Having been warned that, if you lie facing the wrong way, you can wake up with your sleeping bag (not to mention eyes, ears and nose) full of sand, I made sure that my feet were pointing into the wind. For a while I looked up at the stars, enjoying the canyon's absolute silence (a silence you never experience in the city); then I fell dead asleep.

HOT BATH

Next morning, after just half an hour's walking, we caught a strong whiff of sulphur in the air: Palm Springs. We hurried on, keen to reach what had been the previous night's goal, an oasis in the wilderness, created by a perennial hot spring. As we rounded the bend I could see a clump of palm trees. Rumour has it they grew from date stones dropped by escaped German prisoners of war hiding in the canyon during World War I. Near by, the hot spring, keeping a temperature of just under 60°C (140°F), burst from the side of the canyon to flow down into the river.

Moments later we had dumped our packs and stripped off our clothes, and were wallowing in the warm jade-green pool on the river's edge. The mineral-rich water soothed our aching joints and tired muscles. I floated on my back and enjoyed, through the steam, the sight of the bone-dry canyon walls against the green reeds fringing the pool.

The memory of this interlude kept us going through the day, as we pushed on over further stretches of rock and sand. During the morning we kept seeing manure on the path. Then, just before noon, we had our first sighting of the canyon's wild horses—three of them,

grazing on the other side of the river. Over the following days we would see several more small groups of three or four.

WILDLIFE

Despite its desolate appearance, the canyon always has water in it, and so is able to sustain a variety of wildlife. Because the terrain is rough you walk with your eyes on the ground most of the time, so you constantly see the tracks and droppings of many animals. The sand by riverside, particularly, showed us the delicate hoofmarks of the klipspringer, the much deeper ones of kudu and wild horse, tiny footprints of lizards either side of the furrow left by the tail, and the tracks of genets, rodent-like dassies, and baboons. In the afternoon on day two, I discovered the unmistakable large pawprints of a leopard crossing the dunes. Fortunately there was little chance of coming face to face with the beast itself, as leopards are shy and nocturnal.

We often saw baboons, though, or heard them barking among the rocks. A large male sat near us the second morning, watching while we struck camp. As soon as we moved off he ran into the campsite to scavenge, but was disappointed, as we had cleaned up thoroughly. I also saw a baboon ripping the branches at the top of one of the palm trees at Palm Springs, looking for dates.

SAND FREE BOOTS

Make yourself a pair of puttees (cloth protection for the lower leg) to stop sand getting into your boots and causing blisters. Sew a piece of light cloth into a tube that fits loosely round your leg from the ankle to just below the knee, and elasticize both ends. Fit the lower end over the top of your boot. You won't win any fashion awards, but your feet will be grateful.

I wondered how he managed to avoid impaling himself on the needle-sharp spines. Strangest of all was the baboon we saw at the end of the trail, swimming across the river—very rare behaviour.

NIGHTS

It was close to the time of the new moon. In the pitch-black nights, through the crystal-clear air, we could see millions of stars. We lay back, drinking coffee and watching the constellations rise: Scorpio, Orion, the Southern Cross, the gaseous blur of the Milky Way. Punctually each evening, satellites sped past from horizon to horizon. We never failed to see several shooting stars.

The first night, for some reason, was utterly silent. But on the following nights we heard all sorts of sounds: dassies quarrelling with strange bleating noises; the plopping of fish in the river; an owl hooting (just before dawn I saw it flapping past); a jackal howling in the distance.

SHORTCUT TO SCOTLAND

One of the difficulties of walking the canyon is knowing just where you are, as there are no signs or distance markers. You have to study the map, and try to keep track of the bends in the river and the obvious landmarks. Luckily for us, Mike's navigation was excellent. On day three, he found all the shortcuts marked on the map, so cutting off many kilometres of hard walking along the riverbank.

> ## AFRICA'S GRAND CANYON
>
> With a length of 161km (100 miles) and a maximum depth of 550m (1,800ft), the Fish River Canyon is one of the deepest in the world. First created by a fracture in the earth's crust 500 million years ago, the canyon has been further deepened by erosion, the action of glaciers 300 million years ago, and later fracturing. You can read off a whole geological history from its sheer sides: at the lower levels, ancient metamorphosed sandstone, shale and lava, split by dolerite dykes and granite intrusions; above, a narrow layer of pebble conglomerate; then 150–200m (500–650ft) of black sandstone and limestone, capped by a further 10m (35ft) of sandstone and shale.

You need to be very sure you're on the right path before you leave the canyon, otherwise you may find yourself wandering off into the desert. Fortunately each shortcut is marked by a number of cairns of loose stones along the way, made by earlier hikers. These are set up at irregular intervals, but you should see one within 30 minutes of leaving the canyon. If you think you're on a shortcut but don't see cairns, turn back: you've gone the wrong way.

> ## FISH RIVER SCOOTERS
>
> About 12km (7 miles) into the trail, hikers will see a battered old scooter against the hillside on their left. Thereby hangs a bizarre tale. In 1968 a group of young men from Cape Town, none of whom had ever visited the Fish River, set out to ride three scooters (hopefully named "Veni," "Vidi" and "Vici") the length of the canyon. They took an inflatable raft to cope with the many river-crossings, and lots of supplies, but no rucksacks. Only by taking the scooters apart were they able to start manhandling them down to the valley floor. Even so, one scooter had to be abandoned on the descent. The river claimed the second scooter when the raft capsized. After nine days of pushing and pulling the remaining scooter over the rocks and through the soft sand, they abandoned that one, too, and walked out of the canyon carrying the rest of their equipment in their arms.

I found walking uphill out of the canyon a pleasure, after all the tramping along on the flat. Once away from the river, the landscape is barren and scorched, with not a hint of green anywhere.

After the second shortcut of the day we rejoined the canyon and were walking towards yet another long, slow, bend in the river. Gradually we became aware of the most extraordinary wailing sound coming around the corner, faint at first, but getting stronger as we approached. We looked at each other, trying to guess what on earth it could be. The wind moaning through the rocks? An animal in pain? We rounded the bend to be confronted with a completely unexpected sight: a blond man in shorts and a ragged tee-shirt, blasting out *Scotland the Brave* on the bagpipes. His two friends sat listening near by.

Once we'd recovered from our astonishment, and he had stopped playing, we got talking. These were the first people we'd encountered on the trail. All three were Dutch; the piper's name was Michel. Michel had never been on a trail before, so he thought nothing of bringing along his beloved bagpipes, although they weighed about 3.5kg (7.5lb). He told us

that the previous morning, when he was playing near Palm Springs, a group of curious wild horses had come around the corner to take a look. Michel played one last tune for us, *Amazing Grace*, then we moved on.

A LONELY GRAVE

It was hot, and by lunchtime most of us were flagging. Gill and Julia had developed painful blisters which they needed to treat. So though Mike was keen to push on further, we staged a mini-mutiny, heaving off our packs alongside a promising stretch of water, and insisting on our lunchtime swim. Our leader gave in with good grace. But when we waded into the opaque, emerald-coloured water, we discovered that it was only shin-deep, so the

Above: *Mike putting the Nama bread into the hot sand to bake*
Right: *The approach to Palm Springs in the early morning stillness was magical*

"swim" turned into a tepid, muddy wallow. Just after lunch, at a point where we crossed the river, we found several beautiful, deep swimming holes. Mike tactfully refrained from comment.

The third and final shortcut of the day rejoined the canyon near one of the best-known landmarks on the trail, the grave of the German soldier. An iron grave-marker, set on a rocky cairn near Four Finger Rock, carries the inscription (in German): "Here rests in God Lieutenant Thilo von Trotha, born 23.11.1877 in Wahlstadt, died 14.6.1905." These few words barely hint at the extraordinary fate of this Prussian, who originally came to southern Africa in 1899 to fight on the Boer side in the Anglo-Boer War, then joined the German colonial forces in South West Africa (now Namibia) in their bitter war against the indigenous Nama people. Von Trotha was shot in a skirmish in the Fish River canyon and buried on the spot, far from his native country. I walked on through the dry, sandy, almost completely desert landscape of this part of the canyon, thinking how strange it must have seemed to someone used to the greenery of Europe.

NAMA BREAD

Evening found us setting up camp, for the last time, at Kochas Drift. It always seems to work out like this: after the first day of a tough trail you wonder how you could have agreed to put yourself through such punishment; by the last evening you don't want it to end.

Mike announced that he was going to make bread, as a treat for our final dinner. We were intrigued, but sceptical: how was he going to bake over an open fire? Mike told us he had learned the secret from his Nama guide, Simon Fredericks, during a recent hike through the Richtersveld.

We watched, fascinated, as he made a fire in the fine river sand, then mixed flour, water, salt and yeast in a plastic bag. Once the dough had started to firm up, Mike took it out of the packet and kneaded it into a smooth oval, about 5cm (2in) thick. About 45 minutes later, when the sand was well heated, he scraped the fire aside, keeping a few sticks burning, and made a hollow in the hot sand. I began to get the idea, but wondered how he would stop the bread getting full of grit. But he sprinkled the bottom of the cavity, as well as the dough, thickly with flour. He put the dough in the hollow and covered it with hot sand. Almost immediately, grains of sand trickled down the sides of the mound as the bread began to rise. After about 20 minutes Mike put some of the fire back on top, allowed the bread to bake for a further 20 minutes, then pulled a perfect loaf out of the sand. We were delighted to eat fresh food again, and wolfed it down.

Ai-Ais

On the last day, we put our heads down and pressed ahead like horses making for home. Our goal was the spa Ai-Ais (Nama for "hot, hot"), at the mouth of the canyon. A scorching wind blew in our faces, dehydrating us and slowing us down. After a seemingly endless bend in the canyon, we reached the tantalizingly named "Almost There."

The first signs of civilization began to appear: a borehole in the riverbed, pipes running on concrete supports at the side of the path. We met a man wearing light canvas shoes and no pack—a day-hiker. Finally, we came across three children in bathing costumes, carrying towels. They told us that the resort was just round the corner, and in another moment there it was, with its palm trees, chalets and swimming-pool. We'd made it!

We headed straight for the terrace bar. After four days of squatting in the sand, it was sheer delight to sit in real chairs, with real backs. We met up with Michel, the bagpiper, and his two friends, and exchanged loud congratulations. After several celebratory iced beers we were ready for an even greater pleasure—the hot springs for which Ai-Ais is named. At the springs I lay back in the jacuzzi and relaxed among the warm bubbles. But best of all was the spa bath, where I manoeuvred myself into position under the heavy jets of hot water arching through the air, and let them massage my tired, aching muscles. For this I'd happily walk the canyon again—any time.

TRAVELLERS' TIPS

❏ Get the excellent map of the trail from the office at Hobas before setting out.

❏ For a fee, a Parks Board employee will drive you in your vehicle from Hobas to the start of the trail, and then take your vehicle to Ai-Ais to await you at the end.

❏ Ensure that your backpack weighs no more than 14–15kg (31–33lb).

❏ Always aim for the inside of each bend as you walk the canyon, otherwise you will find yourself walking much further than necessary.

❏ The river water in the canyon is perfectly safe to drink, despite often appearing milky or green.

❏ Don't leave litter. If you can't burn it to ashes, carry it out with you.

❏ Wear a small waist-bag to carry snacks, your camera and a handkerchief. It'll save you heaving your backpack on and off all the time.

GOING IT ALONE

INTERNAL TRAVEL

The nearest point to the start of the Fish River trail, the campsite at Hobas, can be easily (though not very quickly) reached by car from Cape Town, Johannesburg or Windhoek. You drive on tar all the way, except for the last 100km (60 miles) or so of gravel road at the end. An ordinary saloon car is perfectly adequate. The only other ways to reach the canyon are by light airplane or bus; to book, contact a local travel agent.

WHEN TO GO

Due to the intense heat and the possibility of floods in summer, the trail is open only in the winter months, from 15 April to 15 September. Winter temperatures are unpredictable, and can rise to as high as 40°C (104°F) in the middle of the day, but drop down to near freezing at night. The best times to go are April–May and August–September, when the weather is more likely to be mild.

OFF ON YOUR OWN

You will need to get some friends to join you, as groups of fewer than three are not allowed on the trail for safety reasons. At least one of you should be an experienced hiker. Otherwise, you are strongly advised to join an organized group, led by Siggi Öhler of Fish River Canyon Hiking Tours (see Contacts)—the only tour operator, to my knowledge, who takes groups the full length of the trail. If you only want to visit the canyon and have a look, there are many tour operators that take groups to the viewsites on the canyon.

We walked the trail in four days, but I would recommend doing it at a more leisurely pace, over five. Take the descent and the first and second days' walking slowly; you will be able to make much better time on the last two days, when the canyon widens out and there are clearer paths.

ACCOMMODATION

Before walking the trail, hikers can stay overnight either at Hobas or Ai-Ais. Hobas is a campsite only, so you will need to sleep in your vehicle, or bring a tent with you. If you stay at Ai-Ais you will have to drive 100km (60 miles) in the morning to get to the start of the trail. Ai-Ais has a variety of accommodation, ranging from campsites to simple rooms with shared facilities, or even luxury flats. If possible plan to stay a few days at Ai-Ais at the end of the trail to enjoy the hot springs.

Bookings for the trail and for accommodation at Hobas and Ai-Ais can be made only through the Namibia Wildlife Resorts Central Reservations Office (see Contacts). As the trail is very popular, you should book as far in advance as possible. (No booking is necessary if you merely want to view the canyon without staying overnight.)

DRIVING IN NAMIBIA

Traffic in Namibia drives on the left. Be very careful when driving on gravel roads not to go above 60–80km (35–50 miles) per hour. Watch out particularly for loose sand on the sides of the road and on corners. If your vehicle starts to slide in the sand, resist the temptation to overcorrect or brake suddenly.

HEALTH MATTERS

Because the trail is a hot and strenuous one, you will be required to present a medical certificate to the control point at Hobas before starting. The necessary form will be sent to you when you make your booking. It covers basic indicators such as blood pressure, heart rate and medical history, and must be completed by a doctor no more than 40 days before you walk.

OTHER THINGS TO DO IN THE AREA

If you are still bursting with energy after your hike, there are a number of adventures readily available in southern Namibia. Visit the Namib Naukluft Park, try ballooning at Sossusvlei, canoeing down the Orange River, or hiking in the Richtersveld (see p. 157–9, 208–12 and Activities).

WHAT TO TAKE

❑ Hat and sunscreen.
❑ Comfortable backpack.
❑ Small pack to wear round your waist to hold items you need to have readily accessible.
❑ Strong, worn-in boots.
❑ A 2-litre (3.5-pint) water bottle.
❑ Warm clothing—nights can be very cold.
❑ Remedies against blisters and plenty of plasters.
❑ A pair of light rubber beach sandals, to use when crossing the river.

Chobe · Kasane · Okavango Delta ⑲ · ⑰ Maun · Nata · Boteti · Makgadikgadi Pans · ⑱ · Francistown · Orapa · Ghanzi · Selebi Phikwe · Serowe · Palapye · *Kalahari Desert* · Limpopo · Letlhakeng · **Gaborone** · Jwaneng · Lobatse

| 0 | 200 | 400 km |
| 0 | 100 | 200 m |

BOTSWANA

Botswana is a desert country in the very heart of southern Africa. As far as humans are concerned, this is an empty land, with a population of just 1.5 million in an area of 600,000sq. km (231,660sq. miles)—about 250,000 of whom live in Gaborone and Francistown. The Okavango Delta, the world's largest delta, runs into the desert in the north, creating an oasis of waterways and seasonally flooded meadows. The strange and spectral landscape of the Makgadikgadi salt pans runs along the northern edge of the Kalahari Desert, which occupies much of the country. Seventeen percent of Botswana is protected wildlife area, and the government follows an active policy of encouraging ecotourism, rather than independent mass tourism. This means that many adventures, such as exploring the Makgadikgadi by quad-bike, are exclusive; but there are also opportunities for self-drive expeditions. However you choose to visit, you will discover a country of unforgettable landscapes and spectacular wildlife.

Sunset over a hippo pool in Little Vumbura

BOTSWANA

17 On Horseback in the Okavango Delta

by Guy Marks

The Okavango Delta is a unique environment of rivers and seasonal flood plains, woodlands and islands of vegetation. To get a perspective on the wildlife that lives here, and a broad outlook on the different habitats, I took a horseback safari as well as trips in a mokoro *(dugout canoe) and conventional game drives.*

The little eight-seated aircraft rattled down the runway at Maun at breakneck speed, its twin propellers whirring wildly. I'd been all night on a plane from London to Johannesburg and from there a two-hour flight had transferred me, minus my luggage, to Maun in Botswana. This is a frontier to the great open wilderness of the Okavango Delta and, like most visitors, I was in and out of the place without so much as venturing beyond the airport. We rose slowly off the ground and banked over the square shanties with tin roofs that dominate the landscape of this sprawling little town. As soon as we cleared the suburbs the earth was brown and dry and the dwellings below changed to round, mud huts with thatched roofs. I

felt a pang of excitement. The boredom of long-haul jet travel was over. This was Africa and my adventure had begun.

Signs of human habitation faded quickly and within 10 minutes the footpaths and occasional dirt roads had dwindled, until all that was left were the buffalo tracks cutting across the scrubland and seemingly dead sparse, dry woodland. Soon I saw the first sign of water: a meandering river, snaking into cul-de-sac pools. Where there is water there is life. I could make out several giraffes below and a lone elephant plodding purposefully across the land. Half a dozen elephants were paddling in the shallows of a pool, their ears flapping at the noise of our engines as we passed overhead. After 20 minutes we landed in a clearing, on a dirt runway deserted but for an empty Land Rover, which had been left for us.

KUJWANA BASE CAMP

P.J. and Barney Bestelink were my hosts at Okavango Horse Safaris over the next five days, for what would turn out to be some of the most exhilarating gameviewing I've ever done. P.J. had met five other guests and myself at Maun and accompanied us on the flight. We loaded up the Land Rover and P.J. took to the wheel aiming for his base camp, Kujwana.

Even on that first drive I knew I was in for something special as we crossed this most extraordinary landscape. One moment we were on dry land with our

---

5 Although there is no skill required for gameviewing from a vehicle or *mokoro* (dugout canoe), the horseback safari is strictly for people with riding experience. You need to be able to ride for six hours a day, post to the trot for stretches of 10 minutes, be confident cantering alongside herds of wild animals, and be able to gallop out of trouble should the need arise.

★★ The accommodation at the lodges and camps is excellent and very comfortable. The saddles are also very comfortable. Mosquitoes can be a pest during the wet season, and in the evenings. I found tsetse flies a constant nuisance at Little Vumbura.

Hard riding hats are not provided, so if you are safety-conscious you need to bring your own. Jodhpurs or riding breeches are essential, as are a good pair of riding boots or shoes.

The Okavango River fans out into an enormous delta as it flows southeast into Botswana

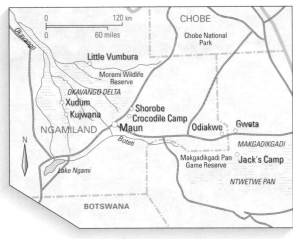

wheels spinning through patches of soft sand, which looked as though they had never seen a drop of water; the next, we were ploughing through the flood plains, with mud up to the wheel hubs and water lapping through the doors into the foot wells. In P.J.'s hands the Land Rover never faltered. He could handle a vehicle or a horse through any terrain, and still had the presence of mind to spot distant wildlife, call out the names of the birds as they flew past, and stop to admire some elephants shading amongst the trees.

After a leisurely hour of driving and game-viewing, we pulled in to Kujwana to be greeted by Barney and the staff, and welcomed to our home for the next few days. This was a luxury camp in true safari style. At one side, a path wound through the trees to individual large walk-in tents. Each had a wash stand at the entrance, and comfortable twin beds inside, with en-suite bucket showers and nearby long-drop toilets. The camp centred around a large dining tent and a circle of chairs around a campfire, right on the edge of a river that stretched away into the water meadows.

SETTLING IN

After a late lunch it was time to get acquainted with the horses and make a start on our riding safari. Before we took to the saddles, though, Barney briefed us on everything from care and proper use of the tack to the light-hearted penalty of a round of drinks, imposed for minor misdemeanours (like losing your hat on the ride, or being more than half an hour late for the morning mount-up). The etiquette of riding with others included important issues such as keeping your position in the group, so that the horses did not compete with each other, and being careful not to give the horses cause or opportunity to kick each other.

The instruction on riding amongst game was new to everybody. The horses needed to be part of the landscape to be accepted, so letting them graze would help them blend in. The downside was that they would also be seen as part of the

FLOODING THE DELTA

Water levels in the Okavango Delta are dependent on rains that fall in Angola, rather than on local rain. Strangely, this means that the highest water levels are during the local dry season. The water surges in from the northwest in March or early April and spreads out gradually. This brings the highest water levels to the Inner Delta during June and to the extremes of the Eastern Delta through July, after which the floods start to recede. By the middle of the rainy season, which starts in late October and continues through March, the plains are dry, the rivers low, and the water channels become inaccessible by boat.

food chain, and Barney frightened us with tales of recent incidents, when lions had jumped out of the bushes. Strategies for such eventualities were carefully planned, and the proper course of action was thoroughly drummed into us.

That done, we headed for our mounts. The team had gone to great lengths to establish everyone's riding experience and physical size before our arrival. That way, they made sure that people and horses were suitably matched.

LEARNING THE ROPES

I was the least experienced rider of the group, and Barney had chosen a steady and reliable horse for me, called Tsabong—a liver chestnut South African Boeoperd. At 15 hands, Tsabong was one of the smallest at the stables, but he could move as fast as any of them and was extremely well schooled.

Under P.J.'s and Barney's watchful gaze and guidance, we headed out of camp into the bush. At first even the most simple of things had to be pointed out to us. We had to learn the terrain, to avoid bushes with long, needle-like thorns, and to beware of burrows and holes in the ground left by springhares.

The ground was constantly changing. One moment we were trotting along dusty paths on the islands and through patches of sand, the next we were wading into the marsh-like water meadows. Large areas of the flood plains were only 20cm (8in) deep, but in the midst of most of them there was a deeper channel. Here,

Above right: *Wading through deep water to cross a water meadow—the art is to keep your feet dry!*
Right: *A tranquil mokoro ride is the perfect way to enjoy the wildlife and scenery*

the water was about a metre (3ft) deep, and I quickly learnt to pull up my legs as the water rose past the stirrups and occasionally up to the saddle.

PLAYING THE GAME

This introductory ride was little more than an hour and a half, which would later seem short compared with those to come, but, even so, there was time for some fine game-viewing. We had our first sightings of tsessebe, a common antelope in these parts, got a glimpse of some reedbucks, and saw plenty of red lechwe, members of the antelope family that exist in large numbers in these wetlands.

The most exciting moment, though, was when we came close to a small breeding group of elephants. A cow, with her three-year-old calf, was being followed closely by two bull elephants just coming into must. Luckily their interests were concentrated on the female rather than us. P.J. led the field, keeping himself between the elephants and his inexperienced new guests. The closer we got, the faster and louder my heart pounded. I became oblivious to the fact that I was riding, but Tsabong seemed to sense where I wanted to go and what I wanted him to do. Most of the group held back, but I stayed ahead with P.J., getting closer by the moment, until the elephants turned and gave us a warning glance. It was a warning not to be ignored: we slowly retreated and left the elephants to their privacy.

We rode back into camp in the early evening. The air was warm and dusty, and filled with the sweet scent of blossom from the flowering knob-thorn trees around the camp. I was less than 24 hours out of London, but it seemed a whole world away.

RIDING OUT AT DAWN

The next morning started as every morning would start for the next five days—with a 5.30 call from Tirelo, one of the camp staff, as he brought hot water to the wash stand and a thermos for morning tea. By 6am we were gathered around the campfire sipping coffee and picking at a very early buffet breakfast, before mounting up at 6.30am. It gets hot here in the middle of the day and the game takes to hiding in the shade. We, too, made the most of the cool mornings, riding out of camp just at sunrise. It was a wonderful time of day: cold at first, but quickly warming up. We passed a lone bull elephant breakfasting on a bush, and heard the roar of lions as they called to each other in the distance.

As I built up my confidence in these unfamiliar surroundings, the rides and the game-viewing got better and better. We rode far closer to the tsessebe than we had on that first ride—but when they took off, they really moved. They are reputedly the fastest of the antelopes, reaching speeds of 70kph (43mph). The kudu were not as fast, but they had a tendency to be quite nervous, flighty animals. We were lucky, that morning, to come across a small group of them that didn't immediately bolt. We let our horses graze, and the kudu just stood there and watched us.

In another spot, eight or 10 giraffes emerged from the trees to see who it was passing them by. As is often the case, they had some zebras grazing amongst them, and although the markings may have been a little different, our horses' shape seemed similar enough to satisfy their curiosity without causing them to panic.

A WAY OF LIFE

Other than Lynn and Suzanne, two American women travelling together, the

ON THE MENU

The food both at Okavango Horse Safaris and at Little Vumbura is of an extremely high quality. Both serve international cuisine, often including local favourites.

Lunches are usually cold dishes, such as a selection of quiches, cold meats and salamis, and fresh salads. There are very good French-style cheeses, and excellent camp-baked bread at both places.

The evening meal is always in three courses. The starter might be hot mushrooms on lettuce, or sautéed chicken livers. The main course is substantial—a chicken casserole, curry or beef stew with fresh vegetables like gem squash, potatoes and green beans. Desserts are dishes such as banana pudding—bananas baked in brandy and sugar—or fresh fruit salad.

rest of us had never met each other before. Within a day, though, the common interest of riding had pulled us together and the whole horseback safari experience was fast becoming a way of life. The six-hour-long morning rides, covering some 25–30km (15–18 miles), were suitably broken up with periods of rest. We would have a short snack break under the shade of a tree, or a bush brunch set on a bank by a hippo pool, where crocodiles lurked in the shallows. Lunch was usually back at camp, followed by an afternoon siesta before an early evening activity. On the fourth day we had an all-day ride, moving on that evening to Moklowane, P.J. and Barney's second camp, about a 40km (25-mile) ride away.

AFTERNOON ACTIVITIES

Usually, our afternoons were filled with different activities. After a long siesta, tea and cake were served at 4pm, followed by *mokoro* (dugout canoe) rides or game-drives. Tirelo, who brought our water in the mornings and our hot showers at lunchtimes, was also a guide. He seemed to love poling us through the shallow waters in his *mokoro* and pointing out every bird, tree and plant. There were vibrantly coloured species such as the lilac-breasted roller, and birds that made distinctive sounds, like the grey lourie, whose call gives it the name "go-away bird." We came close to an elephant paddling in the shallows and another taking shade under a leafy jackal berry tree. There were little African jacanas, like long-legged moorhens, skipping over the surface of the water on nothing more than a lily pad. And there were splashes of colour in the water: the glorious pink flowers of a herb called the vlei ink flower.

The game drives in the Land Rover were led by Person, the operations manager for the camp. He sought out tracks that were almost impossible to see beneath the water, while P.J. pointed out the larger game: antelopes, giraffes, wildebeest, elephants and zebras. As the light faded we stopped for a drink, watching the setting sun with a gin and tonic in our hands. Once the darkness had settled over us, the game-viewing continued, with the aid of a spotlight. There was a whole different world out there at night: the springhares, with their characteristic bounce, like little kangaroos; the hyenas,

out on the prowl. When the light caught a large herd of standing wildebeest, their mirrored eyes lit up like the lights of a distant city.

RIDING WITH BARNEY

Only on our introductory ride did we have the pleasure of riding with both P.J. and Barney. They had more than one group to look after, and split the work between them. So we rode with one or other of them, always accompanied by one of the grooms, so that we had a rear guard. For most of the trip I was led by P.J., but one morning Julia and I split off from our group and joined Barney, who was leading a team of vets on holiday. Tsabong was having a break: that day, my mount was Quito. He moved so smoothly it was like sitting in a big armchair!

Barney seemed to have been around horses most of her life; it was she who had introduced P.J. to riding. She had been racing since she was a child and, during her upbringing in Bahrain, she rode as a jockey for the Emir, winning several bareback races. In return the Emir had given her the best racehorse in his stable.

ELEPHANT–WATCHING

The most memorable game-watching was on my one and only afternoon ride. P.J. was leading and he spotted a breeding herd of elephants on an island, feeding under some moklowane palms. There

---

RESERVES AND CONCESSIONS

At full flood, the Okavango Delta occupies an area of about 15,500sq. km (6,000sq. miles) in a dry year and up to 22,000sq. km (8,500sq. miles) in a wet year, making it the biggest inland delta in the world. Only the central part of the delta is actually designated as the Moremi Wildlife Reserve, which covers about 3,000sq. km (1,160sq. miles). The vast majority of the area outside the reserve is, however, also protected. Operators have to submit proposals to gain or renew a concession and tight control is maintained. The full impact on the environment and local people is considered. All the areas I visited were outside the Moremi Reserve. Little Vumbura is on a community concession; Okavango Horse Safaris operate on two neighbouring government concessions; Kujwana is on a 1,000sq. km (386sq. mile) concession on the Xudum river system, and Moklowane is on the 1,500sq. km (579sq. mile) Matsibi River concession.

BOTSWANA

must have been about 40 of them, of all different ages. Among the bulls, one particularly big specimen wandered through the herd with a stately stride. The females were clearly the bosses, feeding, keeping a lookout and protecting the young, some of which were still suckling. The youngest calf was only about a year old, and hadn't quite come to terms with coordinating the movement of his trunk. It flopped about uncontrollably, as though it didn't really belong to him.

We got closer and closer on the horses. P.J. was keeping a watchful eye on all the adults—the matriarch and the big bull in particular. He could read them like a book, letting us get closer when we could, and stopping us in our tracks when need be. Most of the time the animals ignored us, but occasionally they would look up and we would retreat a short distance. Once they were comfortable again we'd move forwards, and so the stand-off would continue. We were far closer to this vast herd than we had been to the four elephants that had excited me so much on the introductory ride. This time, there was a whole host of activity to watch. The interaction between the herd members and their surroundings was fascinating, and we had a very privileged view. It was like eavesdropping on a private moment

in the elephants' lives. If we had misread the situation, though, the elephants would have had no hesitation in cutting our own lives short.

KEEPING OUT OF HARM'S WAY

It was P.J.'s ability to read the wildlife that made the trip so interesting, while, at the same time, maintaining our safety. One morning we were only a short way into our ride when he made a brief and clear announcement: "OK: we have a lioness on our left. Follow Sarah." Sarah was an Englishwoman working with P.J. and Barney and, on this occasion, was with us as the second staff member. She walked slowly and calmly away, bidding us follow. P.J. had instantly drawn a bear-banger from his belt. This is a loud explosive, held in a pen-like trigger, developed to scare bears in Canada, but equally effective for lions in Africa. He also had a rifle. Knowing that if a lion was going to attack it would attack a lone animal that had broken away from the herd, P.J. held

Above: *Taking a break from riding*
Right: *Cantering alongside a herd of giraffes and zebras*
Above right: *Resting lion spotted on a game drive from Little Vumbura*

back, setting himself up as a decoy for our protection. The lioness was only about 20m (65ft) away. Luckily, she moved away when P.J. spoke. But if she had attacked, his careful plan and selfless attitude would have ensured our safety. If we'd run, things could have turned out very differently. Running game is a lion's breakfast.

RUNNING WITH THE GAME

P.J. also showed his cunning when it came to tracking the herds of plains animals. He would canter near the edge of an island, knowing that the noise of our horses would bring out any giraffes, which are inquisitive animals. At one point he managed to rustle up a herd of 20, and gave us the experience of cantering with the herd. He carefully led us at an angle, rather nonchalantly, towards the back of the herd as it came out of the trees and into the water meadow. Then he turned, so that we were heading straight for them, and brought our horses rapidly to a canter. By the time the

giraffes had responded we were up alongside them. The water splashed and huge, long, graceful legs stretched out next to us. The herd was on the move and we were a part of it.

Running with the herd, whether of giraffes, zebras, wildebeest or red lechwe, was unbelievable. I could feel the adrenalin pumping through my horse, just as it was pumping through me. I could also feel the nervous tension of the

game animals as they ran for their lives. They knew, or at least they assumed, that if our horses were running there must be something to run from, and that was enough for them. For me, it was the thrill of a lifetime.

A CHANGE OF SCENE

I was sad when my time with P.J. and Barney came to an end, but it was not yet time to leave the Okavango. My trip would not have been complete without a visit to one of the more conventional camps. Many visitors split their time in the delta between different camps, as each has a slightly different environment. The only way to travel between camps is by light aircraft: these operate almost like air taxis. My flight put down at two other camps on the way north from Xudum to Vumbura.

I stayed at Little Vumbura, which is a beautiful little luxury camp on a community concession, on the northern side of the delta. Set on an island surrounded by papyrus-fringed waterways and flood plains, it's nevertheless close enough to large areas of dry land to make for some exciting game drives. The lifestyle here was far more relaxed than the very active life on horseback, and required almost no effort at all. Mornings did start early, but the tent was more like a chalet with canvas walls. There was running water and the en-suite facilities included a modern shower cubicle, flushing toilets and tiled floors. There was even a plunge pool, lounge area, terrace and secluded gazebo, where you could spend your free time between gourmet meals and the morning and evening activities.

COMPLETING THE EXPERIENCE

One of the most tranquil ways to start the day was out on the *mekoro* (plural of *mokoro*), gently poling through the reed beds, papyrus and shallow meadows. The rides were combined with informative walks on the islands, giving me a chance to learn about some of the magnificent trees and their uses, as well as the reeds and water-lilies, frogs and even water snakes.

The game-viewing here was very different from the horseback safari, but equally rewarding, with moments of intense excitement. On the first evening I went with Kit, one of the guides, on a powerboat safari, which brought me too close for comfort to a hippo lurking in the deep channel. He launched himself out of the water just centimetres from the boat, almost tipping us over.

The biggest difference was the game-viewing from the Land Rover. The herds included the elegant sable antelope, which I hadn't seen in the south, and a vast gathering of buffalo; but the major change was the chance of seeing lions and trying to find them on a kill. Here the lion was our prize, and under the expert guidance of a man called Doctor, we saw several, both by day and by night. From the back of a horse they were the stuff of nightmares; from the safety of a Land Rover, they were the final ingredient of an African adventure.

TRAVELLERS' TIPS

❏ The best game-viewing is to be enjoyed in the early mornings and the evenings. Even if you are enjoying the luxury of the safari lodges, it is worth getting out of bed for those early mornings.

❏ If you have a choice of two different makes of fibreglass *mokoro*, the slightly wider ones are more stable.

❏ Whether on horseback or on foot, never run from a lion. It will be faster than you.

❏ Talk to the local guides and camp staff—they have a vast knowledge and are eager to share all aspects of local culture, not just the information about flora and fauna.

GOING IT ALONE

WHEN TO GO

The Okavango Delta is best when the water is high, during the dry season, although it can be visited at any time of year. It gets extremely hot during the rainy summer months from November to March. During the winter months of June to September, the days are dry and pleasantly warm, the water is high and the game-viewing is at its best. The horse safari season is from March to November.

GETTING INTO THE DELTA

Most people pre-book their safaris before arriving in Botswana. The tour companies will meet you at the airport and usually include the air transfers to the camps in their prices. Okavango Horse Safaris never have any walk-in trade, and it would be unusual for someone to head for Little Vumbura without a booking, especially as the camp only caters for a total of eight guests. There is no public transport to get you out to the camps and most are fairly inaccessible by land, except those in the Moremi Wildlife Reserve. The reserve has two

entrance gates: the north gate is known as Khwai entrance, and the south gate as Makwee entrance. If, however, you find yourself in Maun and want to get out to the delta, it should be possible to find a place at one of them, as all the camps are in radio contact with the tour operators in town, and flights can be easily chartered.

PLANNING

If you are not a regular rider it is important to plan your horse safari well in advance. This will give you some time to brush up on your riding skills at home, in relative safety and comfort. It is essential that you are competent enough to ride for long periods and to ride out of trouble should the need arise. A few riding lessons and some regular exercise might be a good idea if you haven't ridden for some time.

HEALTH MATTERS

The Okavango Delta is often thought of as a high risk malaria area, but this is somewhat dependent on the season. There is very little risk during the dry season. The first cases are usually reported just after the beginning of the rains in late October/early

November, building up to a high risk period in February. The camps use pyrethroid-based insecticides on large surface areas such as tents, which provides very good control of the malaria-carrying mosquitoes. You should use insect repellents and seek advice on malaria prophylactics.

Water at the camps is drawn from the delta and always boiled before being used as drinking water. The camps exercise high standards of hygiene and there is no undue risk to your health.

On the long rides you may not feel hot because of the constant movement and the occasional splashing with water, but it is easy to get too much sun. You should use sunblock as a matter of course.

WHAT TO TAKE

- ❏ Proper riding gear: jodhpurs or riding breeches and riding boots or riding shoes and chaps.
- ❏ A hard riding hat, or a hat that will keep the sun from your head.
- ❏ Long-sleeved shirts to protect yourself from the sun and from insect bites.
- ❏ It can get cool in the evenings, especially after dark on night game drives, so a fleece or warm jacket is worthwhile.
- ❏ Game-viewing will be greatly improved if you take binoculars.
- ❏ A camera is essential, but anything too big or bulky can be extremely difficult to carry on a horse unless you invest in specialist holster-style equipment bags.

ELEPHANT SAFARIS

If horses don't appeal, try an elephant safari. These are run from Abu Camp on the western side of the delta, in a similar area to the horseback safaris. Abu Camp is one of the most luxurious camps in the delta and the elephant-back safaris have a reputation as the ultimate safari experience. No riding skill is necessary, as experienced mahouts control the elephants for you. All you have to do is sit on a platform on the animal's back and enjoy the experience.

18 Exploring the Surreal Makgadikgadi Pans

by Guy Marks

The Makgadikgadi area in the Kalahari Desert has an almost surreal landscape. The glaring, white salt pans and barren savannahs hold the remains of Stone-Age habitation and fossils of prehistoric megafauna, and are still home to some very special wildlife. I explored the pans by quad-bike, and tracked the wildlife on foot.

My base for exploring deep into the Makgadikgadi was right at the edge of Ntwetwe Pan. Jack's Camp is set amongst a bank of palm trees and acacias, overlooking dry grassland. The temperature soared to 40°C (98°F) the day I arrived, and the place had the air of a true desert environment. It was hard to believe that, in the rainy season, the entire area would be flooded and the bank would be an island.

Jack's is a stylish place recreating the African experience of the 1920s. At the entrance to each walk-in tent is a verandah, freshly oiled to remove the dust. Mine was furnished with two safari chairs, a washstand and large jug of water. Inside, every piece of furniture is in the 1920s style: a large chest made of dark wood, a butler's tray, a dressing table and mirror, canvas shelves stretched over a wooden frame, and an iron bedstead with a deep, comfortable mattress. The centre of the camp was a large mess tent. Here I found a library of leather-bound books and a display cabinet of the most precious local finds. Outside the mess tent there was a umbrella acacia tree, with a long table laid out in its shade. This is where I would eat for the next few days—except, of course, for afternoon tea.

The quad-bikes are easy to ride. They are fun and exciting, and you don't need any previous experience. The recognition of stone tools and fossils can be quickly learnt, but any previous field experience of archaeology, palaeontology, or geology would add to the enjoyment. The game-tracking is not arduous, but footprints can be extremely difficult to spot even for a skilled tracker.

★★ Jack's Camp is a luxury lodge and is comfortable in all respects. Out on the pans it is very hot and dusty. There is extreme glare from the white salty surface and you could suffer from windburn and over-exposure to the sun if you do not cover up properly.

You need a good pair of walking boots for excursions onto the pans. Binoculars are a great benefit for viewing birds and rare wildlife.

TEA AND ATTENTIVENESS

Tea at Jack's was an event in itself, continuing the themes of colonialism, Anglo-Africa and a touch of Arabia. It was served in its own dedicated tent, an open-sided pagoda with rugs and cushions on the floor. At 4pm each day we sipped iced or hot black tea and ate freshly baked cakes. All but one of the guides were botany, zoology or geology graduates who had studied in Britain, and had clipped English accents. They were formally polite and attentive to the point of subservience as they cut the cake and passed the tea.

It was a vast change from Maun, where I had spent the 24 hours before flying in to the Makgadikgadi. Maun is a transit point with very few facilities and I ended up staying at a lodge called Crocodile Camp, some 22km (14 miles) out of town. With no transport of my own and no public transport available this was

Right: Ancient stone tools found on the salt pans
Below: Out on the salt pans at sunset, with nothing but emptiness in all directions

one place where a little attentiveness to clients' needs would not have gone amiss.

At Jack's, though, nothing was too much trouble. On arrival each guest was assigned a guide for the duration of the stay. The personalized itinerary of activities was mapped out between guest and guide, according to their interests. Chris Brooks, a Kenyan-born zoology graduate, was the head guide, and was given the dubious pleasure of my company.

ONTO THE PANS

As soon as tea was over, I joined other guests for my first activity: an excursion by quad-bike onto the pans. Several of us had never driven a quad-bike before, but they were simple to operate, with clutchless foot-controlled gears, and a foot throttle. They were a bit like lawnmowers in their temperament, sometimes starting on the electronic button and sometimes needing to be jerked into action with a hand-pulled recoil cord. Once they were running and warmed up, though, they were very reliable. We were given a quick lesson on wrapping our heads in cloth like Bedouin camel-herders, to protect us from the dust that the bikes would churn up, and then we headed off for the pans.

The bikes were great fun—like big toys that appealed to the child in all of us as we bounced along the tracks. The high-revving engines whined like karts, and the wind caught the clouds of dust and covered us from head to toe. Even with all

the cloth around my face, the dust was getting in and I could feel the salt drawing tears from my eyes.

Within moments we left the edge of the grassland and found ourselves on a wide-open plain of white. The surface of the pan was a salty crust, made up of the remains of algae which had dried to a crisp. As the crust dried, it had cracked and split into an amazing honeycomb pattern.

THE SOUND OF SILENCE

We stopped the bikes way out on the pan just before sunset. Super and Chris handed out drinks and we watched as the sun set over miles and miles of open nothingness. The sky darkened and gradually the stars came out. Chris sent us all off on foot in different directions to take in the atmosphere. We followed his instructions and walked off into the night. I chose a spot and lay down. This was a very strange place: the silence was deafening, and the mind could begin to play tricks.

The temperature dropped the minute the sun had left the sky, and after half an hour or so it was quite cold. I was relieved when we got back on the bikes and headed towards the warmth of the camp. But the night was not over, as the staff from Jack's still had a surprise in store for us. The night and the emptiness of this featureless landscape were disorientating, and we took the approaching lights to be the camp. When we drew up to them,

GEOLOGICAL HISTORY

Makgadikgadi is a vast area of salt pans in central Botswana at the northern end of the Kalahari Desert. The two largest pans are Ntwetwe Pan, at 6,500sq. km (2,509sq. miles) and Sua Pan, at 5,500sq. km (2,123sq. miles). The surrounding area is dry savannah, scattered with dozens of other smaller pans. Collectively, the Makgadikgadi Pans make up an area of about 30,000sq. km (11,583sq.

miles). The pans are the remnants of what was once the largest lake in Africa. Between 7 million and 1.5 million years ago this lake covered an area of about 200,000sq. km (77,220sq. miles). Between 1.5 million and 60,000 years ago it was a lush area of swamp and water meadow, similar to the Okavango delta. The lake finally dried out to this salty crust about 10,000 years ago. The reason is unknown, but it could have been the result of the rivers that fed the lake changing course.

though, we were still miles from home, out in the middle of nowhere. They had built a campfire for us and brought out chairs and a bar. It was a wonderful way to end the day—sitting in the desert around a fire, chatting with new acquaintances, warming our hands and sipping hot glasses of freshly mulled wine.

PICKING UP STONES

The night temperature plummeted, and it was still quite cold in the early morning when we explored the pans once more by quad-bike. This time our objective was to uncover some of their secrets. Chris took us to one of his favourite spots,where there were stone tools—the discarded fragments of ancient human habitation. He told us to walk and see what we could find, looking out for anything that might be relevant. To my astonishment, I found a piece of jet-black rock that had clearly been shaped into a pointed tool. I walked a little further, and there was another. In fact every few minutes I found myself bending down to pick up pieces of rock that had obviously been fashioned by people.

In no more than 10 minutes, we regrouped and showed off our finds. Between five or six of us, we had gathered some 30 stone tools. Chris laid them out and explained their different uses. They broadly fell into three main types: points, scrapers and slices. The points would have been used for rough cutting, digging and hewing; the scrapers were for scraping animal hides, and the slices were a much finer tool with a sharp edge for fine cutting and slicing. We also came across core stones—the blocks from which the tools had originally been cut. It was incredible to think that these stone tools, maybe 50–80,000 years old, were just lying around in vast quantities on the surface of the Makgadikgadi. Somewhere out on the pans there must be human remains, too, but nobody has ever had the time, the inclination or the funding to look. As a scientist, Chris knew the value of our finds, and he was passionate in

ON THE MENU

Food at Jack's is superb, prepared by head chef Benson. He uses local meats in his international cuisine. A typical day's menu during my stay was: lunch—Moroccan chicken pies with cinnamon and ginger, tabbouleh salad and sesame pitta breads; tea—lemon poppyseed cake and muffins; snacks—choux pastry beignets with sunflower seeds, basil and parmesan; dinner—cauliflower soup, home-made brown bread, ostrich piccata with potato galette and garlic and lemon green beans, followed by butternut flan with orange brandy sauce. Wines, beers and soft drinks were served throughout.

explaining the anthropology to us, and how it fitted in with the geology of the area. He also made very sure that every item we had found was carefully replaced.

LIFE AT JACK'S

Back at camp, the lifestyle was taking on a familiar pattern. After the early morning activities, we would return to the camp for a lunch that was fit for the most discerning gourmet. We sat under the shade of the acacia tree talking about the morning's events or swapping travel stories. A flock of hornbills had taken to joining us at mealtimes, and they lined up along the tree, waiting for an opportunity to swoop down and steal the butter or any other unguarded morsel. A francolin with her brood of chicks pecked around in the dust for birdseed that the staff had scattered. As the heat of the day reached its zenith, it was time for a siesta. We all returned to the comfort and shade of our tents, to read, write diaries or to take a nap. At around 3–3.30pm there would be a call outside the tent. The camp staff had brought hot water to the shower. Each

tent had its own private, fenced enclosure just outside. The shower was a canvas bag, hoisted on a pulley. Water trickled lightly from the showerhead, but there was plenty to wash off the dust and revive body and spirit in time for tea and the round of evening activities.

A BROWN HYENAS' DEN

One of the most enthralling evening activities was the chance to observe brown hyenas. The staff had located a den by complete chance and, by careful management, had made it possible to observe the cubs without disturbing their natural lives. In the early evening we parked the safari vehicle at a vantage point and waited. With binoculars Nick, another guide, spotted two cubs in the distance. We watched as they slowly made their way back to the den, walking right past

our vehicle. They were more like dogs than hyenas, with big, pointed ears and shaggy manes. I could just make out a subtle stripe in their body colour, which became quite distinct on the legs. In the evening light the last glimmers of sun caught their coats and shone in shades of copper and deep chocolate brown, and their neck ruffs stood out in a lighter tinge of cream. They were such pretty animals that the name "hyena" didn't seem to fit. In fact, their lifestyle is so unlike that of other hyenas that some have even suggested giving them a more exotic name, such as Makgadikgadi tiger, or Kalahari cutie.

The cubs had built up quite a collection of large bones that were too big for their immature jaws to crush. These and bird feathers from ostrich, kori bustards and black korhaans littered the ground

Above: *We had an excellent vantage point to watch the brown hyena cubs as they came out to play in the evening*
Left: *A baobab tree near Jack's camp*

The black-backed jackals were out in force, and we saw two different types of small antelope: the springbok and the steenbok. There were so many holes made by aardvarks that I had hoped to see one, but they are rarely seen, even by the guides. We did see a porcupine, though, which is a fairly rare sighting.

TRACKING HYENAS ON FOOT

During the day it was difficult to see much of the wildlife, but we could see where it had been, if you knew what to look for. There were two resident San Bushmen (see p. 208) at Jack's, confusingly both called Dabe. They enjoyed taking us on walks, explaining the traditions of their tribal lives, and interpreting the footprints left in the salt and dust.

I went with Chris and one of the Dabes to try to track down an adult hyena. Having seen the cubs the night before, I was keen to learn a little more about these elusive beasts. The cubs have a strange upbringing. The mother doesn't stay with them but goes off to lead a solitary life, like the other adults. There is, however, a loose social group which collectively cares for the young. About five adults were minding this den, not together, but clearly as part of a cooperative clan. At night one or more of the adults brought food to the cubs.

and made perfect playthings for the youngsters. We watched silently as one of the cubs gnawed on a bone, then chased feathers in the wind. After a while it was joined by the other two and, with a large feather still sticking out of the side of its mouth, it plodded off with them across the pans and disappeared into the night.

There was no chance of following them. Strict rules ensure that the animals are not unduly disturbed. But there were plenty of tracks that we could follow, and a night game drive revealed all kinds of hidden life. The desert was not as barren and uninhabited as it first appeared. Desert animals are predominantly nocturnal, avoiding the heat of day. Using a spotlight it was quite easy to find them, as their eyes shone back at us through the darkness. The place was alive with yellow mongooses, springhares, and cape hares.

BROWN HYENAS

Brown hyenas are a rare cousin of the more common spotted and striped hyenas. Their territory is confined to southwest Africa, mostly in Botswana but also in Namibia, and the borders of South Africa, Angola and western and southern Zimbabwe. The total world population is only about 5–8,000, around 3,000 of which are in the Kalahari. These nocturnal animals have an amazing ability to live with limited or no water supply. Their efficient digestive system can break down everything except hair, allowing them to derive nutrients from the driest and most varied carrion. There is still much to learn about their social behaviour and survival techniques. Research is being carried out at a den near Jack's Camp, which is the only habituated brown hyena den in the world.

Chris was sure that a big male lived somewhere near by, as he had seen him here before. We scoured the area and eventually Dabe said: "There," pointing at the sun-baked ground. It yielded no clues to me, but amongst the obscurity of irregular patterns Dabe could clearly see the recent footprints of a brown hyena. "He came this way last night," Dabe concluded, "and went over there, off towards the grass." For the next hour we tracked the footprints over the salt pan and islands of tufty brown grass. Dabe and Chris showed me where the front and back feet had been and the outline of the padded feet and toes. Occasionally there was enough dust for me to see the prints, but most of the time I had to take their word for it. Eventually, Chris found it increasingly hard to follow the spoor, and ultimately even Dabe lost the tracks.

DEEPER INTO NOWHERE

On my last full day in the Makgadikgadi Chris decided to take me even further into the pans. Once again we wrapped up well against the dust and headed off on the quad-bikes. After we'd been going for some time, Chris pulled us up. He knew there were some fossils somewhere around this spot—and, incredibly, he located them. He showed us the bones of megafauna, which had perhaps walked the earth 1.64 million years ago. The pan here had a strange surface, with small lumps of calcrete just breaking the surface, worn smooth into mottled lobes. It looked like the surface of a giant brain.

We travelled still further until we were about 50km (31 miles) from the camp. Our path was cut by one of Botswana's strangest features, a long, straight, high, wire fence, that stretched to the horizon in both directions. This was a veterinary cordon, erected to keep herds of wild game away from herds of domestic animals and stop the spread of animal diseases. It was hard to believe that anything could exist at all out here, let alone vast herds of wildlife. The only footprints in the pan were those of a lone aardwolf, who must have passed this way just at the end of the rainy season. Other than that, there were a few bones of animals that had fallen foul of the fence, and miles and miles of nothing.

ENDLESS ADVENTURE

The more I learned about the Makgadikgadi, the more I appreciated the knowledge and enthusiasm of my guides. Fundamentally, Jack's is a tourist facility providing three or four days of intense desert adventure; but I soon realized that it was also an adventure for the people who work and live there. These young scientists were inspired by this magnificent place and its unanswered questions. One by one, they were finishing their guiding contracts and starting scientific research projects. Each year, 20,000 zebras and 10,000 wildebeest pass through the Makgadikgadi, and Chris was about to start a five-year programme monitoring their annual migrations. Now that's what I call the spirit of adventure.

GOING IT ALONE

WHEN TO GO

Quad-biking can only be done in the winter season, when the delicate surface of the pans is firm and dry. This is from about April to the first rains, in late October. Jack's Camp is open all year round, except for January. During the rainy season the pans are host to large numbers of plains animals—the migration comes through from about December to March. Once the pans are flooded they become home to hundreds of thousands of flamingoes. Complete flooding may last for only a couple of weeks, or the water may linger for two to three months, so it is difficult to predict what the season will bring. Even in the wet season you can still get to the edge of the pans to look for stone tools. The Makgadikgadi has something to offer at any time of the year, but if you go specifically for the quad-biking experience, I would recommend September. At that time the ground is dry and the days are pleasant and not yet too hot.

GETTING TO JACK'S CAMP

A track leads down into Jack's Camp from Gweta on the main road from Maun, via Nata to Francistown. You will need to pre-book your accommodation at Jack's, and take a transfer from Gweta, or arrange to be guided in with your own vehicle. The vast majority of people who visit Jack's Camp fly in from Maun. This transfer is normally included as part of a package deal.

PLANNING

It would be easy to get into a four-wheel drive and head out to the Makgadikgadi, making your own roads if you couldn't find the tracks. No one would stop you, but you would be irresponsible to do so, as you could seriously damage the delicate ecosystem of this unique environment. Quad-bikes are designed to exert minimum ground pressure and therefore minimize the amount of damage done. Even so, they leave their mark, so responsible operators always stick to the same tracks. Unfortunately, there are operators here who also use quad-bikes, without making any attempt to stick to existing tracks. They encourage their clients to go racing around on the pan surface, causing unnecessary damage. The surface is a very thin crust and if you try to take a heavy vehicle across it, you will sink in mud. When planning your trip, try to establish what sort of environmental policy the operators have before committing to their services.

HEALTH MATTERS

The only potential risk to your health out on the Makgadikgadi is the effect of the extreme heat, wind and dry salty air. This means that you are at risk from dehydration, and must make a point of drinking plenty of liquid. Some people suffer from chapped lips, windburn and sunburn. These can be avoided with the use of sunblock creams and lip balms.

WHAT TO TAKE

❏ Take long-sleeved shirts to protect yourself from the sun and wind.
❏ Temperatures can be extreme here, changing dramatically through the day and night, so take several layers of clothing. A warm windproof jacket would be useful for quad-bike rides and evening game drives.
❏ Game-viewing will be greatly improved if you take binoculars.
❏ A camera is essential. A wide angle or even fish-eye lens will help you capture the enormity of this wide-open space.

LIFE AROUND THE MAKGADIKGADI

The fossilized bones that can easily be found in the Makgadikgadi date from the Pleistocene era—between 1.64 million and 10,000 years ago. These include giant hippo, giant sable, giant buffalo and giant wildebeest. The sites at which stone tools are found give a record of the shrinking lake, as the habitation sites would have been close to the water's edge. Although most around Jack's Camp date from 50–80,000 years old, some are 200,000 years old. Further out on the pans, it is thought that some tools are up to 1.5 million years old, and there is still hope of some day finding early hominid remains.

19 Trans-Kalahari Safari

by Chris McIntyre

In the north of Botswana's Kalahari Desert lie Chobe National Park and the Moremi Game Reserve, which protects a swathe of the Okavango Delta. These huge, wild parks have some of Africa's best game and some of its worst roads. We hired a four-wheel drive to travel through the Kalahari sand at the heart of this wilderness.

Many people taking a safari to Botswana fly into camps and lodges, from where guides drive them around in search of the area's wildlife. Purba, a friend from London, and I decided to drive through Botswana at our own pace, to get a better feel for the whole area. Because of the lack of roads or communications, this had to be organized carefully, like a small expedition.

Our adventure started in Victoria Falls, in neighbouring Zimbabwe, early on a hot September morning. There we collected our shiny Land Rover and checked the long list of equipment: tools, two spare wheels, two different jacks, a shade awning, a roof tent and—best of all—a fridge. There were boxes of supplies, a gas cooker, a foldaway table and chairs, cutlery and tablecloths and even a satellite beacon for emergencies.

Food supplies are more easily available in Zimbabwe than in Botswana, so our first stop was Victoria Falls supermarket. An hour later, we emerged carrying cardboard boxes packed with enough bottles, tins, packets and fresh vegetables for five days, and a supply of cold drinks.

ON THE ROAD

The road to Botswana's border at Kazungula was wide and well surfaced, with a verge of low grasses. Beyond it was the thick, rolling bush. We had been given the paperwork to take us and the vehicle across the border, and were soon in Botswana. After diamonds, one of the Botswana's main exports is beef, so we weren't surprised to be stopped at a veterinary control post. The attendant disinfected our tyres and the soles of our shoes, before asking if we had any fresh meat, bones or animal skins. We assured him that we didn't—but he glanced in a few boxes anyway before waving us on. A few hundred metres beyond the control post, we turned towards Kasane. Soon the Chobe River glinted on our right, beyond a narrow strip of irrigated banana fields. Kasane is a small town, spread along one road, but it is an important centre for northern Botswana and has several small lodges and campsites. We picked up some local currency (Pula) and

This is not an ideal first trip to Africa, unless you are used to looking after yourself in wilderness areas. You'll need to navigate using common sense and a GPS, but almost no road signs. The tracks make driving difficult at times. If you are not used to this terrain, then expect to have to dig your vehicle out periodically. On the roads and in the campsites, you may come across dangerous game. You must treat all wild animals with great respect, and keep your cool to avoid problems developing.

The high quality of the vehicle's cooking and camping equipment means that, even when you camp, you're doing so in comfort. However, it would be quite possible to cover this whole route using safari lodges, which would be still more comfortable. The travelling and driving can be tiring, but never arduous. .

Binoculars are important, especially if you're keen on the wildlife, as is a camera. Otherwise most of your equipment is provided with the vehicle. It's vital that you hire a high-quality, properly equipped vehicle from a reputable company that can advise you on the area.

a few guidebooks to Botswana's flora and fauna, before topping up our diesel tank and setting off.

INTO CHOBE

After 5km (3 miles) the only tar road west from Kasane led to an imposing, thatched entry gate into Chobe National Park. Accommodation in Botswana's national parks has to be booked in advance; we had planned our trip from the U.K., booking the vehicle and a mixture of nights in lodges and camping. We showed the game scouts our reservations, paid the park fees and drove into the park. Immediately, the road changed to gravel, without markings. We slowed down to around 40kph (25mph), a safe speed for an area with big game, and started to look for animals.

The vegetation here was mostly stunted mopane trees—the most common tree in southern Africa. Seeing a movement behind the trees, we stopped. A large, male kudu antelope with huge spiral horns appeared, followed by two others. We switched the engine off for a few minutes to watch them. Around us was the white-noise hiss of cicadas.

Soon our gravel road had become a sand track, and we reached a T-junction. In front was the main park track; beyond it the blue expanse of the Chobe River. As is often the case in Botswana's parks, there were no signs, so we checked the map and turned left. The next 4km (2 miles) took us an hour. Late afternoon is prime time for animals to drink, and below us, to the right, lay the river. Every few minutes we stopped to look at something walking, flying or crawling, reaching for our binoculars or cameras from the back seats. A herd of zebras was followed by dozens of impala, a flock of helmeted guineafowl and some entertaining Chacma baboons. None paid much attention to the vehicle, running around us unconcernedly. On the Chobe's flood

plain, the binoculars showed hundreds of dots to be elephants, grazing like cows in a verdant meadow.

BOATS AT DAWN

We spent our first night at Chobe Game Lodge and were both in bed by 9pm. We had requested a small boat excursion at sunrise, so we met Ali, our boatman, by the river at 6am. Even in late September, the air was cool. We were glad that we'd brought our fleeces and delighted that there were no other guests to join us.

As we pushed off from the shore, the river was still. The sun rose and we stopped to watch a couple of fishermen bringing in their nets, balancing on a dugout canoe. Scanning with our binoculars, we picked out an African marsh harrier, which soon curved, silently and smoothly, to dip its talons into the mirror-like water and grasp a fish. Seconds later,

Right: On our fifth day we came across a large lion pride crunching their way through last night's kill, an elephant carcass

BOTSWANA

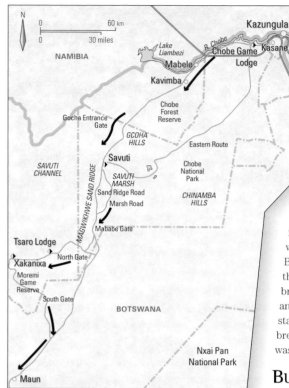

From Chobe Game Lodge into the Kalahari

stream past a bachelor herd of elephants, where the only sound was a low rumble and the rasping made as they pulled up huge tufts of vegetation. We came even nearer to a herd of buffaloes, floating beside the bank within metres of them. By then it was 9.30am: the sun was hot, the wind broke the river's surface, and other boats were starting to appear. The breakfast buffet called: it was time to return.

BUFFALO RIVER

Our next stop was Savuti, in the heart of Chobe, and there were two possible routes: the eastern, via the pans, or the western track following the riverfront. Since this was the dry season, we chose to take the western route following the Chobe River for its first 50km (32 miles), where the game was concentrated.

We set off around midday, which was later than ideal, being already hot and dusty. The track was little more than a series of linked sandpits in places, so we used low gears and momentum to carry us through. Occasional turnings from the road led off to game-viewing loops—tracks which circled around, beside the river or various waterholes, before leading back to the main track. We took one or two of these, but didn't have time for too many delays. We kept the river to our right, stopping occasionally to watch antelope and once, in a thickly wooded valley, a huge herd of buffaloes. At first we just watched them cross in front of the

as it pulled up, the fish dropped back—perhaps too slippery to hold. Swiftly, an opportunist fish eagle stooped to pick it up, and successfully carried the prize to its riverside perch.

In the distance elephants trumpeted, and we heard faint cries of people. "Namibians," explained Ali, who told us that elephants would often cross into the Namibian farmland at night to eat, fleeing back to the sanctuary of Botswana's national park when they were chased off at dawn. Conservation is often a balancing act. Continuing slowly, we stopped several times to take a closer look at an animal on the bank, or a bird flitting by. Pied kingfishers were a favourite, hovering above the water with static eyes, or flying low and fast just above its surface. Once we spotted a pair sitting on a reed, cut the engine and drifted to within an arm's length of them.

With the motor off, we floated down-

car. Ten minutes later they were still coming, so we crawled forward. Gradually
they parted, the closest animals eyeing us
suspiciously as we passed.

FOREST OF SAND

Emerging from the track at a junction
with a tarred road was a shock. This was
the boundary of Chobe National Park. We
filled in the register at the park's office,
and set off towards Savuti. Our next leg
cut through Chobe Forest Reserve, a populated area surrounded on two sides by
the national park. We passed through several small villages then forked right,
leaving the settlements behind.

The track deteriorated further, to two
parallel depressions in the deep sand, an
axle length apart. It seemed to roll on forever. Unlike the Namib and the Sahara,
the northern Kalahari is a fossil desert,
and receives more precipitation than the
250mm (10in) per year that many authorities use to define desert territory. The
gently rolling hillocks over which we were
driving were vegetated sand dunes,
lightly wooded with leadwood trees.

In nearly three hot, dusty hours we
saw only two other vehicles before reaching Chobe's Gcoha entrance gate. Purba
had learnt some Setswana greetings—
"*Dumela Rra*" to greet a man, and
"*Dumela Mma*" for a woman—prompting
smiles and waves from the staff as we left.

HYENAS BY MOONLIGHT

Back in the park the track improved and
with it our speed. We soon passed the
Gcoha Hills, covered with baobabs, and
an hour later we came upon a few parked
vehicles, their occupants watching elephants. This was Savuti, at last, and its
main waterhole. We stopped, too, savour-
ing a cold drink as the sun sank, but left
before the others to set up our first camp
in good light. It was almost dark as we lit
our fire, grateful for the wood that we had
thrown onto the roof-rack during the day.

Around us, several other campers'
fires twinkled, each a few hundred metres
away. As our eyes adjusted to the dark,
we saw shadowy animals skulking
around. Our strong torch beam picked
out malevolent green eyes, which
retreated when lit: Savuti's famous
spotted hyenas. These predators will
crunch anything they find—but fortunately, they are cautious, and wouldn't
approach us whilst we were awake.

LION AT DAWN

Dusk and dawn are the best times for
game-viewing, and next morning our
alarm buzzed before first light. We
grabbed mouthfuls of cereal and fruit
juice between packing up the vehicle and
tent. By dawn we had driven back to the
main waterhole and were watching four
bull elephants drink. Engine off, we
scanned the scene with our binoculars.
Squadrons of Namaqua doves and various
sandgrouse arrived in formation to drink.
Amidst all of this fluttering, two lionesses
appeared. They wanted to drink—but the
elephants didn't want their company. The
lionesses circled, trying to get to the
water, but each time one came close, an
elephant mock charged, shaking its head
and trumpeting. Frustrated, the lions sat
back to watch and wait. Eventually their
attention diverted to a line of impala that
was slowly plodding towards the water.
Both females now crouched, muscles
optimistically taut. We held our cameras
poised, motorwinds on. Watching predators hunt is electrifying. Then the shrill
alarm snort of an impala signalled the
herd's hasty retreat. The lionesses
relaxed, stood up and wandered away,
disgruntled. By now, we had been joined
by six other vehicles, so we took out our
map, switched on our GPS navigation aid,
and headed off to explore.

DRY MARSHES

We followed the map carefully as we
drove, trying not to rely totally on the
GPS. Savuti's sprinkling of *kopjies* (small,
rocky hills) made excellent landmarks
when map-reading, and the sun's position
would confirm our direction, but with all
this navigating work, our game-spotting

Above: *Elephants stopping a lioness from approaching the waterhole*
Left: *Leopard lounging in a camelthorn tree*

suffered. In the end, the day's highlight was a family of cute bat-eared foxes that played around an old tree stump, before disappearing into their burrow.

VANISHING ROADS

That night we slept early and, aside from the alarm clock, nothing disturbed our slumber. Yet in the morning our fire's ashes were dotted with hyenas' pawprints.

Leaving early on the next leg of our journey was wise, as travelling in the cool of the morning is bliss. We followed the main track south. Straight ahead lay the sand ridge road to Moremi and Maun, which shadows the line of the Magwikhwe Sand Ridge. This long, vegetated dune marks the ancient shoreline of the huge

Lake Makgadikgadi, which geologists think once dominated the north of what is now the Kalahari.

We took a left fork, onto the marsh road, which follows the western side of the Savuti Marsh. This would have been impassable during the rains, but in September it was rutted, hardened mud with super views of open plains. Having plenty of time, we didn't rush, stopping to watch small herds of wildebeest and zebras. Navigation continued to be challenging, but the GPS kept us right even when the tracks seemed to disappear.

Eventually we found signs leading out of Chobe's Mababe Gate, and took a right turn towards Moremi Game Reserve. Crossing the Magwikhwe Sand Ridge needed 15 minutes of second gear for the deep sand, after which we dropped onto a flatter, harder track through sparse mopane woodlands.

tsessebe, lions atop an anthill, a stunning leopard posing in a camelthorn tree, and even claimed to have seen a few distant wild dogs—though nobody else saw them. Curiously, the drive's highlights for us was a saddle-bill stork that didn't flee as we approached (as they usually do).

LION KILL

Next morning we waved the other guests off on their drive and got into our own vehicle, pleased at the prospect of a quick drive to view the area at our own pace. Crossing the wooden pole bridge into the park, we didn't expect to see as much as the guide with his practised eyes. But within a short time we had found a large pride of lions in the road, around an elephant carcass that they'd killed during the night. Sated lions lounged under all the bushes. This was the huge local pride of 22 animals, which had a reputation for killing elephants. Three or four females ate, audibly cracking through bones as they went, while two others wandered down to the nearest pool to drink.

LAGOON MEANDERS

That afternoon we headed towards Xakanixa Lagoon. The area ahead of us was one of the most beautiful in southern

BRIDGE OVER THE RIVER KHWAI

The landscape now changed quickly. The stunted mopane vanished, replaced by a wide, green depression where a string of lily-covered pools glinted in the sun. Around were shady forest glades with impala grazing on the undergrowth. After the heat and dust of Chobe, this was wonderful. South of Savuti we'd glimpsed only a few animals; now, something moved wherever we looked.

We dawdled, enjoying the atmosphere, before finally stopping at North Gate to ask directions to Tsaro Lodge, our base for the night. After a quick shower and tea and cakes, we hopped into a full, open-topped Land Rover with a guide and six other guests. The guide didn't say a lot, but clearly his eyes were working overtime. In three hours he spotted antelopes, giraffes, waterbucks and

Right: Pale chanting goshawk scouting for prey over Savuti Marsh

BOTSWANA

Africa, so we had allowed five or six leisurely hours to explore some the side-tracks leading off from the main route. These first followed the Khwai River upstream, then skirted beside a string of lagoons, on the interface between dry land and the Okavango Delta. The scenery was superb: a patchwork of forests, lagoons, flood plains and open grasslands. Even in the heat of the dry season many were verdant and the game was stupendous, dominated by large herds of red lechwe antelopes.

In the middle of the afternoon, driving slowly beside Qua Lediba (*lediba* is the local word for lagoon), we took a road marked on our map as "seasonal" (not recommended during the rainy season). Several times we forded water across the road, until one large pool stopped us. With forest to the left and lagoon to the right, there was no easy way around. The track was flat sand; solid, not slippery. Vehicle tracks had been made recently— a good sign. As we considered our next move, two large trucks, run by a safari operator, approached and drove through. The water reached the middle of their wheels, giving us confidence. We avoided the next pool by crashing through low bushes, but in a third the vehicle lurched alarmingly to the right. The Land Rover didn't falter: it pulled us through.

TIP OF THE TONGUE

Gradually the loop roads ended and we continued on the main track. Three large elephants stopped us. Too close to the road to pass, we watched as they grazed, glad that we'd allowed a day for this journey. A crash came from the forest and a small elephant wandered across the track, underlining the risk of progressing and getting between it and its relatives. As if to reinforce our puny nature, the nearest elephant picked up a branch as thick as a drainpipe. It leisurely stripped off the leaves and twigs, before stuffing it in its mouth to chew the bark. Thirty minutes later the elephants wandered away into the forest and we drove slowly past.

DINNER

At Xakanixa we were serenaded to sleep by the moan of a distant lion, then woken before dawn by our trusty alarm. We packed, ate, checked the vehicle and were swiftly off: our routine had become faster as the trip progressed. That morning we explored a network of tracks on Goaxhio Island, where skeletons of drowned trees dot the landscape. A colony of spoonbills nests on the lagoon here from June to September. We saw only the last few stragglers—bright, white birds, wielding their spoon-shaped beaks like scythes through the shallow water. We saw no cats, but were delighted by a group of inquisitive dwarf mongooses as they played around an old termitaria.

For our last night we stayed in the Xakanixa area, at Camp Moremi. Bernie, the camp's jovial manager, explained that he had a Nile crocodile in his ornamental pool, hippos on the lawn most nights, and a lion that visited frequently. Keen to avoid guests being eaten, he insisted that we were escorted by a guide around the camp at night.

A shower and welcome clean clothes preceded a stylish dinner, during which visitors who had flown into the camp quizzed us about our adventures. Our trip had been less than luxurious, but we had gained a sense of achievement which seemed to have eluded the others.

CHEETAH REFLECTIONS

When staying at a safari camp in Botswana, game drives are normally included in the price. So on our final morning we joined two other vehicles watching four cheetahs. They were magnificent, but Purba and I agreed we preferred the dwarf mongooses.

That afternoon the journey back to Maun was long and dusty but uneventful—aside from a herd of giraffes grazing beside the road outside the national park. As we handed the keys of the Land Rover back at Maun's tiny airport, it seemed like a lifetime since we'd started our adventure, only seven days ago.

GOING IT ALONE

WHEN TO GO

The dry season, from May to October, is generally the best time. The later in the season you go, the more the temperature rises and the better game becomes along the Chobe River and on the edge of Moremi. If you come during the rains, from November to April, then the sand driving is easier, but muddy areas are much more treacherous. Some roads are impassable.

HIRING A VEHICLE

Make sure that either you or the people hiring you the vehicle are experienced in this area. If neither party has a clue, you're asking for trouble. It's not just a case of getting a good vehicle, but also of getting accurate advice. Land Rovers do cost more than other vehicles, but are better in this terrain.

WHAT TO TAKE

❑ Veronica Roodt's maps of Chobe and Moremi and her *Tourist Guide to Botswana*—all published by Shell Botswana. These are essential for this trip.
❑ Torch.
❑ Medical kit.
❑ Camera with a zoom lens.
❑ Binoculars.
❑ GPS navigation aid and the experience to use it. Practise at home if you're unfamiliar with it.

TIPS FOR DRIVING IN SAND

❑ Drive early and late in the day. When sand is cool it is firmer; when hot, the pockets of air between the grains expand and the sand becomes looser.
❑ Where there are clear, deep-rutted tracks in the sand, don't fight the steering wheel: just relax and let your vehicle steer itself.
❑ If you do get stuck, don't panic or spin the wheels—you'll only dig deeper. Stop, relax and assess the situation. Dig shallow ramps in front of all the wheels, reinforcing them with pieces of wood, vegetation, stones, material or anything else which will give the wheels better traction. Lighten the vehicle load (passengers out) and push. Don't let

the engine revs die as you engage your lowest ratio gear, and use the clutch to ensure that the wheels don't spin wildly and dig themselves further into the sand.
❑ In the last resort, lower your tyre pressures until there is a distinct bulge in the tyre walls. However, make sure that you have the means to reinflate them when you reach harder roads again, or you'll ruin them.

CAMPING IN THE BUSH

❑ Avoid camping on what looks like a path through the bush, however indistinct. It may be a well-used game trail.
❑ Camp a reasonable distance from water—far enough to avoid animals arriving to drink.
❑ Make sure that tent is as flat as possible. You will sleep easier.
❑ Gather firewood during the day, not when the light's fading at dusk. You can store it on the vehicle's roof-rack.
❑ Never take citrus fruit into elephant country; some individuals will open *anything* to get at an orange.
❑ Put everything in or on your vehicle at night. Hyenas will eat anything they can pick up.
❑ Use the toilet before bed and always zip up your tent fully at night.
❑ Animals don't attack tents. Whatever you hear at night, don't panic or unzip your tent to investigate.
❑ If you come across lions or leopards on foot in the campsite, stand still. Then back off slowly, making loud, deep confident noises. Never run from a cat.

IN ELEPHANT COUNTRY

Give elephants a wide berth, especially breeding herds with young. Never push to see how close you can get: it may be too close for that individual elephant.

If you accidentally drive too close, reverse if possible. Otherwise you'll probably be on the receiving end of a terrifying mock charge. Ears flapping, trumpet sounding, head up, the elephant will run and stop. If this happens, hold your ground and rev your engine (do not use your horn). Then back off slowly after the elephant has stopped. If you flee, make sure you can outrun it, as the elephant may chase you.

SOUTH AFRICA•LESOTHO

Few other countries can offer the temptations that South Africa takes for granted. The coastline is so enormous that beaches come in every variety from tropical to treacherous. There are flat-topped hills and snow-capped mountains; wild and dangerous big game and areas of tranquil beauty; sophisticated cities next door to poverty-stricken townships. One thing is certain: a visit to this reborn nation promises to be an unforgettable experience.

In the tiny mountain kingdom of Lesotho, with its majestic peaks and quiet river valleys, the people live in tune with the seasons: they grow crops during the hot, rainy summer and live off their harvest during the freezing, snowswept winter. Ponies and feet are the only means of transport, in a land where the pace is still ruled by "Africa time"—somewhat slower than in the rest of the world.

Swadini dam from Blue River Canyon viewpoint

SOUTH AFRICA

20 Shades of Orange

by Carrie Hampton

The mountain desert of the Richtersveld lures you into a dreamland, with its constantly changing landscape of boulders, desert and dunes, mountain peaks and lush river banks. The Orange River carves its way through this remote area and I experienced everything it had to offer, with long hikes and wild canoeing.

The Richtersveld is the remotest of all South Africa's national parks. It is set in the far northwest of the country, and getting to it means a long drive from anywhere. Only the occasional tour operator ventures in with a hiking group; otherwise you have to go it alone—preferably in a four-wheel drive. Four-by-four touring is the fastest growing leisure market, so I set off with Martin, a friend from Cape Town, equipping his Land Rover with a rooftop tent, spare fuel cans, extra water containers and the ultimate luxury of a battery-charged refrigerator.

It was August—a perfect month for the Richtersveld: not too hot during the day and not too cold at night, with a few spring flowers poking their heads through the seemingly lifeless stony desert plains. Contrary to appearance, this unique region, dampened by far-reaching sea mists, has recorded a staggering 300 different plant species per square kilometre (⅓ of a square mile). It seems that the poorer the soil, the more enduring the plants.

Bosluis Basters

We were met by Floors Strauss, an enthusiastic man from the local community of Bosluis Basters. "Baster" is a derivative of "bastard;" the people were so called because of the community's mixed race origins—descended from local Khoisan and early Dutch settlers, the members now carry the Baster name with pride. Floors heads the Transform programme, training local guides and facilitating social and ecological tourism projects.

The failure of winter rains and the subsequent lack of inland drinking water prevented us from doing the challenging four-day guided hike. Instead Floors took us off on a short, boulder-strewn walk, and organized a longer guided hike for us a few days later. He pointed out some petroglyph rock engravings, etched white into black dolomite stone. The carvings, which differ from hieroglyphs in representing no language or script, were made by the original Bushmen, who lived here around 2,000 years ago. Their primitive art shows twirling serpents and geometric spirals, dots and grids, supposedly inspired in a ritual trance-like state.

 Good driving skills are needed in the Richtersveld. Hikes are hot, dry and long, over rocky terrain, so a reasonable level of fitness is required. Moderate stamina is required for the canoe trip, but no physical preparation is needed. You should be able to swim, but life jackets are supplied. Suitable for all ages.

★ Both the Richtersveld and Orange rivers require camping, and many people sleep under the stars on an inflatable mattress. If you want a tent you must bring or hire one prior to arriving in the area. In the Richtersveld you must be self-sufficient in food, water and firewood. On the Orange River canoe adventure all meals are supplied. This is a non-malarial area and there is little danger of nasty diseases, and few insects to bite you. Summers (November to March) are extremely hot.

 Richtersveld requires complete self-sufficiency for you and your vehicle. On the Orange River food and transport are provided; you must bring the rest—a good kit list is supplied.

The Richtersveld does not undulate—it rises straight up and down in rocky mountain ranges. The colours pass from rich gold and rust to pastel pink and purple and even distant ghostly white. In contrast, the dusty, yellow sand flats between the hills are completely level. Floors led us across the crusty surface to a huge rock appropriately named "the hand of God," where a giant hand imprint was clearly etched into the surface.

Standing stark on the slopes of a craggy hillside, a community of bizarre, phallic halfmens plants stood tall. These spiky "half-a-man" or "elephant's trunk" plants have a little topknot of leaves, and grow very slowly, only 1cm (⅓in) or so per year. Most of the plants we saw must have been around for at least a century (see box, p. 212).

In such a parched place the natural desire is to head for water. We emerged from the confines of a gorge to the unexpected fecundity of the Orange River. The grassy banks of De Hoop campsite seemed like Eden in the desert. There were green riverine trees and shrubs and gentle banks leading to shallow eddies of water, allowing easy access for a swim. There were four or five other vehicles, each of which had a private riverside spot to itself. Rooftop tent unfolded, fire lit and warm clothes donned ready for the cold night, Martin and I settled ourselves around the flames. At the edge of the embers went potatoes and butternut squash wrapped in foil, and on our little portable grid sizzled a spiral of *borewors*, a traditional thick sausage eaten at every South African *braai* (barbecue).

PEACE TO DREAM ABOUT

After an early slumber and sunrise awakening, I looked out to the most perfect morning in one of the most beautiful places I have ever seen. The light was a gentle gold and highlighted the orange in the rocks. The sky began a pale, wispy blue and gathered intensity until it was a concentrated azure. The river flowed without haste and the air was still with a hint of warmth to come. This was the kind of peace you dream about. A quick dip in the rather chilly river accelerated the waking process and afterwards I cooked a fry-up on our little portable gas stove.

I should, at this stage, mention toilets: there are none. You have to wander to a secluded spot with toilet paper and possibly a spade, plus a box of matches. Your toilet paper should be burned, as it does not biodegrade readily in such an arid climate, and will soon be spread all over the place by the wind.

The route along the river's edge to the next campsite was difficult and

THE NAMA PEOPLE

Richtersveld and southern Namibia are the home of the Nama tribe. They are the only true descendants of the Khoikhoi pastoralists, who moved down from Botswana 2,000 years ago. Their physical heritage can often be seen in their finer features, paler skin and tufted hair. Even though the apartheid era relocated many families and forbade Nama children to speak their mother tongue at school, 60–70 percent of Richtersveld Nama adults managed to keep their language. It is a strange, multi-clicked tongue, which is classified by UNESCO as endangered. The Nama have a natural talent for music, poetry, proverbs, riddles and tales, which have been handed down orally for generations. Community projects are helping to fuel a strong resurgence in Nama culture, and traditional dancing and old customs are being reinstated. One such is the initiation ceremony for a girl entering puberty. After her first menstruation she spends eight days in a hut, and is then adorned with ochre and beads and danced out with music. The boys then pull her away from the older women to show that she is now a woman, and begin to dance with her.

potentially dangerous for a lone vehicle. The likelihood of getting stuck in the deep channels of soft sand was high. We took it anyway! Martin loved the challenge and, with confidence in both his car and his driving skills, he took the most difficult routes and mastered every one.

Ever more beautiful, the stretch of river leading to the Richtersberg camp site was protected by a high sand ridge. Swathes of tall reeds lined the water's edge with occasional grassy coves and rocky shallows. The fertile beauty of the river contrasted starkly with the dark, pointed peaks of looming mountains, begging to be climbed. I persuaded Martin that a quick vertical climb would work up an appetite. We hiked higher and higher, until Martin finally went on strike. I con-

tinued to the top of the world for a stupendous view of endless, mud-brown mountains, parted by a green-fringed murky river. Martin looked like a half-mens plant, awe-struck at his own dizzy height, and the car was a speck of dust on my sunglasses. Coming down required great care, as every loose rock was a potential hazard.

CRY OF THE FISH EAGLE

The scene at our grassy campsite was fantastic. Colourful birds and white butterflies flitted around, and a statuesque goliath heron spread its massive wings and glided silently overhead. All that was missing from this idyllic place was the haunting cry of an African fish eagle—and then it came, right on cue.

Left: *The sharp peak of Witch's Hat mountain was quite unlike any other rock formation we encountered on the Orange River*
Above: *Investigating a promising-looking cave, I came across a cluster of tiny bats*
Below: *Frequent applications of sunscreen are essential*

I do not know how to do justice to the scenery we travelled through: the vast, sandy, pebble-dotted plain, with a hazy pink watercolour escarpment far in the distance. As we drove higher and higher, strange, cactus-like plants began to appear amongst sculpted yellow, grainy boulders. A quick detour took us to a place I named "Echo Valley," where every shout was returned by three or four hecklers.

On arriving at the amazing Kokerboomkloof campsite, we found a bleached, golden, sculpted landscape with weird and lonely-looking kokerboom (quiver) trees. Kokerbooms are strange, mustard-coloured trees with patchwork bark cracking like dried yellow mud. It was here that archaeological evidence was found of early Bushmen (or San) hunters dating back to 2200–1400 B.C. The hunter-gatherer Bushmen used the lightweight branches of the kokerboom a quivers for their arrows, as the fibrous centre held the arrows firmly in place. These trees live only in the very driest of regions, so are well suited to the meagre annual rainfall in the Richtersveld of around 70mm (2¾in). Unfortunately, many appear to be dying, and researchers are not sure whether this is natural life or if there is a more sinister cause.

We set up camp in a natural bowl between protective boulders and experienced total silence and utter peace. We had an early morning rendezvous with our Nama hiking guide, Simon, who spoke Afrikaans and his native Nama tongue. He took us in search of the "amphitheatre," another echo site, in a narrow ochre gorge with 100m (325ft) vertical walls. Picking our way past rocks of every colour, we saw one patch of ground that seemed to have been covered by a light snowfall. In fact, each glinting snowflake was a bite-sized, shimmering piece of quartz. A delineating line seemed to signify the end of this exhibition, and we passed onto the next geological display. Down in a dry riverbed, by an old goat *kraal* (enclosure) we came across the remains of a remote permanent camp. Prints in the coarse-grained sand along the trail gave away the presence of wild animals in these hills. Simon identified the animal spoor as belonging to kudu (a large antelope with huge, curled horns), klipspringer (a small and secretive olive-green buck) and the most beautiful of all cats, the leopard. This five-hour-long hot hike was just part of the four-day walk, and we wondered if we would really have coped with the full trek.

Back at the Land Rover, the beers were cold and we were happy to sit for a while and drive over the Helskloof Pass and out of the park to drop our guide in his home village of Khubus. We were very tired by now, and remembered being told about a new guest house project in the

FIRE FOOD

The South Africans have mastered the art of *braaing* (barbecuing), and the guides on the Orange River trip have it down to a fine art. Here are some of their tips:

Wrap in foil individual vegetables such as potatoes, sweet potatoes, butternut squash (halved and filled with honey, syrup and raisins), cabbage (stuffed with brown onion soup powder, chutney and grated cheese) and unpeeled onions. Put them on the edge of the hot coals to cook until soft, turning regularly. For the most succulent boned roast leg of lamb, stuff garlic into slits in the flesh and baste in oil and herbs. Wrap in three layers of foil, leaving a little gap to pour in some red wine or sherry. Seal tightly and cook in the middle of the coals for about an hour and a half, turning every 20 minutes.

next village of Eksteenfontein. With the help of half of the Khubus village council, who came to meet us in the general store, we phoned through and made a late booking. The corrugated guest house was newly painted and basic, but immaculately clean, and there was plenty of hot water and big, soft beds. This is probably the remotest and least-visited place in South Africa from which to send a postcard home, so I did.

BASE CAMP

Our next stop was the Felix Unite base camp, from where we were to launch ourselves on to the Orange River for a four-day canoe adventure. To get there we suffered lengthy, bumpy dirt roads, but stopped a couple of times to examine more rock art on giant boulders by the roadside. On reaching the river again, we picnicked while watching red-legged African spoonbills and a pied kingfisher, which hovered and then dropped like a dart. On the north bank was yet another amazing geological formation—this time, a vertical rock fault 650m (2,100ft) high. The south bank was intensively cultivated with fields of dark, rich, loamy soil yielding all sorts of fruit and vegetables. A green pepper crop was dotted with the bright clothes of the female workforce, methodically weeding the rows, while their children sat patiently by.

We spotted a sign saying "Peace of Paradise," and were tempted to have a look. It turned out to be a campsite used by several river canoe operators. The reed partitions and flowering vines leading to the water's edge created an atmosphere akin to the paradise they advertised. However, our destination was another canoe base on the Namibian side, so we continued to the border post and then followed the river back, seeing our earlier path from a different perspective.

When I woke on the morning of our canoe trip, I thought I had died and gone to heaven. The barrenness of the Richtersveld had been replaced with lush greenery, and the river seemed peaceful and beckoning. Our mixed bunch of paddlers, over half from South Africa and the rest a scattering of Europeans and North Americans, ranged from seven to 75 years old. We listened attentively to our chief river guide, Dale, whose youthful appearance and long, blond ponytail belied his extremely competent leadership and charming canoe-side manner. He explained our repertoire of paddling strokes, important signals and safety procedures.

Nappy Run

The previous evening I had met the oldest and wisest of the group, Libby. She was an elegant retired radiographer, brought up in Rhodesia (now Zimbabwe). She asked if I would paddle with her in the two-man Canadian Mohawk canoe, and once we got the hang of going forwards rather than round in circles, we managed quite well together.

We were all destined to get wet on the first day on the Nappy Run, where, in a most undignified manner, we put the life-jackets on nappy-style, and threw ourselves into the bubbling water of Hammerkop Rapid. With legs linked around each other's waists and backsides floating high, this human chain took off at high speed until we reached the base of the rapid. It was such fun that we all did an infantile walk back up the river for another go.

There were so many invisible submerged rocks in the river that you could suddenly find your canoe perched on one like Noah's Ark after the flood. The current swayed the canoe right and left, or

STARS IN AFRICAN FOLKLORE

The three bright stars of Orion's belt give his position away, but Africans see three zebras instead. Aldeberan (the unluckiest hunter in the sky) tried to shoot these zebras for supper, but failed. He could not go home to his wives empty-handed, but dared not collect his spent arrows and try again, for fear of the lurking Lion (the star we know as Betelgeuse). In the end, Aldeberan skulked off home, where his wives laughed derisively at him.

In African legend, the Milky Way was formed by a young girl in a terrible temper. When her mother forbade her to roast her roots in the fire, she picked up the grey ash and glinting hot coals and threw them high into the air, where they remain today.

The four stars making up the Southern Cross are in the sky each night pointing the way south. These are four giraffes, whose heads are always visible to all the animals of the night sky.

jammed it even further between the rocks like a cork in a bottle. The only solution was to poke one foot out and push frantically, without losing balance and falling in. At one point we had a major midstream pile-up. At least half the people, paddles and canoes became separated from each other and floated off to calmer waters to be reunited.

At other times we just rowed with the flow and glided sedately past glistening wet darters. Also called snake birds, for their S-bend necks, these ungainly-looking birds spread their wings out to dry like a vampire's cloak. I was glad my curiosity got the better of me when I stopped to investigate a narrow little cave and found some tiny brown bats inside, but I did not expect my next encounter. I followed a little riverside path up to a clearing and thought aliens had landed when I saw several 2m (6ft)-high and wide, orange, kite-shaped "things" strung up on poles. A guide explained that these were mud-dwelling barbel, of the catfish family, being hung out to dry. I have never seen a stranger sight in my life.

SLEEPING UNDER THE STARS

Setting up camp was not difficult, as it simply involved selecting a soft piece of ground and staking your claim with sleeping mat and bag. Most of us slept out under the most complete night sky imaginable, but some preferred a tent. The guides set to work providing river food nothing short of miraculous. For four days they produced smoked mussel *hors d'oeuvre*, crunchy nut and cauliflower salads, bacon and egg brunches and a last-night speciality, cooked on the coals: tender roast leg of lamb. "It only tastes this good because you've been paddling all day," suggested lead guide Dale. He was too modest, but relaxing by a flaming fire under a zillion stars on a remote bank of the Orange River, certainly enhanced the experience.

I was particularly impressed with the company's adherence to the ecotourism motto of "take only photographs, leave

only footprints." Not one sweet wrapper or cigarette butt was ever discarded thoughtlessly. A portable toilet was carried (I never knew exactly where), and each evening it was placed like a throne in a spot with the most magnificent view. If somebody disappeared and seemed to take forever, you knew that the "loo with a view" had them spellbound.

The Orange River was named after William, Prince of Orange, in 1779, but anyone could be forgiven for thinking it was named for the folded ochre mountain ranges, or the red-tinged water at sunset, or the rising moon, glowing gold with desert dust. Every day, we paddled past some weird and wonderful rock formations. Swirling "snail rocks" or "swiss rolls" started off as horizontal sedimentary strata but curled under intense pressure to form an almost complete circle. On the second day we found a large looming "King Kong," which required a

little imagination. On the third the "Witch's Hat," a sharp peak of pink metamorphic rock, stood alone like a sentinel, and forced the river to change course.

Top: *A break from paddling allowed us to climb up a riverside hill for a view—and to collect a few of the abundant fluorspars for our campfire*
Above: *Tackling an Orange River rapid*

NASTY SJAMBOK

The rapids were all manageable until we came to Sjambok (the Afrikaans name for a particularly nasty whip). The entire group disembarked and boulder-hopped down the river bank to view the rapid, before being briefed on the plan of attack. The main problem was a narrow channel followed by a sharp turn. This combination could spin you around and/or throw you out straight into a stretch of white water. The two young Swedes set forth as if to war, and rushed through at high speed without a problem. The German mother and daughter team spun around mid-rapid and continued down backwards to great cheers, only to fall out in calm water. The South African middle-aged businessmen discussed strategy and came down so slowly that the waves lapped over the rim and sank them in slow motion. They and their canoe completed the rapid below the water line. My partner Libby, being the oldest and most fragile of the group was accompanied by a guide, and I found a new paddling partner for the rest of the day.

Just before Sjambok rapid, we took a break from the river and strolled across an exposed, sandy plain, hazy with the heat. We headed up a pale hill, streaked with bleached veins of pure quartz. In among the rocks were pieces of light turquoise-tinged fluorspar, used as flux in the iron, steel and alloy industries and in the manufacture of enamels and coloured glass. Our use for them was much more fun: when thrown into a hot fire, the rocks glowed a luminous purple and green, then exploded into a frenzy of colourful spitting fireworks.

On the third day of the canoe adventure, we stumbled up to a small prospecting concession at Rudi's Diamond Mine. Here, the one and only worker on site showed us the process of digging, sorting, washing and selecting. We found some semiprecious stones, including the alluring tiger's-eye, but all of dubious quality. Our last campsite was in the shadow of large, burgundy-hued mountains, and the few of us who cannot look at a hill without wanting to climb it set off for a sunset hike.

The fourth day was our last, and by the mid-morning "take out" we had paddled 78km (49 miles). The mountains had dispersed and in their place was green farmland. The Aussenkehr Estate, on whose land we exited, is said to be the largest fruit farm in the southern hemisphere, supplying table grapes to Europe straight from their own airstrip.

After several days of messing around on the water, even Sjambok was a distant, waterlogged memory. We began to feel like the halfmens, who did not want to leave their life-giving river. We returned with some regret to the base camp and had a general clean-up and shower before some fond farewells. I took one more look around me and realized that, if I am ever going to find enlightenment, it will surely be on the banks of the Orange River.

LEGENDS OF THE RIVER

There is nothing lurking in the Orange River that is likely to harm you—unless you believe the centuries-old legend of a great snake as thick as a barrel, that eats goats, calves and children. Another story tells of a poisonous lizard that comes out only at night, uttering a terrible, high-pitched sound, and kills children with its teeth.

The strange tall, phallic halfmens plant stands alone, always leaning towards the north. This is because the original inhabitants of this barren land were chased south across the river, and as they stood to look back into their homeland, the gods took pity and rooted them to the spot so that they could always see their home.

The legendary mountain of copper in the Richtersveld has not yet been found, but there is a boulder near the little town of Kubos which rings like a bell if struck with a hammer.

GOING IT ALONE

WHEN TO GO

It gets extremely hot in summer (November to March) with midsummer temperatures up to and over 45°C (113°F). Winter (June to August) can bring rain and very chilly nights but generally has bright, warm days. After the spring rains, from August to October, the arid landscape of the Richtersveld bursts into incredible bloom and the climate is very pleasant.

INTERNAL TRAVEL

There is no public transport to the Richtersveld National Park. Although a four-by-four vehicle is preferable, a general utility vehicle with high ground clearance will do; a small town car will not. Cape Eco Trails have scheduled guided tours to inaccessible areas of the park that no independent traveller can reach. Richtersveld Challenge offer tailor-made tours to the area, and Executive Safaris will organize your trip and/or accompany your group in a lead vehicle (see Contacts).

The Orange River canoe companies normally offer return transfers from Cape Town. There are scheduled buses that make regular trips from Cape Town (South Africa) to Windhoek (Namibia) taking about eight hours. There is a stop at the border, where the canoe base camp could collect you.

PLANNING

Pre-book entry to Richtersveld National Park through South Africa National Parks central reservations in Pretoria. You can prearrange a guide to accompany you through the Richtersveld in your own vehicle, or for hikes from one to four days. Contact the Transform project or Richtersveld National Park office (note that Afrikaans is mostly spoken). Careful planning is needed for this remote area as there are no shops and petrol is scarce. Take all the food you need for a day or two either side of your planned trip. Shopping is best done before leaving the main N7 north–south highway in the town of Springbok. The only town after that is Port Nolloth, which has a limited selection. Take jerrycans of water and refill them at the park entrance and there-after from the Orange River. You may like to boil the river water, but I have consumed it without adverse reaction. Rubbish must be taken out with you. Fuel is available at the main entrance (Sendlingsdrift), but fill your tank when you can. Take firewood or charcoal with you as you may not collect it in the park.

You can hire a canoe for a few hours on Orange River; if competent, you may be allowed to negotiate the river alone, with pick-up arranged after several days. Plan as for Richtersveld.

HEALTH MATTERS

No special precautions are necessary as the area is free of nasty diseases and there is no malaria.

WHAT TO TAKE

- ❑ Two spare wheels are recommended for the Richtersveld, plus some tools, a high-lift jack and tow rope.
- ❑ Good first-aid kit, as you will be far from help.
- ❑ Insect repellent.
- ❑ Torch.
- ❑ Binoculars.
- ❑ High factor sunscreen.
- ❑ Take a sun umbrella for the Richtersveld or preferably something to make a larger shade cover.
- ❑ Small spade.
- ❑ Windbreaker jacket.
- ❑ Waterproof sandals.
- ❑ Clothing for extreme temperatures (very hot summers, cold winter nights).
- ❑ Waterproof camera or padded dry bag so that you can keep your camera in the canoe.
- ❑ A small fold-up chair—it will make your evenings more comfortable.

TRAVELLERS' TIPS

Richtersveld
- ❑ Never sleep on bare ground, as this is ideal scorpion habitat. Check shoes or clothes that have been left on the ground for any length of time for scorpions.
- ❑ Beware of touching plants, as some have poisonous sap.
- ❑ There are no toilet facilities within the park, so dig a hole, do your business and burn the toilet paper.
- ❑ Wear a T-shirt when swimming to avoid sunburn.
- ❑ Beware of the strong current in the Orange River.

Orange River
- ❑ No glass is allowed down the river, so take boxed wine and sachets of your favourite spirit.
- ❑ Most people sleep under the stars, but in cooler months you may like to take a tent.
- ❑ Stuff your sleeping bag in a plastic garbage liner in the storage compartment so it stays dry even if you don't.

SOUTH AFRICA

21 Call of the Kruger

by Carrie Hampton

South Africa is one of the best places to go on a wild animal safari. Kruger National Park caters for independent visitors, but there are many outstanding private game reserves for those who want to be guided. I wondered how different driving myself and being guided by a ranger would be, and decided to try both.

Africa means animals. You cannot visit South Africa without attempting to see the Big Five—lion, leopard, elephant, rhino and buffalo. Although the animals may be confined within a national park or private reserve, they are wild and dangerous, and should be treated with great respect. It is hard to believe that tourists have been known to get out of their vehicle for a snapshot of "me with lion." Needless to say, they have not always lived to tell the tale.

Richard, a surveyor from central London, accompanied me on safari. We flew from Johannesburg to Nelspruit, where a hire car was waiting, and drove east through subtropical orchards of avocado, mango and lychees, citrus fruits, pawpaws and rows of bananas. Malelane Gate, the southernmost entrance into Kruger National Park, was an hour and a

The safaris are physically easygoing, but thrilling when up close to dangerous wild animals.

Accommodation is excellent, with many choices in every price range. If camping is not your choice, Kruger offers self-catering chalets, too. Open game-viewing vehicles go "off road," so watch out for stray branches and be prepared for a long bumpy ride to search out animals. Kruger is a malarial area, so precautions are advisable. Summers (November to March) are hot, so choose an air-conditioned touring vehicle.

Binoculars and camera are a must. Although you do not have to get completely kitted out in khaki, earthy colours are recommended. Mosquito nets are normally provided in accommodation.

half away. Following the lush Crocodile River valley, we descended into the hotter, drier lowveld (low bush land). It was spring (October), but the grass was so dry it crackled underfoot. The area was in the midst of yet another drought, and the summer rains were eagerly awaited.

ANIMALS EVERYWHERE

Looking intently into the dense dry bush, I almost missed the obvious—a menacingly large rhinoceros, just a stone's throw away. This was a white rhino, easily identifiable by its wide mouth—the highly endangered black rhino has little, pointed lips. These prehistoric animals have survived for 5 million years, yet a perverse desire for their horn has brought the black rhino close to extinction. There were zebras everywhere and blue wildebeest, whose eyes are fixed on the side of their boxed-shaped heads. A harem of elegant tan-and-white impala gazelles sprung gracefully across the road but, surprisingly, the emblems of South African rugby—springboks—were nowhere to be seen. They once roamed the veld (bush) in their thousands, but 19th-century hunters shot them in vast numbers. However, they are still found in large herds at other Southern African reserves.

BUSH-TRACKER SKILLS

I thought I'd try out some bush-tracker skills, by assessing how close we were to the elephants from the freshness of their dung. Richard was quite disgusted as I leaned out of the car and carefully picked

up a donut-sized piece of elephant dung. The remains of poorly digested grass and leaves just crumbled in my hands—this trail was cold. Elephants love to walk along the road, and, since they deposit a large pile of dung approximately every 15 minutes, it is easy to follow their trail—until they hit the bush! It is quite astonishing how an animal so big can become almost invisible as soon as it steps into the undergrowth.

With the help of several guide books to birds and animals, we were doing well on

Above: The twin cascades of Mac Mac Falls, between Sabie and Graskop, seen from the viewing platform on the Panorama Route

identification and variety, but could not wait to see our first lion. A car full of other tourists revealed the location of a pride under a distant tree. All we could see was one pair of teddy-bear ears, twitching occasionally. Night hunters sleep most of the day, and we were beginning to learn that animal-watching takes patience and perseverance. For a closer encounter with lions, we had to wait until we visited Tshukudu private game reserve, a few days later.

DAWN AWAKENINGS

Skukuza restcamp, where I had pre-booked a campsite, was a fully fledged village with supermarket, curio shop, museum, gas station, amphitheatre and a little airport. It was positively bustling, and perfect for families and tour groups. (There are about 20 other, smaller camps within Kruger.) We kept things simple, with earthy, green-dome tents, and ate sweet potatoes, baked in the coals, with tender steaks from a farm stall.

After a night of hyenas' laughter, jackals' howls and several unidentifiable noises, we were up at dawn. As cars are not allowed outside the camp at night, everybody is ready and waiting at the gate at 6am sharp, hoping to see carnivores still eating last night's supper. We had not gone far before a spotted hyena loped across our path. It stood and

stared, then walked directly towards us. This unusual behaviour reminded me that Kruger Park has more than 2 million visitors a year, and most animals appear totally untroubled by cars. Lions are not in the least bit interested in people inside a vehicle, but a ranger informed me that should I put one foot on the ground, the lion would react like lightning.

SHANGAAN VILLAGE LIFE

To see everything the area has to offer, we had to follow a tight schedule. It was still quite early when we left Kruger National Park, and the mild spring morning was warming up. Our impromptu stop at the Shangana Cultural Village, near Hazyview, proved enlightening. It is built around a real village in which live a chief, his three wives and their offspring. Each wife has her own circular thatched mud hut, and the boys and girls have separate communal huts. As custom dictates, permission to enter the village was requested on bended knee by our guide. The chief was out with his cattle, so his handsome eldest son, wearing a feathered headdress welcomed us instead.

Most tribespeople consult a *sangoma* (traditional healer) for medicinal and spiritual purposes. I decided to part with a negligible fee to see what the *sangoma* had to say about me. Bedecked in beads and surrounded by totems, he first

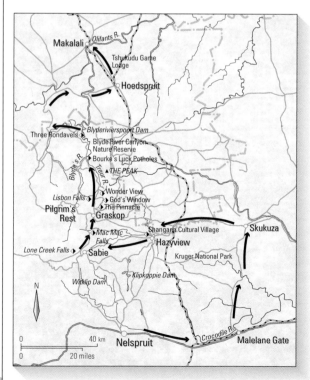

The route of this five-day trip takes in the Kruger and the scenic Panorama Route

showed me all his ground-up medicines, stored in small gourds. He then took up his leather pouch full of bones, shells, coins, stones and other strange objects, and shook them gently. The contents were scattered slowly onto a curly-edged piece of goat skin. From their pattern, he identified that I had no children (correct) and gave me some *muti* (herbal medicine) to put in my bath, to purge this bad luck. He said the bath must face east (strangely enough, mine does).

SO MANY WATERFALLS

Winding up the escarpment road towards Sabie, the scenery grows in lushness and splendour as the rainfall catchment increases. Rivers originating in the high-veld (high plateau) come tumbling into Sabie via hundreds of waterfalls—even in a time of drought. Some are easily accessible; others are hidden deep in the endless pine and eucalyptus plantations. A cold dip in Lone Creek Falls pool was fabulously refreshing, and a clamber to the top of the falls through the forest provided the perfect place for a picnic. Mac Mac Falls (named after the Scots who came seeking alluvial gold) are probably the best known. They are only visible from a caged viewing platform, reached down some exhausting steps.

This undulating woodland was perfect trail-riding country, and I could not resist a quick hour's ride. Timmy, of Sabie Horse Trails, is a huge and gentle Afrikaner Boer (farmer), whose horses are big-boned and sure-footed, and love to roam the hills and valleys at a leisurely pace. Timmy was a mine of information about the birds and trees, and I enjoyed his unpretentious, relaxed style.

Sabie town is small and charming, with a main street perfect for curio-shop browsers. There are plenty of restaurants and cafés, and accommodation signs everywhere. As we travelled north 30km (19 miles) to the little town of Graskop, the afternoon heat was suddenly lifted by a cool breeze. In this area of summer rainfall, the higher you are, the more it rains. In Graskop they expect 2,500mm (98in) between October to March, while in Pilgrims Rest, 17 km (10 miles) away, they have half that amount. It is halved again in the low Kruger region.

PANNING FOR GOLD

There could not have been a more beautiful or romantic spot to have a gold rush than Pilgrim's Rest: the whole village has been declared a National Monument. Luckily, I had pre-booked the busy Royal Hotel, whose rooms and cottages retain their Victorian style and décor. The gold rush started in 1873 when Alec

---

TOP FIVE PANORAMA ROUTE WATERFALLS

Mac Mac Falls (or the Two Scotsmen). This 100m (325ft) twin waterfall tumbles into a narrow ravine, with access via many steps to a small viewing cage. Location: between Sabie and Graskop.

Lisbon Falls. A double waterfall dropping 80m (260ft), creating a fine veil. The car park is at the top of the falls, with good views over the edge. You can hike down to the bottom through alpine scenery, then swim in the pool. Location: north of Graskop near Blyde River Canyon viewpoints.

Berlin Falls. A sheer 80m (260ft) drop with excellent vantage points, revealing the entire falls and deep pool at its foot. Location: just north of Lisbon Falls.

Bridal Veil Falls. Falling 70m (228ft), the canopy of water does justice to its name; the spray will cover you in a fine mist. Accessible via a 15-minute hike on a forest path. Location: 7.5km (4½ miles) west of Sabie.

Lone Creek Falls. As it is in a private pine plantation, there is a small entry fee. There are several short walkways, all within two minutes of the parking area. Location: 12km (7½ miles) west of Sabie.

"Wheelbarrow" Patterson panned for gold in a little stream. When word leaked out that he had been successful, hundreds of other prospectors arrived. Within a year there were 21 stores, 18 canteens, three bakeries and several houses of ill repute.

I tried my hand at gold-panning, kneeling over the stream and swishing fine silt and mud around the bottom of a giant metal saucer. After finding seven tiny specks of gold, and a trace of glinting gold dust in the sludge, I was hooked and wanted to continue. Unfortunately, it's illegal to remove the gold—however miniscule—and I reluctantly returned my small fortune to the river.

WINDOWS ON THE WORLD

The next day was one of magnificent panoramic views and more waterfalls in the Blyde River Canyon Nature Reserve. We started at the Pinnacle viewpoint, a single quartzite column rising out of the deep wooded canyon. God's Window and

ESSENTIAL DRIVING TIPS

❑ You will come across some erratic drivers in South Africa and you should always be prepared for the unexpected. This means drivers (especially Combi taxi buses) stopping, starting or changing lanes without warning, overtaking on bends, and jumping traffic lights.

❑ Most roads have a narrow shoulder lane, and it is usual to move into this lane to let others overtake. A few flashes on the hazard lights is the common way of saying "thank you."

❑ Never stop if somebody flags you down, even if you suspect something is wrong with your car—wait until you get to a service station.

❑ Keep your car doors locked and never give lifts.

❑ Do not leave valuables in your car, even if hidden.

❑ Keep your speed down, as even main roads can have livestock grazing on the verge and wandering across the road.

❑ Petrol stations do not take credit cards, so make sure you have enough cash when you fill up.

Far left: *Cutlet, an orphaned warthog*
Left: *Black-maned lion at Tshukudu Game Lodge, rescued after nearly being shot by farmers*
Below: *Black rhino*

Wonder View spoke for themselves, with staggering views over the thickly wooded escarpment to a distant Mozambique. Next came half-an-hour's scramble on a path that all but disintegrated, down to the pool at the base of Lisbon Falls. The water fell like a fine veil wafting in slow motion, but swimming in it was a shockingly cold experience.

Where the Blyde River ("river of joy") and the Treur River ("river of sorrow") meet, erosion has formed one of the most remarkable geological phenomena in the country—Bourke's Luck Potholes. Over thousands of years, surreal cylindrical rock sculptures, created by whirling water, have formed a series of dark pools which contrast artfully with the yellow rocks. Almost every tour bus stops here and an enterprizing local dance troupe performs at the entrance.

The last and most spectacular viewpoint on this Panorama Route is the Three Rondavels (also called Three Sisters). This unforgettable view is of three huge rock spirals rising out of the far wall of the canyon. Their rounded domes are iced in green, and their sides are stained with orange lichens, giving the whole scene a golden hue.

CLOSE ENCOUNTERS WITH A LION

It was time once again to go in search of African animals. I followed the advice of a South African friend and booked two nights at the family-owned and run Tshukudu Game Lodge, near Hoedspruit. Tshukudu is a relaxed, welcoming place with simple chalets and no fences between you and the wild animals. Ala and Lolly Sussens and their sons raise orphaned animals, and I was able to play with a six-month-old lioness called Eliza—emerging without a scratch. Along with our armed ranger, Eliza came on the early morning game walk. We were also accompanied by Tambo and Becky, 13-year-old elephants rescued from a culled herd when they were just two years old. This mischievous pair appear from the bush on command, and I found myself suddenly being frisked by a firm trunk. Back at the lodge, Cutlet, the orphan warthog, snuffled around my legs and managed to cover me in the engine oil that he had been wallowing in.

Tshukudu's lion-rearing programme began when the family rescued a number of lions in danger of being shot by farmers, and developed a breeding programme to widen the available gene pool in other reserves. The lions are separate from those roaming freely on the reserve and live in prides, with one male to every two to four females. C.J., our ranger, drove us to see the breeding lions, especially a film star named Shumba. This exquisite-looking beast, with golden eyes and a massive mane of black hair, once starred in the film *Jock of the Bushveld*, but is too big and strong to be trusted as a pet. The other lions are not as friendly as Shumba. When a huge, muscular male suddenly leaped up and ran towards me, I almost died of fright. But it ran right past.

SOUNDS OF AFRICA

It was dusk as we left the lion enclosure and C.J. promised us a surprise. He started revving the engine in bursts, and told us to listen. A low rumbling sound, like thunder, began to gain momentum. Suddenly a roar exploded into the African night. Shumba had responded to the engine's resonance and let loose his territorial warning. This sound travels for miles, and up close it vibrates through your whole body and shakes the ground beneath you. One lion set off another, and then another, until the air was full of frightening male power. This truly is the most formidable sound of Africa.

As we casually ate our supper in the reed-enclosed *boma* (outside dining area with central pit fireplace), I heard the roaring again. This was from a free-roaming lion—and it was coming closer. The rangers told us that a lion had been around the camp every evening for a few days, and that they would personally walk each one of us back to our chalets, so not to worry! Eyes darting in every direction in the darkness, we followed C.J. in trepidation to our own chalet. I drifted into a fitful sleep, full of lions roaring and hyenas giggling.

FIVE-STAR SAFARI

To experience fully South Africa's safari repertoire, Richard and I decided on a night in one of the top game lodges.

Makalali, northwest of Tshukudu, is simply stunning in its architecture, accommodation, attention to detail and scenery of wooded hills and hot, dry river valleys. Designed with great care and flair, Makalali combines layered thatch with rustic wood and stone, adorned with distressed metal fixtures and fittings. This theme runs throughout all four separate camps, each catering for up to 12 people. The small staff contingents look after your every need, and each chalet is set far apart for privacy. There is no electricity, and golden lantern light seeps through a metal screen cut with animal shapes, dividing the bedroom from the bathroom. Each chalet has its own private *lapa* (outdoor reed lounge) with giant scatter cushions, and a view into which animals often wander. For lunch, a selection of delicacies arrived, carried effortlessly on a Shangaan waitress's head.

LOOKING FOR LEOPARD

National parks rarely let you venture off the track, but in private reserves you can do whatever you like. When the ranger turned the open safari vehicle towards impenetrable bush I expected us to stop. Not a chance. He just mowed through the undergrowth, crushing small trees and ploughing through dense thickets. A trained Shangaan tracker accompanies each vehicle and can spot big cat spoor at a glance. Working with the rangers, who are in radio contact with each other, you are almost guaranteed to see leopard or lion. We found our lazy leopard dozing in late afternoon sunlight, and I can say without hesitation that she was the most beautiful animal I have ever seen.

After three very different and thrilling safari experiences, I was completely enthralled by the wilds of Africa. No lodge exceeded the other: each offered something special in its own price range. In the words of one diehard, city-loving lawyer I met: "Everybody should go on safari at least once in their lifetime." Personally, I intend to make a habit of it.

GOING IT ALONE

WHEN TO GO

In this subtropical region, the summer months, from October to March, are hot and rainy with dense vegetation. This is when many young are born, and is a lovely time of year as long as you have air-conditioning in your car. A summer haze on the scenic Panorama Route is common. Winter, from April to September, is warm and dry, with quite cool nights. The vegetation dies back and water is restricted to main water holes, making game-viewing easier.

INTERNAL TRAVEL

South Africa's road, rail and airline networks are excellent. You can hire any type of car and drop it off at main points. Local public buses are not advised, but long-distance coaches are fine. You can fly from Johannesburg to Hoedspruit or to Nelspruit Airport. Both airports are very close to Kruger National Park, thus saving you the six-hour drive from Johannesburg. You can also fly from Johannesburg to Skukuza, right in Kruger National Park. Many private reserves have their own small airstrip or, if not, will collect you from the closest airport.

PLANNING

As this is the most visited area in South Africa, accommodation gets pretty booked up from October to February. You can book direct or through an agent.

HEALTH MATTERS

Malaria prophylactics are recommended for the Kruger area. You can drink the tap water all over South Africa but bottled water is readily available. AIDS is widespread in Africa.

ACCOMMODATION

Kruger offers everything from large, bustling campsites to secluded private camps, where you book out the whole place. There is a five-day, accompanied Lebombo motorized four-by-four Eco Trail, for which you have to be totally self-sufficient. Brochures are available from South African National Parks.

There are so many private game reserves and lodges offering excellent accommodation and superb game-viewing, that to choose just one is very difficult. Apart from the accommodation featured in the article, I can recommend Singita Private Game Reserve in Sabi Sands, Blue Mountain Lodge near Kiepersol, M'Bali and Motswari in the Timbavati Game Reserve, Malelane Sun Inter-Continental at the Malelane Gate into Kruger, and The Town House B&B in Sabie.

TRAVELLERS' TIPS

❑ Hold animals in the highest respect and remember that they are wild.
❑ Film is readily available, but have spare reels of your favourite type with you.
❑ Animals are up at dawn, so if you snooze you lose.
❑ Zip up your tent and close doors before leaving, and do not leave food or belongings outside. Some animals will eat anything: hyenas have been known to eat leather shoes, jackals run off with all sorts, and monkeys make a terrible mess.

WHAT TO TAKE

❑ Animal/bird identification books.
❑ Binoculars.
❑ Video recorder or camera with the longest lens possible and spare film.
❑ Khaki clothing.

AFRICAN CUISINE

Pan-African cuisine is the latest foodie trend in the cultured cities of Africa, serving up dishes from across the continent in all their weird and wonderful variety.

Mopane worms are the green-and-blue spiky caterpillars of the nocturnal emperor moth, and are something of an acquired taste, similar to seasoned cardboard with a hint of timber. They may look pretty on the butterfly-leafed mopane tree, but lose some of their appeal once their innards have been squeezed out, and they have been boiled and sun-dried, then rehydrated and fried. Containing 60 percent protein and significant amounts of phosphorus, iron and calcium, they are unrivalled as an easily obtainable source of free food for people living in the broad-leaf savannah of northern South Africa, Botswana and Zimbabwe.

LESOTHO

22 Pony Trekking through the Kingdom in the Sky

by Carrie Hampton

Lesotho, landlocked and completely encircled by South Africa, is the highest entire country in the world. It is also a land of no fences and few roads. The only transport in the interior is pony, donkey or your own two feet. A lengthy but leisurely pony trek seemed the best way to explore the country.

When I asked Sally to come pony trekking in Lesotho, she agreed before understanding what she was letting herself in for. I hadn't told her that we would be in the saddle for five or six hours a day, riding up and down steep gorges, sleeping in mud huts and not showering for four days—because I didn't know. However, all these surprises only added to a fabulous African adventure full of smiling people, idyllic villages and spectacular mountain scenery.

Sally lives in Cape Town and has a smart four-by-four vehicle, which we decided to use for our drive to Lesotho. It turned out that we had absolutely no need for such advanced technology, but at least the lengthy 12-hour journey was done in comfort.

As soon as we had crossed the chaotic but undemanding South Africa/Lesotho border, we could feel a difference in atmosphere. The slight underlying tension and ingrained resentment of South

Africa was gone. People waved happily at us and stared at our shiny, red Mitsubishi, which contrasted sharply with their rusty cars and minibuses.

AT THE GATES OF PARADISE

Hand-painted, lop-sided signposts directed us towards Malealea Lodge and Pony Trekking Centre, on a surprisingly good road. When we stopped at a high point to marvel at the approaching peaks, we did not realize that this was the renowned "Gates of Paradise" pass. Alone one minute, the next we were surrounded by children. I made the mistake of giving them sweets,

---

3 Sitting on a horse, walking up and down mountains for four days, is the easy part. Hikes to waterfalls vary in difficulty, but altitude and gradient make them exhausting. Expect very basic overnight facilities.

★ The lack of facilities (no washing facilities, long-drop toilet, sleeping on foam mattresses on the floors of mud huts) makes this an adventure for those who don't mind roughing it for a few days.

⚒ Cooking equipment is provided for you. You need to take food, sleeping bag, warm clothing and rain protection.

Below left: Without a pony, the only way to get around is to walk, with your baggage on your head
Above: Trekking through the remote Maluti mountains

but quickly learned my lesson. Lesotho's Tourist Board asks visitors not to hand out sweets, or *pom-poms* (a corruption of the French *bonbon*, picked up from French missionaries), as it encourages the children to beg. We left a small crowd fighting over the mints, while others ran after us, shouting: "Hello, *pom-poms*, hello!"

After about an hour, a final sign brought us to a square, one side of which was dominated by a supermarket. Steps led down into a *kraal* (enclosure), squelching with mud and manure and full of horses and their blanket-clad owners. Malealea Lodge and Pony Trekking Centre is a scattering of buildings, all clean and comfortable, with no pretensions of luxury. It is run by Mick and Di Jones, both born in the former British protectorate of Basotholand, before Lesotho gained its independence in 1966. Mick never leaves the country, but Di dashes back and forth to Bloemfontein in South Africa, where they have an office.

Malealea has no telephones, and Sally asked how they stay in contact with the outside world. "Well, actually, we don't," was Mick's reply. He explained that, to contact him from the civilized world, there are three unreliable stages. First, a phone call is made to the Bloemfontein office. The office then contacts a friendly

lady in the sleepy village of Wepener, near the Lesotho border, who may or may not be there. She then tries to establish radio contact with Mick—who also may or may not be there. Not a foolproof system, but it tends to work in an emergency.

RHYTHM OF THE NIGHT

The lodge was almost full to its capacity of 72 guests. They were mainly young people from all over the world, roughing it on overland bus trips, or middle-aged Europeans on coach tours around South Africa. The former hiked to the gorge to see Bushman paintings; the latter hitched an uncomfortable ride in the back of the truck. All then had to clamber down steep rocks to view the stick-man paintings, which are thousands of years old.

At dusk, I wandered from the centre towards the enticing sound of harmonious music. About 20 teenagers from the local village were gathered around the outdoor fire, singing their hearts out. Their strong voices cut through the darkness, and a lively African rhythm filled the night. For about half an hour, they danced and sang; then a band of about five boys performed on an assortment of home-made instruments. The guitar was made from a square oil tin; percussion came from a string of bottle tops, and the drum was a large, round oil can, covered in taut plastic. They plucked and pounded their contraptions with such rhythm and gusto that the audience couldn't keep from dancing. A hat was

223

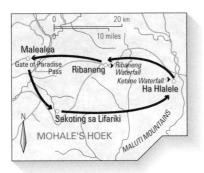

Our four-day trek into the mountains of Lesotho

passed around for both groups: the money would go towards sending some of the youths to school or college.

RIDING A HORSE LIKE A HARLEY

The next morning, Sally and I packed our clothes, food and sleeping bags into the large bags supplied to fit the packhorse. Camera, rain jacket, water bottle and other small essentials were stuffed into leather saddlebags, and we went in search of our steeds. Sally was assigned Bushman, a large chestnut horse, which looked surprisingly well fed. She was brought up on a farm, and I had assumed that she could ride. In fact, she hadn't been on a horse for 20 years, and looked as if she were sitting on a Harley Davidson—legs straight out, hands held high. I explained that a squeeze or a gentle kick with the legs could be classed as

the accelerator, and the reins would act as the steering, as well as the brakes. Sally chose her own method—shouting "Hey!" in imitation of our guide, Julius. On the whole, this worked quite well.

Our packs were loaded onto a little horse with no name. I mounted Black Label; Julius was on Ken. Julius is an experienced Basotho guide (the people of Lesotho are known as Basotho), who owns both Black Label and Ken, and earns more in four days of pony trekking than a labourer would in a month.

TERRIBLE DROUGHT

Julius pointed beyond the carefully tilled plateau on which we stood, across a hundred unseen valleys to the distant mountains. "This is where we are going," he said. Bushman liked being in the front, unlike Black Label, so the least experienced rider took the lead on the most willing horse. After less than an hour the plateau was ripped in two by a steep gorge. At the bottom ran a rather timid-looking river: Lesotho was in the midst of the worse drought in living memory. It was late October, and the spring rains should have filled the rivers and brought flowers into bloom. Instead, the waterfalls merely trickled, and the hillsides were parched yellow and crackling underfoot.

ORIGINS OF THE BASOTHO PONY

Lesotho's mountain terrain is tough to negotiate without transport. Early in the kingdom's history (around 1822), horses were imported, stolen or taken as spoils of tribal war. This continued until 1870, when it was recorded that almost the entire Basotho nation were mounted. The horses were of a noble, oriental, warm-blood stock from Arab, Barb and Persian strains, with some fine English thoroughbred cross which had arrived at the Cape of Good Hope. Soon the Basotho people found themselves exporting ponies instead of importing them. The Basotho pony was in demand because it had not been crossed with the inferior thoroughbred "blood weed" stock infiltrating South Africa's horses. The strong, sure-footed Basotho pony proved its worth during the Anglo-Boer War (1899), when most Boers fought from the backs of their sturdy farm ponies. The Basotho people are fast and fearless riders, but shelter and food for their horses, other than that supplied by nature, is seldom considered, and many horses are very thin.

LANGUAGE

The best way to make friends in a foreign country is to learn a few words of the language. "Yes," "No," "How are you" and "Thank you" are sufficient to endear yourself to the locals. Your guide can correct your pronunciation. The following words will come in useful:

Hello mother/father/brother/sister
Lumela (s), Lumelang. Mé/Ntate/Aboeti/Ausi
How are you? *U phela joang?*
I am well *Ke phela hantle*
Thank you *Kea leboha*
Yes *E-Ea* (said like a sigh)
No *Che*
Children *Bana*
Horse *Pere*
What is your name? *Lebitso la hau U mang?*
It is beautiful *E ntle*
I am sore *Ho bohloko*
Will you sing for us? *Na le tla re bine la?*
"Li" and "lu" are pronounced "di" and "du."

---

steadily. In Lesotho, whenever you think you are quite alone, children appear from nowhere, accompanied by goats, clanging with the sound of Swiss bells hung around their necks. These herders, aged six or seven, wore dirty, ripped clothing under warm Basotho blankets. They seemed timid at first, but soon plucked up courage to sit very close and stare. It was difficult to snooze with so many eyes on me, so I decided to chat. My Sesotho language extends to "*lumela*" (pronouced "*dumela*"), meaning "hello," and "*kea leboha*" (pronounced "*Ja lee bo ha*"), meaning "thank you." Basotho children learn English in school, but they knew only a few words, which they repeated over and over again.

VILLAGE HOSPITALITY

Chief Poli and his wife, Matelang, greeted us at their village of Sekoting sa Lifariki— our first night's stay. This small community stood alone in the mountains, far from any road. A little round mud-and-thatch hut was ready for us, and Matelang quickly fetched a bucket of crystal-clear water from the spring.

Each village visited by pony trekkers has built a special guest hut and stocked it, courtesy of Malealea Lodge, with table, chairs, foam mattresses, pots and pans, plates and cutlery, and a gas bottle for a little stove. The table was 2m (over 6ft) long, and we couldn't imagine how it had got here. At another village, some of the roofs were corrugated iron instead of thatch, and that puzzled us even more, as there were no roads in sight. In Malealea, Mick explained that, if the goods don't fit on a donkey, women carry them on their heads. It takes two women to carry two sheets of corrugated iron.

The villagers have one hut for living and sleeping, and one for cooking, where, tending to a pot on the fire, they sit chatting in asphyxiating smoke that billows out through the door. I was invited in, but could only manage a few seconds without coughing. I spent even less time in the chief's sleeping hut, as he

---

Grazing animals looked thin and hungry, but the people would survive, as long as next year's delayed harvest was not caught by early frost. We had to descend the gorge on a formidable, precipitous, boulder-strewn path, but fording the river was easy—the horses were barely up to their knees. Usually, they have to swim across.

We sauntered through the first of many idyllic-looking villages. Round thatched huts were grouped in family units, each with its own scattering of children, chickens and goats. "*Pom-poms*," shouted the toddlers running around in rags, but I was wiser now.

Lunch of bread and sardines was eaten on a dry, grassy hillside, far from anywhere, with rolling mountains in every direction. We were already over 2,000m (6,500ft) high, and climbing

LESOTHO

was currently sharing it with a recently slaughtered cow.

FREEDOM ON THE PEAKS

Our horses were set loose at night to roam the hillsides in search of grass, and I wondered if we would ever see them again. But they were saddled up and waiting by the time we emerged from the dark interior of our hut the next morning. The night had been full of thunder and lightning, giving the parched soil a few drops of rain, but the day looked clear. Goats

and cows were following their herders out to the hills, and we headed off to rub shoulders with the peaks.

We followed each other in silence, broken only by the occasional "hey!" The track was softer underfoot, and each hill we climbed and valley we crossed took us higher and higher. We reached a pass nearly 3,000m (9,750ft) high and stopped to look around with an overwhelming sense of freedom. We then descended into a world of soft, mossy grasses and terraced hillsides. Oxen were ploughing the fields ready for maize, sorghum, wheat and barley.

The valley floor was moist and tufted with large rosettes of lime-green reed grasses. Another couple of villages came and went as we plodded dreamily ever deeper into the Maluti Mountains. Smiling people responded happily to my shouts of "*Lumela,*" replying: "*Lumela mé*"— which I repeated, from then on. I hadn't realized that the Basotho people never just say "hello"—they always add

"brother/sister/father/mother" etc. I spent the rest of the trek greeting everyone with "hello mother".

A RING OF MOUNTAINS

We arrived at Ha Hlalele village by 3.30pm and looked around us in awe. We were surrounded by a ring of mountain tops. This elevated village, in the middle of the Maluti range, felt extremely remote. The chief's wife was an educated woman who had worked as a teacher in Maseru. Her husband had inherited the chief's title and she had taken her place at his side. She spoke perfect English, and was thrilled to receive our *Newsweek* magazines and other small gifts.

Four village girls accompanied me to the Ketane waterfall. Halfway down the steep gorge, I caught sight of the falls, which dropped 122m (nearly 400ft). The path led straight down, and I didn't feel like the climb back up, so we sat on the edge throwing rocks and waiting for the splash. The eldest girl began to sing: her voice was strong and pure, with a perfect pitch. The others joined in and their natural harmony and soothing songs touched my soul. I sat enraptured, while they sang to me for about 20 minutes.

FELLOW TRAVELLERS

On the third morning we crossed a shallow pass into a valley of soft, sweet grass. Neither of us was in the least bit sore from non-stop riding, and we completed the day in comfort. Julius took us on a slight detour to show us the impressive 100m (325ft) Ribaneng Waterfall from the top, and pointed out the village down below, where we would sleep that night.

The path that led there was a zig-zag ledge of rocks, most uncomfortable for our poor horses' hooves. At the top we met an impressive-looking couple riding long-maned horses with arched necks. A

Above: *Arriving at Ribaneng village for the last night of out trek*
Right: *The remote, empty wilderness of the Maluti Mountains stretched in all directions as we crossed this 3,000m (nearly 10,000ft) pass*

baby was riding snugly on the woman's back, swaddled warmly in blankets. Further down, we passed a young man who had a large suitcase balanced on the pommel of his saddle.

In Ribaneng village the earth and houses were bright orange. There was no grass and the wind blew the ochre dust into whirlwinds around my ankles. The chief was young (perhaps 30 years old) and took little notice of us. Nor did the children. This seemed strange, but when we saw more visitors arriving on ponies from a different direction, we realized that this village was used for all the one-night treks from Malealea. In all, there were four guest huts, some large enough to accommodate 15 sleepers.

The soft evening light formed a yellow halo over the village. I strolled around and was beckoned to a family group sitting on their dusty, mud-caked veranda, with a view they probably thought unspectacular. I showed them photographs from the Malealea brochure, which they passed around, eager to see more.

Our hut was just two strides away from the goat *kraal*, and I slept with the tinkling of bells in my ears. We were getting used to going to bed an hour after dark and awakening at dawn, so when Julius wanted to leave early it was not a problem. It began to rain gently as we were getting into our saddles, but the air still felt warm. Julius packed away his red Basotho blanket and got out a full set of yellow oil skins and a white construction-site hat. He was preparing for serious weather, which should have been a hint to us that we were underdressed.

The rain increased in strength and my shower-proof jacket soon relented to the battering. I got steadily wetter until even my boots were sloshing in water. Finally, after five very wet hours we arrived, shivering uncontrollably. Sally was so frozen that she couldn't get her foot out of the stirrup as she dismounted, and fell flat on her back in the mud. After a hot shower we stopped shaking, and decided that the rain was good news: the land

needed it, and it had completed the range of our four-day experiences.

The sun returned and, with it, some heat to thaw our bodies. We said goodbye to Julius and to our trusty steeds, who had carried us willingly into the very heart of Lesotho. We left the following morning in sublime sunshine with a better understanding of Mick's determination never to leave his home in this beautiful mountain kingdom.

TRAVELLERS' TIPS

❑ It is *very important* that you have rain-proof clothing. A rain cape is best. The lodge have a few for hire.

❑ Take all your own food for overnight treks: pasta, rice and noodles with packet sauces, vacuum-packed meat, tinned fish, a loaf of bread and cheese. Buy fruit and vegetables before getting to Lesotho. A bottle of wine or spirits is a nice evening treat. Gas stove, cooking pots, cutlery and crockery are supplied.

❑ To ensure that everything stays dry, unpack your luggage and put it into a large plastic garbage bag (available at Malealea shop). Then put it into the special packs for the packhorse.

❑ A penknife will be useful.

❑ Don't carry your passport, air tickets and documents on your trek, as they might get wet.

❑ Take small gifts for the villagers: edible treats, toiletries, clothes, gloves, hats or shoes—especially for children. I was asked for salt, glue and painkillers. Sweets are not encouraged, as they make the children beg. Instead, take crayons and paper, books, postcards and pictures.

❑ Ride with long reins, western-style, and be nice to your horse.

GOING IT ALONE

INTERNAL TRAVEL

South Africa's road, rail and airline networks are excellent but Lesotho's vary greatly and some roads are not advisable without a four-by-four. The road to Malealea is very good and is tarred for all but the last 7km (4 miles). Some South African car hire companies do not allow you to take their cars into Lesotho. Others allow it with a letter of authorization, which they provide. You can hire a car in Lesotho's capital city of Maseru. Public Combi taxi buses are not mechanically very safe and the visitor is not advised to use them. Lesotho is very mountainous, with almost no roads in the interior. Most people in Lesotho walk wherever they need to go and this is usually a very long way. The lucky ones own a horse or a donkey.

You can fly into Maseru (Lesotho) only from Johannesburg, not from Cape Town. The flight takes an hour. Malealea Lodge will collect you from Maseru if necessary. The drive from Maseru to Malealea—85km (53 miles)—takes one and a half hours. You can fly to Bloemfontein, South Africa (where Malealea Lodge have an office) and hire a car from there. The flight to Bloemfontein takes an hour and 35 minutes from Cape Town and an hour from Johannesburg. Driving from Bloemfontein to Malealea—200km (125 miles)—takes two and a half hours.

WHEN TO GO

The best months to visit are October through to April, from spring to early autumn. Summer is the rainy season, but the short, sharp afternoon showers are usually quite predictable. We were warned to expect four seasons in one day—we certainly got it over four days. In late October we experienced hot summer sunshine one day, a gentle breeze the next, then a bitter wind, followed by relentless rain, with snow following hard on our heels. February (late summer) is probably the best month, with great swathes of red-hot poker flowers in bloom. Late August/beginning of September (early spring) is also beautiful, with delicate peach blossoms covering the village trees.

PLANNING

Once your transport is arranged and your pony trek booked, you just have to be fit enough to sit on a horse for four days. The saddles are extremely comfortable and my companion, who had not ridden for 20 years, had no ill effects and only very slight stiffness. Nevertheless, a few riding lessons prior to your trek would not be wasted. It is important to note that these ponies cannot carry a person weighing more than 90kg (198lb).

Planning your food is not difficult, as supermarkets in South Africa have everything you need. There is also a shop at Malealea for any basics you have forgotten, such as candles, matches, rice etc. Given advance warning Malealea Lodge will arrange food for your trek, but they prefer you to come prepared. Malealea Lodge has some sleeping bags, towels and rain capes for hire—all of which are essential items.

ACCOMMODATION

Malealea Lodge offers clean, cheerful rooms with comfortable beds and hot showers. This seems like luxury after sleeping on a foam mattress on the floor of a thatched mud hut in the middle of the mountains. The overnight village huts have been built specifically for pony trekking visitors, but are the same as all the village huts: dark and spartan on the inside. A large pile of foam mattresses and some chairs are supplied, and there is a full set of cutlery and crockery. There are one or two gas stoves with several pots and pans and a bucket of fresh spring water for cooking and drinking. There are no washing facilities, and the toilet is a long-drop communal one on the hillside.

WHAT TO TAKE

- ❏ Camera with wide-angle lens.
- ❏ Spare film and battery.
- ❏ Rain-proof clothing (not just shower-proof) and a warm jacket.
- ❏ Food (see Travellers' Tips).
- ❏ Torch, candles and matches (candles can be bought at Malealea).
- ❏ Sleeping bag.
- ❏ Sunscreen.
- ❏ Hat, scarf and gloves.
- ❏ Swimsuit.
- ❏ Towel.
- ❏ Comfortable jeans.
- ❏ Gifts for your hosts.

HEALTH MATTERS

There are no mosquitoes at this altitude—so no malaria. Water at Malealea Lodge and in the remote villages is collected from crystal-clear springs and is safe to drink. You can, of course, boil it or purify it to make sure. The mountain air is refreshingly pure and you are unlikely to catch any diseases.

23 Kayaking along the Garden Route

by Carrie Hampton

South Africa's coastal Garden Route is so civilized that it seems more like the Mediterranean than Africa. But if it's adventure you want, just about every kind of activity is possible here. I decided that sea kayaking provided the perfect combination of exercise, close encounters with sea life and an element of challenge.

When Johan Loots of Real Cape Adventures told me that our sea kayaking trip would be based in Plettenberg Bay, I was delighted. I had visited this place some years before, and had fallen in love with it. We drove the 520km (325 miles) drive east along the coast from Cape Town in spring sunshine. With us was Sally, a 50-year-old South African; two more paddlers were to meet us in "Plett" (as Plettenberg Bay is affectionately called). Johan had to be persuaded to talk about himself, but eventually we learned that he was a psychologist, who had taken time out of his profession to satisfy his passion for paddling. He admitted that he had won a few competitions in his youth, and knew most of South Africa's coastline intimately. We felt in capable hands.

The fibreglass kayaks, in various shades of green and yellow, were rattling away on the trailer as we headed away from the Cape Peninsula. A quick look back before crossing Sir Lowry's Pass into the Overberg gave us the first of many magnificent scenic bay views. The road took us inland for a while, and our next view of the sea was at Mossel Bay—the official start of the Garden Route. The road runs along a narrow strip of land between the Indian Ocean and a chain of alpine-style lakes, amongst heavily wooded valleys.

HAVING A WHALE OF A TIME

We soon reached the most famous Garden Route town, Knysna, with its shops and cafés full of visitors. We continued over the hill to Plettenberg Bay and Johan's holiday home accommodation, "Lagoon

3 Suitable for most fitness levels; no prior preparations necessary. Your upper back and shoulders will probably feel a little overworked at first, but this disappears with daily paddling. You should be able to swim, though life jackets are supplied.

★★ You will be sharing a room (some with bunk beds) at Lagoon House, which is a self-catering family holiday home by the sea. The overnight hut up the Keurbooms River is basic dormitory-style, with only a mattress and blanket supplied. The climate is mild, the water refreshing and there are very few biting insects and no nasty diseases to worry about.

Kayak, paddle, wetsuit shorts and wind breaker are supplied. Extras such as a lycra bodysuit (against sun and wind), neoprene gloves and booties are useful in the cooler months (April–October).

House." Plett is an enormous horseshoe bay, with swathes of golden sand and rocky outcrops perfect for whale-watching and angling. It has just one main street of cafés, restaurants and shops, and a small population that is greatly increased every year during the high season. Plett remains a laid-back town, though, where people shop for their groceries in bare feet and sarongs.

Sonia, a young graphic artist, and Dave, an easy-going Capetonian, had already arrived at Lagoon House. Desperate to see some whales, and having been sitting in the vehicle for six hours, we strolled to Lookout Rocks, where the pounding ocean sent a whitewater veil skywards. Looking intently, we identified the V-shaped blow of the southern right whale, and felt an instant thrill to be only 200m (656ft) away. This is one of the species that migrates to the area

from July to November, to breed and give birth. Our visitor lolled around, before sticking its forked tail in the air and holding it there for a while. When it swam closer and let out a huge blow, its breath had a distinctly fishy odour.

PADDLING UP RIVER

The following morning, I looked out of the window to see Johan and Dave carrying the kayaks across the unmade road to the edge of the lagoon. After delving into the trailers storage compartment to select a colourful wetsuit, wind jacket and life jacket, Johan gave us a short introduction to paddling and rudder-use. The Paddle Yaks™, built to Johan's specifications, are very stable sit-on kayaks. They have front and back storage containers and are built for safety, rather than speed.

Below: *All kitted up and ready to go at Knysna Heads*

We had one each, but Johan does offer doubles.

We were off for an overnight journey up the Keurbooms River, and had stuffed sleeping bags, food, towels, and clothes into the watertight buckets. We were heading for a small overnight hut built especially for kayakers. The large, shallow lagoon, formed by the meeting of the Keurbooms and the Bitou rivers, was a gentle introduction. We paddled quietly past a breeding colony of kelp gulls (or southern blackbacked gulls), and around the privately owned Stanley's Island, then under the N2 highway, where a gentle following breeze made the kayak feel light and comfortable. A caravan park and resort lined the first part of the river. The water had changed from a transparent ocean blue to a golden malt whisky; as we continued, it turned as dark as black tea.

After about 4km (2 miles), a massive gorge prevented any further encroachment by happy campers, and we were alone in a cold, dark ravine. It was lined with sheer, glossy rocks, up to 300m (980ft) high, and filled with 30m (98ft) of water. Montane plants clung to crevices, and birds of prey soared high above us.

Into a Fairytale

The canyon lined our way for about 6km (almost 4 miles), which took us a leisurely hour and a half. When my shoulders started to cramp up, I downed paddle and just drifted for a while. There was no urgency; if you found yourself at the back, it was not long before you overtook somebody else in a daydream. The odd jetski passed us, creating the first waves we were to encounter, and I felt like a cork, bobbing on their unnatural wake. After about three hours' paddling, we encountered a string of orange buoys across the river. These indicated that motorized boats may go no further. From then on, the river was ours alone.

The riverbanks were now crowded with trees: yellow-wood, stinkwood and milkwood, whose names explain themselves. Their wonderfully gnarled trunks

THE FLORAL KINGDOM

The Western Cape has its own unique floral kingdom called fynbos ("fine bush"). This encompasses proteioids (tall, flowering *protea* bushes), ericoids (heath-like *erica* shrubs), restoids (reeds) and geophytes (bulbous plants). There are 8,600 species, of which 5,800 are endemic. Table Mountain alone contains more species than the whole of the United Kingdom, and fynbos has more diversity than the richest parts of the Amazon. Poor soil, lack of nutrients, low rainfall, persistent wind and frequent fires have made the plants adapt and develop. Fynbos thrives on fire, and seeds hidden in the earth by ants, who cannot resist their fluids, are triggered into germination by heat and smoke. When you see a hillside fire in the Cape, it may not be wreaking the havoc you imagine.

and thickly entwined branches gave us the impression of floating through a macabre fairytale. When the river became too shallow to continue, we beached the kayaks and went looking for the hut along a sandy path. The hut was made entirely of wood and raised from the ground on stilts. Bunk beds with mattresses and blankets were inside, and the outside fireplace had some wood. This was our overnight accommodation.

There was time for a quick dip from the beautiful little beach. Just upriver, beyond a small rapid, the river loses its brackish, tidal flavour and becomes fresh water. The sun set fast behind the mountains, and a dark chill descended early. The smell of *braaing* (barbecuing) chops and *borewors* (thick farm sausage) was mouthwatering, and we settled around a wooden table to contemplate the stars. Wilderness experiences tend to bring out the philosopher in you, and we retired to bed having put the world to rights.

It was September—spring in the

Cape—so still a little chilly in the mornings and evenings. Birds hopped about in the bushes, and I caught a glimpse of a rare Knysna lourie, a large and agile bird, springing in green and crimson flashes along a branch.

SEAFOOD ON THE BEACH

The paddle back was our first test of fortitude, as the headwind through the gorge was enough to force you backwards if you stopped for a rest. My shoulders ached, my back felt uncomfortable and my feet had pins and needles. Johan urged us on with the temptation of refreshments at the Keurbooms River Lodge, at the mouth of the river. We paddled up to the poolside balcony and clambered up in our vivid, damp attire. They didn't seem to mind, and we soon perked up enough to continue the short paddle back to the house. The evening culminated in prawns and luscious Knysna oysters in the Lookout Beach Bar, right on the sand, where they mixed the strongest Mai Tai cocktail I have ever tasted.

When we set off the next day, towing the kayaks, nobody was quite sure where we were going. Knysna was on the cards, but Johan wanted to catch the high tide with a low wind—a combination not available that morning. As various decisions came and went, we concluded that all plans were "cast in quicksand," and that we would just have to relax until something happened. So we continued along to Knysna Heads and decided to brave the swell and the wind.

The Knysna Heads are high cliffs forming a narrow, rocky entrance from the sea into the famous Knysna lagoon, on which the town is situated. The tide gushes furiously in and out and strong currents swirl in eddies around submerged rocks. It takes a brave or experienced yachtsman to negotiate this unfriendly stretch of water. At one time, Lloyds of London refused to insure ships passing in and out. Getting into the bobbing boats took some perseverance: we had to put one leg either side, then slide into the seat without tipping over. Heading into the short choppy swell was unnerving and when Sonia found herself side on to it, she flipped up and disappeared. She surfaced, looking a little shocked, and leaped back onto the kayak faster than she had fallen out. Seeing how easy it was to get back on, we soon became braver and paddled across the entrance to the heads. We practised surfing down the short swell and getting some

SEA FOOD AND EAT IT

The Western Cape has the best seafood in South Africa and the greatest variety. You can sometimes buy straight from the boat or even from individuals on the roadside, who hold up their day's catch to tempt you. When eating seafood in a restaurant you can afford to be fussy. Choose oysters from Knysna, as they will be the most mature and tasty. Mussels must come from the west coast harbour of Saldanha, where they grow big and luscious. The open season for collecting crayfish, or rock lobster, nicknamed "red gold," is between November and April. If you are offered it at other times, it will be frozen. Long, thin, silvery snoek, of the barracuda family, should be eaten on the day of the catch, but thick tuna steaks keep longer. West coast sole is delicate and light, and the firm, white flesh of Cape salmon is top of the list for flavour. Until galoen was fished out, it took pride of place as the tastiest fish, and although it can still be caught, it is illegal to sell it. Most restaurants offer "line fish"—whatever has been caught on the line that day. Most small-harbour fishing boats are sectioned off into cubicles and each fisherman literally throws out his hand line to see what he can get. He is paid according to his catch. Your supper probably comes from one of these little boats, rather than a great ocean-going trawler.

speed up before taking avoiding action as rocks suddenly appeared.

It gave us a bit of a fright when a dark shape suddenly broke the surface in front of us. It was a small Bryde's whale, perhaps 7m (23ft) long, with a sleek body and prominently hooked dorsal fin. He swam around for a while, seemingly oblivious, as we sat there, enthralled. We were all quite confident by now, and revelled in the knowledge that we were kayaking in one of the trickiest places along the entire coast with a whale for company.

CRUISE IN CALM WATER

While the three women—Sally, Sonia and myself—cruised into the calmness of the huge Knysna lagoon, Johan and Dave drove around to the new waterfront development of Knysna Quays. We set off past Leisure Isle, full of desirable holiday homes and award-winning guest houses and hotels, and marvelled at how warm the water had become. It was warm because it was shallow—so shallow, in fact, that I ground to a halt on the sandy bottom. Too late, I realized what all the bright marker buoys were indicating. Back in the channel, we paddled past lunchtime diners at the Tapas Bar on Thesens Island and meandered through yachts moored out on permanent buoys. Eventually we arrived at Knysna Quays, where smart yachts park alongside the jetties. Johan and Dave had rejoined us and we became the centre of attention, as our brightly clad fleet of kayaks drifted through the exclusive waterfront environs of shops, restaurants and apartments.

Left: *Kayaking in the turbulent waters off Knysna Heads*
Above: *The Outeniqua Choo Tjoe steam train crossing the Kaaimans River Bridge is an impressive sight*

We parked up and lunched on fresh "line fish" of the day, and then explored Knysna's main street. Famous for its birds and for its wood, it specializes in carving the former out of the latter. Knysna's indigenous forests still exist, but only one Knysna elephant is left—a grumpy old matriarch who roams the forests alone.

OPEN OCEAN SWELL

Buffels Bay is on the coast just west of Knysna, and Johan decided that this was where we should get our first taste of open ocean. He gave us clear instructions on how to get through the breaking waves without falling off, but we remembered how easily Sonia had lost her balance earlier, and looked at him sceptically. "Just follow me," he shouted. Behind me, someone got a dunking in the waist-high water, but I was too busy paddling to look back. The ocean was frighteningly big. As we headed away from the safety of the cove towards an ever-increasing swell, I became a little apprehensive. When you are only centimetres above sea level, the

rise and fall of the waves seems mountainous. Down in a trough it was easy to lose sight of the others momentarily. While Johan was happily surfing down the leading edge of the waves, I was working myself up into a state of panic. Sonia and Sally calmed me down, and presently I had relaxed enough to row with the flow and try a bit of wave-riding. I was picking up speed and wondering how to stop, when the swell suddenly seemed to run out of steam. We surfed back into shore, avoiding the rocks and putting in a last-minute right angle turn. Johan messed around in the wave break a little more, and showed us how it was done.

In a mad dash we loaded up, and just made it back into the water at Kaaimans River mouth, in time to see the renowned Outeniqua Choo Tjoe steam train cross the bridge. Low tide was on the turn, sandbanks impeded our progress and a ripping tide made control difficult. With seconds to spare, Johan alone found deep water and paddled with a professional's speed towards the bridge. We sat stranded, mid-river, and watched with cameras poised. We were quite exhausted by the time we got back to Lagoon House, and decided that home-cooked food, wine and some mutual shoulder-massaging was a fine way to spend an evening.

WATCH THAT BIRDIE

Here are a few colourful or entertaining birds to look out for along the Garden Route:

Knysna lourie—grass-green with blue wings and a scarlet lining, a tufted peak on its head, and white rings around the eyes. Only found in this area.

Hoopoe—a bird with a "Mohican" crest that gives it a startled look. Dressed modestly in brick brown with pied black-and-white wings, it struts around woodlands probing the ground with its long, curved bill.

Greater doublecollared sunbird—an irides-cent, green, long-beaked nectar-eater, with a large band of shimmering red on its chest. It has a high-pitched, high-speed "tweet" and flits from flower to flower.

Helmeted guinea fowl—daft-looking birds, with an ugly blue-and-red head which has a fleshy knob on the top. They wander in large flocks, muttering to each other, and screech if startled. Their black feathers with white polka dots can be found everywhere.

Speckled mousebird—this sociable chatterer makes up for its dull grey and brown colour with a tufty topknot and very long tail.

Our last day was again at sea, but in the lee of the wind and waves, beside the Robberg Peninsula. This long lizard-shaped peninsula, is a pristine nature reserve with a full day's hike around it. We set off from Plettenberg Bay Main Beach, past the moored fishing boats and the monolithic Beacon Isle Hotel. Once the site of a whaling station, then a family hotel, it is now a hotel/time-share complex of dubious design but with an amazing location. This was a dawn excursion, taking advantage of the early morning calm, and the sun rose over wonderfully placid water. I was hoping to see some of the bottlenosed dolphins that frequent the bay, but was told that I would probably have to wait until 4.30pm, when they did their daily dive by. We did see a couple of whales, but were prohibited by law from going closer than 300m (984ft).

SHARK TERRITORY

It was about 4km (2 miles) to the high protective cliffs of Robberg. On the way we floated above the wreck of the little coaster *Athena*. The water was clear enough to see big fish swimming around this artificial reef; Johan told us that he has witnessed a shoal of juvenile hammerhead sharks along this stretch. Hammerheads tend to mind their own business, but great whites have been known to poke their noses into other people's affairs. This whole coast is great white territory, although they are rarely seen.

Back at Main Beach I was astonished to see a motorboat heading straight towards the land at full throttle. I was sure it would crash into the beach—and that's exactly what it did. As there is no harbour, the boats are rammed up onto the soft sand as far as they will go, then winched onto a trailer and driven away.

Our last evening drink may have been on dry land, but we still had sand between our toes. We walked the beach and climbed the rocks at Keurboomstrand, at the furthest end of the bay. Once more the scenery was dramatic, with alpine chalets perched on heavily wooded hillsides. The weather looked moody, but the threatening clouds simply bruised into shades of purple for a stunning sunset.

We all ended the trip with a wonderful feeling of tranquillity, after drifting around on calm water, messing around in waves and paddling with whales. With muscular shoulders and a sense of well-being, we reluctantly packed our paddles and stowed the boats for the last time. Plettenberg Bay retains its place in my list of favourite places: I have a feeling that this was not destined to be my last visit.

GOING IT ALONE

WHEN TO GO

July to November is a great time for shore-based whale-watching, although resident whales and dolphins can be seen from boat excursions all year round. In the winter and spring, the weather has its cool moments, as does the sea, but it is often warm enough for short sleeves. Nights are very cool. December to March is high summer season, sunny but not unbearably hot. The area comes alive during this time, and is buzzing with visitors.

INTERNAL TRAVEL

Plenty of coaches travel the along the coast. The Baz Bus is a hop-on, hop-off minibus service, with a ticket that allows you to stop as many times as you like before reaching your destination. Every Cape Town tour operator offers Garden Route tours. Trains run along the Garden Route, but getting through to Transnet state railway enquiry office is almost impossible. Book through a travel agent or go to the station in person.

PLANNING

Sea kayaking trips can get booked up in the high season (December to February) but they will normally "make a plan," which is the South African way of saying "don't worry." Nature Conservation and Albergo Backpackers in Plettenberg Bay hire canoes for day trips up the Keurbooms River, and South African National Parks hire out canoes for excursions on the lakes at Wilderness (see A–Z Activities). I would not recommend taking to the sea in a kayak without a guide, unless you are very experienced, as conditions can change quickly and this coastline can be quite tricky.

HEALTH MATTERS

You are highly unlikely to catch anything nasty here and no special precautions are necessary. There are very few insects to bother you and no malarial mosquitoes. Tap water in the whole of South Africa is fine to drink, although bottled water is readily available if you prefer it. You can buy any type of food to suit most dietary needs.

WHAT TO TAKE

- ❏ Binoculars.
- ❏ Waterproof camera or padded waterproof bag for camera.
- ❏ Hat, sunglasses and sunscreen.
- ❏ A lycra bodysuit is useful to guard against sun, wind and cooler weather, but not essential. Neoprene gloves and booties for cooler months.
- ❏ If you have a weak back, bring along a foam pad for extra comfort.

WHALE TALES

Whales found around Plettenberg Bay:

Southern right whale—length: 11–18m (36–59ft); weight: 30–80 tonnes (29–78 tons). These placid giants, who swim close inshore, were the "right" whales to catch. The male's testicles can weigh 500kg (1,102lb) each. The whales migrate from the sub-Antarctic to breed and mate in the Cape.

Bryde's whale—length: 11.5–14.5m (38–47½ft); weight: 12–20 tonnes (12–19 tons). Resident around Plettenberg Bay. They feed on shoaling fish, sometimes in conjunction with common dolphins.

Humpback whale—length: 11.5–15m (38–49ft); weight: 25–30 tonnes (24–29 tons). Amongst the most boisterous of all whales, well known for breaching, lob-tailing and flipper-slapping. Their song is the longest and most complex of all animal communication.

Minke whale—length: 7–10m (22–30ft); weight: 5–10 tonnes (5–10 tons). Some individuals are quite inquisitive and may suddenly appear suddenly alongside a boat, but they disappear just as fast. They occur throughout the world and are highly variable in appearance.

Killer whale—length: 5.5–9.8m (18–32ft); weight: 2.5–9 tonnes (2–9 tons). This is actually a dolphin, known as the ultimate predator. Sightings are irregular, but they are one of the most wide-ranging mammals found all over the world, and can easily swim 150km (94 miles) a day.

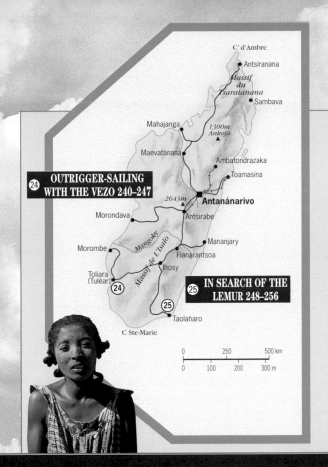

The map shows the following locations:

C' d'Ambre
Antsiranana
Massif du Tsaratanana
Sambava
Mahajanga
1300m Ankofa ▲
Maevatanana
Ambatondrazaka
Toamasina
OUTRIGGER-SAILING WITH THE VEZO 240–247 (24)
2643m ▲ **Antanánarivo**
Morondava
Antsirabe
Mananjary
Moromodava (Mangoky / Massif de l'Isalo)
Fianarantsoa
Ihosy
Toliara (Tuléar) (24)
IN SEARCH OF THE LEMUR 248–256 (25)
(25)
Taolañaro
C Ste-Marie

Scale:
0 250 500 km
0 100 200 300 m

MADAGASCAR

This massive island, which detached itself from the African continent in the distant darkness of time, offers a complete contrast to the mainland. Here you will meet Asian culture on African land, as well as flora and fauna that exist nowhere else. Mesmerizing landscapes start in the high plateaux of the centre and descend to tropical rainforest and arid desert, punctuated by dramatic escarpments, before finally reaching shores of the Indian Ocean. Among this topographical diversity live some 13 million people descended from Indonesians, Africans, Arabs and Indians—a fascinating mosaic of this vast ocean's cultures, which also has the imprint of 60-odd years of French colonization. Lemurs and baobabs are the most obvious of Madagascar's many endemic species, but they are just the beginning of a completely open-ended experience, so great is the potential for adventure in this magnificent but little-developed country.

The imposing canyons of the Isalo Massif

MADAGASCAR

24 Outrigger-sailing with the Vezo

by Fiona Dunlop

Coral reefs, lobsters, sharks and baobab trees are the main natural attractions on Madagascar's scenic west coast. As well as these, the local Vezo people offer an unusual form of transport: the outrigger, which represents the historical connection between this vast chunk of Africa with its Asian origins.

Square white sails dot the horizon; in the foreground, dugouts bob in the waves while their occupants haul in nets full of fish. As we glide past, some wave and shout a few words in Malagasy to my boatmen. Intrigued by the theory that the island's early inhabitants had sailed all the way from southeast Asia across the Indian Ocean, I was keen to witness the maritime prowess of the Vezo, Madagascar's people of the sea, who remain most faithful to their origins. Their livelihood depends on predicting wind strengths and directions by observing coconut palms and judging currents and tides; it is said that some are even capable of locating shoals of fish just by smelling the water.

THE WEST COAST

This sub-group of western Madagascar's Sakalava people lives scattered along the southwest coast from Morondava to south of Tuléar, on the edge of a region notorious for its aridity and inhospitable spiny

Unless you suffer from seasickness, the outrigger experience is straightforward, though it does require organizational skills and some knowledge of French.

★ Don't expect luxury on this adventure. Outrigger seats are just planks, and accommodation is very basic. It can be extremely hot, although there is always a breeze.

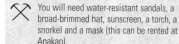 You will need water-resistant sandals, a broad-brimmed hat, sunscreen, a torch, a snorkel and a mask (this can be rented at Anakao).

forest. Beauty and bounty characterize the Mozambique Channel, dividing Madagascar from continental Africa. Gigantic tuna, parrotfish, turtles, prawns and sea cucumbers all figure among the rich display. My plan was to travel as much as I could by outrigger—in French *pirogue*, in Malagasy *laka fihara*—and to discover what was left of the underwater life after centuries of Vezo fishing. Rumour had it that the scuba diving off this coast, around the Great Barrier Reef of Tuléar, was comparable to the wonders of the Red Sea. In Madagascar, where there is little concrete information, rumours have to be taken seriously.

TULÉAR

The starting point is Tuléar (or Toliara), a provincial capital and lively little port of 60,000 people, where a seemingly infinite jetty stretches far out to reach water that is deep enough for cargo boats to moor. Tidal movement is strong here: you may check into a hotel in the evening when the sea is lapping at its feet, and wake up next morning to look over sludgy brown mudflats. All is redeemed, however, by wide avenues lined with swaying coconut palms, fragrant frangipani trees, scarlet hibiscus bushes, seafood restaurants and pockets of French colonial architecture.

From Tuléar, my plan was to head just over 30km (18 miles) south to a Vezo fishing village called Anakao, which lies opposite the protected island of Nosy Ve and its marine reserve. Anakao boasts just one hotel, and this has a diving centre, so it seemed the perfect destination. Halfway there lies another Vezo village, Saint Augustin, whose history of European pirates also sounded promising and where, in theory, I could negotiate an outrigger to reach Anakao.

THE TAXI-BROUSSE TRAIL

I trailed around Tuléar's taxi-brousse (bush taxi) station enquiring about bush-taxis to Saint-Augustin, and received conflicting information. Taxis did go there, but no office displayed that name on its destination board. As the heat rose towards its midday climax, I muttered the name as if it were a mantra, stepping over bamboo cages of chickens and battered cardboard boxes trussed up with recycled string, while their owners took refuge in the shade of nearby trees. Finally, inside a dark, half-built ticket-office, I saw a Saint Augustin sign on the desk and a ticket-seller silhouetted against a mountain of secondhand tyres.

MADAGASCAR'S TRIBES

Malagasy ethnic identities are not easily definable as, apart from the Merina in the highlands, most regional populations are of very mixed descent. Linguists have identified elements of Bantu, Swahili, Arabic, English and French in the national language, which is spoken throughout the island in slightly varying dialects. The closest language to Malagasy outside Madagascar is Ma'anyan, spoken by the Orang Laut (sea-people) of southern Kalimantan in Indonesian Borneo. Of the 18 official tribes that make up the total population of 15 million, the Vezo is the one with the closest affinity to the sea, although anthropologists maintain that, as they are of mixed ethnic origin, definition is by their fishing activities, rather than by any common ancestry.

Unfortunately, he was adamant that no taxi would go there, as the road was too rough.

Eventually, his colleague suggested that I go by road to Ankilybe, a fishing village only 15km (9¼ miles) away, from where I could take a *pirogue* to Saint Augustin. Next morning, before 7am, I stood at the towering tree that doubled as the Ankilybe taxi terminus. Fruit-sellers had already set up in its shade and there was no shortage of activity around me. A car wreck lay across the kerb; a bicycle ridden by two men and four chickens peddled past—then, finally, a pick-up truck drew up. When I asked if it was for Ankilibe, the driver shook his head, and pointed to the wrecked car. That was when I noticed two legs sticking out, attached to a mechanic, who was tightening screws somewhere in the chassis.

ON THE ROAD

Within minutes the driver had appeared, and suddenly passengers materialized from nowhere, piling into the tarpaulin-covered truck with the mechanic, who instantly became the ticket-seller. Luckily he granted my request for a front seat, which I shared with a vociferous lady in a bright pink dress and what appeared to be a spare car battery as a footrest. After syphoning petrol into the tank, the driver push-started the truck and the motor spluttered into life. As we bounced along past zebu-carts and cactus fences, he expounded on the relative merits of the English and French languages in rock music. He turned out to be an ardent electric guitarist, frustrated by the lack of music education in Tuléar, although this town spawns a growing list of popular musicians. Turning off the RN7 onto a dirt road, we passed the region's only mountain, which reaches a dizzy height of 165m (540ft), and memorable for its symmetrical, level-topped profile. Although its Malagasy name is Mahinia, it is known locally as Table, or Onzatable (i.e. "on the table"), a name probably originating from the days of English pirates.

MADAGASCAR

From the land, Ankilybe is hidden behind a bank of sand dunes. I trudged over the ridge and, not for the last time, my heart sank. The cluster of huts and women washing pots did not look too promising, despite the background lure of the azure sea. But the magic word *pirogue* soon brought me to the water's edge, where dozens of dugouts lay on

Above: *The brightly coloured taxi-brousse at Ankilybe soon fills up with passengers*
Right: *The mast is erected and the sail unfurled—my outrigger is ready to go at Ankilybe*

the sand. Intense negotiation with the only fisherman who spoke some French soon halved his asking price, and he and two other young boatmen set up the mast and unfurled the sail of a sturdy-looking outrigger. We were ready to go.

THE TROPIC OF CAPRICORN

It was then that, looking at a detailed map, I realized that we were right on the Tropic of Capricorn. As we sped across a transparent turquoise sea, I felt the magic and, at the same time, the security of sailing in this primitive vessel. Despite its apparent fragility, the deep, narrow hull, hollowed out of a softwood trunk, is perfectly balanced by two perpendicular bars, attached on one side to a wooden float and, on the other forming a suspended triangle. The geometrical precision of this system maintains a perfect balance, even in rough seas, so passengers perched on their narrow plank seats need not fear. The square sail, often a masterpiece of patchwork (I counted 15 patches on one of them), moves with a boom and the adjustable 5m (16ft) mast is simply slotted into a block of wood. After half an hour of being gently propelled by windpower, my boatmen decided things were not moving fast enough: paddlepower stepped in. For the next two hours they paddled practically non-stop, only once stopping to sip some water. I understood why "Vezo" means "paddle."

The approximately 2,000km (1,243 miles) of Madagascar's indented west coast make up a tantalizing stretch of white-sand beaches edged by coral reefs and the odd tiny island. Our route, however, took us past a large swathe of mangroves, before we rounded a headland to cross another bay, where a few thatched shacks eventually took shape on the horizon. Again my heart sank: this could not be Saint Augustin—there was nothing to it. As if reading my mind, the boatman, Frédéric, turned round and, with a toothy grin, told me in his limited French that it was Sarodrano. This village is known for several grottoes that contain sweet water and are considered sacred by the Vezo. We sailed past the village, beautifully outlined against the clean-cut contours of white sand dunes; children splashed and screamed in the waves; bare-breasted women washed in the shallows, and a few men stood picturesquely around outriggers.

THE CUCUMBER MEN

Meanwhile, at sea, we passed countless canoes at anchor. Many of the fishermen were diving to collect sea cucumbers off the bottom. These *dinga-dinga* play an important role in the coral reef system,

acting as cleaners and fertilizers of the ocean floor. Around 47 species are found in Madagascar but, since the early 1990s, their numbers have been seriously depleted to furnish the voracious appetites of Singapore's and China's gourmets. Traders in Tuléar sell them to Asia, where they fetch prices that are higher even than those other local products, lobster and shark's fins. Until recently, sea cucumbers were easy to collect, but Vezo fishermen now have to dive up to 15m (49ft) to find them. This they do without air tanks and often without masks.

Soon the dunes of Sarodrano gave way to limestone cliffs topped by tufts of vegetation and pockmarked at water level by dark grottoes. Until then the sea had been calm; if there were any waves, the boatmen would stop paddling and let the outrigger gently rise and fall. However, around the next headland a suspicious number of white crests broke up the horizon. Our boat was starting to bob up and down more excitedly when Frédéric turned round, smiled, and told me not to worry. Excited exchanges between the boatmen told me something was up—and suddenly, we were in it. Steering the boat directly into the surf, they paddled furiously as the outrigger slapped through this aquatic roller-coaster. It was oceanic white-water rafting!

MADAGASCAR

WATERING HOLE AHOY

Within minutes the adrenalin rush was over and we were back on calmer waters. After rounding another headland, we moved into increasingly shallow waters, over a white, sandy bottom. Saint Augustin came into sight, nestling at the back of a huge half-moon bay between the Onilahy estuary and a tributary of the Andoharano River. For tidal reasons we landed about 500m (550yds) down the beach, then waded through a shallow lagoon to reach the village. Church bells tolled as Flilakison, who had been at the rudder all the way, gallantly carried my bag past zebu, pigs, goats and a gaggle of ducks. We were back on land and back in civilization—of a sort.

I'd been given the name of Saint Augustin's only hotelier, sounding something like "Glow Vear," by a helpful Indian shopkeeper in Tuléar. This turned out to be another remnant of English piratical presence, as it was actually spelt "Glover," though pronounced in a French

NOSY VE'S UNDERWATER SIGHTS

Club-horned corals, huge plate corals, mushroom corals, brain corals, thistle soft corals and branching soft corals are among the diversely textured landscape. Feeding off them or gliding past is an equally vivid population of reef fish. The beautiful angelfish family shows off its brilliantly coloured markings, joined by flashy parrotfish, adorned wrasse and countless yellow butterfly fish. Skulking in the shadows are lobsters and prickly-looking devil firefish. Close encounters with sharks are rare here, unlike on Madagascar's east coast, as they stick to deeper waters further out. These hammerhead, great white, whale and dolphin sharks are nevertheless hunted by Vezo fishermen for their lucrative fins.

INDIAN MUSLIMS

Apart from the Vezo, there is a prominent population of Muslim Indians in this area. They settled in Tuléar several generations ago, but despite their long presence, there is no intermarriage, and there has been occasional racial friction—notably in 1987, when rioters destroyed numerous Indian-owned shops. These family businesses have since recovered. Chinese traders are present, too, but in far smaller numbers.

way. The hotel was more like a family compound, with a handful of bamboo huts designed for the few tourists who came this way. Its name, Auberge du Corsaire, was fitting. Here I said goodbye to my energetic boatmen, who had been touchingly concerned for my wellbeing throughout our journey. They set off again to enjoy better winds and clear sailing back to Ankilybe.

IN SAINT AUGUSTIN

It was not difficult to settle into the lazy rhythms of the hotel. Its main spokeswoman was the beaming 18-year-old Espérance, backed up by her 20-year-old cousin, Damien, who conveniently turned out to be the resident boatman. We had soon struck a deal for the next leg of my outrigger trip, to start at 6am the following day, which was signed and sealed by Damien knocking down a fresh coconut for me to drink. He then volunteered to show me round Saint Augustin.

About 600 inhabitants are catered for by no fewer than five churches, a large new school, a dilapidated clinic and a fresher-looking maternity ward. In the middle of all this stands a venerable, French-style *mairie* (town hall), beside which sprawls the market, consisting of a row of women vendors seated on the ground behind mountains of mangoes and manioc. Later, when I entered the local *épicerie* in search of some repeatedly demanded *cadeaux* (gifts) for a gang of girls pursuing me, I saw how little was available besides fresh produce: all they got was a packet of dry biscuits, which was triumphantly snatched from my hand as if it were a gold bar.

ON THE WAVES TO ANAKAO

I woke before dawn, to hear the cocks crowing, but Saint Augustin has a slow pace: *mora mora*, the Malagasy expression meaning "easy-going," came into its own here. My new boatmen, Damien and Filudi, only used their paddles intermittently, despite an almost total absence of wind. A flotilla of outriggers turned out to be the night fishermen returning: their lack of any kind of light system means that nocturnal fishing only takes place under a full moon. We drifted past the tiny villages of Lovocampy and Soalary, keeping so close to the shore that at times I was tempted to leap out and walk. The water was transparent enough to count the blades of sea grass, and see coral formations and shoals of silvery fish—just an appetizer for the diving that was to come.

Finally, as we rounded a last headland, a white strip broke the monotony of blue. This sandy, uninhabited island was Nosy Ve (which means "is it an island?"). Rimmed by exquisite coral reefs, it draws scuba-divers to its shores. Dozens of outrigger sails were coming into view and finally, three hours of non-sailing later, we landed on the beach of Anakao in front of a row of neat-looking hotel bungalows. Brightly painted outriggers lay on the sand, women sauntered past balancing huge silvery fish on their heads, children threw themselves in and out of the water, smoke rose from cooking fires, a motorboat sped through the waves, and the village stretched south to the next headland. It felt infinitely livelier than Saint Augustin.

INTO THE DEPTHS

Laurent, the French diving instructor who had learnt his trade in the much chillier waters of Brittany, was guiding me through the fantasy underworld of Marumbi, a dive site that lies southwest of Nosy Ve, one of 10 in the vicinity with depths of up to 30m (98ft). It was spectacular: a complete contrast to the wide open seas of the lengthy outrigger journey. We swam through canyons and tunnels, over plateaus and precipitous slopes that dropped down to white, sandy bottoms, all blanketed in densely packed coral formations. Since we rarely descended below 8m (26ft), and visibility was near perfect, the colours remained mesmerizingly bright, sometimes spotlit by shafts of sunlight, at other times muted by the shadows of overhangs, and always echoed in the brilliant markings of abundant reef fish.

After nearly an hour we surfaced to the boat, cruised round the island, then stopped to snorkel at "the aquarium" (the officially protected marine reserve). Here the fish and coral were equally abundant,

TOMB ART

In the last few years, Sakalava-Vezo funerary art has had to change its style, due to the effect of tomb-plunderers. The monumental square tombs were once made of sculpted wood, incorporating erotic statues and images of oxpecker birds, which symbolized the separation between the world of the living and that of the dead. Virtually nothing remains of these edifices that drew visitors to Mangily, near Morondava. Instead, today's tombs are built in rendered stone, some of which can be seen beside the RN7, about 25km (15 miles) from Tuléar. Mermaids, romantic seaside trysts, aeroplanes, wrestlers, a lustful kiss and, of course, outriggers are among the whimsical murals, while the roofs are spiked with carved wooden totems and—the most important element—rows of zebu cattle horns from the deceased's precious herd.

Above: *Colourful outriggers pulled up on the beach at Anakao*

but a strong current made swimming difficult. We sped back to Anakao, and our small diving group exchanged impressions. A Frenchman in his 50s announced that, for him, the diving around Nosy Ve was far superior to anything he had seen around La Réunion or Mauritius.

RETURN JOURNEY

Days later, as the tiny plane I had hitched a ride in flew low up the coastline to Murumbé in a cloudless sky, I could pick out the contours of atolls and reefs in the turquoise sea below. We circled over the Baie des Assassins before Patrice, the French pilot, landed on the rough airstrip at Murumbé, my last Vezo village. As I strolled along Murumbé's beach, the scene felt pleasantly familiar: outriggers, gangs of children, chatty women with tightly braided hair and faces covered in bark paste, and with smiling, open-faced men. All this was edged by an infinite blue, sprinkled with white sails. Nostalgia set in.

This increased a few hours later, as our little plane was heading northeast towards Antananarivo. Suddenly we found ourselves in the heart of a thunderstorm: lightning cracked, the grey clouds swirled, water trickled into the cabin, the plane bounced madly and all orientation disappeared. I longed to be back on the Tropic of Capricorn. Not one drop of the ocean had landed on me during my outrigger adventures.

CURIOSITIES

Nosy Ve is not only shrouded in its colourful piratical past (numerous human bones have been found there) but also in ongoing Vezo *fady* (taboos), which include a ban on pork or pig on the island. To the south lies the even tinier island of Nosy Satrana, where another curiosity of the region has been uncovered: the fossilized eggs of the *Aepyornis*, a distant relative of the ostrich that reached heights of over 3m (10ft), but became extinct about 500 years ago. Also known as the elephant bird, this flightless creature laid gigantic, football-sized eggs, of which fragments occasionally turn up. At Anakao, however, you will be more likely to come across countless perfect seashells, their contours softened from being churned by the waves. Remember, however, that removing seashells from the ocean floor is illegal, even in Madagascar, and that shell-sellers at Anakao or Tuléar should not be encouraged.

GOING IT ALONE

WHEN TO GO

This hot region, the driest in Madagascar, sees tropical downpours in January and February, although these are sporadic, in some cases providing only 5cm (2in) of annual rain. From May to July, a strong southern wind, the *tsioke-atsimo*, often prevents outriggers from sailing. In July and August, Europe's main holiday season, Madagascar's limited infrastructure becomes severely stretched, so that period is also best avoided. Altogether, the best times of year for this region are March to April and September to November.

VISAS

Thirty-day tourist visas can be obtained either from your local Madagascar embassy or consulate or on arrival at Ivato, Antananarivo's international airport.

INTERNAL TRAVEL

Flights to Tuléar from the capital, Antananarivo, are operated by Air Madagascar six times a week and once a week by TAM, a subsidiary airline. There is a 30 percent reduction on fares for anyone who has arrived with an Air Madagascar international flight. Seats are much in demand and often overbooked with long waiting lists, so make sure you book at least a month in advance (more in high season), and that you reconfirm your flight several days beforehand. Sometimes a flight may be unexpectedly cancelled, so if possible avoid having too tight a schedule. The alternative is to take a collective taxi from the capital to Tuléar. These long-distance mini-vans offer greater comfort than local taxi-brousses but can take up to 20 hours. It is advisable to book a seat the day before at the relevant taxi-brousse station. There is also a weekly private coach service, Jumbobus, which leaves Antananarivo on Tuesdays and Tuléar on Saturdays—tel: 2022 20521 (Tana); tel/fax: 94 42729 (Tuléar). Cars with drivers can be rented from the capital or from Fianarantsoa.

HEALTH MATTERS

Madagascar is a malarial country but there is less risk in the dry southwest. In Anakao, due to an almost total absence of fresh water, mosquitoes are virtually unknown. It is still essential to take weekly prophylactics of the mefloquine variety (Lariam is a common tradename), which need to be prescribed by your doctor. Resistance to chloroquine is widespread. Always use insect repellent at dusk as an extra precaution. Precautions should also be taken against hepatitis A, typhoid, tetanus, polio and rabies. There is little that you can do about the occasional cholera outbreaks except be careful about where and what you eat and drink. Bottled water (*eau vive*) is widely available. Bilharzia (*schistosomiasis*) is present in some freshwater pools.

MONEY QUESTIONS

Credit cards can only be used in top hotels, which often add on a surcharge. French francs and US dollars (only mint condition and post-1996 $100 notes are accepted, due to counterfeits) are the easiest foreign currencies to exchange in hotels or banks. Traveller's cheques in these same currencies, as well as English pounds, Deutschmarks and Swiss francs, are also accepted. There are no banks outside large towns (in this case Tuléar), so make sure you have enough Malagasy francs with you before setting off. Keep small notes on you for the inevitable *cadeaux* (gifts) and for *pousse-pousse* (rickshaw, average fare about 70 cents).

WHAT TO TAKE

- ❏ Lightweight, cotton clothes and long-sleeved cotton shirts.
- ❏ Broad-brimmed hat or baseball cap.
- ❏ Sunglasses and sunscreen.
- ❏ Water-resistant sandals, swimming costume, towel.
- ❏ Toiletries (including soap, as this is rarely provided).
- ❏ Torch, money belt, camera film and batteries (available in Tuléar).
- ❏ Take a few little gifts such as pens, hairclips or T-shirts for the village children.

FINDING A GUIDE, A CAR OR AN OUTRIGGER

Tuléar has several travel agencies which will provide guides and drivers although their prices for four-wheel drives are very high. If you speak some French, enquire at your hotel to see if they know someone personally, as this cuts out the large agency commission. Outriggers can only be negotiated directly with the boatmen at Tuléar, Ankilybe, Saint Augustin or Anakao. Motorized canoes are also easily available, though at a price.

MADAGASCAR

25 In Search of the Lemur

by Fiona Dunlop

Madagascar's unique wildlife is symbolized by its numerous species of lemur. By combining the rainforest of Ranomafana National Park with the canyons of Isalo, visitors have an excellent chance of sightings, as well as travelling through some of the island's most riveting landscapes.

Madagascar has an abundance of endemic species, flora and fauna alike. When this "great red island" drifted away from continental Africa some 40 million years ago, nature was allowed to evolve in complete isolation. As a result, an estimated 80 percent of species are unique to Madagascar. Many have already disappeared, but this island, the fourth largest in the world, is nonetheless a fantastic wildlife laboratory that continues to attract naturalists.

LEMUR LOGISTICS

Number one on Madagascar's list is the engaging lemur, of which 33 species remain, with over 15 thought to have become extinct. This herbivorous mammal, with its pointed nose and long tail, is found throughout Madagascar, from the tropical rainforest of the north and east coast to the dry deciduous forest of the south. Yet however single-minded you may be about tracking down these charming, goggle-eyed creatures, you will be thwarted by Madagascar's poverty. In some cases the infrastructure is bearable; in others it is non-existent.

3 Hiking in Ranomafana is relatively easy, as the trails are well-maintained, though steep. Isalo's canyon treks are more demanding, requiring fitness and agility.

★★ The parks have only one comfortable hotel each, so if you have not booked into these you will be staying in very basic accommodation. Campsites in Isalo are well-organized.

✂ Camping and cooking equipment, sleeping-bags and porters can all be hired at Isalo park headquarters.

Luckily, enterprising Malagasy will organize private cars with a guide and/or driver in most large towns. Thus my plan seemed relatively straightforward: I would fly south from the capital of Antananarivo to Fianarantsoa, then negotiate a car to take me to two national parks: Ranomafana and Isalo. The former claims 12 species of lemur and the latter seven. They also represent two highly contrasting ecosystems, veering from tropical rainforest to arid, sandstone massif sliced by narrow canyons of semi-deciduous tropical forest.

TANA'S CONTRASTS

Antananarivo (nicknamed "Tana") is a very likeable and beautifully sited capital. Straddling 12 hills midway up the dorsal spine of the island at a refreshing altitude of 1,300m (4,265ft), it combines outlying paddy fields with steep roads that twist upwards past a placid lake into the upper town, where the French developed their colonial capital. Most buildings are dilapidated and the shantytown outskirts are worse even than Brazil's *favelas*. Despite this, there is a national unity and pride and the "great red island" possesses a magic that few can resist.

I wandered up and down steps, narrow lanes and streets lined with tall, tiled-roof houses, past rickety food stalls, piles of crusty baguette loaves, mangoes, manioc or papayas, against the background noise of the gear-grinding, rusting Citroën 2CV taxis. Strangers greeted me on the street in impeccable French, as if I had been there for years.

FIANARANTSOA

The 20-seater Twin Otter plane bumped along the landing strip at Fianarantsoa to be greeted by a cheering crowd of 100-odd Betsileo. The flight is scheduled to run twice weekly, but is obviously still a major event in this sleepy provincial capital of 150,000 inhabitants. Most of my fellow passengers were French businessmen, who were immediately whisked away by colleagues in shiny jeeps. Otherwise, there was not much automobile life, but a taxi eventually lumbered around the corner and I was soon heading for the town centre.

My hotel in Fianar was a colonial flashback. The Hotel Moderne, with the Chez Papillon restaurant downstairs, was opened in 1950 by Monsieur Papillon, who maintains an extraordinarily varied menu written in curvacious, brasserie-style hand. Food is served, accompanied by local wine, on Chez Papillon's original crockery, in true Parisian fashion, by one bad-tempered, white-jacketed waiter and a more benign *maître d'hôtel*.

THE VAGARIES OF TRAVEL

Negotiating a car for my trip wasn't straightforward. It was Sunday and Fianar, being a fervently religious centre, was deserted. Everything was shuttered up and no touts approached me. Eventually, at another hotel up the hill, a driver named Jean was found, and we negotiated a (very high) price. Later that evening, he appeared fleetingly at Chez

---

FADY AND TABOOS

There are cairns at various points of Isalo park. Each passing walker is expected to add a stone, to appease the ancestors of the massif. The entire massif has long been a sacred site, much used for burial sites. Remnants are hidden in the rock crevices. The burial system requires five years in a temporary coffin before the bones are removed, then celebrated at an inebriated party at the village, before being reburied by drunken revellers. This last, permanent grave is usually in seemingly inaccessible crevices high up on the cliff-face—but no accidents ever happen.

Papillon to tell me that, contrary to our arrangement, an advance would not be necessary, then disappeared into the night. That was the last I ever saw of him.

Next morning, I was introduced to another driver: Angelo. According to Angelo, there was one major problem: a petrol shortage. Under threat of privatization, Madagascar's petrol workers were on strike and no petrol had been delivered for three days. Sure enough, just around the corner, a queue of over 50 immobile cars, trucks and vans snaked towards the inactive petrol station.

Six hours, several appointments and numerous potential drivers later, I was still waiting. Meanwhile, I made the acquaintance of Christian "Chameleon," an enterprising 14-year-old who, with the

---

GALLIC HANGOVER

In 1896 France officially colonized Madagascar after centuries of on-off presence together with English and Dutch missionaries, traders and pirates. French control was obtained through a typical colonial trade-off: Britain kept Zanzibar in exchange for foregoing any claim on Madagascar. Although independence was won in 1958 and came into force in 1960, the French profile remains high. Gallic names have stuck along with the language, endless handshaking, cars, croissants and baguettes. A scattered population of expatriates, many of whom have Malagasy spouses, works in industry (of which there is little), tourism, commerce and vineyards. Even the typefaces used by local printers are pure 1930s art deco French.

aid of a bamboo cane, showed me six different chameleon species that inhabited the shrubs in front of the hotel. Finally Angelo produced Joro, the man with a Range Rover and some stockpiled petrol. We were off.

RANOMAFANA

Ranomafana lies 65km (40 miles) northeast of Fianar along a route with a 25km (15-mile) stretch of rutted and potholed dirt road. However, within two hours we had entered the cloud and humidity of the rainforest. This 43,000ha (141,122-acre) national park was created in 1991, and its upkeep is financed by several American universities, which maintain a permanent research unit there. With 300 of Madagascar's 1,800 orchid species, 124

bird species and 85–90 percent of its fauna endemic, Ranomafana is recognized as one of the island's top naturalists' destinations. Rushing through its centre is the beautiful Namorana River, providing the source of energy for the region's hydroelectric power.

There is very little to the village itself, a cluster of huts and basic hotels in the valley beside the fast-fading Hotel and Station Thermale. This 1930s relic was frequented by the French, who relished the health-giving properties of two sulphurous springs. You can still swim in the open-air pool, soak in an individual bath cubicle or indulge in a massage, although the entire structure has seen better days. Far more compelling is the wildlife waiting uphill at the park entrance.

Left: *The last section of the road to Isalo crosses an arid plateau riddled with termite mounds*
Inset: *Betsileo villagers in Barangotra; the brightly painted wooden balcony is a typical feature of a Betsileo house*

FOLLOWING FIDI

Fidi, my guide, was a walking zoological and botanical encyclopaedia. His passion was insects, but he could also name any bird, mammal, reptile or tree in French, English and Latin without a second's hesitation. I was lucky, as he had just finished working several days non-stop with an eminent Japanese professor of ornithology, who was recording and analyzing bird-song. Ranomafana attracts specialists from all over the world, though only a small section of the park is user-friendly, with well-marked trails.

That first day we only had time to take a night walk, setting off across the river at a fast pace as the light began to fade. Fidi was wearing a head-torch, and chain-smoked most of the way. It wasn't long before we reached a turn-off in the trees, which lead to my first lemur-sighting. There, in a bamboo stand among the trees, was a family of greater bamboo lemurs, all contentedly chewing away at the leaves, stems and shoots of this plant, that can grow 10cm (4in) in a day. With endearingly big, round eyes, brown- to honey-coloured fur and long bushy tails, they moved around continually, oblivious to us and some American student researchers, occasionally making spectacular flying leaps to reach fresher arboreal pastures.

We climbed further up the steep incline past pandanus, umbrella-like tree-ferns (there are 10 varieties in Ranomafana), epiphytes, lianas and Chinese guava, before finally reaching our destination: a hilltop shelter, designed for night trekkers to gather and feed certain animals. This is not good ecological practice, as it encourages dependency among wild animals, but it involves a limited number. As we arrived, a group was concentrating on feeding bananas to a striped civet, but Fidi quickly spotted an extraordinarily tiny creature peeking out of the branches—a brown mouse lemur. Although little more than 8cm (3in) long, this reddish-coloured lemur is known to leap up to 3m (9ft). It soon swivelled its globular eyes and disappeared into the night.

Darkness had fallen, and a gentle drizzle had set in as we descended the hill. This was when I felt the rainforest come alive, with a mounting cacophony of birds, frogs and cicadas invading the stillness around us. That night, the rain increased to such a point that I found myself confined to a narrow corridor in the middle of my bed—the only part unaffected by a relentless leak in the roof.

MADAGASCAR

LEMURS CONTINUED

Twelve hours later we were back in the muddy forest, this time joined by Henry, a young Belgian journalist. Fidi agreed to take a slower pace (*mora mora* became our keyword—Malagasy for "gently" or "slowly"). Despite the grey morning and continuing drizzle, we soon had some incredible sightings. As we were admiring a misty view over the rainforest canopy, a ring-tailed mongoose scuttled through the undergrowth; then a red-fronted coua swooped onto a nearby branch, soon followed by a beautiful blue coua. Not much further along the trail we came across a couple of red-bellied lemurs, both with rust-coloured fur, with patches of white on the belly of the female and around the eyes of the male. Clinging to the female's back was a toy-like baby.

Our luck, or more likely Fidi's expert guidance, did not run out. We stumbled through tangled undergrowth for a better view of a pair of red-fronted lemurs, high up in the branches. The grey-coated male was grooming himself for the day ahead, while his wife and baby munched leaves near by. They soon heard us and made acrobatic leaps through the air, stopping once more before eventually disappearing through the foliage. This particular species requires 20–25ha (65–82 acres) of territory, lives in groups of between two and 15 and, like the bamboo lemur, is monogamous and matriarchal. Fidi explained that most lemur species will not share their territory with other groups of the same species, but do tolerate the presence of other species.

Our last sighting was a woolly lemur, a nocturnal creature, peacefully dozing on a branch. Fidi's trained eyes meanwhile picked out a giant chameleon, a member of the Parson's family, with a remarkable, coiled tail. Contrary to received beliefs, chameleons change colour not to blend with their background, but to convey emotion and regulate body temperature. Fidi told us that their ability to swivel their eyes through 180 degrees has inspired a Betsileo proverb: one should

FIRE PROBLEMS

Much of the southern savannah is scorched black by ill-intentioned fires, lit by Bara cattle farmers to regenerate grass growth. This is an ongoing ecological problem, which a series of government directives has not succeeded in resolving. The long-term result of this slash-and-burn practice is that an estimated 85 percent of Madagascar's original forest has been destroyed.

move through life like a chameleon, slowly and surely with eyes on the past and the future simultaneously. As we neared the river and the outside world we saw our last Ranomafana speciality: a ground roller with subtle green-and-blue colouring. Emerging from this cloistered, verdant universe was like coming out of a dream. But more lemurs lay ahead.

CONTRASTS ON THE ROAD

Madagascar is justly famed for its landscapes. Perhaps the poor quality of most roads is a plus, as it allows time to enjoy an incredible diversity of spectacular views, as well as changing ethnic groups and vernacular architecture. Around Ranomafana live the people of the forest, the Antanala—late arrivals on the island, who were once hunter-gatherers. These desperately poor people attempt to make a living selling sacks of charcoal and woven palm-leaf pouches of river crayfish or honey at the roadside.

The better-off, though hardly wealthy, Betsileo of the Fianar region have tall, tiled-roof houses of two or three storeys, made of brick or mud, and often featuring fretwork balconies and even pillars. Beside them there is always a jewel-like emerald-green paddy field, usually yielding two, sometimes three harvests a year.

BREATH OF THE DEEP SOUTH

Between Ranomafana and Fianar, the scenery is characterized by the undulating *hauts plateaux*, the island's most fertile region. Tea, rice and vines are cultivated in the rich red earth and bricks are fired at the very source of the clay, usually by women. South of Fianar, towards Ihosy, lie some of Madagascar's most breathtaking landscapes. Cultivated valleys and grasslands give way to sculptural rocky outcrops and zebu cattle.

All this I observed from the back seat of a Peugot 505. Back in Fianar, I had reluctantly had to switch vehicles and guides. I was now in the hands of a pair of 20-year-olds: Tina, at the wheel and, beside him, Santos, the guide, who had been guiding tourists since the age of 10.

When we reached a pass at 1,500m (4,921ft), still more striking scenery unfolded before us. We stopped to admire the huge valley encompassing Ambalavao and its vineyards. Beside us stood one lone pine tree and a stone monument dedicated to some French military officers who died "*pour la France*" in 1947, the year the Malagasy rebelled. Beyond Ambalavao, vegetation and villages were visibly on the retreat, increasingly replaced by stark, barren hills and huge herds of zebu. Yet the trees, grasses and occasional paddy fields revealed that there was still water below ground. Gradually the sun dipped and, as we skirted the hat-shaped rocky outcrop of Ifandana Peak, the sky ignited into startling colours. Later, in the darkness, distant pinpoints of light proved to be savannah fires, rivals to the jewel-box of stars that slowly became visible above.

ISALO'S SPLENDOURS

Isalo National Park lies beyond a termite-ridden plateau 90km (56 miles) west of Ihosy, with its headquarters in the tiny cowboy village of Ranohira. The dramatic Isalo Massif rises abruptly to the north, its eroded sandstone escarpments sliced by canyons and rising to heights of 1,300m (4,265ft). It is an unexpectedly unearthly paradise, wild and beautiful, with waterfalls, natural pools, open valleys, jagged rock formations, pockets of lush vegetation and, of course, lemurs. I was back on track. The best option for experienced hikers is to organize a camping trek over several days, with a guide, porters and tents, all of which can be arranged at the park headquarters. However, two days earlier there had been an armed attack on some tourists which prompted me to choose the rough atmosphere of Ranohira, which, since the discovery of sapphires in late 1998 at Ilakaka, only 32km (20 miles) to the southwest, has been transformed into a frontier town.

Zozoly, the charming and informative guide whom I chose from the identikit photos on the wall of the park headquarters, made sure I experienced the essence of this vast, 81,540ha (201,482-acre) wilderness. We made three separate treks of several hours each and, apart from crowds of swimmers at the freshwater pool, rarely encountered

BAMBOO LEMURS

The monogamous and matriarchal greater bamboo lemur (also known as the broad-nosed gentle lemur) is one of two that are unique to Ranomafana. The other is the golden bamboo lemur, that was only discovered in 1986. The former is particularly rare, thought at one point to be extinct. Resighted in 1972 in the Ranomafana area, it vanished again until the late 1980s. Another of the mysteries surrounding these two lemurs is that parts of the bamboo contain high levels of deadly cyanide. One theory is that this is countered by the soil that they also eat, which contains laterite and iron oxide—a natural antidote. Both species live for about 35 years, moving around in groups of a dozen. The young later pair off with a member of another family group, an important factor that avoids in-breeding.

another soul. This pool is the most accessible natural sight, less than one hour's walk from the edge of the park, itself only 3km (2 miles) from Ranohira. The trail leads through savannah and tapia trees to a magnificent, huge canyon, rimmed on three sides by extraordinary formations, the grey sandstone striped with ochre and splashed with brilliant orange and lime-green lichen. Sprouting from the boulders is the *Pachypodium rosulatum*, a curious plant with delicate yellow flowers, whose bulbous stalk resembles a baobab, due to its cactus-like ability to store water. Here, too, grows the endemic aloe, the *Aloe isaloensis*.

CANYONS AND LEMURS

Our longest trek, totalling about five hours, led through two parallel canyons: the Canyon des Maky and the Canyon des Rats. These deep clefts in the rockface lie 17km (10 miles) from Ranohira along a dirt road that was only just passable. Leaving Tina and Santos beneath some wild mango trees, Zozoly and I set off across a placid stream before passing a few adobe houses—the original village of Ranohira. Here a Bara man-and-wife team pounded sugar cane and tamarind, a combination that is eventually fermented into a lethal local rum. Beside the thatched huts with walls of bamboo, mud and zebu dung, narrow channels threaded through the rice fields.

From then on the trek became an intoxicating succession of wildlife sightings and paradisical natural settings. Although Isalo is not known for its lemurs, seven species exist there, of which I was lucky enough to see three. In an area of dry deciduous forest we had prolonged sightings of a mother and baby red-fronted brown lemur. This lemur is able to walk on all four legs on the ground, unlike others that remain in the branches. In winter, it retires to caves to sleep with its long tail curled round its neck—a natural scarf.

By then we had combined forces with two other visitors and their guide and, between them, the two guides trawled the forest, making grunting noises to attract any nearby lemurs. Sure enough, we soon saw five delightful Verreaux's sifaka, whose white fur, dark facial markings, long legs and incredible agility make it instantly memorable. It is the biggest of the lemurs, attaining 3–4kg (about 6lb) in weight and is able to leap distances of 8m (26ft), clinging to branches with the suckers on its hands. Our third lemur sighting came in thick shrubs at the entrance to the Canyon des Rats, where Zozoly spotted four ring-tailed lemurs. Unlike the sifaka, this lemur needs to drink, so prefers riverine forest.

PARADISE

Like the lemur, I revelled in the walled riverside setting as the sun gradually rose over the rim some 400m (1,312ft) above us. Huge sandstone boulders created a spectacular obstacle course along the path of a transparent stream. Ferns grew in ridges and over rocky shelves, umbrella palms and spiky pandanus were everywhere, and specimens of Isalo's 50-plus bird species swooped past, including the Benson's rock-thrush and a melodious turquoise, black and russet Malagasy cuckoo. Our last trek, later that day, was to the Namazaha waterfall. As we climbed up sheer rocks and over more boulders, in an equally magical setting, I decided that Madagascar's endemic species had made the right choice 40 million years ago.

Far right: *Wonderful wildlife-spotting terrain—the Canyon des Maky in Isalo National Park*
Right: *The lesser mouse lemurs (genus* Microcebus) *are the smallest members of the family; this is a brown mouse lemur*

GOING IT ALONE

WHEN TO GO

Ranomafana's east coast climate sees heavy rain and cyclones from November to March, when trekking conditions become difficult, but this is also a good time for wildlife. A happier medium is in April to May or September to November, when showers are only sporadic. Isalo's climate is much drier, with a shorter rainy season from mid-November to February. From July to September, the high season for European visitors, night temperatures can be very cold and day temperatures rarely exceed 20°C (70°F). As in Ranomafana, the mid-seasons of April to May and October to November offer a more enjoyable compromise.

INTERNAL TRAVEL

Public transport is limited to the notorious taxi-brousse (bush taxi), which varies from reasonable mini-vans to packed pick-ups or over-populated trucks. It all depends on the state of the road in question. Little more than 10 percent of Madagascar's roads are actually sealed; even these are often badly potholed. The rest are dusty dirt road or sand, and cases of truck drivers falling asleep at the wheel are tragically quite common. This said, the RN7, which links Fianarantsoa with Isalo, is mostly in good condition, apart from a stretch of dirt road just west of Ihosy. Comfortable mini-vans ply this route regularly. On the other hand, the taxi-brousse to Ranomafana is a painful experience.

PLANNING

If you want to stay in comfort at these two national parks, it is essential to book your hotel well in advance, as the only two with any degree of comfort are much in demand. Otherwise the absence of telephones in Isalo means that you have to take pot-luck on arrival. If you want to camp, arrangements can be made on the spot.

HEALTH MATTERS

Madagascar is a heavily malarial country and it is essential to take weekly prophylactics of the mefloquine variety (Lariam is a common trade name). These need to be prescribed by your doctor. Resistance to chloroquine is widespread. Always use insect repellent at dusk as an extra precaution. Precautions should also be taken against hepatitis A, typhoid, tetanus, polio and rabies. There is little that you can do about the occasional cholera outbreaks, except be careful about where and what you eat and drink. Bottled water (*eau vive*) is widely available. Bilharzia (*schistosomiasis*) is present in some freshwater pools.

WHAT TO TAKE

- ❏ Good walking boots.
- ❏ A broad-brimmed hat or baseball cap.
- ❏ A rain poncho, a pullover or fleece, loose cotton clothes and long-sleeved shirts.
- ❏ Sunscreen.
- ❏ Sunglasses.
- ❏ Binoculars, camera, film and batteries (none are available at either park).

FINDING A GUIDE

You cannot enter Isalo without a guide, and at Ranomafana it is strongly advisable, although trails are well-marked and maintained. Both parks offer good, trained guides, whose fees are fixed by the park authorities. Their photos, exam results and linguistic abilities are posted at park headquarters, though the better guides may already be committed. All speak Malagasy and French, with English, Italian and German spoken by some. National park entrance tickets are valid for three days; always keep them with you for occasional controls.

CAR HIRE

This can be arranged through a travel agency in Antananarivo or through a hotel in Fianarantsoa. A four-by-four is essential for the road to Ranomafana, though not necessary for the Fianar-Isalo road. Make sure that your agreed price includes all petrol, driver and guide costs.

OTHER ATTRACTIONS

Southwest from Isalo lies the sapphire-rush town of Ilakaka. Since these precious stones were discovered there in September 1998, this huge, unstructured shantytown of 40,000 miners and their families has mushroomed in the scrub beside the main road. Ilakaka now offers far more services and goods than Ranohira. The open mines are south of the road, and the traders' centre (Comptoir des Acheteurs) a few kilometres away. Sri Lankans and West Africans are the main buyers, and their rapid, good-humoured negotiations with the miners are fascinating to watch.

INTRODUCTION

Contained in the first section of these "Blue Pages" are lists of selected contacts relevant to the 25 adventures related on pages **18–256**. Because the adventures are personal accounts, the information provided here will reflect each author's own experience, and therefore details will vary accordingly. Remember also that some contacts are in remote places, so be sure to call or write in advance before setting out. None of the places in the Contacts or the A-Z have been vetted in any way by the publishers and, although some of the companies were used by our writers, this is no guarantee they will still be run by the same people or to the same standard of proficiency.

The Contacts section gives details of companies used by our authors and complements the Activities A–Z in the second part. Below is some general information to help you plan your own adventures.

INTERNATIONAL DIALLING CODES

Telephone and fax numbers given in this section of the book begin with the area code where applicable. When dialling from outside the country, prefix this number with the international network access code of the country you are in, followed by the country code.

International Network Access Codes

For calls from the U.K. 00
For calls from the U.S. 011

Country Codes

Botswana 267
Kenya 254
Lesotho 266
Madagascar 261
Malawi 265
Mozambique 258
Namibia 264
South Africa 27
Tanzania 255
Uganda 256
Zambia 260
Zimbabwe 263

EMBASSIES AND CONSULATES

British Embassies

For regularly updated travel advice prior to a trip:
website: www.fco.gov.uk

Botswana
British High Commission
Private Bag 0023
Queens Road
The Mall
Gaborone
☎ 352841/2/3 **fax:** 356105
email: british@bc.bw

Kenya
British High Commission
Upper Hill Road
P.O. Box 30465
Nairobi
☎ (2) 714699
fax: (2) 714760 **email:**
bhcinfo@iconnect.co.ke

Lesotho
British High Commission
P.O. Box Ms521
Maseru 100
☎ 313961 **fax:** 310120
email:
hcmaseru@lesoff.co.za
website:
www.lesoff.co.za/bhcmaseru

Madagascar
British Embassy
1st Floor
Immeuble Ny Havana
Cité de 67 Ha
P.O. Box 167
Antananarivo
☎ (2) 2022 27749/27370
fax: (2) 2022 26690
email:
ukembant@simicro.mg

Malawi
British High Commission
P.O. Box 30042
Lilongwe 3
☎ 782400 **fax:** 782657
email: britcom@malawi.net

Mozambique
British High Commission
Avenue Vladimir I Lenine 310
P.O. Box 55
Maputo
☎ (1) 420111/2/5/6/7
fax: (1) 421666 **email:**
bhc.maputo@teledata.mz

Namibia
British High Commission
116 Robert Mugabe Avenue
Windhoek
☎ (61) 223022
fax: (61) 228895
email: bhc@iwwn.com.na

South Africa
British Consulate
Liberty Life Place
Block B, 1st Floor
256 Glyn Street
Hatfield 0083
Postal address:
P.O. Box 13611
Hatfield 0028
Pretoria
☎ (12) 483 1400
fax: (12) 483 1444
Consulates can also be found in Cape Town, Durban and Johannesburg.
website: www.britain.org.za

Tanzania
British High Commission
Hifadhi House
Samora Avenue
P.O. Box 9200
Dar Es Salaam
☎ (51) 117659/112950
fax: (51) 112951
telex: 41004
email:
bhc.dar@dar.mail.fco.gov.uk

Uganda
British High Commission
10–12 Parliament Avenue
P.O. Box 7070
Kampala
☎ (41) 257054/9
fax: (41) 257304
email:
bhcinfo@starcom.co.ug

Zambia
British Embassy
Independence Avenue
P.O. Box 50050
Lusaka
☎ (1) 251133 **fax:** (1) 251923
email: brithc@zamnet.zm

Zimbabwe
British High Commission
Corner House
Samora Machel Avenue/
Leopold Takawira Street
P.O. Box 4490
Harare
☎ (4) 772990 **fax:** (4) 774617

ACCOMMODATION PRICES

Hotels listed in the Contacts
and A–Z sections have been
split into four price cate-
gories. Some parts of the
world are generally cheaper
than others but a rough
guide is as follows:

$ = under $40
$$ = $40-$85
$$$ = over $85

AMERICAN EMBASSIES

Botswana
P.O. Box 90
Gaborone
☎ 353982
After hours ☎ 357111
fax: 356947
email:
usembgab@global.co.za

Kenya
Moi/Haile Selassie Avenue
Nairobi
Postal address:
P.O. Box 30137
Unit 64100
APO AE 09831
Nairobi
☎ (2) 334141 **fax:** (2) 340838
telex: (2) 22964

Lesotho
P.O. Box 333
Maseru 100
☎ 312666 **fax:** 310116
email: amles@lesoff.co.za

Madagascar
14-16 Rue Rainitovo
Antsahavola
P.O. Box 620
Antananarivo
☎ (2) 21257/20089/20718
fax: (2) 34539
telex: USA EMB MG 22202,
Antananarivo

Malawi
P.O. Box 30016
Lilongwe 3
☎ 783166 **fax:** 780471
telex: 44627

Mozambique
Avenida Kenneth Kaunda 193
Maputo
Postal address:
P.O. Box 783
Maputo
☎ (1) 492797 **fax:** (1) 490114
email:
library@mail.tropical.co.mz
telex: 6-143 AMEMB MO

Namibia
Ausplan Building
14 Lossen Street
Private Bag 12029
Ausspannplatz
Windhoek
☎ (61) 221601
fax: (61) 229792

South Africa
877 Pretorius Street
Arcadia 0083
Pretoria
P.O. Box 9536
Pretoria 0001
☎ (12) 342 1048
fax: (12) 342 2244

Tanzania
36 Laibon Road (off
Bagamoyo Road)
P.O. Box 9123
Dar Es Salaam
☎ (51) 666010/1/2/3/4/5
fax: (51) 666701
telex: 41250

Uganda
Parliament Avenue
P.O. Box 7007
Kampala
☎ (41) 259792/3/5
fax: (41) 259794

Zambia
Corner of Independence and
United Nations Avenues
P.O. Box 31617
Lusaka
☎ (1) 250955/252230 After
hours ☎ (1) 252234
fax: (1) 252225

Zimbabwe
American Embassy
172 Herbert Chitepo Avenue
P.O. Box 3340
Harare
☎ (4) 794521

1 RAFTING THE SOURCE OF THE NILE ➤ 20–27

OPERATORS

Adrift (Uganda) Ltd

P.O. Box 8643
Kyadondo Road
Kampala
☎ (41) 268 670
fax: (41) 268 670
email: adrift@starcom.co.ug
website: www.adrift.co.nz
Adrift made the first descent of the source of the White Nile in July 1996, and has been running commercial rafting trips ever since. All the raft guides and safety kayakers are extremely experienced and enthusiastic, not to mention highly qualified. In addition to 1- and 2-day river trips, Adrift also offers a multi-day itinerary that includes rafting, sea kayaking, and a sunset cruise on Lake Victoria.

Pearl of Africa Tours and Travel Limited

P.O. Box 5326
Kampala
☎ (41) 534801
fax: (41) 534801
email: pearlatt@swiftuganda.com
This American-owned company offers a comprehensive programme of itineraries to suit most schedules and budgets, from a 1-day fishing trip on Lake Victoria to a 12-day tour of Uganda's 6 National Parks. In addition to rafting and gorilla tracking, also available to suit individual requirements are game drives and guided tours, not to mention airport transfers and car rental, with and without a driver. Special interest safaris, such as photography and birdwatching, are available on request.

GETTING THERE

Adrift (Uganda) Ltd

See under Operators, above.
Transfers from Kampala to the river and back are arranged by Adrift at no extra cost.

City Cars Ltd

Room 20, Tank Hill Parade
Muyenga
P.O. Box 151
Kampala
☎ (41) 268611
email: citycars@starcom.co.ug
Getting to Murchison Falls is all but impossible by public transport, so hiring a vehicle is essential. Owned and run by a father and son team from the U.K., City Cars offers excellent service and value for money, specializing in journey itineraries, preparing route maps, and advizing on where to go and what to see. Hatchbacks, saloons, and a selection of off-road vehicles can be hired on a chauffeur-driven or self-drive basis, with discounts available for long-term hire.

Paul Ssekkono

Uganda House Taxi Hire Association
P.O. Box 806
Kampala
☎ (77) 448759
The drive from Entebbe Airport to Kampala takes a little less than an hour, and if you haven't arranged airport transfers through your tour operator, reliable transport is as rare as it is welcome. Wherever you want to go in and around Kampala, Paul provides a punctual service at a reasonable rate.

STA Travel

Priory House
6 Wrights Lane
London W8 6TA
U.K.
☎ (020) 7361 6262 **fax:** (020) 7937 9570
website: www.statravel.co.uk
Although specializing in student and independent travel, STA also arranges flights for non-students, and offers exceptional deals on fares to Uganda from London. Travel consultants are invariably friendly, helpful, and extremely knowledgeable.

INFORMATION

Uganda Tourist Board

IPS Building
Parliament Avenue
P.O. Box 7211
Kampala
☎ (41) 342196/7
fax: (41) 342188
email: utb@starcom.co.ug
website: www.visituganda.com

Uganda Wildlife Authority

P.O. Box 3530
Kampala
☎ (41) 346287
fax: (41) 346291
email: director@uwahq.uu.imul.com
website: www.visituganda.com

CONTACTS

ACCOMMODATION

The best, but not necessarily the cheapest, way to arrange accommodation in Kampala or on the banks of the Nile is through one of the local tour operators. If you prefer a more flexible itinerary, accommodation is easy to arrange on arrival, either through the Uganda Tourist Board or at individual establishments.

Alinda Guest House $

P.O. Box 137
Masindi
☎ (465) 20482
The Alinda Guest House is the first hotel on the right as you drive into Masindi from Kampala, and is arguably the most inviting. Featuring a picket-fenced patio, an open-air courtyard restaurant and selection of simple but spotless rooms, it provides an ideal rest-stop on the demanding drive to Murchison Falls. The restaurant serves simple but wholesome food, although it's not worth hanging around for breakfast; buttered bread is about as exciting as it gets.

Bugugali Rest Camp $

Situated on the banks of the Nile within spitting distance of the thunderous Bugugali Falls, Bugugali Rest Camp is a cheap and cheerful option for those who want to drink in views of the Nile over a chilled beer of the same name. Accommodation is in *bandas* (traditional-style thatched huts), and a little old lady takes orders for fresh tea and muffins at the bar every morning.

Paraa Rest Camp $

c/o Uganda Wildlife Authority

See under Information, above.
Overlooking the Nile's south bank at the heart of Murchison Falls National Park, Paraa Rest Camp is as welcoming as it is peaceful. Home-made food and cold beers are served on the patio, and accommodation is in *bandas*, complete with hot showers, clean sheets, and mosquito nets. From here, it's barely a minute's walk to the National Park headquarters, where you can arrange launch trips and game drives.

Speke Hotel $$$

P.O. Box 7036
Kampala
☎ (41) 250554
fax: (41) 255200
A colonial-style hotel with a patio overlooking Nile Avenue in the heart of Kampala. A number of dining options are available, including the Rock Garden, which prepares passable lunchtime snacks and comes alive on Fri and Sat nights. Even if you don't stay here, it's an excellent place to meet for a drink and watch the world go by.

FOOD AND DRINK

Fasika Ethiopian Restaurant

Kabalagala
Kampala
☎ (41) 26857
If you've never tried Ethiopian food but like your flavours rich and spicy, the Fasika is well worth a visit. All the main dishes are served on one enormous pancake, or *injera*, made with rice and wheat flour. Chicken, mutton, beef, and vegetable dishes are cooked in a variety of sumptuous sauces and scooped up into small, pancake parcels. After feasting on this fine cuisine, hands are washed in warm, scented water poured into a pewter bowl.

Khana Khasana Tandoori Restaurant

20 Acacia Avenue Kololo
P.O. Box 21528
Kampala
☎ (41) 233049
fax: (41) 347346
You'd be hard pushed to find a better Indian restaurant anywhere in Africa. Served by candlelight and accompanied by a chorus of crickets and frogs, the food is exquisite and the service exceptional. The chicken stuffed with cashew nuts and served with royal gravy comes highly recommended, as does the boneless mutton with spinach.

Sam's Continental & Tandoori Restaurant

78 Kampala Road
P.O. Box 20197
Kampala
☎ (41) 251694
If the idea of African game makes your mouth water, Sam's Continental and Tandoori brestaurant is *the* place to be in downtown Kampala. Impala, crocodile, and ostrich are all on the menu, and, although the portions are never huge, the final bill is unlikely to be either. Breakfast, morning coffee, lunch, and afternoon tea are also served at this popular eatery in the heart of the city.

2 GORILLA-TRACKING IN THE IMPENETRABLE FOREST ➤ 28–37

For Operators, Getting There and Information see the preceding adventure.

ACCOMMODATION

Apart from the **Speke Hotel** (see p. 260), options include:

Buhoma Community Rest Camp $

c/o Uganda Wildlife Authority
See under Information, p. 259.
Situated to the left of the road just inside the gates of Bwindi National Park, the Buhoma Community Rest Camp offers simple but comfortable accommodation in *bandas* (traditional thatched huts). All the staff are friendly and welcoming, and the food is basic but delicious. Breakfast and packed lunches are available on request.

Bushara Island Camps $

P.O. Box 794
Kabale
☎ (486) 22447
fax: (486) 22447
Accessible only by traditional canoe, the campsite on Bushara Island is as peaceful and idyllic as anyone could wish for. Accommodation is in luxurious, safari-style tents, while the restaurant serves some memorably mouth-watering dishes. The entire island only takes half an hour to walk round and, if you're lucky, you might have the whole place to yourself.

FOOD AND DRINK

For places to eat and drink in Kampala, see p. 260.

3 LAKE TURKANA BY OVERLAND TRUCK ➤ 40–47

OPERATORS
Gametrackers

1st Floor, Kenya Cinema Complex
Moi Avenue
P.O. Box 62042
☎ (2) 338927
fax: (2) 330903
email: game@africaonline.co.ke
website: www.gametrackers.com
This popular, reasonably priced and highly rep-

utable company has been operating two-weekly trips to Turkana via the Chalbi Desert for longer than a decade. They also offer a number of other quality camping safaris—to areas such as the Maasai Mara and southern Rift Valley Lakes—as well as camel safaris and organized treks up Mount Kenya.

Let's Go Travel

Caxton House
Standard Street
P.O. Box 60342
Nairobi
☎ (2) 340331/213033
fax: (2) 214713
email: info@letsgotravel.com
website: www.letsgotravel.com
One of the most experienced and highly regarded booking agencies and safari operators in Nairobi, Let's Go is a recommended first contact for setting up personalized trips in Kenya at all budgets, as well as for car rental, and advice on visiting Turkana independently. For travels further afield, they have offices in Kampala (Uganda) and Arusha (Tanzania).

INFORMATION
Kenya Tourist Board

P.O. Box 30630
Nairobi
☎ (2) 604246
fax: (2) 501096
email: KTB@form-net.com
U.K. office:
25 Brook's Mews
Mayfair
London W1Y 1LF
U.K.
☎ (020) 7355 3144
fax: (020) 7495 8656
website: www.kenyatourism.org

ACCOMMODATION
NAIROBI

Travellers taking the overland truck to Turkana are likely to spend at least one night on either side of the trip in Kenya's capital city.

Holiday Inn Nairobi $$$

Parklands Road
Parklands
P.O. Box 66807
Nairobi
☎ (2) 740920/21
fax: (2) 748823
email: mayfair@africaonline.co.ke

One of the more affordable of Nairobi's tourist-class hotels, the Holiday Inn (formerly the Mayfair Court) offers standard Holiday Inn value for money, while the rambling colonial era buildings have more character than one would expect of a hotel in this chain. The hotel is located some 10 minutes' drive from the city centre in the suburb of Westlands, within walking distance of several shopping malls, banks, and some of the city's best restaurants.

Hotel Terminal $
Moktar Daddah Street
Nairobi
☎ (2) 228817
The combination of secure rooms, reasonable prices, helpful staff, and a convenient downtown location has, for some years, made this one of the outstanding budget hotels in Nairobi.

Nairobi Serena Hotel $$$
P.O. Box 48690
Nairobi
☎ (2) 711077
fax: (2) 718103
email: serenamk@africaonline.co.ke
This plush hotel, situated in attractive green gardens only a few minutes walk from central Nairobi, is the flagship for one of East Africa's finest hotel and lodge chains. Facilities include a swimming pool, world-class restaurant, and business centre.

Nairobi Youth Hostel $
Ralph Bunche Road
P.O. Box 48661
Nairobi
☎ (2) 723012
A long-time favourite with backpackers, the youth hostel was completely renovated in 1994 and remains one of the city's best bases for travellers on a budget, set in leafy suburbia about 10 minutes' bus ride from the city centre.

ON THE ROAD
If you are taking an overland truck to Turkana you will camp in sites selected by the company. Independent travellers will find that in most parts of northern Kenya their options are restricted to campsites and cheap local guesthouses.

Marsabit Lodge $$
☎ (183) 2044
This recently privatized lodge lies within Marsabit National Park, some 5km (3 miles) from the town of Marsabit. Accommodation is nothing special by standards elsewhere in Kenya, but nothing else of this quality exists in northern Kenya and the location is superb. Campers can pitch a tent in the lodge grounds or at the campsite at the National Park entrance for a small charge.

Mosaretu Women's Group Campsite $
No contact details available.
Lying on the main road through Loiyangalani, near the shore of Lake Turkana, this community-run campsite offers inexpensive camping facilities as well as accommodation in simple reed huts. There are no contact details—but the chances of it being full are slim, to say the least.

Yare Safari Club $
P.O. Box 63006
Nairobi
☎/**fax:** (368) 2295
Situated 3km (2 miles) outside Maralal along the Nairobi Road, this is one of the best backpacker haunts in northern Kenya, offering camping, moderately priced rooms, a lively bar, and a limited selection of meals.

FOOD AND DRINK
NAIROBI
The city is renowned for its wide selection of affordable world-class restaurants. Perennial favourites include the **Minar Restaurant** on Banda Street for Indian cuisine, and the superb **Trattoria Restaurant** on the corner of Wabera and Kuanda Street for Italian dishes.

OUTSIDE NAIROBI
Once you head north of the central highlands, restaurants are few and far between, and what you eat is most likely to be determined by what you can find. Almost certainly, you will come across the East African staple dish of *ugali*, a thick "porridge" made from maizemeal. This is normally eaten with a bland bean or vegetable stew. A number of refugees from the conflicts in Ethiopia have established restaurants in northern Kenya, serving the Ethiopian staple of *injera*, a flat "pancake" eaten with fiery *wot* sauce. This is not to everybody's taste but can make a very welcome change from the seemingly ubiquitous *ugali*.

4 WALKING WITH THE MAASAI IN THE SERENGETI REGION
► 48–57

OPERATORS

Hoopoe Adventure Tours Tanzania Ltd

India Street
P.O. Box 2047
Arusha
☎ (57) 7011/7541 **fax:** (57) 8226
email: hoopoe@form-net.com
website: hoopoe.com
Established in 1988, Hoopoe has become one of the best-known operators in Tanzania. They offer a full range of treks and conventional safaris throughout the northern Tanzanian circuit. The U.K. agent is Tribes Travel. See below.

Serengeti Balloon Safaris Ltd

Seronera Lodge
Serengeti
☎ (57) 8578
email: serengeti@balloonsafaris.com
website: www.balloonsafaris.com
The only company offering balloon flights over the Serengeti.

Contact for all enquiries outside Tanzania:
Serengeti Balloon Safaris Ltd

Harleston
Norfolk
U.K.
☎ (01379) 853481

Tribes Travel

12 The Business Centre
Earl Soham
Woodbridge
Suffolk IP13 7SA
U.K.
☎ (01728) 685971 **fax:** (01728) 685973
email: info@tribes.co.uk
website: tribes.co.uk
Tribes Travel, directed by Guy and Amanda Marks, is a pioneering UK-based tour operator specializing in community-centred tourism on the principles of fair trade. Tribes offers tailor-made and small group wildlife, trekking, and cultural trips throughout Tanzania, using carefully selected lodges, local operators, and local and indigenous guides. Tribes Travel is also the U.K. agent for the African adventure travel specialists Hoopoe Adventure Tours (see above for further details).

GETTING THERE
Air Tanzania

Dar es Salaam
☎ (51) 110245
Local and international airline with connecting flights from Dar es Salaam to Arusha.

Precision Air

Arusha International Conference Centre
Ngorongoro Wing
P.O. Box 1636
Arusha
☎ (57) 6903 **fax:** (57) 8204
email: info@precisionairtz.com
website: www.precisionairtz.com
Dar es Salaam office:
☎ (51) 30800
Local airline with connecting flights from Dar es Salaam to Arusha.

INFORMATION
Tanzania Tourist Board (T.T.B.)

Boma Street
Box 2348
Arusha
☎ (57) 3842/3
website: www.tanzania-web.com/
Dar es Salaam office:
Salmora Avenue
UNESCO House
Box 2585
Dar es Salaam
☎ (51) 113144

ACCOMMODATION
Kirurumu Lodge $$$

Lake Manyara
Booking office:
India Street
P.O. Box 2047
Arusha
☎ (57) 7011 **fax:** (57) 8226
Luxury tented lodge overlooking Lake Manyara from the Great Rift Valley escarpment. Stylish and carefully considered design, blending with the surroundings. Ecologically sound and supporting local community projects.

OPERATORS
Art of Travel

21 The Bakehouse
Bakery Place
119 Altenburg Gardens
London SW11 1JQ
U.K.
☎ (020) 7738 2038 **fax:** (020) 7738 1893
email: info@artoftravel.co.uk
website: www.artoftravel.co.uk
Established in 1989, Art of Travel specializes in
tailor-made itineraries to southern Africa and
the Indian Ocean islands. Their consultants
have personal experience of a wide range of
adventurous activities in the region, from
climbing Kilimanjaro to diving in Zanzibar.
They provide an efficient and highly individual
service, and take the hassle out of arranging
flights, transfers, and accommodation.

Hoopoe Adventure Tours

See Operators in preceding adventure.

Marangu Hotel

P.O. Box 40
Moshi
☎ (55) 51307 **fax:** (55) 50639
email: marangu@africaonline.co.ke
The Marangu Hotel has been arranging treks on
Kilimanjaro for over 4 decades and provides a
high-quality service. Their guides and porters
are extremely attentive, knowledgeable and
friendly. They offer fully-equipped treks for the
5-day Marangu Route and for the 6-day
Machame Route. Budget travellers have the
option of arranging a "Hard Way" Marangu trek,
where they bring all their own food and equipment and cater for themselves. The hotel
arranges a guide and 2 porters per trekker, and
books hut accommodation.

GETTING THERE

The Dutch carrier **DutchKLM** flies direct to
Kilimanjaro. **Ethiopian Airlines** flies to Dar es
Salaam and Kilimanjaro (via Addis Ababa).
Several international airlines fly to Dar es
Salaam including **British Airways**, **Alliance
Air**, and **Swiss Air**.

Ethiopian Airlines

4th Floor
Foxglove House
166 Piccadilly House
London W1V 9DE
U.K.
☎ (020) 7491 9119 **fax:** (020) 7491 1892
website: www.ethiopian-airline.com
Friendly service, but long flight from London to
Dar es Salaam and Kilimanjaro, via Rome and
Addis Ababa.

KLM

websites: www.klm.com; and
tanzania.klm.com

INFORMATION

For more information about climbing
Kilimanjaro or about the national park contact:

Kilimanjaro National Park

(The Chief Park Warden)
P.O. Box 96
Marangu
or
Tanzania National Parks

(The Director-General)
P.O. Box 3134
Arusha

Tanzania Tourist Board

See Information, p. 263.

ACCOMMODATION
Marangu Hotel $–$$

See Operators, above, for details.
Set in lush and exotic gardens with views
across to Kilimanjaro, the Marangu Hotel is
well-run and friendly with comfortable accommodation and good food. The Director,
Desmond Brice-Bennett, provides a reassuring
safety briefing for all trekkers departing for
Kilimanjaro.

GETTING THERE

Air Kenya—not to be confused with the
national carrier, Kenya Airways—flies daily
between any combination of Nairobi and
the three main tourist centres along the
coast, Mombasa, Malindi and Lamu. Air Kenya
is based at Wilson Airport just outside central
Nairobi.

Air Kenya

P.O. Box 30357
Nairobi
☎ (2) 501601/605745 **fax:** (2) 602951
email: sales@airkenya.com

OPERATORS

There is little to prevent independent travellers from exploring the north coast without using a tour operator, but visitors who want to make a string of hotel and flight bookings, or to visit the coast in conjunction with a safari upcountry, are pointed towards **Let's Go Travel** (see p. 261).

INFORMATION
Kenya Tourist Board

See p. 261.

ACCOMMODATION
MOMBASA
Mombasa Serena Hotel $$$

P.O. Box 48690
Nairobi
☎ (2) 711077 **fax:** (2) 718103
email: serenamk@africaonline.co.ke
One of the finest hotels anywhere on the Kenya coast, the Serena makes imaginative use of traditional Swahili architecture and has a perfect beachfront location on Shanzu Beach, about 15 miles north of central Mombasa. A world-class hotel in every respect.

WATAMU
Hemingway's $$$

P.O. Box 267
Watamu
☎ (122) 32008 **fax:** (122) 32266
email: hemingways@form-net.com
With its attractive location on Turtle Bay and excellent facilities, Hemingway's has few, if any, peers in the Watamu area. Catering to game fishermen and conventional holidaymakers alike, it is named after the great writer who spent time fishing in the area—portraits of E.H. line the walls of the bar, along with some immense stuffed fish.

MALINDI
Driftwood Club $$

P.O. Box 63
Malindi
☎ (123) 20155 **fax:** (123) 30712
email: driftwood@swiftmalindi.com
Comfortable rather than luxurious, this low-rise beach hotel has been a Malindi institution for as long as anyone can remember. Popular with Kenya residents, the Driftwood Club is a recommended mid-range coastal retreat.

Fondu Wehu Guesthouse $

P.O. Box 5367
Malindi
☎ (123) 30017
It's a shame that what is arguably the finest backpacker establishment anywhere on the East African coast has to lie at the heart of one of the region's less inspiring towns. Offering the choice of dormitory beds, private rooms, and camping space, this is *the* place to head for if you drift into Malindi on a tightish budget—or just want to hang out in the company of other travellers.

LAMU

In addition to the places listed below, some 20-odd guesthouses are scattered in the old town. Room rates are inexpensive and highly negotiable; places come and go (and go uphill or downhill) with giddying regularity. If in doubt, ask one of the touts on the waterfront to find you a room. This is effectively a free service: the tout will get a commission from the guesthouse, and mostly he will be motivated to find you a good room on the basis that a happy customer will almost certainly mean repeat business in the form of *dhow* excursions, etc. There is also a guesthouse in Pate (anybody will point you in the right direction) and a few local people are happy to put up travellers for a small fee in Siyu.

Kipungani Sea Breezes $$$

P.O. Box 232
Lamu
☎ (121) 33191
email: prestigehotels@form-net.com
Set on a stunningly beautiful, palm-lined beach on the landward side of the island, this small, low-key retreat is the perfect place to live out your desert island fantasies. Cheap it is not, but the organic architecture is inspired, and the aura of absolute isolation and down-to-earth management style make it the ultimate place to get away from it all. Quite simply one of the best lodges of its type in Africa.

Peponi Hotel $$$

P.O. Box 24
Lamu
☎ (121) 33154 **fax:** (121) 33029
email: peponi@africaonline.co.ke

Owned and managed by the same family for 30 years now, Peponi—Swahili for heaven—combines architectural elegance and culinary excellence with a winningly laid-back management style. It is set on Shela Beach, a short walk or *dhow* ride from the old town.

Petley's Inn/Lamu Palace Hotel $$

P.O. Box 83
Lamu
☎ (121) 33272 **fax:** (127) 3319
email: islands@africaonline.co.ke
The only tourist-class hotels in Lamu, co-managed as of 1998, are both prominent features along the waterfront. Established in the 1930s and furnished in the traditional Swahili style, Petley's is comfortable and atmospheric—and the rooftop bar is an excellent place to watch over the harbour. The Lamu Palace lacks the atmosphere, a consideration which, given the sticky heat of Lamu, may be overridden by the blasting air conditioners in every room.

FOOD AND DRINK

Abundant seafood and the widespread availability of traditional Swahili cuisine—which makes extensive use of coconut milk—combine to make the coast of Kenya one of the few places in sub-Saharan Africa where eating out is a regular highlight of the day. In any of the main tourist centres you'll be spoilt for choice of restaurant, and Lamu in particular is justifiably known for the excellent selection of affordable, good eateries that line the waterfront.

7 EXPLORING THE SPICE ISLANDS ►76–85

OPERATORS
Art of Travel
See page 264.

Chumbe Island Coral Park

P.O. Box 3203
Zanzibar
☎/**fax:** (54) 31040
email: chumbe.island@raha.com
website: www.xtra-micro.com/work/chumbe/
A visit to this unspoilt speck of paradise is a must for anyone interested in wildlife and conservation or who dreams of being a castaway! If you can't afford the overnight rates then splash out on a day trip.

Ocean Tours

P.O. Box 3075
Zanzibar
☎/**fax:** (54) 33642
email: ocean-tours@twiga.com
Established in 1993 and located opposite the Serena Inn in Zanzibar Town, Ocean Tours offers the full range of excursions around the island, including advice on the best diving locations. Their guides speak good English and are sensitive to cultural and environmental issues. Mountainbiking tours (Jun to Nov) may be offered in the future.

GETTING THERE
FLIGHTS

Gulf Air flies direct to Zanzibar from Muscat. International airlines serving Dar es Salaam include **British Airways**, **KLM**, **Alliance Air**, **Swissair**, and **Ethiopian Airlines**. **Precision Air** connects Dar es Salaam with Zanzibar.

Ethiopian Airlines
See page 264.

Precision Air

A brisk and efficient daily service taking only 20 minutes between Dar es Salaam and Unguja.

FERRIES

Several ferry companies provide services between Dar es Salaam and Zanzibar, including **Sea Star Ferries**, **Megaspeed Liners** (also serving Pemba), **Sea Express**, **Azam Marine Sea Bus**, and **Flying Horse**. Price and speed vary with service; the crossing usually takes 1–2 hours.

MegaSpeed Liners
☎ (811) 326413 **fax:** (811) 232361
email: Megaspeed@zanzinet.com

INFORMATION
Zanzibar Travel Network
website: www.zanzibar.net
Established in 1997, this dedicated online travel guide to Zanzibar provides an excellent introduction to the islands and how to visit them.

ACCOMMODATION
Emerson's & Green Hotel $$$
236 Hurumzi Street
P.O. Box 3417
Zanzibar
☎ (54) 30171 **fax:** (54) 31038

email: emegre@zanzibar.org
website: www.zanzibar.org/emegre
Located in the heart of Stone Town, this beautifully restored palace once belonged to one of the richest men in Zanzibar. Although expensive, Emerson's & Green is well worth an overnight stay to appreciate the wonderful atmosphere of its spacious rooms. Each one is opulently furnished with ornate local carvings, traditional antiques, and the distinctive stone baths.

Matemwe Bungalows $$–$$$

P.O. Box 3275
Zanzibar
☎ (54) 236535 **fax:** (54) 236536
email: matemwe-znz@twiga.com
website: www.matemwe.com
With a wonderful position overlooking a sandy beach scattered with *dhows* from the local fishing village, Matemwe Bungalows also has an excellent dive centre offering snorkel trips, single dives, night dives, discover scuba diving "try dives," 4-day P.A.D.I. Open Water Certification Courses, and 3-day Advanced Open Water Courses.

8 A WALK ON THE WILD SIDE
➤ 88–95

OPERATORS
Chilongozi Safaris Ltd

Private Bag 286X
Ridgeway
Lusaka
☎ (1) 265814 **fax:** (1) 262291
email: info@chilongozi.com
website: www.chilongozi.com
Based in Lusaka, Chilongozi Safaris Ltd arranges quality safaris to some of Zambia's most beautiful and remote locations. These include Livingstone Island and both the Kafue and South Luangwa National Parks. Its founders, Tim Came and Justin Matterson, are two of southern Africa's most experienced safari specialists and are no strangers to adventure themselves. Tim has spent time in the past as a river guide on the Zambezi and in Botswana, while Justin's momentous achievements include running 3,218km (2,000 miles) across the Himalayas and canoeing the entire length of the Zambezi.

For more information see entries under Accommodation, p. 268.

Chilongozi safaris can be booked through the following agents outside Zambia:

Okavango Tours and Safaris

Marlborough House
298 Regents Park Road
London N3 2TJ
U.K.
☎ (020) 8343 3283 **fax:** (020) 8343 3287
email: info@okavango.com
website: www.okavango.com
This British-based safari operator organizes tailor-made itineraries, often around specialist activities such as horse riding, elephant riding and walking.

Karawane Individuelles Reisen

Postfach 909
D-71609 Ludwigsburg
Germany
☎ (7141) 28 48 48
fax: (7141) 28 48 69
email: africa@karawane.de

Ker & Downey

2825 Wilcrest Drive
Suite 600
Houston
TX 77042-6007
U.S.A.
☎ (713) 917 0048 ext 14 **fax:** (713) 917 0213
email: info@kerdowney.com
website: www.kerdowney.com

GETTING THERE

Flights from Lusaka to Mfuwe can be booked through **Zambian Airways**, **Proflight**, and **Eastern Air**. Zambian Airways' flight from Lusaka to Mfuwe takes approximately 1 hour in an extremely comfortable 18-seater twin-propeller Beechcraft. Two-and-a-half-hour road transfers to Chibembe Tented Lodge from Mfuwe can be arranged through **Chilongozi**— see Operators, above. Alternatively, a 12-minute transfer by light aircraft is available (this only carries 5 people maximum).

Zambian Airways

P.O. Box 310277
Lusaka
☎ (1) 225151 **fax:** (1) 223227
email: roanair@zamnet.zm
website: www.africa-insites.com/zambia/roanair.htm

CONTACTS

INFORMATION
Zambia National Tourist Board
P.O. Box 30017
Century House
Cairo Road
Lusaka
☎ (1) 229087 **fax:** (1) 225174
email: zntb@zamnet.zm
U.K. office:
2 Palace Gate
Kensington
London W8 5NG
U.K.
☎ (020) 7589 6343 **fax:** (020) 7225 3221
U.S.A. office:
237 East 52nd Street
New York
NY 10022
U.S.A.
☎ (212) 308 2155 **fax:** (212) 758 1319
Australia office:
C/o Orbitair International Pty Ltd
Level 10
36 Clarence Street
Sydney
NSW 2000
Australia
☎ (2) 995300 **fax:** (2) 902665

ACCOMMODATION
Chibembe Tented Lodge $$$
For details see **Chilongozi Safaris** under
Operators, above.
Accommodation is in spacious and luxurious
en-suite tents—5 twins and 2 doubles. The
rate, which includes meals, all game-viewing
activities, drinks, laundry service, park fees,
and levies, represents good value when you
consider both the high standards and difficult
logistics of running a remote, seasonal camp.

Chibembe Walking Camps $$$
For details see **Chilongozi Safaris** under
Operators, above.
Accommodation is in comfortable, beautifully
constructed wood and thatch huts. Just imagine taking an open-air bush shower while
listening to lions roaring in the distance!

Chisamba Safari Lodge $$$
P.O. Box 51018
Lusaka
☎ (1) 704600/1/2/3 **fax:** (1) 704800/221175
email:chisamba@zamnet.zm
website: www.africa-insites.com/
zambia/chisamba.htm

For those spending a night in Lusaka, this is a
recently built luxury lodge, tastefully decorated and catering to the upmarket traveller.

Ndeke Hotel $$
Garden Group Hotels
P.O. Box 30815
Lusaka
☎ (1) 251734 **fax:** (1) 252422
Very popular with budget travellers, in a safe
and reasonably quiet area of Lusaka.

9 CANOEING ON LAKE KARIBA AND THE LOWER ZAMBEZI ► 96–103

OPERATORS
Natureways
c/o Safari Consultants
2 Meredith Drive
Eastlea
P.O. Box 5826
Harare
☎ (4) 700383/722003 **fax:** (4) 704603
email: gwen@safcon.icon.co.zw
website: www.natureways.co.zw
Natureways was established in 1985 by Garth
Thompson as one of the first canoeing operations on the Zambezi in the Mana Pools area.
Subsequently he began walking safaris in the
national park too. One of the directors is James
Varden, who has been a guide for 11 years after
a course lasting 4 years. To obtain a canoeing
licence, guides must spend a minimum of 500
hours on the river. Natureways is a well-
respected company and one of the best
canoeing operations in Zimbabwe. They provide high quality food and accommodation and,
while client safety is paramount, the guides are
not stifling in their treatment of guests.
Canoeing trips on the river stop at the end of
Oct for the rainy season and begin again at the
beginning of May.

Sunvil Discovery
Sunvil House
Upper Square
Old Isleworth
Middlesex TW7 7BJ
U.K.
☎ (020) 8232 9777 **fax:** (020) 8568 8330
email: chris@sunvil.co.uk
website: www.sunvil.co.uk
The company is a specialist team from the long-
established independent tour operator, Sunvil
Holidays. Sunvil Discovery started life in 1991

with a ground-breaking programme of fly-drive trips to Namibia, and now works exclusively in southern Africa. All the members of the team have lived and worked in Africa. It is run by Chris McIntyre.

Wilderness Safaris

Victoria Falls
☎ (13) 2396/3371/2/3
fax: (13) 4224/5942
The Wilderness Safaris Group was formed in 1983 and is a travel company with small comfortable camps in remote corners of Africa. The company took over Matusadona Water Lodge in about 1995 and refurbished it. It is a small lodge with only 8 bed spaces. From there you can walk and take boat rides on the lake and along the shore to watch mammals and birds, and you can fish. The facilities include a plunge pool in lake water but protected against crocodiles. The lodge is only in radio contact with the office in Victoria Falls.

GETTING THERE

The international and domestic terminals in Harare are close enough to walk from one to the other. Note that there is a second domestic airport called Charles Prince, about 20km (12 miles) west of Harare on the Kariba road, which is used by some charter companies. While there are taxis at the international terminal to take you to Charles Prince, there are rarely taxis at the latter, so it is more difficult to do the journey in reverse. The trip, which usually takes about an hour, will usually be organized with a transfer company. There are both charter and scheduled flights to the Kariba area. If you fly on a charter it will take you right into Mana Pools; the scheduled flight lands in Kariba town and you will have to arrange some form of transport (flight or vehicle) into the park.

10 VICTORIA FALLS
► 104–113

OPERATORS
Adrift (Kandahar Safaris)

The Train Carriage
P.O. Box 233
Victoria Falls
Zimbabwe
☎ (13) 3522/2014/2279 **fax:** (13) 2014
email: adrift@africaonline.co.zw
Adrift Zimbabwe, which is an offshoot of the internationally known rafting company, Adrift, is linked to Kandahar Safaris and based in "The

Train Carriage" in the centre of Victoria Falls. The Zambezi Gorge rapids are the highest graded, commercially run, day rafting trips in the world, for which Adrift's safety record is unblemished. In addition to a first-aid kit and radio telephone, the company is linked to the Medical Air Rescue Service in case of an emergency. Adrift is also a member of RAZZ, the Rafting Association of Zimbabwe and Zambia, the trade organization which ensures that operators are acting responsibly.

Kandahar Safaris

Address as for Adrift, above.
Kandahar Safaris is a family run company owned by Clive and Kerry Bradford and has been operating for 10 years. They run both Adrift rafting and canoeing expeditions above the Falls, which can last from 1 to 3 days. One day trips usually use inflatable canoes but for the longer journeys the canoes are generally made of fibreglass.

Insatiable "adventure junkies" can book the following at Adrift/Kandahar Safaris: whitewater rafting and canoeing; horse rides; ultra lights; tandem skydiving; bungee jumps; riverboarding; abseiling; bushwalks; tour of the Falls; crocodile farm; helicopter flight; microlight flight; airport transfers; sunset cruise; entry into Victoria Falls; game drives.

Safari Drive

Wessex House
127 High Street
Hungerford
Berks RG17 0DL
U.K.
☎ (01488) 681611 (general safari enquiries)
☎ (01488) 684509 (Adrift enquiries)
website: www.safaridrive.com
Founded in 1992 as a specialist, self-drive safari operation and has now evolved into a general safari operator with expertize in more active types of safari. It has recently become the operational arm in the United Kingdom for Adrift.

ELEPHANT RIDING OPERATORS
Okavango Tours and Safaris

See page 267.

Songwe Experience

P.O. Box 29
Victoria Falls
☎ (13) 3211/20 **fax:** (13) 3205/7
email: saflodge@saflodge.co.zw
The Songwe Experience was recently set up by

Giles and Caroline Whittle-Herbert, who set out to provide a comfortable but genuine experience for visitors to Makuni Village and to Songwe Point. A percentage of the price of each visit goes to a development trust within the village.

Wild Horizons

P.O. Box 159
Victoria Falls
☎ (13) 4219/2004/2029 **fax:** (13) 4349/2004
email: wildhori@samara.co.zw
This is is a well-respected and long-established concern run by the White family, with 3 safari camps in the Victoria Falls/Hwange National Park area and running mobile and walking safaris in the park. The third camp, Elephant Camp, was opened in 1995 with 4 African elephants. These are now dedicated for the use of residents at the camp while a further nine animals cater for half-day experiences and for those camping for 1 night with the elephants.

The Zambezi Helicopter Company

P.O. Box 125
Victoria Falls
☎ (13) 3569 **fax:** (13) 5806
email: reservations@helicopters.co.zw
website: www.bookorbuy.com/helicopters
The Zambezi Helicopter Company was formed in 1996 and now has three helicopters with which it flies over the Falls or makes longer game flights over nearby national parks. While helicopters do offer a good aerial view of the Falls, they also fly lower than fixed-wing aircraft and their noise can be disturbing to those on the ground trying to enjoy a completely different experience. The company provides transfers to and from hotels in Victoria Falls and its liability is up to European standards.

ACCOMMODATION
Sprayview Hotel $$

P. O. Box 70
Victoria Falls
☎ (13) 4345/4344
email: sprayvw@africaonline.co.zw
A very pleasant and reasonably priced hotel in a fairly central location.

The Victoria Falls Hotel $$$

P. O. Box 10
Victoria Falls
☎ (13) 4751/4761 **fax:** (13) 4258
email: vicfallshotel@tvfh.zimsun.co.zw

website: www.zimbabwesun.com
This magnificent Edwardian hotel is located near the station and its lawns run down towards the falls. It has 171 rooms, 9 suites and a royal suite.

Victoria Falls Safari Lodge $$$

P.O. Box 29
Victoria Falls
☎ (13) 3208/20 **fax:** (13) 3205/7
email: saflodge@saflodge.co.zw
website: www.vfsl.com
This is a modern, multi-level, 72-bedroomed hotel, built in safari lodge style and overlooking its own waterhole, 3km (2 miles) outside Victoria Falls.

---

11 KAYAKING ON LAKE MALAWI ► 116–125

OPERATORS
Kayak Africa

P.O. Box 48
Monkey Bay
Cape McLear
☎ 584456
Bookings through Cape Town office:
☎ (21) 689 8123 **fax:** (21) 689 2149
email: kayakafrica@earthleak.co.za
website: www.kayakafrica.co.za
South African kayak safari operator based at Chembe, with permanent wilderness camps on Domwe and Mumbo islands. Offers 1-week packages, including 25km (16 miles) of kayaking, accommodation and food, usually run from Sun to connect with the weekly flight from Lilongwe, but shorter trips can be arranged at any time depending on space availability. P.A.D.I. Openwater diving courses, unlimited dives or advanced courses can be combined with the kayak trip for an extra payment, on the basis of a minimum 5-day trip. Operating since 1994, Kayak Africa's organisation and environmentally friendly attitude are exemplary. Guides and instructors are well-trained and knowledgeable about Cape McLear and the lake. Food is invariably excellent. The company also runs kayak safaris in Mozambique and Madagascar. It plans to upgrade its wilderness camps.

GETTING THERE
Air Malawi

Head Office
Robins Road
P.O. Box 84

Blantyre
☎ 620811 **fax:** 620042
In the U.K. book through:

Flight Directors
☎ 0870 6080767/6060122

Trailfinders
42-50 Earls Court Road
London W8 6FT
U.K.
☎ (020) 7938 3366 **fax:** (020) 7937 9294
This travel agency can book competitively
priced international flights to Malawi
(Lilongwe) with **British Airways** or **Air
Malawi**. They do not deal with Air Malawi
domestic flights—book separately or through
the tour company that you are linking up with.

INFORMATION
Ministry of Tourism, Parks & Wildlife
Post Bag 326
Murray Road
Lilongwe
☎ 782702 **fax:** 780650
email: tourism@malawi.net.
The Tourist Information Office is located in the
same building.

Malawi Tourism Information
Geo Group & Associates
4 Christian Fields
London SW16 3JZ
U.K.
☎ (0115) 982 1903 **fax:** (0115) 981 9418
email: enquiries@malawitourism.com

ACCOMMODATION
Chembe Lodge $
P.O. Box 187
Monkey Bay
Cape McLear
☎/**fax:** 584334
Reservations through Johannesburg office:
P.O. Box 70301
Bryanston 2021
South Africa
☎ (11) 706 1210/3 **fax:** (11) 463 3001
email: hello-afrika@iafrica.com
website: www.helloafrika.com/chembe.htm
This tent hotel at the peaceful, eastern end of
Chembe village offers Cape McLear's best
accommodation for the moment. Stand-up
sylvan tents with outside decks are dotted
among bougainvillaea bushes right on the

beach. Only a few have private washing facilities, and all lighting is by generator or
hurricane lamp. Rates include breakfast and
dinner, not gourmet but adequate. Activities on
offer include catamaran cruises and scuba diving (e.g. a P.A.D.I. open-water course including
accommodation).

FOOD AND DRINK
Chembe's handful of low-key bars and restaurants are strung out along the lakeshore. **Fat
Monkeys** is a popular bar as it offers satellite
T.V. to the information-hungry and **The Gap**
remains a favourite for late nights. Chembe's
original guesthouse, **Stevens**, is the best
option for food.

**12 A HORSE SAFARI ON THE
NYIKA PLATEAU
► 126–133**

OPERATORS
Heart of Africa Safaris
P.O. Box 2338
Lilongwe
☎ 740579
☎/**fax:** 740848
email: nyika-safaries@malawi.net
website: www.nyika.com
This is the only company that runs the horse
riding and accommodation in Nyika National
Park, as well as the Kazuni Camp in nearby
Vwaza Marsh Wildlife Reserve. Horse riding by
the hour or the day is available, as well as game
drives and guided walks. Horse safaris based at
the tent camps (2–10 night duration) are for a
minimum of 2 and a maximum of 6 people.
Between Apr and Dec there are set departures
of 7 and 10 nights. Four-day safaris from Sun to
Thu include 2 nights at Chelinda Camp. (See
also below, under Accommodation.)

GETTING THERE
Ulendo Safaris
P.O. Box 30728
Capital City
Lilongwe
☎ 743501/7 **fax:** 743492
email: ulendo@malawi.net
This hotel booking agent also runs a useful
transfer service from the airport to Lilongwe,
has a wide range of information, and can
arrange transfers or tours to other parts of
Malawi. Their office is located in the shopping
centre opposite the post office in the old town.

ACCOMMODATION
Heart of Africa Safaris $–$$$

See above for contact details.
This operator offers a range of accommodation in Nyika to suit every budget: a campsite; self-catering chalets in the pine forest (for up to 4 people); rooms at Chelinda Camp itself (full board); and, the latest addition, luxury log cabins (also full board) high on the hill behind, with a separate restaurant and bar.

Imperial Hotel $$

Post Bag A113
Lilongwe
☎ 743243
email: imperial@malawi.net
This small, friendly hotel next to the post office in the old town only opened in 1999 but has become Lilongwe's favourite expatriate cross-roads. It has colourfully decorated en-suite rooms and serves copious breakfasts. A lively bar and restaurant spills on to a roof terrace.

FOOD AND DRINK
Huts Restaurant

P.O. Box 515
Lilongwe
☎ 744756
This is where to go for a flavoursome Indian meal in air-conditioned comfort. Tandoori, curry, and vegetarian dishes. Tucked away at the back of the SS Rent-a-car building on Kamuzu Procession Road in the old town.

---

13 SEEKING A DIVE IN SOUTHERN MOZAMBIQUE ► 134–141

OPERATORS
Mozambique Connection

P.O. Box 2861
Rivonia 2128
South Africa
☎ (11) 803 4185/6910/6930 **fax:** (11) 803 3861
email: mozcon@pixie.co.za
website: www.mozambiqueconnection.co.za
This Johannesburg-based travel agency has been specializing in Mozambique since the early 1990s, and can organize everything you need there, from car rental to visas, accommodation along the coast, scheduled flights to Maputo, and charter flights between Johannesburg and Inhambane with Eagle Air. They are used to dealing with customers based outside Africa and also cater for business groups.

SPECIALIST OPERATORS
Scuba diving

Barra Lodge Dive Charters (African Dive Adventures), c/o Barra Lodge (see below).
email: afridive@iafrica.com
website: www.cybercraft.co.za/dive
This South African company from Natal is the only scuba diving operation on Barra beach and, as such, suffers from its own popularity. Instructors are good but it is time some of the equipment was renewed. One-day resort course includes tuition, a lagoon dive, and openwater dive.

Horse-riding

Barra Lodge Stables, c/o Barra Lodge (see below)
Birgit, the owner, has excellent horses and takes you through a good variety of landscapes during the 1-hour ride, morning or afternoon. Longer rides can be arranged with advance notice.

INFORMATION
Fundo Nacional do Turismo (Futur)

Avenida 25 de septembre 1203
C.P. 4758
Maputo
☎ (1) 307320/3 **fax:** (1) 307324
email: futur@futur.imoz.com

ACCOMMODATION
Albatroz Restaurant $$

See Food and Drink, below, for details.
Not just a restaurant: offers comfortable self-catering chalets accommodating six. Allen, the owner, runs fishing charters and, in Jun to Sep, whale watching. Diving will soon be on offer too.

Barra Lodge $$

P.O. Box 207
Inhambane
☎/**fax:** (23) 20561
Or book through:
P.O. Box 6921
Midrand 1685
South Africa
☎ (11) 314 3355 **fax:** (11) 314 3239.
email: barra@pixie.co.za
website: www.barralodge.co.za
Established since 1996, this beautifully sited beach resort is expanding fast. Thatched chalets, self-catering or otherwise, a campsite, and dormitory accommodation are now joined

by two new upmarket lodges, the Ilha do Barra (at Barra Point) and Flamingo Bay (built on stilts above the mangroves). Endless activities include scuba diving, fishing charters, fly-fishing, sailing, canoe safaris, and horse riding. A thatched houseboat sleeping 6 people is also available for touring the bay. Friendly and attentive service, though less impressive on the restaurant front. Charter flights from Johannesburg for weekend or weekly packages; transfers from Inhambane.

Casa Azul $

Praia da Tofo
☎ (23) 29021
(Or book through Mozambique Connection—see above.)
Basic beach house located among shady casuarinas right on Tofo beach, a few steps from the water and fishermen. Self-catering rooms/flatlets with shared bathrooms; breakfasts served on the terrace by José, the caretaker and able cook. Casa Azul is now the base for Tofo Divers, a new scuba diving operation.

Rovuma Carlton Hotel $$/$$$

Rua da Sé
4376 Maputo
☎ (1) 305000 **fax:** (1) 305305
(Or book through Mozambique Connection—see above.)
A recently modernized, high-rise hotel in a convenient central location next to the cathedral. The service is excellent and there's a restaurant and coffee-shop. Run by the Pestana Hotels group that also operates Inhaca Island Lodge and Bazaruto Lodge.

FOOD AND DRINK
Albatroz Restaurant

Praia da Tofo
☎ (23) 29005
Perched in the dunes above Tofo beach with an outside terrace. Excellent fresh seafood and South African wines.

Turtle Cove

Praia da Tofo
☎ (23) 29021
Set among palm trees a couple of kilometres back from the beach, this relaxed surfers' and backpackers' lodge offers imaginative, fresh Mozambiquean cuisine in an atmospheric structure, inspired by indigenous building styles.

---

14 DRIVING THE SKELETON COAST & DAMARALAND
➤ 144–153

OPERATORS
Sunvil Discovery

See page 268 for details.
U.K. agent for Turnstone Tours (below).

Turnstone Tours

P.O. Box 307
Swakopmund
☎**/fax:** (64) 403123
Run by Bruno Nebe, a Namibian by birth and an expert on the desert. He runs small, high-quality trips, such as day trips into the bird reserve of Sandwich Harbour and around the coast, and longer expeditions up into the most remote areas of Damaraland. Many are tailored to particular interests, including birds, wildlife, rock art, local history, or even gems and minerals.

ACCOMMODATION

There are a number of bleak and basic camp-sites dotted all the way along the shore between Swakopmund and Henties Bay, and several good hotels and B&Bs in Swakopmund. It's best to book these in advance, especially during the busier periods. They include:

Brandberg Restcamp

P.O. Box 35
Uis
☎**/fax:** (64) 504038
This small restcamp (at Uis, which is near Brandberg) has five 2-bedroom flats and several 3–4-bedroom houses. Each flat has 4 beds, 2 baths, 2 toilets, and a kitchen. The houses each take 6–8 people. There's also a camping site, a 25m swimming pool, tennis courts, a full-size snooker table, and a badminton court. The restaurant serves breakfast, lunch, and dinner, and will organize day trips to mines in the area and to Brandberg.

Pension Adler

3 Strand Street
P.O. Box 1497
Swakopmund
☎ (64) 405045/6/7 **fax:** (64) 404206
Located opposite the aquarium and 50m (164ft) from the sea, this modern, stylish pension has been designed with space and taste, and has good facilities. Its 14 rooms are all slightly different, and there's a heated indoor pool, a sauna, and a rooftop sun-terrace.

Schweizerhaus Hotel
P.O. Box 445
Swakopmund
☎ (64) 402419 **fax:** (64) 405850
The Schweizerhaus is a good value hotel with a commanding location, overlooking the ocean yet near to town. It has 34 rooms, simply furnished and in German style; most have a balcony, though some overlook a courtyard with free-flying parrots. The Café Anton, below, opens for extensive breakfasts and is renowned for super pastries.

15 THE HEART OF THE NAMIB
► 154–163

OPERATORS
Namib Sky Adventure Safaris
☎ (663) 3233/3234 **fax:** (663) 3235
Runs dawn ballooning trips over the desert, usually from Kulala, Movenpick or Mwisho camps. A fascinating, eerie experience, and an excellent platform for landscape photography. Balloon flights must be booked in advance.

Sunvil Discovery
See page 268 for details.
Sunvil Discovery specializes in fly-drive trips to Namibia; these usually include an important 100 percent CDW insurance that is unique, covering the car completely in case of accident.

ACCOMMODATION
Wilderness Sossusvlei Camp
P.O. Box 6850
Windhoek
☎ (61) 225178 **fax:** (61) 239455
Stylishly built from rock and timber, each of the 9 twin rooms has its own small plunge pool and an en-suite bathroom. The central lounge, dining room, and bar are linked to the bedrooms by raised walkways. This is the area's most impressive lodge—advanced booking essential. Rates include all meals, drinks, and guided activities. You can drive or fly to it.

Zebra River Lodge
P.O. Box 11742
Windhoek
☎ (63) 293265 **fax:** (63) 293266
This is one of Namibia's friendliest guest farms, offering 6 double rooms in a relaxed and unpretentious atmosphere, with superb cuisine. Advanced booking recommended. In addition, Zebra River has short walking trails, ideal for day hikes, and it's close to the Naukluft

Mountains. Also offered are 4WD day trips into the pans, including Sossusvlei, Dead Vlei and Sesriem Canyon.

CAR HIRE
Sossusvlei 4x4 Car Rental
☎ (64) 500142/(63) 293250
fax: (64) 500941
Located at Sesriem, one of the gates into the Namib-Naukluft National Park. 4WDs for hire. The company also runs "shuttles" between the 2WD car park and Nara Vlei.

For driving trips around the country, the best companies are:
Avis
P.O. Box 2057
Eros Airport
Windhoek
☎ (61) 233166 **fax:** (61) 223072

Budget Rent A Car
P.O. Box 1754
Windhoek Airport
Windhoek
☎ (61) 228720 **fax:** (61) 227665

Imperial
P.O. Box 1387
Eros Airport
Windhoek
☎ (61) 227103 **fax:** (61) 777721

16 HIKING THE FISH RIVER CANYON
► 164–173

OPERATORS
Canyon Tours
P.O. Box 431
150 4th Street
Keetmanshoop
mobile ☎ 081 127 3137 **fax:** (63) 222216
email: canyon@iwwn.com.na
Runs tours in the south of Namibia, to Lüderitz, Sossusvlei, and the Fish River Canyon.

Drifters Adventure Tours
P.O. Box 48434
Roosevelt Park 2129
Johannesburg
South Africa
☎ (11) 888 1160 **fax:** (11) 888 1020
email: drifters@drifters.co.za
Organizers of camping safaris out of Johannesburg to many destinations in Southern Africa.

Fish River Canyon Hiking Tours

P.O. Box 3823
Cape Town 8000
South Africa
☎/fax: (21) 462 0532
mobile ☎ 083 269 8658
email: siggi@tablebay.co.za
website: www.tablebay.co.za

Siggi Öhler, who runs this company, has walked the canyon with large and small groups more than 50 times. His charge does not include transport to and from the trail (though he will pick you up at Grünau), but covers all food and camping costs for the trail itself. Strongly recommended for novice hikers.

SWA Safaris

P.O. Box 20373
Windhoek
☎ (61) 221193 fax: (61) 225387
email: swasaf@iwwn.com.na
website: www.iwwn.com.na/swasaf

German-managed operation, in business since 1954. They offer a range of tour programmes, but will tailor-make an itinerary for you, with or without tour guide.

Trans Namibia Tours

P.O. Box 20028
Windhoek
☎ (61) 221549 fax: (61) 230960
email: namibia@tnt.com.na
website: www.trans-namibia-tours.com

Weekly, guided sightseeing tours throughout Namibia, as well as custom-made itineraries, and in-depth study tours and expeditions for serious travellers.

INFORMATION
Namibia Wildlife Resorts

Central Reservations Office
Private Bag 13267
Windhoek
☎ (61) 236975/6/7/8 fax: (61) 224900
email: reservations@iwwn.com.na

All reservations for Namibian nature reserves —including the Fish River Canyon and resorts within it such as Hobas and Ai-Ais—have to be done through this office.

ACCOMMODATION
Ai-Ais Hot Springs $–$$

The available accommodation at Ai-Ais Hot Springs comprises camping sites, huts with basic cooking and communal washing and toilet facilities, self-contained flats, and luxury flats.

Day visitors are allowed between sunrise and sunset. The extensive facilities include a spa, swimming-pool and restaurant. This is the ideal place to relax at the end of the trail. Open mid-Mar to end-Oct. Bookings can be made through the Central Reservations Office (see above) only.

Grünau Hotel $

P.O. Box 2
Grünau
☎/fax: (63) 262001
email: grunauhot@mar.namib.com

Closest hotel to the Fish River Canyon. All rooms en suite, with T.V. and roof fan. Basic accommodation for backpackers, and camping- and caravan site also available. Transport to the canyon easily available from Grünau.

Hobas Campsite $

Ten camping sites are available, each for a maximum of 8 people, 2 vehicles and 1 tent, or 1 caravan. Fireplace, water, washing and toilet facilities, and a swimming-pool are available. Bookings can be made through the Central Reservations Office (above) only. You are recommended to overnight here before starting the trail.

GETTING THERE
Coach services
Intercape Mainliner

Windhoek office:
☎ (61) 227847
Cape Town office:
☎ (21) 386 4400 fax: (21) 386 2488
email: marius@intercape.co.za
website: www.intercape.co.za

The company has scheduled departures around South Africa and surrounding countries, including regular coach departures from Cape Town and Windhoek, all stopping at Grünau for the Fish River Canyon.

VEHICLE HIRE
Budget Rent A Car

P.O. Box 1777
Kempton Park 1620
Johannesburg
South Africa
☎ (11) 392 3907 fax: (11) 392 2172
email: bracsain@mccarthy.co.za
website: www.budget.co.za

Budget rent out a wide range of vehicles at fairly reasonable rates and have branches all over Southern Africa.

CONTACTS

Campers Corner

P.O. Box 48191
Roosevelt Park 2129
Johannesburg
South Africa
☎ (11) 789 2327 **fax:** (11) 787 6900
email: campers@iafrica.com
website: www.campers.co.za
Established in 1976, one of the oldest camper and motorhome rental companies in South Africa. They also rent out cars and minibuses. Branches in all main Southern African cities, including Windhoek.

Freedom Africa Touring Club

P.O. Box 418
Rondebosch 7701
Cape Town
South Africa
☎ (21) 686 9112 **fax:** (21) 685 7129
email: africatour@icon.co.za
website: www.freedomafrica.com
This group hires out Harley-Davidson and Honda motorbikes. They will also arrange custom-made tours.

Odyssey Car Hire

P.O. Box 20938
Windhoek
☎ (61) 223269 **fax:** (61) 228911
email: odyssey@iwwn.com.na
website:
www.iwwn.com.na/odyssey/odyssey.html
Range of vehicles available, from saloon cars to campers to 4x4s.

EQUIPMENT
Camp & Climb

155 Smit Street
Braamfontein 2017
Johannesburg
South Africa
☎ (11) 403 5410 **fax:** (11) 403 5429
Outdoor camping and hiking equipment specialists, with several branches in the Johannesburg-Pretoria area, and in Cape Town. Assistants can give expert advice.

Cape Union Mart

34–40 Barrack Street
Cape Town 8000
South Africa
☎ (21) 464 5800 **fax:** (21) 461 9789
email: info@ capeunionmart.co.za
website: www. capeunionmart.co.za
One of the largest suppliers of trailing,camping and adventure equipment in South Africa. They have several branches in each of the main cities, with helpful, knowledgeable staff.

---

17 ON HORSEBACK IN THE OKAVANGO DELTA ► 176–185

OPERATORS
Okavango Horse Safaris

P.J. and Barney Bestelink
Private Bag 23
Maun
☎ 661671 **fax:** 661672
email: ohsnx@global.bw
P.J. and Barney own and run all the operations at Okavango Horse Safaris. Their organizational skills and attention to detail are faultless. They offer a 5-day or 10-day safari with up to 8 guests in each small group. Departures are from Mar to Nov. They also operate the secluded Nxamaseri Lodge, in the northwest of the delta panhandle, which is ideal for birdwatching, fishing, and *mokoro* trails.

Sunvil Discovery

See page 268.
Agents for Okavango Horse Safari.

Wilderness Safaris

P.O. Box 78573
Santon 2146
South Africa
6th Floor
Twin Towers West
Santon City, Santon
South Africa
☎ (11) 883 0747 **fax:** (11) 883 0911
email: info@sdn.wilderness.co.za
Wilderness is one of the largest operators in Botswana and manages around 15 different camps and lodges. Little Vumbura is one of the newest of their lodges. (See page 269.)

GETTING THERE
Air Botswana

Lobatse Road
Gaborone
Botswana
Postal Address:
P. O. Box 92
Gaborone
☎ 351921 **fax:** 374802
telex: 2413

U.K. office:
177/178 Tottenham Court Road
London W1P OHN
U.K.
☎ (020) 7757 2737 **fax:** (020) 7757 2277
Two direct flights daily from Johannesburg to
Maun plus connecting flights via Gaborone.

Local Charters

The different flight charter companies are normally contracted direct by the lodges. Moremi
Air, Mack Air, Delta Air, and Northern Air all
have offices by Maun airport.

INFORMATION
Department of Tourism

P.O. Box 429
Maun
☎ 660492 **fax:** 661676

---

18 EXPLORING THE SURREAL
MAKGADIKGADI PANS
► 186–193

OPERATORS
Sunvil Discovery

See page 268.
Agents for Jack's Camp.

Uncharted Africa Safari Company

P.O. Box 1996
Northriding 2162
South Africa
☎ (11) 462 9448 **fax:** (11) 462 9447
email: bianca@unchartedafrica.co.za
Uncharted Africa operates Jack's Camp and the
nearby San Camp. Their prices include all food
and accommodation as well as the excursions
on quad bikes, game viewing from vehicles, and
walks with the bushmen.

GETTING THERE

See under **Air Botswana** and **Local Charters**
in the adventure above.

INFORMATION
Department of Tourism

See under the adventure above.

ACCOMMODATION

There is a limited number of hotels and lodges
in Maun.

Riley's $$$

☎ 660320
This long-established hotel is run on internationally high standards and is currently owned
by the Best Western Group.

Sedie Hotel $$

☎ 660177
This hotel lies about 10km (6 miles) out of
town.

Crocodile Camp $$

☎ 660265
Unless you are part of an organized tour with
transport, or you have your own vehicle,
Crocodile Camp is very inconvenient, for it is
situated some 22km (14 miles) out of town, at
Matlapeneng. Some of the rooms are not
secure, service is poor, and facilities are basic.

FOOD AND DRINK

Apart from the lodges and hotels, there are 2
restaurants in Maun, **The Power Station**
(below) and **The Sports Bar**. There are also a
few cafés, snack bars, and fast food joints.

The Power Station

This large venue is not only a restaurant—it
includes a bar and cinema at the back of the
electricity station, set in a courtyard and indus-
trial buildings. It is a popular meeting place,
frequented by the local tour guides and pilots.
It serves a good choice of grills and salads, with
main courses such as steak with pepper sauce,
and is very reasonably priced.

---

19 TRANS-KALAHARI SAFARI
► 194–201

OPERATORS
Sunvil Discovery

See page 268.
A leading specialist tour operator, Sunvil
Discovery offer safari-equipped Land Rovers
for hire around Botswana, Namibia, Zimbabwe,
and Zambia. Their expert team plan and organize expeditions to Botswana's most remote
areas, as well as less challenging "fly-in" trips to
safari lodges.

Local operators

A number of activities, such as 4WD excursions
and boat trips, can be arranged through lodges
—see under the Accommodation entries below.

ACCOMMODATION
Camp Moremi $$$
c/o Afro Ventures
8 Milcliff Road
P.O. Box 1200
Paulshof 2056
South Africa
☎ (11) 807 3720 **fax:** (11) 807 3480
email: jnb@afroventures.com
Linked to its water-bound sister camp, Camp Okavango, Camp Moremi has a good location beside Xakanika Lagoon, at the end of the Moremi Tongue. Accommodation is in 11 large safari tents with private showers and toilets, each a few metres from the back of the tent. Mostly 4WD trips with experienced guides, though boat trips are sometimes possible.

Chobe Game Lodge $$$
P.O. Box 32
Kasane
☎ 650340 **fax:** 650280/650223
email: chobe@fast.co.za
Though more like a hotel than a small bush lodge, this 52-room lodge's reputation for service and its superb location in the heart of the Chobe area ensure that it remains a firm favourite. Activities include boat rides on the river and game drives along the waterfront.

Ilala Lodge $$$
Livingstone Way
Zambia
P.O. Box 18
☎ (13) 4737 **fax:** (13) 4740
email: ilalazws@africaonline.co.zw
A favourite in Victoria Falls, right between the town and the Falls themselves, this 16-room lodge has all the facilities of a big hotel and the best location in town, yet it's small and friendly. Make sure that you book in advance.

Impalila Island Lodge $$$
P.O. Box 70378
Bryanston 2021
South Africa
☎ (11) 706 7207 **fax:** (11) 706 7207
On the northwest side of Impalila Island, overlooking the Zambezi's Mowomba rapids, this super lodge is better value and much less expensive than its neighbours in Botswana. Impalila's 8 stylish, wooden, double chalets are large, its food very good, and its staff attentive. Activities include motorboat trips, dugout canoe excursions, birdwatching walks, and top-class tiger-fishing.

Ichingo Chobe River Lodge $$$
P.O. Box 55, Kasane
☎/**fax:** 650143 (on the island) **fax:** (in Kasane town) 650223
On the Chobe side of Impalila Island, Ichingo is less luxurious but is still a super, friendly lodge. Its 7 large twin-bed tents, with en-suite showers and toilets, have a rustic feel. Unusually for a bush lodge, children are welcome. Activities are basically the same as Impalila (above).

Tongabezi $$
Postbag 31
Zambia
☎ (3) 323235 **fax:** (3) 323224
Set on a sweeping bend of the Zambezi, Tongabezi has set the region's standard for innovative camp design with its 5 twin-bed cottages and 3 double houses. Expect high quality food and stylish accommodation.

Tsaro Elephant Lodge $$
Postbag BR319
Gaborone
☎ 584139 **fax:** 302555
This established, small lodge overlooks the Khwai River and Moremi beyond, near North Gate. Its 8 rooms are traditional brick rooms, a welcome change from canvas, and staff are efficient and friendly.

Camping sites
Camping sites inside the parks can be booked directly through:

Parks and Reserves Reservations Office
P.O. Box 20364
Boseja
Maun
☎ 661265 **fax:** 661264
Reservations must be within 12 months of travel and paid in advance, before arrival.

CAR HIRE
Avis
P.O. Box 790
Gaborone
☎ 313093 **fax:** 312205
email: avisbots@global.bw
Avis have offices in Maun and Kasane, and one-way rentals are possible. They have very modern petrol engined Toyota Hilux twin-cabs. However, they don't have any camping equipment, or even spare jerrycans, which you'll need for a petrol-engined vehicle on this route.

20 SHADES OF ORANGE
➤ 204–213

RICHTERSVELD OPERATORS
South African National Parks Head Office
P.O. Box 787
Pretoria 1110
☎ (12) 343 1991 **fax:** (12) 343 0905
email: reservations@parks-sa.co.za
website: www.sa-parks.co.za
Advance bookings for all South African national parks are done through this head office.

Richtersveld National Park (part of South African National Parks)
P.O. Box 406
Alexander Bay 406
☎ (27) 831 1506 **fax:** (27) 831 1175
email: johant@parks-sa.co.za
website: www.sa-parks.co.za
If head office say the park is full, contact the Richtersveld National Park direct, as they may tell you otherwise.

ORANGE RIVER CANOE OPERATOR
Felix Unite River Adventures
P.O. Box 2807
Clareinch 7740
Western Cape
☎ (21) 683 6433 **fax:** (21) 683 6488
email: bookings@felix.co.za
website: www.felixunite.co.za
The best-known canoe adventure operator in South Africa with have excellent guides and a highly professional but relaxed operation.

SPECIALIST OPERATOR
Transform Programme
P.O. Box 406
Alexander Bay 406
☎/**fax:** (27) 831 1417
Floors Strauss will arrange guides in the Richtersveld—essential on any long hikes. He will also advise on cultural events in the area.

GETTING THERE
RICHTERSVELD
Cape Eco Trails
P.O. Box 313
Noordhoek 7985
Western Cape
☎ (21) 785 5511 **fax:** (21) 794 0736
email: ecotrail@mweb.co.za

This company offers trips into remote and inaccessible areas of the Richtersveld where no independent traveller has access.

Executive Safaris
P.O. Box 1646
Bellville 7535
Cape Town
☎ (21) 949 0826 **fax:** (21) 949 0827
email: info@executivesafaris.co.za
website: www.executivesafaris.co.za
This company will organize the logistics of your trip to Richtersveld with your own vehicle, and will lead the tour in another vehicle if you wish.

Richtersveld Challenge
P.O. Box 142
Springbok 8240
☎/**fax:** (71) 81905
email: richtersveld.challen@kingsley.co.za
Fully inclusive tours into the Richtersveld.

COACH SERVICES
Intercape Mainliner
See page 275 for details.
Has scheduled pick up/drop off near the South Africa/Namibia border at the Orange River.

INFORMATION
Northern Namaqualand Tourism Task Team
website: www.diamondcoast.co.za
For information on Richtersveld area.

ACCOMMODATION
Eksteenfontein Guest House $
P.O. Box 25
Eksteenfontein 8284
☎ (27) 851 8994
A small town in the middle of nowhere on the way from the Richtersveld National Park to the Orange River canoe base. It is a community project run by local ladies and offers basic accommodation that's spotlessly clean.

Richtersveld National Park
See South African National Parks Head Office or Richtersveld National Park, above, for details. A variety of self-catering cottages is available in all South African National Parks. All are clean and reasonable, but not of luxurious standard. Guest cottages available at park entrance sleep from 4 to 10 people and bungalows sleep 2 or 3. Camping is also available. Bedding and towels provided plus fully equipped kitchens.

CONTACTS

SOUTH AFRICA & LESOTHO

OTHER INFORMATION
Useful books include:
Newman's Birds of Southern Africa by
Kenneth Newman, published by Southern Book
Publishers (ISBN 1-86812-611-0)
Southern African 4x4 Trails Yearbook by
Andrew St. Pierre White, published by
International Motoring Productions (ISBN 0-
620-20507-5)

21 CALL OF THE KRUGER ► 214–221

OPERATORS
Afro Ventures (Pty) Ltd
Cape Town office reservations:
P.O. Box 16336
Vlaeberg 8018
☎ (21) 424 2220 **fax:** (21) 424 2221
email: cpt@afroventures.com
website: www.afroventures.com
Johannesburg office reservations:
P.O. Box 1200
Paulshof 2056
☎ (11) 807 3720 **fax:** (11) 807 3480
email: jnb@afroventures.com
A reputable destination management company
for the whole of southern Africa. They will suggest itineraries, book accommodation, arrange
transport and transfers. The company also has
a representative in the U.S.A., for sales only:

Kelley & Associates
(Robert E. Kelley)
115 S. Brighton Place
Arlington Heights
IL 60004
U.S.A.
☎/**fax:** (847) 342 1226
email: RKelley175@aol.com

Lowveld Environmental Services
P.O. Box 5747
Nelspruit 1200
Mpumalanga
☎ (13) 744 7636 **fax:** (13) 744 7063
email: lowveld@iafrica.com
This company has a good reputation for providing tailor-made safaris and scheduled daily
tours of Kruger National Park. Well-trained and
knowledgeable driver/guides.

Mfafa Safaris
P.O. Box 4214
White River 1240
☎ (13) 750 1782/3 **fax:** (13) 750 1909

email: tours@mfafa.co.za
Registered safari tour operator, established in
1992, operating in Kruger National Park area
and other areas of South Africa, Swaziland, and
Mozambique. Its driver/guides are registered
with South African Tourism and the Field
Guides Association of Southern Africa.

SPECIALIST OPERATORS
Sabie Horse Trails
P.O. Box 571
Sabie 1260
mobile ☎ 082 938 2060
fax: (13) 764 2422
Timmy really loves his horses and shares his
local knowledge. He offers trail rides from 1
hour to 2 days in the hills and river valleys near
Sabie town. The western-style saddles are comfortable and the horses are very well behaved.
For novices or experienced riders.

Shangana Cultural Village
☎ (13) 737 7799 **fax:** (13) 737 7007
email: shangana@fast.co.za
Located between Hazyview and Graskop on the
R535, this is the only cultural village devoted to
the Shangaan people of the northeast. It is very
well done without seeming too touristy. It
encompasses a real Shangaan village comprising a chief, his 3 wives and their offspring. You
can also have a consultation with a traditional
healer, Sangoma. Arts and crafts on sale—recommended.

GETTING THERE
Most European airlines fly to South Africa, as
does **American Airlines**. Other U.S. airlines
connect in Europe for onward flights.

SA Airlink
P.O. Box 7529
Bonaero Park 1622
☎ (11) 356 1111 **fax:** 978 1106/1635
website: www.saa.co.za
Part of South African Airways, they fly from
Johannesburg to Nelspruit.

SA Express
P.O. Box 101
Johannesburg International Airport, 1627
☎ (11) 978 1111 **fax:** (11) 978 1106
website: www.saexpress.co.za
SA Express flies from Johannesburg to
Hoedspruit and Skukuza airports.
U.K. office:
☎ (020) 7312 5010 **fax:** (020) 7312 5011

U.S.A. offices:
New York: ☎ (212) 418 3700
fax: (212) 980 2606
Los Angeles: ☎ (213) 641 4111
fax: (213) 641 0860
Miami: ☎ (305) 461 3484 **fax:** (305) 461 3861
European offices:
Munich: ☎ +49 (89) 539 436
fax: +49 (89) 530 9679
Paris: ☎ +33 (1) 42 61 57 87
fax: +33 (1) 42 60 18 15

Avis
P.O. Box 221
Isando 1600
☎ (11) 923 3500 **fax:** (11) 923 3501
website: www.avis.co.za

INFORMATION
Mpumalanga Tourism Authority
P.O. Box 679
Nelspruit 1200
☎ (13) 752 7001 **fax:** (13) 759 5441
email: mtanlpsa@cis.co.za
website: www.mpumalanga.com

South African Tourism
Private Bag X164
Pretoria 0001
☎ (12) 482 6258 **fax:** (12) 347 8753 (Attn.
Information Dept)
email: satour@icon.co.za
website: www.satour.co.za

OTHER INFORMATION
Useful books include:
Behavior Guide to African Mammals by
Richard Despard Estes, published by The
University of California Press (ISBN 0-520-
05831-3)
Absa FIND IT Kruger National Park, pub-
lished by Jacana (ISBN 1-874955-85-9)
Newman's Birds of Southern Africa by
Kenneth Newman, published by Southern Book
Publishers (ISBN 1-86812-611-0)
A useful accommodation guide book is:
_AA Hotels, Lodges, Guest Houses, B&B's:
Southern Africa_, published by AA South
Africa (ISBN 0-9583907-6-2).

ACCOMMODATION
Blue Mountain Lodge $$$
P.O. Box 101
Kiepersol 1241
Mpumalanga
☎ (11) 784 4144/5 **fax:** (11) 784 4127

email: bluemtnres@icon.co.za
Nelson Mandela used to come for weekend
breaks to this secluded farm estate in the hills
west of Kruger. Quiet, calm, and delightful with
superb food and discreet service. There is a
wide range of accommodation choice. Each
cottage has its own interior theme and the
courtyard duplex apartments are very continental. There are several grand mansion
houses down by the bass lake, where you can
have your own chef.

Makalali Private Game Reserve $$$
P.O. Box 785156
Sandton 2146
☎ (11) 883 5786 **fax:** (11) 883 4956
email: makalali@icon.co.za
website: www.makalali.co.za
This is one of the most impressive game lodges
in South Africa but slightly limited in game as it
does not border Kruger. Its prices are lower
than many other 5-star lodges in the more popular game reserves. Incredible, innovative
architecture is combined with superb food,
excellent service and fine game-viewing.

Malelane Sun Inter-Continental $$$
P.O. Box 392
Malelane 132
☎ (13) 790 3304 **fax:** (13) 790 3303
email: intmktg@southernsun.com
website: www.southernsunleisure.co.za
At the entrance to Kruger National Park, with
rooms in a semicircle out from the main lodge.
Lovely sundowner deck overlooking a river frequented by hippos.

M'Bali & Motswari $$$
P.O. Box 67865
Bryanston 2102
☎ (11) 463 1990 **fax:** (11) 463 1992
email: martinek@motswari.co.za
website: www.motswari.co.za
M'Bali provides a luxury tented option.
Motswari, the sister camp on the same reserve,
has lovely thatched cottages along the river and
even the option of an outside shower with a
view of passing wildlife. Set high on the hillside
overlooking a dam, game roams through the
bush right in front of your room. Excellent
game drives and good food and service.

The Royal Hotel $$

P.O. Box 59
Pilgrim's Rest 1290
☎ (13) 768 1100 **fax:** (13) 768 1188
email: royal@mweb.co.za
website: www.royal-hotel.co.za
This entire old-gold-rush town is a National
Monument. The Royal Hotel has 11 bedrooms
in the hotel and 39 in cottages along the historic little street. All are faithful in design and
décor to their Victorian heritage. When the
hordes of tourists head out of town you can
stroll down the quiet lane to your cottage in
this delightful, picturesque setting.

Singita Private Game Reserve $$$

P.O. Box 650881
Benmore 2010
☎ (11) 234 0990 **fax:** (11) 234 0535
email: reservations@singita.co.za
website: www.singita.co.za
One of the very top lodges in South Africa, with
exceptional personal service and fabulous food.
Singita comprises two lodges: Ebony, with a
colonial feel; and Boulders, with a more con-
temporary ethnic feel. Each suite has its own
plunge pool overlooking the Sand River frequented by game, and the rooms at Boulders
have glass frontage for an outdoor feel inside.

South African National Parks $

See page 279.

The Town House Guest House $–$$

P.O. Box 134
Sabie 1620
☎ (13) 764 2292 **fax:** (13) 764 1988
email: sabieth@iafrica.com
Finalist in the AA/SAA Bed & Breakfast
Accommodation Awards. This guest house is
charming, as is the owner, Ginny. Breakfasts
are served by the pool with busy little weaver
birds building nests in the palm fronds. Good
information provided on adventures in and
around the beautiful hills and valleys of Sabie.

Tshukudu Game Lodge $–$$

P.O. Box 289
Hoedspruit 1380
☎ (15) 793 2476 **fax:** (15) 793 2078
email: tshukudu@iafrica.com
You immediately feel part of the family at this
owner-run game lodge. The atmosphere is
charming and friendly, and many guests return

time after time. (The full board rate includes
game drives.) The one thing that sets this place
apart from all others is the presence of orphan
animals like Eliza, the playful lioness, and
Becky, the elephant.

FOOD AND DRINK
Harrie's Pancakes
Graskop

The most famous eating house in Graskop—so
popular that some tour operators book a year in
advance. Delicious sweet and savoury pancakes.

Loggerhead Restaurant

Corner of Main and Old Lydenburg Road
Sabie
☎ (13) 764 3341 **fax:** (13) 764 3089
Famous for local, fresh, de-boned trout.

The Wild Fig Tree Restaurant

Sabie
☎ (13) 764 2239 **fax:** (13) 764 3089
Specializes in traditional South African dishes
including game meat.

> ## 22 PONY TREKKING THROUGH THE KINGDOM IN THE SKY
> ➤ 222–229

OPERATORS
Malealea Lodge

Lesotho
Bookings:
P.O. Box 12118
Brandhof 9324
Bloemfontein
South Africa
☎ (51) 447 3200 **fax:** (51) 448 3001
email: malealea@mweb.co.za or
malealea@pixie.co.za
website: www.malealea.co.ls
website: www.africa-insites.com/
lesotho/travel
Malealea is a well-organized but also very
relaxed owner-run lodge, where you can stay
before and after your pony trek into the mountains. Mick and Di Jones are lovely, down to
earth people and make a great contribution to
tourism in Lesotho. There are no telephones at
Malealea, so bookings for accommodation and
pony treks are done through their South
African office.

Agents in Europe where you can book a
Malealea Lodge pony trek:

Acacia Adventure Holidays
Lower Ground Floor
23A Craven Terrace
London W2 3QH
U.K.
☎ (020) 7706 4700 **mobile** ☎ 0467 370 795
fax: (02) 7706 4686
email: acacia@afrika.demon.co.uk

In The Saddle
Laurel Cottage
Ramsdell
Tadley
Hampshire RG26 5SH
U.K.
☎ (01256) 851665 **fax:** (01256) 851667
email: rides@inthesaddle.com

Tribes Travel
See page 263.

Aksent!
Lange Van Ruusbroecstraat 2
2018 Antwerp
Belgium
☎ (3) 239 6452 **fax:** (3) 239 6479
email: aksent@glo.be

ARO Tours, Marck van der Donk
Woeringenstraat 5A
Nijlen 2560
Belgium
☎ (3) 411 2507 **fax:** (3) 411 0810
email: sales@zuidafrika.com

NBBS Reisen
Schipholweg 101
2316 XC Leiden
The Netherlands
☎ (71) 568 8668 **fax:** (71) 522 6475
email: rsver@nbbs.nl

SNP Natuur Reisen
P.O. Box 1270
6501 BG. Nijmegen
The Netherlands
☎ +31 (24) 360 41 66 **fax:** +31 (24) 360 1422
email: brekelmans@snp.nl

Terres D'Aventure
6 Rue Saint-Victor
75005 Paris
France

☎ (1) 53 73 77 77 **fax:** (1) 43 29 96 31
email: Terdav-Prod@wanadoo.fr

GETTING THERE
Flights
The closest airports are Maseru (Lesotho) or
Bloemfontein (South Africa).
Malealea Lodge offers a transfer from Maseru
airport only (minimum 2 passengers). Flights
from Johannesburg to Maseru are operated by
SA Airlink (see page 280). There is no direct
flight from Cape Town to Maseru— you have to
go via Johannesburg. Flights from Johannesburg to Bloemfontein (1hr) and Cape Town to
Bloemfontein (1hr 35mins), are both operated
by **South African Airways**.

LOCAL BUSES
It is possible to take local Combi taxi buses
from Bloemfontein or Maseru, but you will have
to change at least 6 times before you get to
Malealea. No official timetables are available.

CAR HIRE
You can hire a car in Maseru, the capital of
Lesotho, or in South Africa and come across
the border. You will need a letter of authorization from the car hire company to take the car
from South Africa to Lesotho and not all hire
companies allow this. There are many signs to
Malealea Lodge.

Avis
P.O. Box 294
Maseru 100
Lesotho
☎ 31 4325/32 5326 **fax:** 31 0216

Budget Rent A Car
P.O. Box 0936
Maseru West 105
Lesotho
☎ 31 6344/35 0686 **fax:** 31 0461

COACH AND OVERLAND TOURS
Several coach tours and overland trucks stop
here for a night or 2. Coach tour operators
include: **Boabab Reisen**, Amsterdam, The
Netherlands; **Summums Reisen**, Amsterdam,
The Netherlands; **Lernidee Reisen**, Berlin,
Germany. Overland tours include: **Dragoman**,
Suffolk, U.K. (☎ (01728) 861133; **website:**
www.dragoman.co.uk) and **Truck Africa**,
London, U.K.

CONTACTS

SOUTH AFRICA & LESOTHO

SOUTH AFRICA/LESOTHO BORDER

Formalities at the Van Rooyens Gate border post (closest entry point to Malealea) were very easy for the author. There was no forms to fill in and just a quick stamp in the passport. This is probably because Lesotho is completely surrounded by South Africa, and hundreds of people cross the border every day. Nevertheless, you should have your papers in order and proof of onward travel when re-entering South Africa. You must also pay a Lesotho exit toll fee of 2 Rand (35 cents!).

BORDER POSTS CLOSEST TO MALEALEA LODGE

Van Rooyens Gate, near Mafeteng: open 6am–10pm.
Maseru Bridge: open 24 hours.
Makhaleng Bridge, near Mohaleshoek: open 8–6.
Tele Bridge, near Moyeni: open 8–6.

VISA REQUIREMENTS

No visas required for citizens of U.K., Europe and U.S.A. Check with a travel agent anyway as rules have a habit of changing.

INFORMATION
Lesotho Tourist Board

P.O. Box 1378
Maseru 100
Lesotho
☎ 31 2896/3760 **fax:** 31 0108

ACCOMMODATION
Malealea Lodge $

See above under Operators.
Good, clean, unpretentious accommodation with very comfortable beds, bright linen, and hot water (you will be dying for a hot shower after your trek). They have rooms and cottages with and without en-suite bathrooms. There is also a backpackers' section with twin rooms and communal bathroom and kitchen. Large, home-cooked meals are offered in a communal dining room with long tables. Their little bar stocks wine and spirits, and drinking water comes straight from a crystal-clear spring; bottled water is also available. Room rates are based on bed only plus whatever meals you want.

23 KAYAKING ALONG THE GARDEN ROUTE ➤ 230–237

OPERATORS
Nature Conservation

☎ (44) 535 96488 **fax:** (44) 533 0322
email: rob/keur@mweb.co.za
Day canoe hire.The Uitsig overnight hut up the Keurbooms River takes a maximum of 12 people. Mattress, blanket, and gas lamp provided plus axe for chopping firewood.

Real Cape Adventures

c/o Johan Loots' Sea Kayak Store
P.O. Box 51508
Waterfront
Cape Town 8002
☎/fax: (21) 790 5611
email: johan@mweb.co.za
website: www.seakayak.co.za
Johan Loots is an acknowledged expert on sea-kayaking in southern Africa.

GETTING THERE
BUS AND COACH COMPANIES
Baz Bus

8 Rosedean Road
Seapoint
Cape Town 8001
☎ (21) 439 2323 **fax:** (21) 439 2343
email: inso@bazbus.com
website: www.bazbus.com
Small buses with scheduled departures all over South Africa and surrounding countries. Your ticket allows you to get off and stay at any of their pick-up locations, before continuing your journey.

Greyhound Express

☎ (11) 830 1301 **fax:** (11) 830 1528
email: enquiries@greyhound.co.za
website: www.greyhound.co.za
Scheduled bus departures all over the country.

Intercape Mainliner

See page 275.

Translux (coaches)

☎ (21) 449 3333 **fax:** (21) 405 2545
(No email or website)
Scheduled departures all over the country.

INFORMATION
RECSKASA (Recreational and Commercial Sea Kayaking Association of South Africa)
P.O. Box 51508
Waterfront 8002
Cape Town
☎ (21) 64 2057 or (21) 790 6404
Info hotline ☎ 0823 4455 98
website: www.doorway.co.za/recskasa

Knysna Tourism and Information Centre
40 Main Street
Knysna 6570
☎ (44) 382 5510 **fax:** (44) 382 1646
email: knysna.tourism@pixie.co.za
website: www.knysna.info.co.za

Plettenberg Bay Tourist Information Centre
P.O. Box 894
Plettenberg Bay 6600
☎ (44) 533 4065 **fax:** (44) 533 4066
email: info@plettenbergbay.co.za
website: www.plettenbergbay.co.za

South African Tourism
See page 281.

ACCOMMODATION
There is every type of accommodation available in Plettenberg Bay and along the entire Garden Route. Tourist information centres will give you good local information.

Brenton on Sea Hotel $$
P.O. Box 36
Knysna 6570
☎ (44) 381 0081 **fax:** (44) 381 0026
email: brenton.on.sea@pixie.co.za
website: www.brentononsea.co.za
This lies on the coast, about 20 minutes' drive from Knysna town. Alpine-style, wooden chalets on the hillside overlooking a long sandy beach—a perfect place for families.

Hog Hollow Country Lodge $$
P.O. Box 503
Plettenberg Bay 6600
☎/**fax:** (44) 534 8879
email: hoghollow@global.co.za
website: www.hoghollow.co.za
In the heart of indigenous rolling woodland set back from the coast, Hog Hollow has cosy, individual chalets, tastefully decorated with ethnic touches. Owner-run, with everybody around a big table for dinner. Booking office for most of Plettenberg Bay's best activities.

Nature Conservation
See under Operators, above.

OTHER INFORMATION
"Paddleyaks" (kayaks used in adventure) are on sale from Johan Loots' Sea Kayak Store —see Real Cape Adventures under Operators.

Useful books include:
Eyewitness Handbooks—Whales, Dolphins and Porpoises by Mark Carwardine, published by Dorling Kindersley Ltd
(ISBN 0-7513-1030-1)
MTN 'Whale Watch' by Vic Cockcroft and Peter Joyce (ISBN 1 86872 163 9)
WWF—Whale Watching in South Africa by Peter B Best (ISBN 1 86854 185 1)
Best Walks of the Garden Route by Colin Paterson-Jones, published by Struik in South Africa (ISBN 1 86872 115 9)
See also Other Information in the South African adventures above.

24 OUTRIGGER SAILING WITH THE VEZO
► 240–247

OPERATOR
Safari-Vezo Club de Plongée
B.P. 427
Tulear 601
☎ (20) 94 41381
Good equipment, diving suits, and instructors. Hobbie-cats, snorkelling, and windsurfing equipment also for hire. Day trips to Nosy Ve and Nosy Satrana. Fishing charters.

OUTRIGGERS
These can be hired in Tulear, at Ankilybe, Saint Augustin or Anakao. Hire prices should be reasonable, but need to be negotiated locally with the individual boat owners.

ACCOMMODATION
L'Auberge du Corsaire $
Chez Glover
Saint Augustin
☎ None
Basic, thatched huts in a compound and even more basic, shared washing facilities. Good local food.

Hotel Plazza $

Boulevard Lyautey
Tulear 601
☎ (20) 94 41900 **fax:** (20) 94 41903
email: plazza.h@dts.mg
Efficiently run, large hotel with a tropical garden overlooking the sea. Decent, well
ventilated, though slightly worn rooms, with
bathrooms and balcony. Bar, restaurant.

Hotel Safari-Vezo $

Bivouac d'Anakao
B.P. 427
Tulear 601
☎ (20) 94 41381 **fax:** (20) 94 41251
French-owned beach hotel in Anakao. Twenty-
two roomy bungalows strung along the beach
with a restaurant at one end. There is no running water, so all washing is with buckets,
although there are shared septic toilets. Guests
must stay on a half-board basis. Motorboat
transfers are arranged by their office in Tulear.
Catamaran trips to Nosy Ve and diving are also
available.

FOOD AND DRINK
La Bernique

Boulevard Galliéni
B.P. 425
Tulear 601
☎ None
Located opposite the Hotel Plazza, this is a very
popular little French *tapas* bar that sometimes
serves excellent food.

L'Etoile de Mer

Boulevard Lyautey
Tulear 601
☎ (20) 94 42807
Lofty, thatched restaurant on the seafront
boulevard, next to the more visible Le Corail,
whose food is to be avoided. Malagasy, French,
and seafood specialities.

Zaza Club

Boulevard Lyautey
Tulear 601
☎ (20) 94 41243
Large, popular restaurant with extremely
attentive service, good fresh seafood, Indian
and French specialities. Later in the evening it
metamorphoses into a nightclub.

ANAKAO BEACH RESTAURANTS

Several families at Anakao offer budget seafood
meals in rustic, open-air settings. You can even
buy fresh lobster from the fishermen and have
it cooked for you. **Chez Emile**, next to Safari-
Vezo, is a dependable set-up and the cooking is
good. Make sure you agree on a price beforehand.

---

25 IN SEARCH OF THE LEMUR
► 248–256

OPERATORS
Contemporary Travel Inc.

870 Jericho Turnpike
St James.
NY 11780
U.S.A.
☎ (516) 360 3663 **fax:** (516) 360 3625
Specializes in travel to Madagascar.

Cortez Travel

1174 Lomas Santa Fe Drive
Solana Beach
CA 92075
U.S.A.
☎ (619) 755 5136 **toll free** ☎ 800 854 1029
fax: (619) 481 7474
email: cortez-usa@mcimail.com
website: www.cortez-usa.com
This San Diego-based agency is the Air
Madagascar representative in the U.S.A. and
also runs tours.

GETTING THERE

International flights to Madagascar are with **Air
Madagascar** (via Munich, Paris or Nairobi, or
from Johannesburg), **Air France** or **Air
Liberté** (through Nouvelles Frontières). If you
fly with Air Madagascar, you get a 33 percent
discount on domestic flights.

Trailfinders

See page 271
This reliable travel agency can book your international and domestic flights. Payment can be
made by credit card over the phone and tickets
sent by post.

INFORMATION
ANGAP

1 rue Naka Rabemanantsoa
B.P. 1424
Antanimena, Antananarivo
☎ (20) 22 30518 **fax:** (20) 22 31994
email: angap@dts.mg
ANGAP is the acronym for Madagascar's parks
authority, the National Association for
Protected Areas Management.

Maison de Tourisme de Madagascar

B.P. 3224
Place de l'Indépendance
Antaninarenina
Antananarivo
☎ (20) 22 32529 **fax:** (20) 22 32537

ACCOMMODATION
Hotel Colbert $$–$$$

Place de l'Indépendance
Antananarivo
☎ (20) 22 20202 **fax:** 20 22 34012
email: colbert@bow.simicro
The main rival of the Madagascar Hilton is a much livelier and friendlier place. Well-appointed rooms, good service, restaurants, bar, and even a small casino. Good, central location in the *haute ville*.

Hotel Jean Laborde $

Off rue Arabe-Grandidier
Isoraka
☎ (20) 22 33045 **fax:** (20) 22 32794
Small hotel with reasonably priced, simple, spacious rooms with bathrooms and sometimes balcony. Rather dark and dingy ground-floor bar and restaurant but the French food is good. Reservation is essential, although bookings are sometimes lost.

Hotel Manja $

Ranomafana
☎ None
The last hotel in the village, in a pretty, riverside location. Rustic, thatched bungalows with shared washing facilities. The owners are very friendly, there is a decent restaurant, and the service is excellent.

Hotel Moderne–Chez Papillon $

B.P. 1161
Fianarantsoa 301
☎ (20) 75 50815/50003
Fianar's legendary hotel and restaurant, seriously in need of an update, stands conveniently opposite the railway station and a few steps from the taxi-brousse station. Rooms with bathroom, giant cockroaches included.

FOOD AND DRINK
La Boussole

21 rue du Docteur Villette
Isoraka
Antananarivo
☎ (20) 22 35810
Spacious, lively brasserie-style bar, café, and restaurant tucked away down a backstreet. Very popular with French residents, so booking is advisable. Wide range of dishes include ostrich meat, Malagasy, French, and Italian dishes.

Hotel Glacier

46 Avenue de l'Indépendance
Antananarivo
☎ (20) 22 20260 **fax:** 20 22 20332
This is the place to go on Fri and Sat evenings to drink rum and watch Madagascar's great musicians play live while locals dance the night away.

CAR HIRE
Eco-tours
c/o Hotel Moderne–Chez Papillon $

See under Accommodation, above, for details. Ask for Joro or Angelo to organize a car and driver guide for touring the national parks from Ranomafana to Isalo.

ADVENTURE TRAVEL: GENERAL

INTRODUCTION

This book has, we hope, whetted your appetite for adventure, and the Activities A–Z is intended to supply a useful, if not comprehensive, list of as many adventurous activities as the authors could discover within an area.

The activities vary from volunteer work, cultural, and language opportunities to really intrepid sports. Most of the experiences call for interaction with local people and many are directly connected to ecotourism—where strict controls are applied to guarantee the benefits to the environment and to minimize the damage caused by the impact of increasing numbers of visitors to sensitive areas. We have supplied the names and addresses of organizations that can help the traveller to achieve these challenging pastimes, but they have not been inspected or vetted by us in any way. Even where the authors have used a company to organize their own trip, this is no guarantee that any company is still run by the same people or to the same degree of efficiency. Bear in mind that many of the regions covered can be volatile both climatically and politically. Weigh up all the factors first, get a feel for your chosen destination, and let us guide you towards the outfits that can help.

WEBSITES

Some of the more useful websites for planning an adventure trip are listed below.

www.doorway.co.za

Contains information about accommodation, and travel, as well as safaris, adventure activities, and tours in Southern Africa.

www.go2Africa.com

This is one of the most comprehensive online travel information sources on southern Africa – a very useful planning tool with photographs of over 1,000 establishments, plus a paragraph about every town, park, reserve, and place of interest in the whole of Southern Africa.

www.travelsa.com

Identifies adventure tour operators by activity, as well as listing many accommodation options and travel information—over 3,000 pages.

ADVENTURE TRAVEL: GENERAL

In recent years adventure travel to Southern Africa has become big business. Bungee jumping, skydiving, mountainbiking, river rafting, scuba diving, sea kayaking—the list goes on and on. Some outfits specialize in a particular activity, but, increasingly, adventure tour operators are becoming generalists, covering a wide range of types of tour and activity, sometimes across several different countries. For ease of reference such operators are listed together here, with cross-references included in other sections on specific activities.

U.K. OPERATORS

African Explorations

Holwell, Burford
Oxfordshire OX18 4JS
☎ (01993) 822443 **fax:** (01993) 822414
email: safaris@globalnet.co.uk
Contact them to plan your adventure holiday or safari to all parts of southern Africa.

Africa Travel Centre

21 Leigh Street, London WC1H 9QX
☎ (020) 7387 1211 **fax:** (020) 7383 7512
email: africatravel@easynet.co.uk
Will arrange adventure tours to all countries of southern Africa.

Four Corners

Sherwood House, Nottingham Road
Bristol BS7 9DH
☎ (0117) 942 2070 **fax:** (0117) 944 6617
email: info@fourcorners.co.uk
Will help you plan for a variety of adventure activities in southern Africa.

KE Adventure Travel

32 Lake Road, Keswick
Cumbria CA12 5DQ
☎ (01768) 773966 **fax:** (01768) 774693
email: keadventure@enterprise.net
website: www.keadventure.com
Founded in 1984 and formerly known as Karakoram Experience. Southern Africa programme includes a trip combining Mount Kenya and Kilimanjaro, and a 2-week "Spirit of Africa" tour combining Mount Kenya with white-water rafting, a camel safari and wildlife watching.

Rainbow Tours
64 Essex Road, London N1 8LR
☎ (020) 7226 1004 **fax:** (020) 7226 2621
email: info@rainbow.co.uk
website: www.rainbow.co.uk
Specialists in independent adventure travel.

Sunvil Discovery
See p. 268.

U.S.A. OPERATORS
Adventure Center
1311 63rd Street, Suite 200
Emeryville, CA 94608
☎ (510) 654 1879 **toll free** ☎ 800 227 8747
fax: (510) 654 4200
website: www.adventure-center.com
Worldwide operator offering trips from 6 days
to 7 weeks in hotels, lodges, and campsites.

Africa Desk
329 Danbury Road, New Milford
CT 06776
☎ (860) 354 9341 **toll free** ☎ 800 284 8796
fax: (860) 354 9345
email: cafrica@africadesk.com
website: www.africadesk.com

KE Adventure Travel
1131 Grand Avenue, Glenwood Springs
CO 81601
☎ (970) 384 0001 **toll free** ☎ 800 497 9675
fax: (970) 384 0004
email: ketravel@rof.net
website: (above)
See under U.K. entry above.

Lemur Tours Inc
501 Mendell Street, Unit B, San Francisco
CA 94124
☎ (415) 695 8880 **toll free** ☎ 800 73 lemur
fax: (415) 695 8899
email: Carol@lemurtours.com
website: www.lemurtours.com
Incorporated in 1983, claims to be the only
Malagasy-American tour operator in the U.S.A..
Offers a wide variety of wildlife, natural history,
and cultural tours to Madagascar.

REI Adventures
P.O. Box 1938, Sumner
WA 98390
☎ (253) 437 1100 **toll free** ☎ 800 622 2236
fax: (253) 395 8160
email: travel@rei.com
website: www.rei.com

Trips offered include a 6-day trek up the
Marango route on Kilimanjaro and game drives
to the Serengeti and Ngorongoro Crater.

Wilderness Travel
1102 Ninth Street, Berkeley
CA 94710
☎ (510) 558 2488 **toll free** ☎ 800 368 2794
fax: (510) 558 2489
email: webinfo@wildernesstravel.com
website: www.wildernesstravel.com
Trips offered include Botswana's wildlife, a
desert safari in Namibia, a Zambian walking
safari, and adventure travel in Zimbabwe.

SOUTHERN AFRICA OPERATORS
MADAGASCAR
Green Madagascar Tours
P.O. Box 888, 21 rue Ramelina
Antananarivo 101
☎(2) 66656 **fax:** (2) 66659
email: greenmadagascartours@simicro.mg
website: www.simicro.mg/gmt
Arranges tailor-made adventure tours.

Stella Tours
Regional Tourist Office,
P.O. Box 1192, 301 Fianarantsoa
☎ (7) 550667
Michel Leonis (aka Stella) organizes adventure
tours and excursions in Madagascar's southern
region, from 1 to 5 days.

SOUTH AFRICA
Adventure Village
229 Long Street, Cape Town 8000
☎ (21) 424 1580 **fax:** (21) 424 1590
email: info@adventure.village.co.za
Every kind of adventure activity in Western
Cape (and north to Victoria Falls).

Affordable Adventures
P.O. Box 1008, Sunninghill 2157
Johannesburg
☎ (11) 465 9168 **fax:** (11) 467 3913
email: adventures@global.co.za
website: www.tourism.co.za/adventures
Specializes in Johannesburg and Gauteng areas.

Drifters Adventure Tours
P.O. Box 48434, Roosevelt Park 2129
Johannesburg
☎ (11) 888 1160 **fax:** (11) 888 1020
email: drifters@drifters.co.za
Well-established company, runs a camping
safari operation throughout southern Africa.

Felix Unite Tourism Group

See page 279 for details.

Flamingo Adventure Tours/ Flamingo Disabled Ventures

P.O. Box 60554, Flamingo Square 744l, Cape Town

☎/fax: (21) 557 4496

email: flamtour@iafrica.com

website:

www.time2travel.com/ct/flamingo/index

Run by Pam and Jeff Taylor, specializing in adventure tours for the disabled, but also caters for able-bodied tourists. Sites have been inspected for accessibility, and vehicles are specially adapted. Mainly Western Cape area.

Let's Go To Africa

P.O. Box 1183, Bedfordview 2008, Johannesburg

☎ (11) 455 1166 **fax:** (11) 455 6859

email: chriss.olympicunited@galileosa.co.za

website: www.letsgotoafrica.co.uk

Design itineraries and arrange adventure tours into all over southern Africa.

Philip Briggs and Ariadne Van Zandbergen

P.O. Box 2636, Bedfordview 2008, Johannesburg

☎/fax: (11) 792 6736

email: philari@hixnet.co.za

Author Philip, and photographer and tour leader Ariadne will design itineraries to suit all budgets with the most reputable operators.

Pulse Africa Tour Operators

P.O. Box 2417, Parklands 2121, Johannesburg

☎ (11) 327 0468 **fax:** (11) 327 0281

email: pulselac@sprintlink.co.za

website: www.africansafari.co.uk

Established operator of adventure tours to all countries of southern and east Africa.

Shearwater Adventures

P.O. Box 76270, Wendywood 2144, Johannesburg

☎ (11) 804 6537 **fax:** (11) 804 6539

email: shearwater@icon.co.za

Specializes in outdoor adventure activities at Victoria Falls, from the Zimbabwean side.

Wild Frontiers

P.O. Box 844, Halfway House 1685, Gauteng

☎ (11) 315 4838 **fax:** (11) 315 4850

email: wildfront@icon.co.za

A vastly experienced South African adventure company with its own ground operation in Uganda. Can also set up tours to Kenya, Tanzania, Zimbabwe, Zambia, Mozambique.

Wild Thing

P.O. Box 51074, Waterfront, Cape Town 8000

☎ (21) 423 5804/5805

fax: (21) 461 1653/423 4995

email: wildthing@icon.co.za

website: www.wildthing.co.za

Founded in 1989. Offers a range of activities in South Africa, especially Western Cape.

ZAMBIA
Africa Tour Designers

P.O. Box 31802, Lusaka

☎ (1) 224616/223641/225386

fax: (1) 224915

email: atd@zamnet.zm

Will tailor-make adventure tours for you.

Makora Quest

P.O. Box 60420, Livingstone

☎ (3) 324253/321679/320401

fax: (3) 320732/323206

email: quest@zamnet.zm

Runs a wide variety of adventure activities in the Livingstone/Victoria Falls area.

AIRBORNE ADVENTURES

View wildlife quietly from a balloon, buzz about noisily in a microlight aircraft over Victoria Falls, or experience the ultimate thrill of sky-diving and parachuting. Southern Africa's good climate and varied landscape make it the ideal venue for all these activities. Apart from ballooning, the other types of airborne adventure require some prior training. In most cases this can be done on a weekend course, with the first flight or jump being included as part of the course.

NAMIBIA
NAMIB DESERT
Namib Sky Adventure Safaris

See p. 274.

SOUTH AFRICA
JOHANNESBURG

The stable atmospheric conditions on the Highveld (the high inland plateau of South Africa) make it ideal territory for ballooning.

Airtrack Adventures

P.O. Box 630, Muldersdrift 1747, Johannesburg
☎ (11) 957 2322/957 2360
fax: (11) 957 2465
email: flypixsa@iafrica.com
website: www.easyinfo.co.za
Offers hot air balloon safaris and flights for
photo opportunities.

Bill Harrop's "Original" Balloon Safaris

P.O. Box 67, Randburg 2125, Gauteng
☎ (11) 705 3201 **fax:** (11) 705 3203
email: travelsa@iafrica.com
Runs short balloon flights, but will also organize
game-viewing safaris and planned tours.

WESTERN CAPE

The variable and often windy weather of the
Cape means that you have to choose your times
carefully for taking to the air. Spells of complete calm can occur in any season, but are
most frequent in Mar–May.

The Flight Zone Hang Gliding School

P.O. Box 12576, Serengeti 7530, Cape Town
☎/**fax:** (21) 919 0676
email: flightzone@mjvn.co.za
website: http://users.iafrica.com/i/in/intense
Champion hang glider pilot, Johan Anderson,
with 12 years tuition experience, offers instruc-
tiion from beginners' level upwards, including a
specially developed tandem in-flight method.

Skydive Citrusdal

Farm Modderfontein, Citrusdal, Western Cape
☎/**fax:** (21) 462 5666
email: info@skydive.co.za
website: www.skydive.co.za
Experience skydiving without any previous
training, by going tandem. After an introductory video, you take off, hook up to your
instructor, and out you go at 3,500m (11,000ft).
You can also do an all-day course, with a static-
line parachute jump the same evening.

ZAMBIA/ZIMBABWE
VICTORIA FALLS,

On the border between Zambia and Zimbabwe,
"Vic Falls" is a mecca for adventure tourists.
Airborne adventures are available from both
sides of the border. View the Falls from an
unusual angle from a helicopter or microlight
aircraft, or on a tandem parachute jump.

Batoka Sky

P.O. Box 60971, Livingstone, Zambia
☎ (3) 320058 **fax:** (3) 323095
Regional office: P.O. Box 50017, Randjesfontein
1683, Gauteng, South Africa
☎ (11) 805 6068/70 **fax:** (11) 805 6069
email: reservations@batoksky.co.za
website: www.batoksky.co.za
Offers microlighting and tandem parachute
jumps in Victoria Falls area.

United Touring Company

See below under Safari.

Adrift/Kandahar Safaris

See p. 269.

The Zambezi Helicopter Company

See p. 270.

TAFIKA CAMP, SOUTH LUANGWA NATIONAL PARK
Remote Africa Safaris

P.O. Box 5, Mfuwe, Zambia
☎ (62) 45018 **fax:** (62) 45059
email: remote@zamnet.zm
website:
www.tecc.co.uk/bbs/remote/remote.htm
Offers microlight flights from the camp for
sightseeing and game-viewing.

BIRDWATCHING

Southern Africa is a birdwatcher's paradise,
with more than one thousand species. The
range of habitats in the region is immense, from
wetlands to semi-desert and bushveld, from
mountains to dense jungle. Spot the spectacular purple-crested lourie in Mozambique, the
rare, bearded vulture found only in the
Drakensberg Mountains of KwaZulu-Natal, in
South Africa, or listen to the haunting cry of the
fish eagle over the region's lakes and rivers.
Many operators offer you the opportunity to
combine birdwatching with other activities,
such as wildlife safaris and houseboat holidays.

SOUTH AFRICA
Dzombo Tours and Safaris

P.O. Box 18, Milnerton 7435, Cape Town
☎ (21) 551 6918 **fax:** (21) 551 6664
email: dzombo@iafrica.com
Offers birdwatching safaris in South Africa and
all adjacent countries.

Lawson's Specialised Tours

P.O. Box 507, Nelspruit 1200, Mpumalanga
☎ (13) 755 2147/755 2108
fax: (13) 755 1793
email: lawsons@cis.co.za
website: www.lawsons.co.za
Caters for beginners and the more experienced.
Peter Lawson is an acknowledged expert.

Monty Brett

P.O. Box 650727, Benmore 2010, Johannesburg
☎ (11) 783 6629 (mornings)
fax: (11) 783 6535
email: mbrett@global.co.za
website: www.sappibrett.co.za
A noted expert on southern African birds.

SA Tours and Safaris with African Alternatives

P.O. Box 2806, Durbanville 7551, Cape Town
☎ (21) 975 2189/4472 **fax:** (21) 975 5194
email: travel@ecoafrica.com
website: www.ecoafrica.com
Specialized birdwatching safaris.

Wilderness Safaris

P.O. Box 5219, Rivonia 2128, Johannesburg
☎ (11) 884 1458 **fax:** (11) 883 6255
email: enquiry@wilderness.co.
Birdwatching and other special interest tours.

LESOTHO
Fraser's Semongkong Lodge

c/o P.O. Box 243, Ficksburg 9730, Free State,
South Africa
☎/**fax:** (51) 9333106
email: verney@lesoff.co.za
website: www.africa-insites.com/lesotho/travel
On slopes of Thaba Putsoa range. Over 70
species recorded in the area; a colony of bald
ibis is nesting in the cliffs in front of the Lodge.

MALAWI

The Nkhotakota Wildlife Reserve is a vast tract
of untouched moimbo woodland, with 230 bird
species recorded.

Njobvu Safari Lodge

P.O. Box 388, Nkhotakota, Malawi
☎ 292506
Practical lodge next to the reserve.

SOUTH AFRICA
WESTERN CAPE

Many species to be seen in mountains, macchia
scrub, marshes, and estuaries.

Eksplor

P.O. Box 13060, Mowbray 7705, Cape Town
☎ (21) 424 7797 **fax:** (21) 424 8793
email: wildcat@intekom.co.za
Birdwatching trips in the Western Cape.

SIBAYA LAKE, KWAZULU-NATAL

In the remote northeast of South Africa, this
lake offers outstanding birdwatching opportunities. Over 300 species have been recorded.

Island Rock (Pty) Ltd for Sibaya Lake Lodge

P.O. Box 1194, Kloof 3640, KwaZulu-Natal
☎/**fax:** (31) 763 4267
email: islrock@iafrica.com
The lodge is situated right on the lake.

KNYSNA LAGOON

Combine birdwatching with a boating holiday in
South Africa's "Lake District."

Lightley's Holiday Cruisers

See below under Boat Trips.

UGANDA

Ten national parks—Murchison Falls, Queen
Elizabeth, Kidepo Valley, Lake Mburo,
Rwenzori Mountain, Bwindi Impenetrable,
Mgahinga Gorilla, Mount Elgon, Semuliki, and
Kibale—offer some of the best birdwatching in
Africa with over 550 species recorded.

Uganda Wildlife Authority Headquarters

Plot 3 Kintu Road, Nakasero, P.O.
Box 3530, Kampala
☎ (41) 346287/346288 **fax:** (41) 346291

Uganda Tourist Board

IPS Building, Parliament Avenue,
Box 7211, Kampala
☎ (41) 342196/7 **fax:** (41) 342188
email: utb@starcom.co.ug
Apply to these bodies for the necessary permits
to go birding in the national parks.

ZAMBIA
Lilayi Lodge

P.O. Box 30093, Lusaka
☎ (1) 228682/3; direct to Lodge ☎ (1)
230611/230326 **fax:** (1) 222906
email: lilayi@zamnet.zm
website: www.africa-
insites.com/zambia/lilayi.htm
Offers good birdwatching (over 300 species).

Mutemwa Lodge
See below under Fishing.

Star of Africa
Alan & Scotty Elliot, Private Bag 6, P.O. Hillside
Bulawayo, Zimbabwe
☎ (9) 41715/41837 **fax:** (9) 229909
email: star_of_africa@telconet.co.zw
Birdwatching from a houseboat on the Kafue
floodplain.

Tiger Fishing Tours
See below under Fishing.

ZIMBABWE
Gwembe Safaris
See below under Boat Trips.

BOAT TRIPS

You can enjoy the superb coastal scenery
around Cape Town from the deck of a cruise
boat, go whale watching on the Garden Route,
cruise in a *dhow* off Madagascar, Mozambique
or Zanzibar, or drift at leisure in a houseboat on
Lake Kariba. Nov–Apr is the best time for boating in South Africa, but to the north the winter
months, May–Oct, are preferable.

MADAGASCAR
A variety of craft is available for hire to cruise
the subtropical waters around the island.

Auberge Ambohimahavelona
P.O. Box 43, Tulear 601
☎/**fax:** (9) 443045
email: camoin@dts.mg
Rural hotel, 1 hour from Tulear (free transfer
from Tulear).Take an out-rigger trip on the
Onilahy River, to St. Augustin and Anakao.

Lakana Vejo Centre Nautique
P.O. Box 158, Tulear
☎ c/o Motel Capricorne (9) 442620/9442879
fax: (9) 441320
This hotel in Ifathy, catering mainly for French
groups, provides a good base for boat trips and
other aquatic activities.

Tony Adkins (Catamaran Hoonos)
c/o P.O. Box 89, Tulear
☎/**fax:** (9) 443317
Charter a fibreglass outrigger or catamaran
that sleeps 4. Take a 1-week cruise via the

islands up the coast to Morondava, or hire by
the day/night. Good value, including food.

MOZAMBIQUE
The Bazaruto Islands, off the northern coast of
Mozambique, have been declared a national
park. Cruise around them in an Arab *dhow*.

Mozaic Coastal Tours
P.O. Box EH 75, Emerald Hill, Harare
Zimbabwe
☎/**fax:** (4) 301164/300981
email: traveller@primenetzw.com
website: www.icon.co.zw/mozaic
Dhow sailing holidays around Bazaruto Islands;
set monthly departures. Will also tailor-make
self-sail and self-drive holidays in Mozambique.

SOUTH AFRICA
WESTERN CAPE
Boat trips offer the chance to view seal colonies
and superbly beautiful coastal scenery from the
ideal vantage point!

Oceanrafters
P.O. Box 51444, Waterfront 8002, Cape Town
☎ (21) 788 9640 **fax:** (21) 438 0234
email: oceanrafters@yebo.co.za
Offers 3 departures a day, daily, for a 2-hour
highspeed powerboat ride around Table Bay.

Waterfront Charters
P.O. Box 50446, Waterfront 8002
Cape Town
☎ (21) 418 0134 **fax:** (21) 425 3816
email: info@waterfrontcharters.co.za
website: www.waterfrontcharters.co.za
Variety of boat trips offered around the coast of
the Cape Peninsula, and to Robben Island.

GARDEN ROUTE
Running between Mossel Bay in the south and
Storms River in the north, the Garden Route is
one of the most scenic and popular tourist
areas in South Africa. Lake cruises available,
and the opportunity to see whales (especially
Sep–Dec), seals, and dolphins on a sea cruise.

Lightley's Holiday Cruisers
P.O. Box 863, Knysna 6570, Western Cape
☎ (44) 386 0007 **fax:** (44) 386 0018
email: sandpoint@pixie.co.za
website: www.knysna.co.za/lightleys
Rent a houseboat and cruise around the beautiful Knysna lagoon. Excellent birdwatching and
fishing available in the area.

Ocean Adventures

P.O. Box 1812, Plettenberg Bay 6600
Western Cape
☎/fax: (4457) 35083
email: oceanadv@global.co.za
website: www.plettbay.co.za/oceanadventures
Holds the whale watching licence for this area
(in the middle of South Africa's Garden Route).
Boat trips of 2–3 hours, accompanied by guide,
to view whales and dolphins.

SIBAYA LAKE, KWAZULU-NATAL
Island Rock (Pty) Ltd for Sibaya Lake Lodge

See above under Birdwatching.

ZIMBABWE/ZAMBIA

Completed in 1959, the Kariba Dam holds back
the Zambezi River to form one of the largest
man-made lakes in the world. The border
between Zambia and Zimbabwe runs down the
centre of Lake Kariba. This is a favoured resort
for many people in the region, especially pleasant in the mild winter weather from May–Oct.

C.T.R. Management and Charter Consultants

P.O. Box 116, Kariba, Zimbabwe
☎ (61) 2845 fax: (61) 2522
Anchored at Marineland, by the Caribbea Bay
Hotel, this company offers 20 boats for hire.

Gwembe Safaris

P.O. Box 630162, Choma, Zambia
☎ (32) 20169/20021
fax: (32) 20054/20570
email: gwemsaf@zamnet.zm
For houseboat trips from Zambian side.

Kariba Boating and Safaris

Carobeck Andora Harbour, P.O. Box 268
Andora Harbour, Kariba, Zimbabwe
☎/fax: (61) 2553/2227
email: chipsaf@zambezi.net
Twenty-five boats for charter on Lake Kariba.

TD Tours

P.O. Box 68798, Bryanston 2021,
Johannesburg, South Africa
☎ (11) 787 5427 fax: 787 5501
website:
www.africanfocus.co.za/travel/tdtours
Specialists in renting out houseboats (65 boats
available), from the Zimbabwean shore.

BUNGEE JUMPING

Bungee jumping has to be the biggest adrenalin
rush of all adventure activities. Southern Africa
has the world's two highest locations sport: the
bridges at Victoria Falls on the Zimbabwe/
Zambia border, and at the Bloukrans River, in
South Africa. If you don't fancy diving headfirst
suspended by your ankles, then try a bridge
jump from the Gouritz River Bridge, in South
Africa's Western Cape region. This way you get
to launch yourself from the bridge standing
upright. One end of the rope is attached to a
harness around your upper body, the other end
is fastened on to a second bridge, some distance
away, so you scythe through the air in a huge
arc. It's not quite as hair-raising as bungee
jumping, but will still get your pulses racing.

SOUTHERN AFRICA

These operators offer bungee jumping adventures in South Africa and at Victoria Falls.

SOUTH AFRICA
BLOUKRANS RIVER BRIDGE

This bridge, on the N2 near Plettenberg Bay,
offers what is now the highest bungee jump in
the world. You freefall for five seconds, plus a 2-
second cord stretch, reaching 165–175m
(500–540ft) at full stretch.

Face Adrenalin

P.O. Box 137, The Crags 6602,
Western Province
☎/fax: (42) 281 1458
email: bungy@global.co.za
Operates the bungee jump from the Bloukrans
Bridge; has a perfect safety record.

GOURITZ RIVER BRIDGE

On the N2, between Albertinia and Mossel Bay,
are infact two bridges. The disused rail bridge,
and the current road-bridge—50m (150ft) apart
and 75m (230ft) high—make this a unique location for bridge jumping. Bungee jumping from
the rail bridge is also available.

Face Adrenalin

See above under Bloukrans River Bridge.
Operates the bridge jumping and bungee
jumping from the Gouritz Bridge.

Wild Thing

See above under Adventure Travel: General.

ZAMBIA/ZIMBABWE

At 100m (310ft) the bridge at Victoria Falls is the second highest bungee jump in the world. Bungee jumping operators include:

Adrift/Kandahar Safaris

See p. 268.

Africa Extreme

P.O. Box 60353, Livingstone, Zambia
fax: (3) 324157
email: extreme@zamnet.zm

Batoka Sky

See above under Airborne adventures.

Fawlty Towers

216 Mosi-o-Tunya Road, Livingstone, Zambia
☎ (3) 323432
email: ahorizon@zamnet.zm
website: www.africa-insites.com/zambia/adventurecentre.htm
Lodge based in Livingstone Adventure Centre; ideal base for bungee jumping and other adventure activities on Zambian side of Victoria Falls.

United Touring Company

See below under Safari.

CLIMBING AND ABSEILING

From Mount Kilimanjaro to the Drakensberg, to the Table Mountain chain, Southern Africa offers a full range of mountain challenges. You can do easy day hikes, multi-day hikes, climbs of all grades of difficulty, or abseiling down sheer cliffs. Both traditional climbing and sport climbing (where permanent bolts are set in a route up the rock) are catered for. Even if you are a novice, there are many organizations providing training so you can tackle your first mountain adventure in an organized group. Mountaineering equipment is expensive, but you can hire everything you need and try out the sport before committing yourself.

MALAWI
Mountain Club of Malawi

P.O. Box 240, Blantyre, Malawi
☎ 643436
Contact them for advice about climbing in Malawi and organized climbs in the region.

SOUTH AFRICA
WESTERN CAPE

This mountainous region offers rock climbing of all grades, as well as many short, bolted sport climbs. Abseiling available on the mountains in and around the city of Cape Town.

Abseil Africa

P.O. Box 16382, Vlaeberg 8018, Cape Town
☎ (21) 424 1580 **fax:** (21) 424 1590
email: abseil@iafrica.com
website: www.millenia.co.za/abseilafrica
Offers a variety of abseiling adventures (off Table Mountain, through waterfalls).

Cape Town School of Mountaineering

P.O. Box 678, Rondebosch 7700, Cape Town
☎/**fax:** (21) 671 9604
email: simon@orca-industries.co.za
website: www.mountainspecialists.active3.com
Directed by Simon Larsen, who has been involved in the development of mountain training since 1991.

KALAHARI

Semi-desert and desert region, with low mountains, in the northern Cape province of South Africa.

Kalahari Adventure Centre

P.O. Box 20, Augrabies Falls 8874, Northern Cape
☎/**fax:** (54) 451 0177
email: info@augrabies.co.za
website: www.augrabies.co.za
Will take you abseiling in some of the remote scenic areas of the Kalahari. Trained supervisors cater both for beginners and the more advanced.

DRAKENSBERG MOUNTAINS, KWAZULU-NATAL

The rock faces of the Drakensberg are composed of friable basalt, making them unsuitable for other than expert climbers. Abseiling is, however, available, and the area is ideal for walking (see below under Hiking).

Uvongo Tours

P.O. Box 398, Uvongo 4270, KwaZulu-Natal
☎ (3931) 76008 **fax:** (3931) 77238
email: uvongo@iafrica.com
website: www.uvongo.com

FREE STATE

The eastern part of this province offers rolling hills, with beautiful, golden sandstone cliffs.

Mount Everest Game Reserve and Self-Achievement Courses

P.O. Box 215, Harrismith 9880, Free State
☎ (58) 623 0235 **fax:** (58) 623 0238
email: adgeo@gem.co.za
website: www.adventuregeographic.co.za
Specializes in organizing cliff adventures for small groups. Activities include abseiling and sport climbing on bolted routes.

KENYA/TANZANIA

Straddling the Kenya/Tanzania border, Mount Kilimanjaro is, at 5895m (19340ft), Africa's highest mountain. Ascending it is an extremely strenuous hike, rather than a climb; but altitude sickness may affect you.

Ascend Adventures

6648 E. Corrine Drive, Scottsdale, AZ 85254, U.S.A.
☎ (480) 596 9126 **toll free** ☎ 800 2-ASCEND (227-2363)
email: brannon@pop.phnx.uswest.net
website: www.ascendadventures.com
Principally a climbing and white-water rafting outfit. It supplements its Arizona operation with international trips such as rafting the Zambezi and climbing Kilimanjaro.

Kilimanjaro Guide Tours and Safaris

P.O. Box 210, Moshi, Kilimanjaro, Tanzania
☎ (55) 50120 **fax:** (55) 51220

Roy Safaris

See below under Safari, Tanzania.

Sunway Safaris

P.O. Box 2657, Pinegowrie 2123, Johannesburg, South Africa
☎ (11) 888 6856 **fax:** (11) 888 6855
email: sunway@icon.co.za
website: www.icon.co.za/~sunway
Offers a budget trip, sleeping in tents.

UGANDA

The chief mountain challenge is Mount Elgon (4321m/14,178ft), offering a 3–4 day hike rather than a climb. Experience hot springs and waterfalls; no specialized climbing experience or special equipment needed.

Uganda Wildlife Authority Headquarters and Uganda Tourist Board

See above under Birdwatching.
Apply for more information and the required permits to climb Mount Elgon.

ZAMBIA/ZIMBABWE
VICTORIA FALLS

In addition to bungee jumping, the Vic Falls bridge between Zimbabwe and Zambia also offers a variety of abseiling adventures.

Abseil Zambia

P.O. Box 61023, Livingstone, Zambia
☎ (3) 323454 **fax:** (3) 324440
email: abseil@outpost.co.zm
website: www.africa-insites.com/zambia/abseilzambia.htm

Adrift/Kandahar Safaris

See p. 268.

CYCLING

The main roads of the region and their users are not particularly cyclist-friendly, especially in and around the cities, but the country areas provide wonderful cycling: through forests, up and down mountains, along rivers. You can bring your own bike, or hire one, and plan your own itinerary, or you can join a group on a cycling tour organized by an operator. The sort of equipment you bring with you or hire will obviously depend on the type of cycling you have in mind. Padded cycling shorts, a helmet, and a waistbag for small items are essentials, but your choice of bicycle— sturdy mountain-bike with wide tyres, light road bike with narrow ones, or intermediate touring bike—will be dictated by your route.

LESOTHO
Fraser's Semongkong Lodge

See above under Birdwatching for details. Mountainbike (and motorbike) trails start from here into the remote Lesotho mountains.

MOZAMBIQUE

The Limpopo estuary, 250km (155 miles) north of Maputo, is an exciting mountainbike venue.

Zongoene Lodge

☎ Maputo (1) 499523 or
☎ Pretoria, South Africa (12) 346 1286

email: zongoene@satis.co.za
website: www.satis.co.za/zongoene
Luxury lodge base for mountainbiking.

SOUTH AFRICA
Fat Trax African Mountain Biking Tours
Suite 142, Postnet X18, Rondebosch 7700, Cape Town
☎/**fax:** (21) 794 6679
Half-day to multi-day mountainbiking tours, with bikes and basic equipment included.

SA Tours and Safaris with African Alternatives
See above under Birdwatching.

Zulwini Tours and Safaris
See below under Rafting.
Mountainbiking trails offered in South Africa.

WESTERN CAPE
As well as the scenic Garden Route, this area has many small coastal fishing towns to the north, and inviting mountains behind.

Downhill Adventures
Corner of Orange, Kloof and Long Streets, Cape Town 8000
☎ (21) 422 0388
email: downhill@mweb.co.za
website: www.downhilladventures.co.za
Mountainbiking adventures in Western Cape.

KWAZULU-NATAL
Gibela Safaris
P.O. Box 47736, Greyville 4023, Durban
☎/**fax:** (31) 297005
email: info@gibela.co.za
website: www.gibela.co.za
Cycling tours and mountainbiking trails.

MPUMALANGA, FREE STATE AND NORTHERN PROVINCE
Jacana Country Homes and Trails
P.O. Box 95212, Waterkloof 0145, Gauteng
☎ (12) 346 3550/1/2 **fax:** (12) 346 2499
email: jacana@lia.co.za
website: www.trails.co.za
They administer 7 mountainbike trails, of varying lengths, in Northern Province, Free State, and Mpumalanga areas. On most of them overnight facilities are available.

DIVING AND SNORKELLING

Some of the most beautiful parts of Southern Africa lie hidden beneath the region's waters. Most of the diving and snorkelling activity is, naturally enough, concentrated around the coastal areas, and particularly in the warmer Indian Ocean, which offers beautiful tropical and sub-tropical reefs. A great variety of diving, and the opportunity to view some fine historic wrecks, is available around Cape Town. The really adventurous can view sharks from a protective cage. But underwater adventurers can also find things to do even in landlocked countries, such as Zimbabwe and Malawi. Several institutions with international affiliation, such as the National Association of Underwater Instructors (NAUI), run courses for beginners.

Dive The Big Five
P.O. Box 2209, White River 1240, Mpumalanga, South Africa
☎ (13) 750 1832 **fax:** (13) 750 0018
email: divebig5@iafrica.com
website: www.divethebig5.co.za
Offers 8 standard tours to the east coast of Southern Africa, each consisting of a scuba diving safari linked to a wildlife safari. Great White Shark cage diving offered, plus seal, penguin, and dolphin diving tours, and wreck and tropical reef diving. Will also tailor-make tours.

Kayak Africa
See page 270.
Scuba diving with sea kayaking expeditions to Lake Malawi, Madagascar, and Mozambique.

MADAGASCAR
TULEAR
The sea here offers tropical, warm-water snorkelling and scuba diving. Training courses, shore- and boat-dives are available.

Hotel Le Paradisier
P.O. Box 490, Tulear
☎ (9) 442914 **fax:** (9) 441175
email:paradisier@simicro.mg
website: www.simicro.mg/paradisier
Latest hotel in Ifathy is a good base for diving.

Nautilus Deep Sea Club
P.O. Box 519, Tulear
☎ (9) 441874 **fax:** (9) 441380
Well-equipped, French run diving centre right on Ifathy beach, a short distance from the reef.

DIVING AND SNORKELLING

Lakana Vejo Centre Nautique
See above under Boat trips.
Snorkelling and scuba diving (also night dives).

MALAWI
Several operators run training courses and
shore- and boat-dives in Lake Malawi.

Lake Divers
P.O. Box 182, Monkey Bay
☎/fax: 584528
email: lakedivers@malawi.net
Offers a variety of scuba courses, including
P.A.D.I. openwater diving.

ScubaDo
Livingstonia Beach Hotel, P.O. Box 11, Salima
☎ 744022 fax: 744483
email: info@scubado.demon.co.uk
Scuba courses, P.A.D.I., master courses and
boat charters. Also runs trips into Mozambique.

Scuba Shack
P.O. Box 176, Monkey Bay
☎/fax: (in South Africa) (11) 949 1698
Offers P.A.D.I. scuba diving courses in Chembe.

Rift Lake Charters
P.O. Box 284, Mangochi
☎ 584473 fax: 584576
Qualified N.A.U.I. instructors available to train
beginners. They hire out scuba equipment, and
offer night- and boat-dives in Lake Malawi.

MOZAMBIQUE
The main centres for diving and snorkelling in
the warm subtropical seas off Mozambique are
Inhaca Island, close to the capital, Maputo,
Inhambane on the central coast, and the
Bazaruto Islands off the northern coast.

Barra Lodge Dive Charters
See p. 272.

Destination Africa Tours
P.O. Box 26014, Gezina 0031, Gauteng,
South Africa
☎ (12) 333 7110 fax: (12) 333 7911
website: http://destination.co.za
Scuba diving tours to Inhaca Island.

Unusual Destinations
P.O. Box 11583, Vorna Valley 1686, Gauteng,
South Africa
☎ (11) 805 4833/4 fax: (11) 805 4835
email: unusdest@global.co.za

Diving and whale watching at Punto do Ouro;
also self-drive holidays in southern
Mozambique and the Bazaruto Islands.

Mozaic Coastal Tours
See above under Boat trips.
Organizes scuba diving and snorkelling trips
into Mozambique.

Indaba Tourism Services
P.O. Box 340, Hazyview 1242,
Mpumalanga, South Africa
☎ (13) 737 7115 fax: (13) 737 7403
email: ndaba@mweb.co.za
website: www.ndaba.co.za
Scuba diving in Mozambique offered. Can be
combined with wildlife safaris in Kruger
National Park and parks in KwaZulu-Natal.

SOUTH AFRICA
CAPE TOWN
The advantage of diving and snorkelling here is
that when it is blowing a gale on one side of the
Cape Peninsula it is often calm on the other.

Adventure Safaris & Sports Tours
P.O. Box 32176, Camps Bay 8040, Cape Town
☎ (21) 438-5201 fax: (21) 438 4807
email: adventurepic@icon.co.za
website: www.mothercity.co.za/asst.htm
Organizers of shark cage diving, fishing, swimming with dolphins, as well as a range of other
adventure activities.

Orca Industries
3 Bowwood Road, Claremont 7708, Cape Town
☎ (21) 671 9673 fax: (21) 671 9733
email: duncan@orca-industries.co.za
Established for 13 years. Instructors with internationally recognized qualifications offer basic
and advanced diving courses.

Two Oceans Diving Academy
P.O. Box 285, Cape Town 8000
☎ (21) 419 0521 fax: (21) 419 0349
email: keene@iafrica.com
An affiliate of N.A.U.I., this academy provides
instruction in diving for beginners, through to
advanced levels.

KWAZULU-NATAL
The northern coast of this province offers the
only real tropical diving in South Africa.
Sodwana Bay, the most popular diving destination, has the world's most southerly coral reefs.

Andy Cobb Eco Diving

P.O. Box 386, Winkelspruit 4145,
KwaZulu-Natal
☎/fax: (31) 964239
email: andycobb@iafrica.com
website: www.adventurescuba.co.za
Guided adventure diving and game park safaris
in KwaZulu-Natal and southern Mozambique.

Hluhluwe Inn Hotel and Hluhluwe Safari Tours

P.O. Box 92, Hluhluwe 3960, KwaZulu-Natal
☎ (35) 562 0251/2/3 fax: (35) 562 0254
Base yourself here for scuba diving on tropical
coral reefs off nearby Sodwana Bay.

Overland and Undersea Safaris

P.O. Box 11015, Dorpspruit 3206,
KwaZulu-Natal
☎/fax: (331) 903171
email: kathi@undersea.co.za
website: www.undersea.co.za
Affiliated to KwaZulu-Natal's Shark Research
Institute, this operator offers you the opportunity to tag whale sharks in the Indian Ocean.

Sodwana Bay Lodge and Hotel Resort

P.O. Box 5478, Durban 4000, KwaZulu-Natal
☎ (31) 304 5977 fax: (31) 304 8817
email: sbls@mweb.co.za
website: www.leisurelodges.co.za
Situated near to tropical reefs of Sodwana Bay.
Base for diving tours of the reefs. Diving
courses available.

Island Rock (Pty) Ltd for Sibaya Lake Lodge

See above under Birdwatching.
Use as a base for lake dives in north of province.

TANZANIA

ZANZIBAR
Ras Nungwi Beach Hotel

P.O. Box 1784, Zanzibar
☎ (54) 33767
email: rasnungwi@zanzibar.net
website: www.zanzibar.net
Snorkelling trips, beginners and advanced
scuba instruction, and organized dives.

Zanzibar Dive Centre

P.O. Box 608, Zanzibar
☎/fax: (811) 323091
email: oneocean@twiga.com

website: www.webworks.com.au/zanzibar/zdc-
sites
Runs scuba diving courses from beginners to
advanced, and offers shore- and boat-dives.

FISHING

All types of fishing are to be had in southern
Africa. You can go deep sea and game fishing off
most areas of the coast; angling from the thousands of miles of coastline and in the lakes and
large rivers; fly-fishing in the many streams and
dams. Battle the combative tigerfish on the
Zambezi or in Lake Kariba, or go after really big
game: swordfish, sailfish, and tuna off the east
coast. Or angle gently for trout and bream.

SOUTH AFRICA
SA Tours and Safaris with African Alternatives

See above under Birdwatching.
Offers big game fishing off South African coast.

WESTERN CAPE
Cape Nature Conservation

Private Bag X9068, Cape Town 8000
☎ (21) 483 4051 fax: (21) 230939
Issues permits for angling in a number of dams
and rivers in the Western Cape.

Lightley's Holiday Cruisers

See above under Boat trips.
Excellent fishing for grunter, kob, and shad
from your own boat on the Knysna Lagoon.

KWAZULU-NATAL
Hluhluwe Inn Hotel and Hluhluwe Safari Tours

See above under Diving.
Big game fishing trips from Sodwana Bay.

LESOTHO
Fraser's Semongkong Lodge

See above under Birdwatching.
Trout-fishing available.

Oxbow Lodge

See below under Four-Wheel-Drive Trails.
Base for trout fishing in the Maluti mountains.

MADAGASCAR
Lakana Vejo Centre Nautique

See above under Boat Trips.
Centre for deep-sea fishing and fly-fishing.

MALAWI
Angling Society of Malawi
P.O. Box 744, Blantyre, Malawi
Can advise you about the abundant fishing for tigerfish, catfish, salmon, and trout available in the rivers and lakes of Malawi.

MOZAMBIQUE
INHAMBANE
Both deep-sea fishing and fly-fishing available.

Barry Dowson
Casa Barry, P.O. Box 16, Inhambane, Mozambique
☎ (23) 29007
Offers spacious, self-catering chalets as base for deep sea fishing. All situated on Tofo beach. Very popular, so book well in advance.

Barra Lodge Fishing Charters
See p. 272 for further details.

TANZANIA
ZANZIBAR
Best times for deep sea fishing here are Aug–Nov for yellowfin tuna, and Nov–Mar for billfish.

Ras Nungwi Beach Hotel
See above under Diving.
Deep-sea fishing for yellowfin tuna, and billfish.

UGANDA
Lake and river fishing in Uganda offers the opportunity to catch the Nile perch.

Uganda Wildlife Authority Headquarters and Uganda Tourist Board
See above under Birdwatching.
Apply here for fishing permits.

ZAMBIA/ZIMBABWE
Gwembe Safaris
See above under Boat Trips.
Fish for bream and tigerfish in Lake Kariba from your own houseboat.

Mutemwa Lodge
P.O. Box 1637, Parklands 2121, Johannesburg South Africa
☎ (11) 888 2431 **fax:** (11) 888 5798
Situated on the Zambezi River, in Zambia. Use as a base for catching tigerfish and bream.

Tiger Fishing Tours
P.O. Box 31730, Lusaka, Zambia
☎/**fax:** (1) 262810
email: tiger@zamnet.zm or tigercamp@aol.com
website: www.africa-insites.com/zambia/ads/tiger.htm
Runs a camp on the Zambezi River, in western Zambia, available as base for fishing.

LAKE KARIBA
See entries for **C.T.R. Management** and **Charter Consultants** and **Kariba Boating and Safaris** under Boat trips, above.

FOUR-WHEEL-DRIVE TRAILS

Four-by-four off-road driving is a relatively new, rapidly growing activity in southern Africa. Many trails have opened recently, enabling you to reach some of the most remote and beautiful areas in the region. If you do not have your own vehicle, you can take part in an organized tour, or hire a 4x4 from one of the many rental agencies. Some tour operators (details below) also provide training for those unused to this form of driving.

SOUTH AFRICA
4XForum
P.O. Box 1000, Sun Valley 7985, Cape Town
☎ (21) 785 5752
email: fwdrive@iafrica.com
website: www.4xforum.co.za
Publishers of a newsletter about all aspects of 4x4 activities in southern Africa, giving information about new and established trails.

4X4 Adventure Tours
P.O. Box 914005, Wingate Park 0153, Pretoria
☎ (12) 345 3548 **fax:** (12) 345 1797
Run by Jacques Wilkin, a specialist tour guide with more than 10 years experience. He gives driver training at various levels and runs expeditions of between 1–9 days to all parts of sub-Saharan Africa.

Maui Camper Hire
P.O. Box 4368, Kempton Park 1620 Johannesburg
☎ (11) 396 1445 **fax:** (11) 396 1757
email: maui@iafrica.com
website: www.maui-rentals.com
Rents out 4x4 vehicles. Has depots at Victoria Falls and in several South African cities.

Tribes Travel
See p. 263 for details.
Offers 4x4 and self-drive adventures in South
Africa and Botswana.

LESOTHO
Malealea Lodge
See p. 282.

Oxbow Lodge
Oxbow Malibamatsoe River, Maluti Mountains
Postal Address:P.O. Box 60, Ficksburg, Free
State 9730, South Africa
☎ (51) 933 2247
fax: (51) 933 2247
website: www.africa-
insites.com/lesotho/travel
Base for 4x4 trailing in the Maluti mountains.

MALAWI
SS Rent-a-Car
Kamuzu Procession Road, P.O. Box 997
Lilongwe, Malawi
☎ 741634/744189 **fax:** 625074
Rents out 4x4 and other vehicles.

NAMIBIA
Odyssey Car Hire
See p. 276.

SOUTH AFRICA
Adventure Unlimited
P.O. Box 22045, Glenashley 4022,
KwaZulu-Natal
☎ (31) 569 3604 **fax:** (31) 569 4062
email: adventure@unlimited.co.za
website: www.bluebox.co.za/adventureunlimited
4x4 jeep and camper hire, and jeep safaris to
many destinations in the province.

Jacana Country Homes and Trails
See above under Cycling and Mountainbiking.
Four 4x4 trails in Northern Province, KwaZulu-
Natal, Mpumalanga, and Free State.

HIKING

Whether you enjoy hiking through mountains,
desert, coastal scenery, grassland, or bush,
southern Africa has them all. If you have the
right equipment and know what you are doing,
you can simply take off into the wilderness. But
for the less experienced there are many clearly
laid out multi-day trails, mostly with cabins at
the end of each day's walking. These can be

booked through the Parks Boards, or Nature
Conservation authorities of the various countries. The most important item of equipment
will be your boots and your pack. Make sure
that the boots are comfortable, well worn-in,
and support your ankles; and that your pack
fits well and is properly balanced on your back.

NAMIBIA
NAUKLUFT MOUNTAINS
Büllsport Guest Farm
Postbag 1003, Maltahöhe
☎ (63) 293363 **fax:** (63) 293372
Büllsport is the perfect base for hiking in the
Naukluft Mountains. Excellent, traditional
guestfarm—comfortable accommodation in 8
rooms (including 1 family room), good food,
and a warm welcome. Advanced booking recommended. Büllsport also offers inexpensive
horse riding trails into these mountains.

SOUTHERN AFRICA
African Routes
P.O. Box 1835, Durban 4001, KwaZulu-Natal
☎ (31) 569 3911 **fax:** (31) 569 3908
email: aroutes@iafrica.com
Adventure tour operator, catering for the 18–35
age group. Offers a variety of camping and trailing tours throughout southern Africa.

Backroads
801 Cedar St, Berkeley, CA 94710-1800, U.S.A.
☎ (510) 527 555 **toll free** ☎ 800-GO-ACTIVE
(800 462 2848)
fax: (510) 527 1444
email: backtalk@backroads.com
website: www.backroads.com
Walking and hiking trips in South Africa.

Dzombo Tours and Safaris
See above under Birdwatching.
Combines hiking trails with birdwatching
safaris.

Tribes Travel
See p. 263 for details.

Zulwini Tours and Safaris
See below under Rafting.

LESOTHO
Fraser's Semongkong Lodge
See above under Birdwatching.

Oxbow Lodge
See above under Four-wheel-drive trails.

SOUTH AFRICA
Jacana Country Homes and Trails
See above under Cycling.

Dozens of self-guided hiking trails, spread right across South Africa, through privately owned conservation areas.

Mac Safaris
P.O. Box 1531, Olivedale 2158, Gauteng
South Africa
☎/fax: (11) 462 6212
email: macsafari@icon.co.za
Hiking eco-tours for small groups. Often include other adventure activities such as whale-watching, canoeing, and horse riding.

South African National Parks
See p. 279.

Multi-day hiking trails include the Kruger National Park, led by an armed ranger, and the spectacular, but tough, Otter Trail on the Garden Route, through coastal wilderness. Reservations should be made a year in advance.

CAPE TOWN
Cape Eco Trails
See p. 279.

DRAKENSBERG MOUNTAINS, KWAZULU-NATAL
This spectacular mountain chain offers many superb 1- and multi-day hikes. Hot in the summer months (Nov–Apr), the mountains can experience heavy snowfalls in winter (Jun–Sep).

Midlander Trips and Tours/Hilander Hiking Experiences
P.O. Box 20028, Howick 3290, KwaZulu-Natal
South Africa
☎/fax: (332) 304293
email: info@kzntours.co.za
website: www.kzntours.co.za
Operates in the mountains, both in KwaZulu-Natal and Lesotho.

Sani Pass Hotel and Leisure Resort
P.O. Box 44, Himeville 3256, KwaZulu-Natal
☎ (33) 702 1320 fax: (33) 702 0220
email: sanipasshotel@eastcoast.co.za
website: www.sanipasshotel.co.za
In southern Drakensberg Mountains. Starting point for a number of excellent hiking trails.

FREE STATE
Mount Everest Game Reserve and Self-Achievement Courses
See above under Climbing.

Arranges hikes in the surrounding hills.

TANZANIA
Hoopoe Adventure Tours
See p. 263.

UGANDA
Uganda Wildlife Authority Headquarters and Uganda Tourist Board
See above under Birdwatching.

Many hiking trails are available in the national parks. Apply for information and permits.

ZAMBIA
VICTORIA FALLS
Taita Falcon Lodge
P.O. Box 60012, Livingstone, Zambia
☎/fax: (3) 321850
email: taita-falcon@zamnet.zm
website: www.africa-insites.com/zambia/taita.htm
Use as a base for walking trails in the Victoria Falls area. One trail takes you to Chief Makuni's village, where you can experience tribal life.

MOTORBIKING

For many adventure travellers, a motorbike is the ideal way to cover large distances and see the most sights. Whilst many of southern Africa's roads present a hostile face to motorbike enthusiasts—gravel or worse—those who plan their itineraries carefully, either by going independently or taking a standard tour, will not be disappointed.

LESOTHO
Fraser's Semongkong Lodge
See above under Birdwatching for details.
Motorbike (and mountainbike) trails start from here into the remote Lesotho mountains.

SOUTH AFRICA
WESTERN CAPE
Use this area as a starting point for a motorbike tour up the scenic Garden Route, or northwards up the west coast, with its small fishing towns and magnificent wild flowers in Aug and Sep. Alternatively, the lovely mountains of the region make for rewarding touring.

Classic Twin Tours

P.O. Box 141, Koelenhof, Stellenbosch,
Cape Town
☎ (21) 882 2558 **fax:** (21) 882 2207
email: enquiries@classictwintours.com
website: www.classictwintours.com
Harley-Davidsons for hire with full back-up. Set
tours available around the Western Cape and
along the Garden Route.

Freedom Africa Touring Club

See p. 276.

South African Motorcycle Tours

Sierra Cottage, Gemini Way, Constantia, 7800
Cape Town
☎/**fax:** (21) 794 7887
email: a.france@mweb.co.za
website: www.doorway.co.za/samt
Tours from Cape Town of 1, 2, 7 and 12 days.

MOUNTED TRAILS

Let something else's legs do the walking! A
great variety of mounted trails are available in
southern Africa, taking you through often stunningly beautiful landscape. Most are horse or
pony trails, but you can also get to ride elephants. It's a good idea to have a little riding
practice before leaving home, so that the appropriate parts of your anatomy can toughen up.

U.K. OPERATORS
Okavango Tours and Safaris

See p. 267.

Ride World Wide

Staddon Farm, North Tawton
Devon EX20 2BX
☎ (01837) 82544 **fax:** (01837) 82179
email: rideww@aol.com
website: www.rideworldwide.co.uk
Horse riding trips into Botswana, Kenya,
Tanzania, Malawi, and Zimbabwe.

U.S.A. OPERATORS
Big Five Tours & Expeditions

See below under Safari.

Equitour Fits

See below under Safari.

BOTSWANA
Elephant Back Safaris

Private Bag 332, Maun, Botswana

☎ (267) 661 260 **fax:** (267) 661 005
website: www.elephantbacksafaris.com
Luxury safari operation run from Abu's Camp in
the Okavango Delta, exclusively for elephant-
back safaris.

Hartley's Safaris

See below under Safari.
Agent for Elephant Back Safaris, above.

KENYA
Offbeat Safaris Limited

P.O. Box 56923, Nairobi, Kenya
☎ (2) 506139/601130 **fax:** 502739
Horse safaris in Maasailand and Laikipia,
Kenya.

LESOTHO
Malealea Lodge

See p. 282 for details.

Tribes Travel

See p. 263 for details.
Offers horse safaris in Lesotho with local
Basotho guides.

MADAGASCAR
RANOHIRA AREA
Le Relais de la Reine

P.O. Box 01, Ranohira
Book through Madagascar Discovery Agency
Rte de l'Universite, P.O. Box 3587 Antananarivo
☎/**fax:** (2) 35165/67
email: mda@bow.dts.mg
website: www.madagascar-contacts.com/mda
Use as a base for horse riding. Beautifully sited
and designed hotel surrounded by rocky outcrops, near Isalo National Park, 15km (9miles)
south of Ranohira. French owned and run;
needs advance booking.

MALAWI
Heart of Africa Safaris

See p. 271.

NAMIBIA
Büllsport Guest Farm

See above under Hiking.

SOUTH AFRICA
Jacana Country Homes and Trails

See above under Cycling.

Mac Safaris

See above under Hiking.

JOHANNESBURG AREA
Triple B Ranch
P.O. Box 301, Vaalwater 0530,
Northern Province, South Africa
☎ (14) 755 3737 **fax:** (14) 755 3705
email: tessa@waterberg.net
Base for a variety of adventures, including
riding with game, cattle-mustering, and out-
rides.

NORTHERN PROVINCE
Equus Horse Safaris
See below under Safari.

ZAMBIA
Lilayi Lodge
See above under Birdwatching.

ZIMBABWE
VICTORIA FALLS
Wild Horizons
See p. 270.

RAFTING AND CANOEING

Southern Africa offers a full range of river conditions for rafting and canoeing, from Grade I
(steadily-moving, unobstructed water) through
to Grade VI (wild water, for experts only).
Since the region is generally dry, there are only
a few rivers, listed below, available for paddling
all year round; the one exception that has been
included is the Doring (Western Cape), in spate
only during the winter. Wear light, quick-drying
clothing, gloves if you blister easily, and plenty
of sunscreen. The operators will supply life
jackets and other necessary equipment. Since
many companies operate on several rivers,
we've listed the rivers first, then the operators.

RIVERS
Breede River, Western Cape, South Africa
The perennial Breede winds from the mountains near Ceres, past Swellendam and out into
the sea at Infanta. Provides gentle, easy canoeing and river rafting, with some Grade II rapids.

Doring River, Cedarberg Mountains, South Africa
Has a short season when it can be run, after the
winter rains, usually Aug and early Sep. The
strength and difficulty of the rapids varies
according to the rainfall.

Kunene River, border of Namibia/Angola
This hard-to-reach river offers a 5-day trip
between Ruacana Falls and Epupa Falls; a mixture of quiet water and Grades I–IV rapids.

Limpopo River, border of South Africa/Zimbabwe, Mozambique
Low and full of sandbanks during the frequent
droughts in this area, the Limpopo can always
be paddled at its estuary in Mozambique.

Lower Orange River, border of South Africa/Namibia
This perennial river is one of the most popular
canoeing and rafting destinations in the region.
There are Grade II and III rapids above the
Augrabies Falls. Below Augrabies scenic 5-day
trips are available, mainly on Grade I water, but
with some Grade II rapids.

Nile River, Uganda
Rafting is available on the highest reaches of
the river near its source.

Vaal River, Gauteng Province, South Africa
Provides a gentle day-long drift downstream
from the town of Parys, an hour from
Johannesburg. You will encounter small Grade
II rapids. The season is from Sep–May.

Zambezi River, Border of Zambia/Zimbabwe
Perhaps the most popular of all the river destinations in southern Africa is the Batoka Gorge
on the Zambezi, below Victoria Falls. The
rapids are Grade V, and are run only in rafts.
Sep-late Dec/early Jan, when the river is low, is
the best time. On the upper Zambezi, above the
Falls, half- to 2-day trips with a few rapids are
offered.

OPERATORS
Adrift/Kandahar Safaris
See p. 269 for details.

Aquatrails
4 Constantia Road, Wynberg 7800,
Cape Town, South Africa
☎/**fax:** (21) 762 7916
email: inbound.iafrica@ct.lia.net
website: www.aquatrails.co.za

Ascend Adventures
See entry under Climbing and Abseiling.

Batoka Sky
See above under Airborne adventures.

Bundu Adventure
P.O. Box 60773, Livingstone, Zambia
☎ (3) 324407 **fax:** (3) 324406
email: zambezi@zamnet.zm
website:
www.africa-insites.com/zambia/bundu.htm
Organizes river rafting and canoeing on the
upper and lower Zambezi River.

Chundukwa Adventure Trails
P.O. Box 61160, Livingstone, Zambia
☎ (3) 324006/324452 **fax:** (3) 324006
email: chunduka@zamnet.zm
website:
www.africa-insites.com/zambia/ chundukwa.htm
Offers canoeing river safaris on the Zambezi.

The Dragonfly Group
P.O. Box 987, Northlands 2116, Gauteng,
South Africa
☎ (11) 884 9911 **fax:** (11) 884 9915/6
email: info@dragonfly.co.za
website: www.dragonfly.co.za
Also at: P.O. Box 346, White River 1240,
Mpumalanga, South Africa
☎ (13) 764 1823 **fax:** (13) 764 1810
Offering white-water rafting and many other
adventure activities since 1979.

Dzombo Tours and Safaris
See above under Birdwatching.

Eca Travel & Tours
P.O. Box 26350, Arcadia 0007, Pretoria,
South Africa
☎ (12) 329 3765 **fax:** (12) 329 6441
email: umlani@mweb.co.za
Acronym stands for Ecology, Culture,
Adventure.

Fawlty Towers
See above under Bungee jumping.

Kalahari Adventure Centre
See above under Climbing and abseiling.

Karibu Safari
P.O. Box 35196, Northway 4065, Durban,
South Africa
☎ (31) 563 7994/9774 **fax:** (31) 563 1957
email: karibusa@iafrica.com
Specializes in the lower Zambezi area (from the
Zambian side).

Mac Safaris
See above under Hiking.

Raft Extreme
Livingstone, Zambia
☎ (3) 324024 **fax:** (3) 322370
email: grotto@zamnet.zm
River rafting in Livingstone/Victoria Falls area.

Remote Africa Safaris
See above under Airborne Adventures.

The River Rafters
P.O. Box 314, Bergvliet 7864, Cape Town,
South Africa
☎ (21) 712 5094 **fax:** 712 5241
One-day to multi-day river adventures offered
on the Breede, Doring, and Orange.

Safari Consultants (for Natureways)
See p. 268 for details.

Wilderness National Park
P.O. Box 35, Wilderness 6560, South Africa
email: reservations@parks-sa.co.za
website: www.parks-sa.co.za
Cape Town office:
☎ (21) 422 2810 **fax:** (21) 424 6211
Pretoria office:
☎ (12) 343 1991 **fax:** (12) 343 0905
Three-day guided canoe trail through inland
lakes at Wilderness, on the Garden Route.

Which Way Adventures
See below under Safari.

Whitewater Excitement
P.O. Box 5992, Auburn, CA 95604, U.S.A.
toll free ☎ 800/750-2386
email: norm@wweinc.com
website: whitewaterexcitement.com
This white-water specialist runs trips to destinations worldwide, including the Zambezi.

Zongoene Lodge
See above under Cycling.

Zulwini Tours and Safaris
P.O. Box 100482, Scottsville 3209,
KwaZulu-Natal, South Africa
☎ (331) 471579 **fax:** (331) 472334
email: zulwini@pmb.lia.net
Canoeing safaris on the Orange and Zambezi
rivers, and the Maputaland Lakes in northern
KwaZulu-Natal. Also offers adventure tours.

SAFARI

Safari is *the* adventure activity of the region. Innumerable operators offer services in the area, not all of them reliable and efficient, but you should be safe if you choose from the listings below. You can safari in air-conditioned luxury or rough it at very little cost. Everyone wants to see the "Big Five"—lion, buffalo, elephant, rhino, and leopard. But safari is also about getting in touch with your surroundings and being observant of smaller things. The classic way of viewing animals in their natural habitat is from vehicles, but the more adventurous can go on foot, from a canoe or a bicycle, or mounted on a horse or even an elephant.

U.K. OPERATORS
Africa Exclusive
66 Palmerston Road, Northampton NN1 5EX
☎ (01604) 628979 **fax:** (01604) 639879
email: africa@africaexclusive.co.uk
website: www.africaexclusive.co.uk
Specialists in tailor-made safaris throughout central, south, and east Africa. They organize active safaris to less-visited places. In mass safari destinations they use tented camps and light aircraft to avoid the minibus tours. Also agents for Jack's Camp.

African Explorations
See p. 288.

Contiki Holidays for 18–35's
☎ (020) 8225 4200 **fax:** (020) 8225 4246
website: www.contiki.com
Has been operating worldwide for 35 years. Runs adventure-style tours and camping safaris in Namibia, Botswana, South Africa, and east Africa. Also has a Johannesburg office: P.O. Box 652112, Benmore 2010, Johannesburg
☎ (11) 305 7002 **fax:** (11) 305 7011
email: contiki@global.co.za

Hartley's Safaris
The Old Chapel, Hackthorn, Lincolnshire LN2 3PN
☎ (1673) 861600 **fax:** (1673) 861666
email: info@hartleys-safaris.co.uk
website: www.hartleys-safaris.co.uk
Long-established operator, originating in Botswana. Also agents for Jack's Camp.

KE Adventure Travel
See p. 288 .

Safari Drive
See p. 269.

U.S.A. OPERATORS
Aussies African Safaris
146 Sandy Cove, Nassau Bay, TX 77058
☎/**fax:** (281) 335 0911
email: jessaim@aol.com
Established in 1949, operates safaris throughout Africa, concentrating on southern Africa.

Big Five Tours & Expeditions
1551 SE Palm Court, Stuart, FL 34994
☎ (561) 287 7995 **toll free** ☎ 800 BIG FIVE (244-3483)
fax: (561) 287 5990
email: info@bigfive.com
website: www.bigfive.com
Typically 11–18 day safaris, including Namibia's deserts and elephant-back safaris in Zimbabwe.

Bush Homes Africa Safaris
750 Piedmont Avenue N.E., Atlanta, GA 30308
☎ (404) 888 0909 **fax:** (404) 888 0081
website: www.bushhomes.com
Runs safaris into all parts of Africa.

Bushtracks African Expeditions
P.O. Box 4163, Menlo Park, CA 94026-4163
☎ (650) 326 8689 toll free ☎ 800 995 8689
fax: (650) 463 0925
email: info@bushtracks.com
Runs safaris and customized tours into Zambia and other southern and east African countries.

Explorers World Travel Inc
P.O. Box 278, Lake Bluff, IL 60044
☎ (847) 295 7770 **fax:** (847) 295 8314
email: ewt@ewtravel.com
website: www.ewtravel.com
Agents in the U.S.A. for walking safaris in the Serengeti.

Equitour Fits
P.O. Box 807, Dubois, WY 82513
toll free ☎ 800 545 0019
Specialists in horse safaris.

United Touring Company
One Bala Plaza, Suite 414, Bala Cynwyd, PA 19004
toll free ☎ 800 223 6486
fax: (610) 617 3312
email: utcusa@unitedtour.com
website: www.unitedtour.com
In operation for over 50 years.

SOUTH AFRICA
African Explorer Tours & Safaris
P.O. Box 39, Greyville, Durban 4023, KwaZulu-Natal
☎ (31) 232673 **fax:** (31) 230492
email: africanex@saol.com
website: www.epages.net/africanexplorer
Customized safaris to all southern Africa.

African Outposts
P.O. Box 4593, Rivonia 2128, Gauteng
☎ (11) 884 6847 **fax:** (11) 883 9684
email: afout@fast.co.za
website: www.tourism.co.za/af-out
Also ecotourism, conservation, cultural tours.

Africa Outing/Tamba Africa
5 Alcyone Road, Claremont 7708, Cape Town
☎ (21) 614028 **fax:** (21) 683 7377
email: afouting@iafrica.com
website: www.afouting.com
Safari tours and self-drive packages to South Africa, Zimbabwe, Namibia, and Botswana.

Afro Venture Safaris
P.O. Box 1200, Paulshof 2056, Gauteng
☎ (11) 807 3720 **fax:** (11) 807 3480
email: reservations@afro.co.za
website: www.afroventures.com
Established in 1972, with branches in South Africa, Botswana, Zimbabwe, and Namibia.

Classic Safari Camps of Africa
P.O. Box 2441, Northriding 2162, Gauteng
☎ (11) 465 6427 **fax:** (11) 465 9309
email: classics@pop.onwe.co.za
website: www.classicsafaricamps.com
Group of safari operators working in 24 safari venues spread throughout southern Africa.

Coenraad Vermaak Safaris
P.O. Box 1084, Hilton 3245, KwaZulu-Natal
☎ (331) 431 1973 **fax:** (331) 431 993
email: info@seeafrica.co.za
Tailor-makes safaris to fit your preferences and budget, as far north as Tanzania.

Eca Travel & Tours
See above under Rafting and Canoeing.

Epic Expeditions
62 Strand Street, Cape Town 8001
☎ (21) 419 1721 **fax:** (21) 419 1703
email: expepic@iafrica.com
website: www.atol.co.za/epic

Adventure safaris. Be prepared to rough it; not for the pampered or spoilt.

Equus Horse Safaris
36 12th Avenue, Parktown North 2193, Gauteng
☎ (11) 788 3923 **fax:** (11) 880 8401
email: equus@equus.co.za
website: www.equus.co.za

Falcon Africa Safaris
P.O. Box 3490, Randburg 2125, Johannesburg
☎ (11) 886 1981 **fax:** (11) 886 1778
email: fasafari@icon.co.za

Fly-in-Safaris
P.O. Box 92, Cape Town International Airport 7525, Cape Town
☎ (21) 934 4488 **fax:** (21) 934 4462
email: civair@mweb.co.za
Offers fly-in safaris to remote country hotels and bush camps in southern Africa.

Gaylards Safaris/Botswana Safaris and Tours
P.O. Box 13195, Humewood 6013, Port Elizabeth, Eastern Cape
☎ (41) 468 0055 **fax:** (41) 468 0146
email: gaylards@pixie.co.za
website: www.pix.za/gaylards/about.htm
Safaris in Namibia, Botswana, and South Africa.

Habari Safaris
P.O. Box 3631, Honeydew 2040, Gauteng
☎ (21) 854 8498/9 **fax:** (21) 854 8499
email: grant@habari.co.za
Tailor-made safaris to suit destination and budget.

Karibu Safari
See above under Rafting.

Safariplans
P.O. Box 4245, Randburg 2125, Johannesburg
☎ (11) 886 1810 **fax:** (11) 886 1815
email: safap@iafrica.com
website: www.safariplan.co.za
Established in 1974 by people who previously operated their own camps and lodges.

South African National Parks
See p. 279.

Star of Africa
See above under Birdwatching.

Sunway Safaris

See above under Climbing and abseiling.

Which Way Adventures

P.O. Box 2600, Somerset West 7129,
Western Cape
☎ (21) 845 7400 **fax:** (21) 845 7401
email: whichway@iafrica.com
Established operator running overland safaris
and expeditions throughout region.

Zulu Parks and Wildlife Safaris

P.O. Box 802, Hilton 3245, KwaZulu-Natal
☎ (331) 434127 **fax:** (331) 431962
email: zulusaf@iafrica.com
website: www.kzntours.co.za
Operator with a background in professional
conservation; recommended by Game Rangers
Association of Africa.

EASTERN CAPE

Parks in this area include the Mountain Zebra
National Park, a 6,500ha (17,000-acre) sanctuary for the rare Cape mountain zebra and other
animals, with over 200 bird species; and the
11,700ha (27,500-acre) Addo Elephant
National Park, created to preserve the remnants of the area's once vast herds of elephants.

Amatola Tours

P.O. Box 18227, Quigney 5211, East London
Eastern Cape
☎ (431) 430472
email: amatour@gis.co.za
website: www.touringsa.co.za
Safaris in the Eastern Cape, and the chance to
gain an insight into the life of the Xhosa people.

JOHANNESBURG
Triple B Ranch

See above under Mounted Trails.

KRUGER NATIONAL PARK,
MPUMALANGA

One of the world's great wilderness areas, the
nearly 2,000,000ha (4,942,000-acre) Kruger
National Park houses more than 500 species of
bird, 114 species of reptile, and 147 species of
mammal, including elephants, lions and rhinos.
The park caters for tourists of all kinds, from
the jet-setter who wants luxurious lodge
accommodation to the budget tourist who
wants to caravan or camp.

Exclusive Safaris

P.O. Box 427, Heidelberg 2400, Gauteng
☎ (151) 2710 **fax:** (151) 5370
email: excl@netactive.co.za
Safaris to the Kruger National Park with add-on
visits to game parks in KwaZulu-Natal.

Gibela Safaris

See above under Cycling.

Indaba Tourism Services

See above under Diving and snorkelling.

Indula Safaris and Tours

P.O. Box 551, Wierda Park 0149, Pretoria
☎/**fax:** (12) 666 8643
email: safaris@indula.co.za
website: www.indula.co.za
Specializes in Kruger National Park.

Kruger Eco Safaris

P.O. Box 960, Fourways 2055, Gauteng
☎ (11) 465 9629 **fax:** (11) 465 9746
email: keco@iafrica.com
website: http://users.iafrica.com/k/ke/keco
Seeks to give visitors a holistic experience of
the environment and ecology of the park.

Lowveld Environmental Services

See p. 280 for details. "Sight, Sound and Smell"
tour into the Kruger National Park.

Nirvana Lodge and Safaris

Private Bag X3017, Hoedspruit 1380
Mpumalanga
☎/**fax:** (15) 793 1350
email: janvdev@global.co.za
website: www.wildnetafrica.co.za/travel-
sa/nirvanalodge
Lodge offers a variety of safari packages.

Step into Africa Tours and Safaris

P.O. Box 3745, White River 1240, Mpumalanga
☎ (13) 751 3603 **fax:** (13) 751 1384
email: graftrav@mweb.co.za
Family-owned business with more than 30
years' experience in the industry.

Wildlife Safaris

P.O. Box 3134, Randburg 2125, Johannesburg
☎ (11) 888 6896 **fax:** (11) 888 6898
email: info@wildlifesaf.co.za
website: www.wildlifesaf.co.za
Operating since 1971, specializes in safaris to
the Kruger National Park.

NORTHERN KWAZULU-NATAL

The major safari destinations here are the

96,000ha (237,000-acre) Hluhluwe-Umfolozi National Park, with the world's largest population of black and white rhino; and the 36,700ha (91,000-acre) Greater St. Lucia Wetland Park, proclaimed a World Heritage Site in 1999 for its unique ecosystems.

Dinizulu Safaris
P.O. Box 11, Hluhluwe 3960, KwaZulu-Natal
☎ (35) 562 0025 **fax:** (35) 562 0209
email: dinizulu@iafrica.com
website:
aasa.simplenet.com/travel/tourops/dinizulu
Operating in this area for 30 years, specializing in safaris to the many game reserves.

Hluhluwe Inn Hotel and Hluhluwe Safari Tours
See above under Diving.
Safaris in the Hluhluwe wetlands reserve.

Uvongo Tours
See above under Climbing and abseiling.

NORTHERN PROVINCE
Garonga Safari Camp
P.O. Box 84717, Greenside 2034, Johannesburg
☎ (11) 327 016l **fax:** (11) 327 0162
email: tsa@wn.apc.org
website: www.garonga.com
Operates a bush camp in South Africa's Northern province.

BOTSWANA
OKAVANGO DELTA
The Okavango River flows southwest from Angola towards the sea, but peters out a vast 13,000sq. km (5,000sq. mile) inland delta. Its vast network of waterways, home to crocodile and hippos, and over 350 bird species, can mostly be explored only by canoe.

Desert and Delta Safaris
P.O. Box 1200, Paulshof 2056, Gauteng South Africa
☎ (11) 807 3720 **fax:** (11) 807 3480
email: reservations@afro.co.za
website: www.afroadventures.com
Operates several safari lodges in Okavango Delta, as well as in Sossusvlei area of Namibia.

Hartley's Safaris
P.O. Box 69859, Bryanston 2021, Johannesburg, South Africa
☎ (11) 708 1893 **fax:** (11) 708 1569
email: hartley@hot.co.za

website: www.hartleyssafaris.co.za
For U.K. office, see under U.K. Operators.

Wildlife Helicopters
Private Bag 161, Maun, Botswana
☎/**fax:** (267) 660664
email: wildheli@info.bw
Aerial photography and game viewing over the Okavango Delta.

KENYA
The major safari attraction of this country is Tsavo National Park, at 21,800sq. km (8,400sq. miles) Kenya's largest park, containing the full range of African wildlife. It is divided into Tsavo East and West. Also a major attraction is the 870sq. km (330sq.-mile) Meru National Park, the setting for Joy Adamson's *Born Free*.

Gametrackers
See p. 261.

Let's Go Travel
See p. 261.

MALAWI
Safari in Liwonde National Park, 250km (130 miles) south of Lilongwe. Thousands of hippos are on view, as well as crocodiles and hundreds of elephants. Most of the park is closed over the wet season (Apr–Oct). Nyika National Park is 2,000m (6,500ft) above sea-level, and famous for its wildflowers (Nov–Apr).

Central African Wilderness Safaris
P.O. Box 489, Lilongwe, Malawi
☎ 781153 **fax:** 781397
email: wildsaf@eo.wn.apc.org
Offers tailor-made safaris in Malawi, as well as Namibia, Botswana, Zimbabwe, and South Africa. Booking agents for Mvuu Wilderness Lodge in Malawi's Liwonde National Park and for Chintheche Inn near Mzuzu.

The Nyika Safari Company
P.O. Box 2338, Lilongwe, Malawi
☎ 740579 **fax:** 740848
email: nyika-safaries@malawi.net
website: www.nyika.com
Operate safaris within Nyika and Vwaza Reserves in northern Malawi.

MOZAMBIQUE
Dive The Big Five
See above under Diving and Snorkelling.

NAMIBIA

Namibia's main safari destination is the Etosha National Park, 22,200sq. km (8,500sq. miles) of wilderness in the extreme north of the country, centred around a vast seasonal lake. In the south, the Namibia Naukluft Park, with its massive sand dunes, is also well worth a visit.

The Cardboard Box Travel Shop

15 Johann Albrecht Street, P.O. Box 5142
Windhoek, Namibia
☎ (61) 256580 **fax:** (61) 256581
email: namibia@bigfoot.com
website: www.ahj.addr.com
Organizes a range of 3–10 day safaris to all parts of Namibia.

Chameleon Adventure Camping Safaris

22 Wagner Street, Windhoek, Namibia
☎/**fax:** (61) 247668
email: chamnam@chameleon.com.na
Budget safaris (7–8 days or tailor-made).

Oryx Tours Namibia

P.O. Box 2058, Windhoek, Namibia
☎ (61) 217454 **fax:** (61) 263417
email: oryxtours@iwwm.com.na
website: www.iwwm.com.na/oryx
Incoming tour operator offering safaris throughout Namibia.

TANZANIA

The famous Serengeti, with its 14,800sq. km (5,750sq. miles) of rolling, almost treeless grasslands is this country's great tourist destination. Expect to see giraffe, millions (literally) of antelope, and the big cats that prey on them. Adjacent is the Ngorongoro Conservation Area, famous for its 20km (12.5 mile)-wide crater. Arusha is the main starting point, but beware of the many untrustworthy operators in this town! The following are tried and tested operators who will give you excellent service.

Hoopoe Adventure Tours

See p. 263.

Roy Safaris

P.O. Box 50, Arusha, Tanzania
☎ (57) 8010/2115 **fax:** (57) 8892
email: roysafaris@intafrica.com
website: www.intafrica.com/roysafaris
A dynamic company, geared towards budget travellers, and offering a combination of sensible prices and quality services.

Sunny Safaris

P.O. Box 7267, Arusha, Tanzania
☎ (57) 7145 **fax:** (57) 8094
email: sunny@arusha.com
A well-established company that combines reliability with affordability at the budget camping level, while also offering good lodge safaris.

ZAMBIA

Zambia's national parks are best visited in the dry season, from Apr–Oct. Expect to see hundreds of species of bird, and elephants, hippos, and the big cats; the rhino has virtually been poached out of existence here. Besides S. Luangwa, there is Kafue, at 22,400sq. km (9,500sq. miles) the second largest park in the world; North Luangwa, a wild area to be visited only with a safari operator; and Lower Zambezi, Zambia's newest national park.

Africa Original Expeditions

P.O. Box 31457, Lusaka, Zambia
☎ (1) 265362 **fax:** (1) 261472
email: anzac@zamnet.zm
website: www.africa-insites.com/zambia/africaoriginals.htm
Specializes in safaris to all parts of Zambia.

Chundukwa Adventure Trails

See above under Rafting and canoeing.

SOUTH LUANGWA NATIONAL PARK

One of Africa's finest wildlife parks set in 9,000sq. km (3,300sq. miles) of wilderness in the valley of the Luangwa River. Contains a huge variety of birds and game, including large herds of hippos and elephants.

Chinzombo Safari Lodge

P.O. Box 85, Mfuwe, Zambia
☎ (62) 45053 **fax:** (62) 45076
email: chinzsaf@zamnet.zm
website: www.africa-insights.com/zambia/chinzombo

Kafunta River Lodge

P.O. Box 83, Mfuwe, Zambia
☎/**fax:** (62) 45036
email: kafunta.luangwa.com
website: www.luangwa.com/kafunta

Robin Pope Safaris

P.O. Box 80, Mfuwe, Zambia
☎ (62) 45090 **fax:** (62) 45051
email: popesaf@zamnet.zm
website: www.onsafari.com/southern_af/robin

Wild Zambia Safaris

P.O. Box 100, Mfuwe, Zambia
☎ (62) 45015 **fax:** (62) 45025
email: kapani@zamnet.zm

The Wildlife Camp

P.O. Box 53, Mfuwe, Zambia
☎**/fax:** (62) 45026
email: wildlife@luangwa.comâ

ZIMBABWE

The 220,000ha (542,000-acre) Mana Pools
National Park is in the middle Zambezi Valley. It
is rich in game, including black rhino.

Safari Consultants

See p. 268.

SEA KAYAKING

The sea kayak is distinguished from other similar craft by its seaworthy features: watertight
hatches, flotation devices, sealed cockpits, and
robust rudder systems. The wide hull provides
stability, and the curved bow makes for better
performance. You will need basic skills, which
operators will teach you, but grasp these and
the continent opens up.

Coastal Kayak Trails

179 Beach Road, Mouille Point, Cape Town
8000, South Africa
☎**/fax:** (21) 439 1134
email: leon@kayak.co.za
website: www.kayak.co.za
Basic and advanced sea kayaking courses

Kayak Africa

See p. 270.

Real Cape Adventures

See p. 284 for details.

Raft Extreme

Victoria Falls, Zimbabwe. See under Rafting.

Ras Nungwi Beach Hotel

See under Diving and snorkelling.

Zulwini Tours and Safaris

See under Rafting.

VEHICLE HIRE

If you don't want to work through an operator,
you can hire a vehicle and take off on your own.
Many hire companies cater for low- or medium-
budget travellers planning their own safari.

Britz Africa

P.O. Box 4300, Kempton Park 1620,
Johannesburg, South Africa
☎ (11) 396 1860 **fax:** (11) 396 1937
email: jburg@britz.com or cb2@britz.com
4WD campervans and mobile homes. Depots in
Jo'burg, Cape Town, Durban, and Windhoek.

Camper Vacations Motorhome and 4X4 Hire

P.O. Box 41, Kenton on Sea 6191, Eastern Cape
South Africa
3-, 4- and 5-berth campers and 4x4 campers.

Campers Corner

See p. 276 for details.

Foley Hire Limited

Livingstone, Zambia
☎**/fax:** (3) 320888
Land Rover specialist.

Holiday Camper Hire and Africa Wonderland Tours

Private Bag X3, Bryanston 2021, Johannesburg
South Africa
☎ (11) 708 2176 **fax:** (11) 708 1464
website: www.argo-navis.com/campers
Mobile homes for travel all over Southern Africa.

Knysna Camper Hire

P.O. Box 1286, Knysna 6570, Western Cape
South Africa
☎ (445) 825516 **fax:** (445) 825887
email: knysna.campers@pixie.co.za
website: www.time2travel.com/campers
3-, 4- and 5-berth campers.

Maui Camper Hire

See above under Four-wheel-drive trails.

Nomad Adventure Centre

204 Long Street, Cape Town 8000, South Africa
☎ (21) 426 5445/6 **fax:** (21) 426 5420
Offers a variety of vehicles for self-drive.

GENERAL INDEX

A

aardvarks 191
acacia 131, 152
accessories, travel 16
accommodation
and restaurants
Botswana 276–8
Kenya 261–2, 265–6
Lesotho 284
Madagascar 285–6, 287
Malawi 271–2
Mozambique 272–3
Namibia 163, 273–4, 275
South Africa
279, 281–2, 285
Tanzania 263–4
Uganda 260, 261
Zambia 268
Zanzibar 266–7
Zimbabwe 113, 270
AIDS 117, 221
airborne adventures 290–1
airports
Kenya 47, 75
Lesotho 229
Madagascar 247
Malawi 133
South Africa 221
Tanzania 57, 67
Zambia 95
altitude sickness
61, 63, 65–6
animal droppings 92, 214–15
ant lion 89
Antanala people 252
A.T.M.s (automatic bank
teller machines) 15

B

backpacks 16
ballooning 290–1
Namibia 157–9
South Africa 290–1
banditry
Kenya 47
Madagascar 253
Uganda 30, 32

baobab tree 116, 117, 118
Basotho pony 224
Baster people 155, 204
bee-eaters 93, 97, 103
Betsileo people 252
Big Five 49
bilharzia 117, 125, 247, 256
birdwatching 291–3
birdlife
Botswana 181, 195–6, 200
Kenya 43–4, 69
Lesotho 292
Madagascar 254
Malawi
117, 123, 129, 132, 292
Namibia 157, 160
South Africa 206, 208–9,
210, 232, 233, 236, 291–2
Tanzania 64
Uganda 292
Zambia 93, 292–3
Zimbabwe 97, 100
body-boarding 104
braaing (barbecuing)
205, 208
Brachystegia 130–1, 132
bread-making 172
buffalo bean 121
buffaloes 51–2, 196–7
bungee jumping 294–5
burial customs
(Madagascar) 249
bush
bushwalking 53
bush-tracker skills 214–15
camping 201
bush lavender 91

C

canoeing/kayaking 311
Malawi 116-24, 311
South Africa
208–12, 230–6, 304–5, 311
Tanzania 311
Uganda 21
Zimbabwe
96–102, 104, 109–10, 311
car hire
Botswana 201, 278

Lesotho 283
Madagascar 256, 287
Namibia 163, 274
South Africa 311
Uganda 27, 259
see also vehicle hire
Chagga people 58, 60
chameleons 252
cheetahs 49, 51, 200
cholera 13, 247, 256
cichlids 120, 121
civets 92
climate and seasons
Botswana 185, 193, 201
Kenya 47, 75
Lesotho 229
Madagascar 247, 256
Malawi 125, 133
Mozambique 141
Namibia 153, 163, 173
South Africa
213, 221, 237
Tanzania 57, 67, 85
Uganda 27, 37
Zambia 95
climbing and abseiling
Kenya 296
Malawi 295
South Africa 206, 295–6
Tanzania 296
Uganda 296
Zambia 296
Zimbabwe 104
clothing requirements 16
cloves 79, 80
coconuts 80
coir 80
coral reefs
Kenya 68–9
Madagascar 244
Mozambique 138, 140
Tanzania 81, 82, 84, 85
credit and debit cards 15
crocodiles 45, 46, 92
cultural encounters
Kenya 41–2, 45–6, 72–4
South Africa 216–17
Zimbabwe 110–12
currencies 13
customs regulations 14
cuts and scrapes 27
cycling 296–7

INDEX

GENERAL INDEX

INDEX

GENERAL INDEX

ACKNOWLEDGEMENTS

Phillip Briggs and Ariadne van Zandbergen wish to thank John Addison of Wild Frontiers, RSA; Alan Dixson of Let's Go Travel, Kenya; Anu Vohoru of Air Kenya, Kenya

Fiona Dunlop would like to thank in particular: in Malawi, all the members of the Kayak Africa team, Oliver of Chembe Lodge, Nyika Safaris; in Mozambique, Nic Tasiolas of Mozambique Connection for essential support and guidance, the staff of Barra Lodge at Inhambane; in Madagascar, life-saving pilot Patrice Dal Lage, Fidi at Ranomafama, Zozoly at Isalo and Santos between the two. Thanks too to Paul Norrish of Njaya Lodge, Belinda Bishop of Explore Worldwide and David Rogers of *Getaway* magazine for welcome travel advice.

William Gray thanks Joanna Hayes and Gordon Owles of Art of Travel, London; Tim Came and Justin Matterson of Chilongozi, Zambia; Nancy Galloway of Ocean Tours, Zanzibar

Paul Grogan, for service above and beyond the call of kindness, would like to thank the following: Ignatius Nakishero at the Uganda Tourist Board for all his assistance; Kelley MacTavish at Pearl of Africa for all her time and advice; Linda Stewart at Harrison Beaumont Insurance for not putting any limits on his adventures; Jo and Jarina for being such welcoming hosts; Emma Warren, for putting up with his camera 24 hours a day; and last, and probably least, Steve Watkins for making it all possible.

Carrie Hampton would like to thank Ala Sussens (Tshukudu), Donald Lamont (Royal Hotel), Floors Strauss, Mfafa Safaris, Johan Loots (Real Cape Adventures), Mark Uren, Liz Rawlins (SA Tourism), Mick and Di Jones (Malealea Lodge), Sue Stephen, Rob Maclean, Carlos, Lowveld Environmental Services, and Lew Rood (Singita).

Chris McIntyre would like to thank Giles and Caroline for all their help with his trip in Chobe National Park.

Guy Marks would like to acknowledge the following for their assistance in the course of researching this book: Alliance Air and British Airways for providing flights to Tanzania and South Africa; PJ and Barney Bestelink for their kind hospitality at Okavango Horse Safaris; the staff at Jack's Camp for their help in the Makgadikgadi; Sunvil Discovery for all their assistance; Peter Lindstrom, Gunter Guzinski, and the staff of Hoopoe Adventure Tours, Tanzania for their help and support.

Richard Whitaker thanks warmly for their assistance: Siggi Öhler of Fish River Canyon Tours for helpful advice; Namibia Wildlife Resorts for accommodation; Cape Union Mart and Camp & Climb, both of Cape Town, for help with equipment.

Michael Woods would like to thank Clive and Kerry Bradford, James Varden, Shane White and Chris McIntyre.

Copy editors: Nia Williams, Nick Reynolds **Paste-up:** Jo Tapper **Proofreading:** Hilary Weston
Indexer: Marie Lorimer

Abbreviations for terms appearing below: (t) top; (b) bottom; (l) left; (r) right; (c) centre

Cover acknowledgements

Front Cover (t): **AA Photo Library/Cliver Sawyer** Front Cover main picture: **Getty One/Stone** Front Cover inset: **AA Photo Library/William Gray** Spine: **AA Photo Library/Clive Sawyer** Back Cover (t): **AA Photo Library/Guy Marks** Back Cover (c): **AA Photo Library/Paul Grogan** Back Cover (b): **Ariadne van Zandbergen** Back Cover (br): **AA Photo Library/Eric Meacher** Inside flaps: (t): **William Gray**; (ct): **AA Photo Library/Guy Marks**; (cb): **AA Photo Library/Carrie Hampton**; (b): **AA Photo Library/William Gray**

The Automobile Association wishes to thank the following photographers and libraries for the assistance in the preparation of this book.

Jan Baldwin 8(cr); **Purba Choudhury** 8(cb); **Bruce Coleman Collection** 19, 143, 219, 254; **William Gray** 106, 107, 142/143, 146/147; **Carrie Hampton** 211; **Chris McIntyre** 164, 150(tl), 150(b), 151, 154/155, 158/159, 159, 162, 163, 175, 195, 198/199, 198, 199; **Guy Marks** 39, 50/51, 50, 51, 54, 54/55, 55; **Margo Pfeiff** 8(br); **Ariadne van Zandbergen** ifc/1, 110, 111(tr), 111(b); **Richard Whitaker** 166, 166(tl), 167, 170, 171/171; **Michael Woods** 98, 98/99, 99, 102; **World Pictures** 3, 86/87

The remaining photographs are held in the Association's own library (AA PHOTO LIBRARY) and were taken by the following photographers:
Fiona Dunlop 2/3, 114/115, 118/119, 118, 122, 123, 127, 130/131, 131, 134, 135, 138, 139, 238/239, 239, 242, 243, 246, 250, 251, 255; **William Gray** ifc(tl), 6/7, 38/39, 59, 62/63, 63, 66(t), 66(cr), 67, 78/79, 79, 82, 83, 83(bl), 87, 90, 90/91, 91, 94, 103; **Paul Grogan** 1(br), 8(c), 18/19, 22/23, 23, 36, 27, 30, 30/31, 31(b), 34/35, 34, 35; **Carrie Hampton** ifc(bl), 1(br), 7, 202/203, 203, 206/207, 207(tr), 207(br), 210/211, 215, 218, 218/219, 222, 223, 226, 227, 230/231, 234, 235; **Guy Marks** 174/175, 178, 178/179, 182, 182/183, 183, 186, 186/187, 187, 190/191, 191; **Ariadne van Zandbergen** 1(cr); 42, 42/43, 43, 46, 47, 70/71, 71(tr), 71(b), 74/75

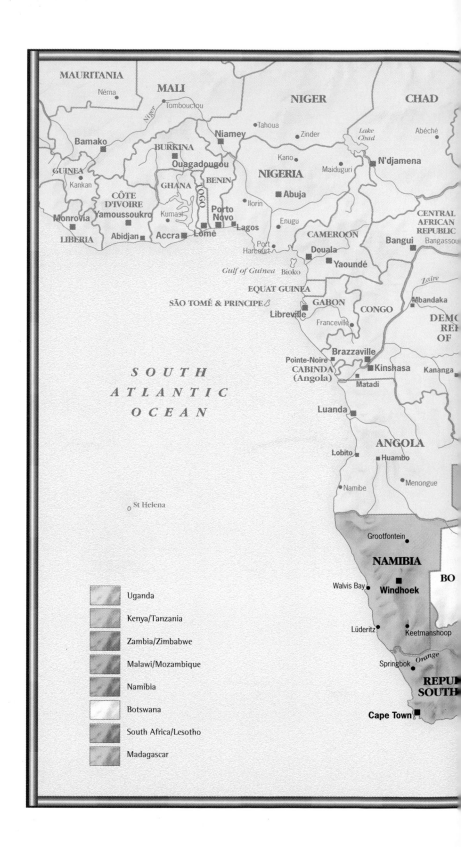

MAURITANIA

Néma

MALI

Tombouctou

Niger

NIGER

CHAD

Tahoua

Zinder

Lake
Chad

Abéché

Niamey

Bamako

BURKINA

Ouagadougou

Kano

N'djamena

GUINEA

Kankan

CÔTE
D'IVOIRE

GHANA

BENIN

TOGO

NIGERIA

Maiduguri

Abuja

Ilorin

Monrovia

Yamoussoukro

Kumasi

Porto
Novo

Enugu

CENTRAL
AFRICAN
REPUBLIC

LIBERIA

Abidjan

Accra

Lomé

Lagos

CAMEROON

Bangui

Bangassou

Port
Harcourt

Douala

Yaoundé

Gulf of Guinea

Bioko

Zaïre

EQUAT GUINEA

SÃO TOMÉ & PRINCIPE

GABON

CONGO

Mbandaka

Libreville

Franceville

DEMO
REP
OF

Brazzaville

SOUTH

Pointe-Noire

CABINDA
(Angola)

Kinshasa

Kananga

ATLANTIC

Matadi

OCEAN

Luanda

ANGOLA

Lobito

Huambo

Namibe

Menongue

St Helena

Grootfontein

NAMIBIA

Walvis Bay

Windhoek

BO

Uganda

Kenya/Tanzania

Zambia/Zimbabwe

Malawi/Mozambique

Namibia

Botswana

South Africa/Lesotho

Madagascar

Lüderitz

Keetmanshoop

Springbok

Orange

REPUI
SOUTH

Cape Town